THE
ROYAL MONMOUTHSHIRE MILITIA

HENRY CHARLES, 6TH DUKE OF BEAUFORT, K.G.
Colonel, 1803-1835.

THE ROYAL MONMOUTHSHIRE MILITIA

BEING A DETAILED DESCRIPTION OF THE REGIMENT
FROM THE YEAR 1660 TO THE TIME OF ITS TRANSFER
TO THE SPECIAL RESERVE

BY

B. E. SARGEAUNT

CAPTAIN 12TH BATTALION THE LONDON REGIMENT

ASSISTANT SECRETARY OF THE ROYAL UNITED SERVICE INSTITUTION

The Naval & Military Press Ltd

Published by

The Naval & Military Press Ltd
Unit 10 Ridgewood Industrial Park,
Uckfield, East Sussex,
TN22 5QE England

Tel: +44 (0) 1825 749494
Fax: +44 (0) 1825 765701

www.naval-military-press.com
www.nmarchive.com

In reprinting in facsimile from the original, any imperfections are inevitably reproduced and the quality may fall short of modern type and cartographic standards.

MONMOUTH CASTLE

PREFACE

WITHIN the chapters of this book I have endeavoured to lay before the reader a faithful account of the Royal Monmouthshire Militia from its creation in the year 1660 up to the present time. Those who may do me the honour of reading the pages which I have penned—pages which have been written only after exhaustive and detailed research—cannot fail to appreciate the high position which the Regiment has at all times occupied in the Militia Force. It has the distinction of having been embodied on many occasions. During the Seven Years' War it was on permanent service between the years 1760 and 1763; at the time of the American War it was embodied for five years following the year 1778; during the Napoleonic Wars it was doing duty for twenty-two years; and in more recent times there have been the embodiments during the Crimean War, when the Regiment drafted large numbers of men to the Royal Welsh Fusiliers in the Crimea, and the South African War, when two complete companies and a special service section were contributed to the forces engaged in the war.

My object has been to make the book of interest not only to officers and men who have served in the Regiment, but also to all those connected with the county of Monmouth. For this reason I have included in the initial chapter much concerning the county and the regiments which have at different periods belonged to it. At the present time, when everything is being done to enlist local patriotism throughout the country, it seems that a book dealing solely with the military associations of a county is the best means of encouraging local sympathy in the direction of impressing the individual with the duty which he, as a member of the State, owes to the State.

In the compilation of this volume I have received much kind assistance from several gentlemen, and I particularly wish to acknowledge the very great help which has been so readily extended to me by Lieutenant-Colonel C. M. Crompton-Roberts, whose indefatigable efforts and vast local knowledge have contributed so largely to the production of the work. Colonel Crompton-Roberts has spared no pains in forwarding to me notes and extracts of interest for the book, and by means of these few words I wish to convey to him my best thanks.

To Lieutenant-Colonel A. Leetham I owe a debt of gratitude for assistance in many ways, and also to Colonel J. A. Bradney. Colonel W. F. N. Noel, late Royal Engineers, a former adjutant of the Royal Monmouthshire Militia, very kindly allowed me to make use of the valuable notes which he had previously collected and published. Amongst others whom I wish to thank for kind assistance are His Grace the Duke of Beaufort, Colonel Lord Raglan, Lieutenant-Colonel H. E. M. Lindsay, Colonel W. D. Steel, Lieutenant-Colonel J. C. Llewellin, and Mr. R. Baker Gabb, while at the same time I would mention the Staff of the Royal United Service Institution, including Lieutenant-Colonel A. Leetham, the Secretary, Major C. H. Wylly, the Librarian, and the Library Clerks, Mr. Richard Dane and Mr. J. H. Harper, both of whom have rendered me much assistance. Quartermaster-Sergeant S. Fairman, R.E., of the Permanent Staff at Monmouth, has also helped me very materially in many ways. I must not forget, too, my brother officer, Captain K. R. Wilson, of the firm of Messrs. Spottiswoode and Company, whose expert knowledge has been of such value in the technical details of the book.

I am indebted to Mr. George F. Harris, of Monmouth, for photographs which he has kindly sent to me, and from which many of the plates in the volume have been produced.

In conclusion I can only add that I hope the result of my efforts may be found of some interest to those who may do me the honour of reading the book.

B. E. SARGEAUNT.

WHITEHALL: *December* 1909.

CONTENTS

CHAPTER		PAGE
I.	THE COUNTY OF MONMOUTH, AND ITS FORCES OTHER THAN ITS MILITIA	1
II.	A GENERAL GLANCE AT THE MILITIA	33
III.	THE MONMOUTHSHIRE MILITIA AT ITS FORMATION	45
IV.	THE EMBODIMENTS OF 1696, 1760, AND 1778	56
V.	THE REGIMENT AT THE CLOSE OF THE EIGHTEENTH CENTURY	79
VI.	THE EMBODIMENTS DURING THE PENINSULA AND WATERLOO CAMPAIGNS	102
VII.	FROM 1816 TO THE END OF THE CRIMEAN WAR EMBODIMENT	134
VIII.	THE REGIMENT BETWEEN 1857 AND 1876	149
IX.	EVENTS BETWEEN 1877 AND 1881	163
X.	THE REORGANISATION OF THE ARMY AND MILITIA IN 1881	173
XI.	THE ROYAL MONMOUTHSHIRE MILITIA BETWEEN 1881 AND 1889	178
XII.	THE REGIMENT BETWEEN 1890 AND THE SOUTH AFRICAN WAR	198
XIII.	THE REGIMENT IN SOUTH AFRICA AND DURING EMBODIMENT AT HOME	218
XIV.	FROM 1901 TO 1909	229
	LIST OF OFFICERS	257
	APPENDICES	293

PLATES

HENRY CHARLES, 6TH DUKE OF BEAUFORT, K.G.	*Frontispiece.*
KING HENRY V.	To face p. 4
MAP OF MONMOUTHSHIRE, 1610	,, 8
OFFICERS' MESS, MONMOUTH CASTLE	,, 18
MESS-ROOM AND PORTION OF CARVED CEILING	,, 34
HENRY, 1ST DUKE OF BEAUFORT, K.G.	,, 44
FACSIMILE OF THE ORIGINAL MS. OF THOMAS DINELEY	,, 48
SIR JOHN WILLIAMS, BARONET, AND SIR HOPTON WILLIAMS, BARONET	,, 52
COMMISSION OF LIEUT.-COLONEL HENRY PROBERT, 1702	,, 56
A MILITIA MEETING, 1770	,, 62
THOMAS MORGAN (BRIGADIER-GENERAL)	,, 68
HENRY, 5TH DUKE OF BEAUFORT, K.G.	,, 74
TYPES OF MILITIA UNIFORM, 1793	,, 82
SET OF DRILL BLOCKS	,, 104
SIR SAMUEL FLUDYER, 2ND BARONET	,, 120
BALLOT PAPER, 1817	,, 130
COLOURS PRESENTED BY THE 6TH DUKE OF BEAUFORT, 1813	,, 136
SKETCHES BY LIEUTENANT J. M. ZAMOISKI DURING THE CRIMEAN WAR EMBODIMENT	140, 144
THE ROYAL MONMOUTHSHIRE LIGHT INFANTRY AT PEMBROKE DOCK, 1855	,, 148

PLATES

COLONEL JOHN FRANCIS VAUGHAN . . . . *To face p.*	166
COLOURS WORKED BY THE LADIES OF MONMOUTHSHIRE AND PRESENTED DURING THE CRIMEAN WAR EMBODIMENT . ,,	180
GODFREY CHARLES, 1ST VISCOUNT TREDEGAR . . . . ,,	190
COLONEL WILLIAM EDWARD CARNE CURRE . . . . ,,	206
GEORGE FITZROY HENRY, 3RD LORD RAGLAN, C.B. . . . ,,	230
FIELD-MARSHAL H.R.H. THE DUKE OF CONNAUGHT, K.G., AND THE OFFICERS, 1906 . . . . ,,	244
HEAVY TRESTLE BRIDGING ON THE RIVER MONNOW AT PWLL HOLM, 1906 . . . . ,,	246
RAILWAY AND HIGH COMMAND REDOUBT IN COURSE OF CONSTRUCTION . . . . ,,	248
HOWITZER GUN BATTERY; DEMOLITION OF RAILWAY; AND IMPROVISED GIRDERS FOR RAILWAY BRIDGE . . . . ,,	250
LIEUT.-COLONEL HENRY E. MORGAN LINDSAY . . . . ,,	252

SUBSCRIBERS

His Grace the Duke of Beaufort
Colonel the Viscount Tredegar
His Excellency Colonel Lord Raglan, C.B.
The Lord Llangattock
The Hon. Mr. Justice A. T. Lawrence
Sir Chas. Cayzer, Bt.
General Sir R. Harrison, G.C.B., C.M.G.
Colonel Sir Ivor Herbert of Llanarth, Bt., C.B., C.M.G., M.P.
Sir Henry Mather-Jackson, Bt.
Colonel Sir A. W. Mackworth, Bt., C.B.
J. Murray Bannerman, Esq.
R. St. John Beasley, Esq.
Holt Beevor, Esq.
S. Courthope Bosanquet, Esq.
Colonel J. A. Bradney
E. W. T. Llewelyn Brewer-Williams, Esq.
A. J. R. Butler, Esq.
Isaac Butler, Esq.
C. H. R. Crawshay, Esq.
Lieut.-Colonel C. M. Crompton-Roberts
Colonel H. R. Crompton-Roberts, D.S.O.
Colonel W. E. C. Curre
M. David, Esq.
Miss Davies
(The late H. de la Pasture, Esq.)
Captain C. G. Evans
Rev. W. C. Feetham
Leolin Forestier-Walker, Esq.
Major R. S. Forestier-Walker
Miss B. Baker Gabb
R. Baker Gabb, Esq.
Captain C. J. F. Galloway
Captain W. A. D. Galloway
Captain F. L. W. Giles, R.E.
Captain F. E. Gill
Douglas Graham, Esq.
R. E. Greenwell, Esq.
Major G. G. Griffin
J. E. Gunning, Esq.
J. Reginald Harding, Esq.
Canon J. T. Harding
F. C. Harris, Esq.
G. R. Harris, Esq.
Major J. Gilbert Harris

SUBSCRIBERS

Colonel E. A. HERBERT, M.V.O.
G. S. HOMFRAY, Esq.
Alderman W. HUGHES
C. J. HUTH, Esq.
Captain W. B. M. JACKSON
G. C. JAMES, Esq.
F. B. JARVIS, Esq.
E. T. L. JENKINS, Esq.
W. H. P. JENKINS, Esq.
A. E. JONES, Esq.
DAVID JONES, Esq.
ROBERT JORDAN, Esq.
C. T. H. KEMEYES-TYNTE, Esq.
H. MARTYN KENNARD, Esq.
Major G. M. LAMOTTE
PERCY LAYBOURNE, Esq.
Lieut.-Colonel A. LEETHAM
H. LEWIS, Esq.
Colonel H. E. M. LINDSAY
Captain H. MACKWORTH
Colonel MANSEL
Captain J. L. MANSEL
J. HOBSON MATHEWS, Esq.
VIVIAN MATHEWS, Esq.
Major R. L. MATTHEWS
(The late Colonel the Hon. F. C. MORGAN)
Lieut.-Colonel C. C. E. MORGAN
Captain W. F. H. MORGAN
Colonel W. F. N. NOEL
Captain J. G. O'BRIEN
Captain G. B. OLLIVANT
A. G. PARDOE, Esq.
Major-General L. LLOYD PAYNE, C.B., D.S.O.
F. G. PHILLIPS, Esq.
Captain R. J. S. PRICE
T. G. PROSSER, Esq., M.D.
R. J. PRYCE-JENKIN, Esq.
Hon. W. F. R. SOMERSET
EDWARD STEER, Esq.
Miss STEWART
JAMES STRAKER, Esq.
T. G. H. STUDDERT, Esq.
Captain T. R. SYMONS
D. A. THOMAS, Esq., M.P.
J. R. L. THOMAS, Esq.
Major C. J. VAUGHAN
A. VIZARD, Esq.
C. A. VYVYAN-ROBINSON, Esq.
R. J. WATTS, Esq.
E. B. WAUTON, Esq.
Lieut.-Colonel W. H. WHEELEY
T. L. WHITEHEAD, Esq.
Lieut.-Colonel D. E. WILLIAMS
E. J. WILLIAMS, Esq.
H. A. WILLIAMS, Esq.
W. C. ADDAMS WILLIAMS, Esq.
L. V. WOOLER, Esq.
The WORSHIPFUL COMPANY OF HABERDASHERS (per J. Eagleton, Esq., Clerk)

THE
ROYAL MONMOUTHSHIRE MILITIA

CHAPTER I

THE COUNTY OF MONMOUTH, AND ITS FORCES OTHER THAN ITS MILITIA

THE county of Monmouth, washed on the south by the estuary of the Severn and the Bristol Channel, and situated in one of the most fertile districts of the British Isles, possesses an area of 395,849 acres.[1] The whole of the county is not, however, composed of arable land, for there are mountainous parts rich with mineral productions, the principal one being coal, where agriculture is abandoned and where mines and quarries consequently abound. The population is therefore controlled by the industries of the particular district; where agriculture is pursued the towns have remained small and insignificant, but in the localities where mineral wealth has been found, innumerable mines have been sunk, employing many thousands of hands; consequently it is not

---

[1] John Speede, in describing the county in a work published in 1610, records: 'The form thereof is scallop-wise, both long and broad, shooting her north point to Llantony and her south to the fall of Rempney, betwixt which two are twenty-four English miles, and from Chepstow east to Blanagwent west are not altogether nineteen; the whole in circuit draweth somewhat near to seventy-seven miles. The air is temperate, healthful and clear, the soil is hilly, woody and rich; all places fruitful, but no place barren. The hills are grazed upon by cattle and sheep, the valleys are laden with corn and grass, never ungrateful of the husbandman's pains, nor makes frustrate his hope of expected increase; whose springs abundantly rising in this county with many streams do fatten the soil even from side to side.'

Again: 'This shire is strengthened with fourteen castles, traded with six market-towns, divided into six hundreds, wherein are situated one hundred and twenty-seven parish churches, and is not accounted amongst the Welsh shires, being subdued by Henry the Second, who, passing the Nant Pen-carne, a small brook and of no danger, yet held fatal by the Welsh, over-credulous to a prophecy of Merlin Silvester, the British Apollo, who had foreshewed that when a stout and freckle-faced king (such as Henry was) should pass over that ford, then the power of the Welshmen should be brought under; whereby their stout courage was soon abated, and the whole county the sooner in subjection to the English.'

surprising to find that all the largest towns are situated in these iron and coal producing districts. Indeed the discovery of mineral wealth in any locality is seen to have converted a once unimportant market town into a busy and populous place. Thus Monmouthshire has a heterogeneous population, but one comprising men of the very finest physique.

Looking back upon the early history of the county, it is recorded that in the year 78 the Silures, who inhabited Monmouthshire, were subdued by Julius Frontinus. It is even now possible to trace the 'via Julia,' a road made by the Romans between the mouth of the Severn and Caerwent,[1] and thence to Caerleon and Neath. The chief place of the Romans was Caerleon, an important military town at that time, for it was the headquarters of the second imperial legion. Other military stations were Abergavenny, and Monmouth (then termed Blestium).

In the ninth and tenth centuries Monmouthshire was frequently invaded by the Danes. After the Norman Conquest the district was administered by certain Norman nobles, called the 'Lords of the Marches.' Many struggles took place between them and the Welsh princes until the year 1535, when the power of the 'Lords of the Marches' was removed by Henry VIII, and Monmouth was constituted an English county.

Some of the more important historical associations of the county are the following :—

    A.D. 610.—At Tintern, Ceolwalf, King of Wessex, was defeated by Theodorick or St. Thewdric, Prince of Morganwg or Glamorgan. The conqueror died of his wounds three days after the battle, and was buried at Mathern. Tintern Abbey was founded in 1131 by Walter de Clare, great-uncle to Richard 'Strongbow,' the conqueror of Leinster.

    A.D. 728.—On Carno mountain, Ethelbald, King of Mercia, was defeated by the Britons.

    A.D. 1034.—Rytherch ap Jestyn, Prince of South Wales, was defeated by Canute.

    A.D. 1063.—At Trelech, Gryffydd ap Llewellyn, Prince of Wales, was defeated and Monmouthshire was subjugated by Harold, afterwards King of England.

---

[1] An important place of learning and worship in the time of the Romans.

A.D. 1171.—Caerleon was taken by Henry II in his progress to Ireland.

A.D. 1172.—Abergavenny Castle, under William de Braos, was taken by Sytsylt ap Dyfnwald, a Welsh chieftain, but shortly afterwards restored to Braos, who invited Sytsylt and his son Geoffrey to conclude a treaty of Amity at this place, when they were both treacherously murdered. A similar act of sanguinary treachery had been before perpetrated within the same walls by William, son of Milo, Earl of Hereford.

A.D. 1173.—Near Newport, Owen ap Caradock, son of Jorwerth ap Owen ap Caradock, Prince of Wales, whilst proceeding unarmed to meet Henry II, under the faith of a safe conduct granted to him for that purpose, was treacherously murdered by a detachment from the garrison of Newport.

A.D. 1215.—Abergavenny Castle taken from the forces of King John by Llewellyn, Prince of Wales.

A.D. 1233.—At Grosmont,[1] November 12, in a night attack Henry III was surprised and defeated by Richard Marshal, Earl of Pembroke, who took 500 horses, with many wagons laden with provisions, baggage and treasure.

A.D. 1405.—At Usk, Owen Glyndwr was defeated and driven to the mountains by the forces of Henry IV.

A.D. 1535.—Monmouthshire, by an Act of Parliament, was separated from Welsh jurisdiction and made an English county.

[1] Marsh, in his 'Annals of Chepstow Castle,' records, when referring to the writings of John of Wendover, 'We can therefore only notice, by way of summary, how, while the King lodged in the Castle of Grosmont, the forces of Llewellyn and the Marshal (Earl of Pembroke) (the latter abstaining from any attack on the King's person) surprised the royal camp outside, seized their horses and baggage, and dispersed the army almost naked—how they defeated the royal troops at Monmouth—how they met an intended surprise by John of Monmouth by surprising the surpriser, and ravaged his territory till he was reduced from affluence to beggary.' Later, Richard Marshal, while reconnoitring with a hundred men in the neighbourhood of Monmouth Castle, which was held by a distinguished Flemish knight, Baldwin de Gysnes, the latter sallied out with a thousand well-armed men, intending to make them prisoners; but a vigorous conflict with sword and lance ensued for an entire day, when Baldwin de Gysnes, with twelve of his stoutest warriors, assailed the Earl, hoping to take him to the castle, and so end the conflict, but he gallantly kept them at a distance with his sword. Finally, as the Earl was being dragged to the castle by the bridle, Baldwin was wounded in the breast by an arrow, which afforded the Earl an opportunity for escape.

A.D. 1645.—Chepstow Castle, under Colonel Robert Fitzmorris, surrendered to the Parliamentarians under Colonel Morgan.

A.D. 1648.—Chepstow Castle was surprised by the Royalists under Sir Nicholas Kemeys, but on May 25 was retaken by assault by the Parliamentarians under Colonel Ewer, when Sir Nicholas and forty more of its brave and loyal defenders were slain.

A.D. 1648.—Raglan Castle, after an heroic defence under Henry Somerset, first Marquis of Worcester, then over eighty years of age, surrendered to Sir Thomas Fairfax, August 19. This castle has the glorious distinction of being the last in England that held out for the King.

Caldecot, one of the six hundreds of Monmouthshire, lies to the south of Chepstow. Camden, in his 'Britannia,' says, 'Not far from Caldecot are Woundy and Penhow, the seats formerly of the illustrious family of St. Maur, now corruptly called Seymour. For we find that about the year 1240 (in order to wrest Woundy out of the hands of the Welsh), Gilbert Marshal, Earl of Pembroke, was obliged to assist William St. Maur, from whom was descended Roger of St. Maur, knight, who married one of the heiresses of the illustrious John Beauchamp, the noble Baron of Hache.'

Of the principal towns of the county, Monmouth,[1] being the county town, ranks first. It was a Roman station, and afterwards a Saxon fortress. A map, dated 1698, shows it at that time as being on the main road between London and St. Davids. The castle, of which some portions still remain, part being the headquarters and officers' mess of

[1] Speede, in describing Monmouth, observes: 'The castle was the birthplace of our conquering Henry, the great triumpher over France, but now (1610) decayed, and from a princely castle is become no better than a regardless cottage. In this town a beautiful church, built with three aisles, is remaining, and at the east end a most curiously built (but now decayed) church stands, called the Monks' Church; in the monastery whereof our great antiquarian Geoffrey, surnamed Monmouth, and Ap Arthur, wrote his History of Great Britain; whose pains, as they were both learned and great, so have they bred great pains among the learned both to defend and to disprove. The town's situation is pleasant and good, seated betwixt the rivers Monnow and Wye; three gates yet stand, besides that tower or lock of the bridge, and a trench or tract of wall running betwixt them on each side down to the river, containing in circuit about eight hundred paces. The town is in good repair and well frequented, governed by a mayor, two bailiffs, fifteen common counsellors, a town clerk, and two sergeants for their attendance. It is in latitude removed from the equator fifty-two degrees and eight minutes, and from the west point of longitude is set in the degree of 17, 36 min.'

KING HENRY V.
(Born at Monmouth Castle.
(*From an oil painting in the possession of Lieut.-Colonel C. M. Crompton-Roberts.*)

the Royal Monmouthshire Royal Engineers, was the favourite residence of John of Gaunt, Duke of Lancaster, and of his son Henry of Bolingbroke, afterwards Henry IV, and was also the birthplace of Henry V. It was rebuilt by John, Lord of Monmouth, in the year 1257. The town was incorporated by Edward VI, and benefited by additional privileges in the reigns of Queen Mary, James I, and Charles II. The place possesses a decreasing population, which at the present time does not much exceed 5000.

Newport is a seaport town situated on the right bank of the river Usk. It has more than doubled its population, which is now 68,000, during the past thirty years, a fact mainly due to the immense coal-export trade which takes place and to the numerous iron foundries. The place was chartered by Edward III and James I. It was once the scene of extensive Chartist riots, and in the Royal United Service Museum at Whitehall are preserved four pikes used by the Chartists in an attack on the town. About 10,000 of them from the neighbouring mines armed with guns, pikes, and other weapons, arrived at Newport on November 4, 1839. They divided themselves into two bodies; one, under the command of Mr. John Frost, an ex-magistrate, proceeded down the principal street, whilst the other, headed by his son, took the direction of Stow Hill. They met in front of the Westgate Hotel, where the magistrates were assembled with about thirty soldiers of the 45th Regiment and several special constables. The rioters broke the windows and fired on the inmates, by which the Mayor, Mr. (afterwards Sir Thomas) Phillips, and several other persons were wounded. The soldiers returned the fire and dispersed the mob, which fled, leaving about twenty dead and others wounded. A detachment of the 10th Royal Hussars arrived from Bristol, and the town became tranquil.

'Chartism' was a movement in Great Britain for the extension of political power to the working classes, rising out of national distress and popular disappointment with the result of the Reform Bill of 1832. The Chartists' demands were six in number: Universal suffrage, vote by ballot, annual Parliaments, payment of the Members, the abolition of the property qualification, and equal electoral districts.

The castle at Newport was erected by Robert, Earl of Gloucester, natural son of Henry I, celebrated for his patronage of literature and for his skill and valour in the service of his half-sister the Empress Maud.

Caerleon, as before stated, was the headquarters of the Romans at the time of Julius Frontinus, and it was made by Dubritius the seat of an archbishopric, which was removed to Menevia, now St. Davids, in the eleventh century. The name of the place is a corruption of the Latin Castrum Legionis.' Though now a place of but small importance, Caerleon was once undoubtedly the principal town of South Wales. It was long the capital of the British dominions, and is described by the bards as equalling Rome in splendour. Geoffrey of Monmouth says that at the time of the Saxon invasion it contained 200 astronomers.[1] It was the principal residence of Arthur and his knights, 'full famous in romantic tale.' Close to the Roman amphitheatre stands a mound which is called 'Arthur's Round Table.'

Pontypool, a town with some 7000 inhabitants, is associated with the art of imitating Japan varnish; for it was here that this form of industry was discovered, in the early part of the eighteenth century, by Major John Hanbury. This kind of trade, together with the manufacture of Pontypool ware, or articles of polished iron, is still carried on, and a large portion of the population is employed in ironworks, forges, and iron mills for making tin-plate. There is also a considerable trade in iron and coal.

Abergavenny is another place which has doubled its population during the past thirty years, consequent on the mineral discoveries in the district. It is the principal town in the north of the county, and lies in the midst of most magnificent scenery. Its population is approximately 8000.

Chepstow, though quite a small town, is worthy of mention, owing to the interesting and extensive ruins of its ancient[2] castle, which dates

---

[1] Speede records: 'By the report of Giraldus, in this city was the Court of great Arthur, whither the Roman ambassadors resorted unto him, and as Alexander Elsebiensis writeth, therein was a school of two hundred philosophers, skilful in astronomy and other arts. Which is the more credible for that Amphibalus, St. Alban's instructor, was therein born; and Julius and Aaron, two noble proto-martyrs of Great Britain, in this city received the crown of martyrdom, where their bodies were also interred.'

[2] The commission, dated August 3, 1660, of Henry, Lord Herbert, as governor of Chepstow Castle, is worded: 'By virtue of the power and authority to me given by His Most Excellent Majesty Charles the Second by the Grace of God King of England, Scotland, France and Ireland, Defender of the Faith, &c., I do hereby constitute and appoint you Henry, Lord Herbert, to be Governor of the Garrison of Chepstow Castle, with the Works, Effects and Strength therein or belonging thereunto; together with all Ordinances, Arms, Ammunition, Provisions and other Utensils of War therein or belonging thereunto, which you are by virtue of this commission to receive into your charge. And the said Garrison, with the Works and fortifications thereof, you are to uphold and maintain in good repair, which you shall defend and keep for the use of His Majesty. And you shall not render nor suffer the said garrison to be delivered unto any person or persons unless he or they be sufficiently authorised thereunto by His Majesty or myself. And you shall duly exercise or cause to be exercised the Officers and Soldiers of the said Garrison in Arms, and use your best

from the eleventh century. Henry Martyn, one of the judges of Charles I, died in this castle after being confined in it for thirty years.

For very many years Chepstow, on account of its geographical situation, contained a garrison of importance.[1] In the year 1661, Henry, Lord Herbert, who succeeded as third Marquis of Worcester in 1667, and who in 1682 was created Duke of Beaufort, was governor and captain of Chepstow Castle, with Thomas Nanfan as lieutenant and Thomas Jeyne as ensign. He held the office as late as the year 1685, when he had for lieutenant William Wolseley, and for ensign Ezra Walters. In the year 1661 the cost of the garrison, which consisted of one company, amounted to 127l. 8s. per month. To ensure the better regularity in the payment of this monthly sum, the revenues derived from imports and exports at Bristol were devoted to the purpose under a warrant dated Westminster, February 4, 1660. A royal garrison was maintained at Chepstow until early in the eighteenth century : in the year 1695 it consisted of one captain, one lieutenant, two sergeants, three corporals, one drummer, one gunner, and sixty-two rank and file.

Having described briefly some of the principal towns of the county, it is noticed that, out of the total population of 316,864, the majority of the inhabitants either live in the smaller towns or are scattered about the agricultural districts. This state of things, from a military point of view, would have been of considerable importance in days gone by, but in these days of rapid locomotion it is rendered insignificant. It must be remembered that originally the local regiments of a county were

care and endeavour to keep them in good order and discipline, commanding them to obey you as their Governor. And you are to follow and observe such orders and directions as you shall from time to time receive from His Majesty and myself. Given under my hand and seal at the Cockpit the third day of August, 1660, in the 12th year of His Majesty's Reign.—ALBEMARLE.'

A warrant dated October 25, 1660, runs : ' Whereas we have constituted you (Henry Lord Herbert) Governor of Our Town and Castle of Monmouth and do think fit to continue a company therein as a garrison for the defence and safeguard thereof, We do by these presents give you power and authority to raise and arm the said company, consisting of one hundred men besides officers ; and do hereby constitute and appoint you to be Captain thereof to be employed in the defence of the said place. You are duly to train and exercise them in arms both officers and soldiers, and to keep them in good order and discipline, commanding them to obey you as their captain. And you are from time to time to observe such directions and commands as you shall receive from Us. Given at Our Court at Whitehall, the 25th day of October in the twelfth year of Our Reign. By His Majesty's Command.—EDW. NICHOLAS.'

[1] In 1643 Chepstow Castle was in the command of Lord Herbert, as General of South Wales and Monmouthshire. On March 28 Lord Herbert wrote to Captain Thomas Morgan, in command of the trained band at Chepstow, ordering him to remain there and not to allow any of the arms to go out of the town, but to transfer two of the four heavy pieces of ordnance to the town of Monmouth.

recruited in that particular county, and it was only after the invention of railways and other facilities for rapid locomotion that the county ceased to recruit entirely from within its boundaries. Latterly, a militia officer could live in Northumberland and belong to a regiment in Sussex, or a private might have work in the West of Ireland and his regiment would be in Norfolk. The result of this change of circumstances cannot be said to be altogether satisfactory. Originally the gentlemen of the county were the officers of the county regiments, and the men who worked for them or who were their tenants in daily life formed their companies when the regiments were embodied. This led to great local interest and *esprit de corps*; the officer knew his men thoroughly, just as the latter knew their officer, and they had much in common. The County Associations for the Territorial Force, recently formed, have for their object the revival of this local sympathy. At the present time it is possible for each county in England, with perhaps the exception of the three smallest, to recruit complete auxiliary regiments from within its borders; and no doubt it will be the aim of the County Associations to see that all effort is made in this direction.

Monmouthshire is one of the happy counties of England which is able to reflect on its name having been associated with regiments of all kinds—Regular, Militia, Yeomanry, Volunteer, and those of the present Territorial Force.

The 43rd, or Monmouthshire Light Infantry, a regular regiment, now the 1st battalion of the Oxfordshire Light Infantry, was raised in the year 1741, it then being known as the 54th Regiment. The command of it was first given to Lieut.-Colonel Thomas Fowke (who had for many years commanded the 7th Dragoons). The order for raising it was addressed to him as follows :—

'War Office : 17th January, 1741.

' SIR,—His Majesty having thought fit to order a regiment of foot to be forthwith raised under your command, which is to consist of ten companies, of three sergeants, two corporals, two drummers, and seventy effective private men in each company, besides commissioned officers; and to grant a warrant for allowing two pounds for each private man as levy-money, and to authorise the Commissary-General of the Musters to make out muster-rolls complete, for two musters, from the 25th of December last, the commencement of your establishment, the better to enable your officers to raise good and able men; I am therefore commanded by Mr. Secretary-at-War to acquaint you with this, and that

JOHN SPEEDE'S MAP OF MONMOUTHSHIRE, 1610.

his Majesty expects you will take care to have your regiment complete at the expiration of the two said musters.

'I am further to acquaint you that the proper orders will be sent for issuing the necessary arms, as usual, out of His Majesty's Stores of Ordnance; as also to the Paymaster-General of the Forces to pay you fourteen hundred pounds, being two pounds per man, as levy-money for seven hundred effective private men, and likewise to issue to you two months' subsistence for the whole regiment, from the 25th day of December last inclusive.

'I am,
'RD. ARNOLD.'

The regiment was present at the siege of Quebec in 1759, when its casualties were three privates killed; an ensign, two sergeants, and eighteen privates wounded; and two missing. It was also present in the expedition against Montreal, and in that against Havannah in 1762. At the Battle of Bunker Hill, in 1775, it fought with great bravery; and this was the first occasion upon which the 52nd acted in unison with the 43rd, afterwards honourably and fraternally linked during the Peninsula War. In Lord Cathcart's expedition against Copenhagen in 1807, the 43rd formed a brigade of reserve with the second battalion of the 52nd and the 92nd Highlanders, the brigade being commanded by Major-General Sir Arthur Wellesley. On October 20 the troops, after their victorious efforts, were re-embarked for return home.

The 43rd fought throughout the Peninsula War, when they were commanded for a time by Sir William Napier, who served with great distinction, and was several times wounded. He is famous as being the author of 'The War in the Peninsula.'

They were present at Corunna, the brigade to which the regiment was attached being the extreme right of the army, covering the retreat of the British troops to their shipping. The two battalions here suffered casualties amounting to 300 in number. As a reward for the regiment's services a letter was addressed to the commanding officer from the Horse Guards, on March 2, 1821, informing him that 'His Majesty has been pleased to approve of the regiment being permitted to bear on its colours and appointments, in addition to any other badges or devices which may have heretofore been granted to it, the words—Vimiera, Busaco, Fuentes d'Onoro, Ciudad Rodrigo, Badajoz, Salamanca, Vittoria, Nivelle, Nive, and Toulouse.' A communication was also received from the Horse Guards, dated March 22, 1821, stating that 'His Majesty had been pleased to approve the additional word "Corunna" being worn by the regiment on its colours and appointments in commemoration of the distinguished services of the 2nd Battalion in the action fought near that town on the 16th January, 1809.'

The regiment also took part in the attack on New Orleans in the second American War. The city, held by a garrison of 12,000 Americans under General Jackson, was attacked in December 1814 by a British force of 6000 men under General Keane, aided by the Fleet. After a few skirmishes Sir Edward Pakenham arrived and took command, and on January 1, 1815, a determined attack was made upon the American position. This, however, failed, and owing to difficulties as to supplies the British force retired. On the 7th a final assault took place, but the assailants were again repulsed with a loss of 1500, including Sir Edward Pakenham, after which the expedition withdrew. On April 3 the 43rd, with the 7th Fusiliers, sailed for England. After receiving strong drafts at Deal from the 2nd battalion, the regiment on June 16, mustering 1100 bayonets, embarked for the Netherlands to join the Allied Army, and arrived just too late to participate in the victory at Waterloo.

The colours carried by the 43rd between the years 1818 and 1827 are now at Whitehall.

The first, or royal colour, is the Great Union, and the second, or regimental colour, the Red Cross of St. George on a white field. They only bear the one distinction, 'Peninsula,' the other honours, shortly afterwards authorised, not having been added. The colours were made to replace those carried with such distinguished honour in the Peninsula, and were presented to the regiment in 1818, at Valenciennes, by Lady Blakeney, wife of Colonel Sir Edward Blakeney, K.C.B., commanding the 7th Fusiliers, which, with the 23rd Fusiliers and 43rd Light Infantry, formed Major-General Sir James Kemp's brigade of the Army of Occupation in France. Lieut.-Colonel C. C. Patrickson, C.B., commanded the 43rd. The colours were carried on parade at the celebrated review held on October 23, 1818, the day before the break-up of the army, when the whole of the British, Hanoverian, Saxon, and Danish contingents, commanded by the Duke of Wellington, were paraded before the Emperor of Russia and King of Prussia near Valenciennes. They were again on parade when the 43rd were inspected at Gibraltar in 1822 by General Foissac le Tour, commanding the French army in Spain—the occasion when he was forced to admit that the regiment moved quicker than the French infantry, who he had hitherto prided himself were the fastest in Europe. Their last public act was to accompany the regiment to the Peninsula in 1827, when 5000 British troops were despatched under General Sir Henry Clinton, owing to the disturbed state of Portugal and the hostile attitude of Spain. A few months later the colours were retired from service, when a new set, bearing the eleven additional honours authorised in 1821, were presented by Mrs. Haverfield, wife of the commanding officer, Lieut.-Colonel William Haverfield. On the death of Colonel Haverfield, in 1830, the old colours came into the possession of Lieut.-Colonel Henry Booth, K.H., who died in 1841. On April 8, 1895, they were presented to the Royal United Service Museum by Colonel J. Johnstone and the officers of the 43rd (now the 1st battalion Oxfordshire Light Infantry), to be placed alongside those of the sister-battalion, the 52nd Light Infantry.

Another pair of colours of the regiment may be seen in St. Mary's Church, Monmouth. They saw service with the regiment until 1887, in which year Lady Aberdare, at Shorncliffe, presented the regiment with new ones. The regimental colour, though in a very dilapidated condition, still bears the name 'Monmouthshire' and the number 43; also the names of two of the Peninsula victories in which the regiment took part—Vimiera and Salamanca. The Queen's colour is so shattered that it is scarcely discernible. The colours were deposited with great ceremony in the church by the officers of the 43rd, a colour party escorting them from Shorncliffe. After the ceremony, Mr. and Mrs. C. H. Crompton-Roberts gave a luncheon party in honour of the occasion, at which Captain J. Hanbury-Williams, the senior officer of the colour party, in reply to a toast to 'the health of Colonel Vesey and the officers of the 43rd,' responded as follows :—

'I beg to thank you most cordially on behalf of Colonel Vesey, the officers, non-commissioned officers, and men of the regiment, for the kind way in which you have drunk the health of the regiment. The task which devolved upon me to-day was one that brought with it a feeling of pride in my regiment, and of love for the old county to which I have the honour to belong, and which more than a century ago gave us our title of "Monmouthshire Light Infantry." Those colours which we have handed over to-day are, I may say, the last relics of the old 43rd, for on the regimental colour there still remains the glorious old number—the number of a regiment which formed part of that splendid Light Division whose undying fame was gained in the Peninsula War. Forty years ago (1847) when the silk on those poles was full and bright, they were presented to us by Lady Pakenham.[1] Forty years ago we were quartered for the last time in Monmouthshire, and though our connection with the county has been but slight, yet there is a name which stands prominently in our regimental records, and which all Monmouthshire men honour, the name of a Lord Raglan,[2] who, when wounded at Busaco, was a captain in the 43rd.'

The Loyal Monmouthshire Yeomanry Cavalry dates from the year 1798, when its first troop, called the Chepstow Volunteer Cavalry,[3] was raised. This title does not seem, however, to have been adopted officially, for in the 'Gazette' and official lists the troop is called the 'Chepstow Troop of Gentlemen and Yeomanry.' Very soon afterwards a second troop was raised at Monmouth, and called 'The Loyal Monmouthshire Yeomanry Cavalry.'[4] The Chepstow troop was slightly stronger than the Monmouth one, but each possessed three officers. The Chepstow troop was first commanded by Charles Lewis of St. Pierre, and that at Monmouth by Richard Lewis of Llantillo.

Both troops wore a scarlet coatee with dark blue facings and white breeches, and the ordinary light cavalry helmet with a red and white hackle. They were armed with swords and pistols. In the 'Hereford Journal' of October 31, 1798, it is recorded: 'On Thursday last the Chepstow Volunteer Cavalry were presented with an elegant standard by the lady of Colonel Wood of Piercefield. The troop was drawn up in the Park, and made a very excellent appearance. The company afterwards assembled at the house, where a grand entertainment was prepared.' Again on December 5 the same journal states, 'On Friday the Loyal Monmouthshire Troop of Yeomanry, commanded by Captain Lewis of Llantillo, arrived at Monmouth for the purpose of being trained and exercised there for a short time. They were received by the

---

[1] The colours in question were presented to the regiment on March 22, 1847, at Portsmouth by the Honourable Lady Pakenham, wife of Lieut.-General the Honourable Sir Hercules Pakenham, K.C.B., the colonel of the 43rd. They succeeded a pair which had been presented in 1827 at Gibraltar by Mrs. Haverfield, wife of the commanding officer, on the day preceding that on which the regiment embarked on the 'Melville' and sailed for Lisbon to join the army under General Sir Henry Clinton.

[2] Lord Raglan obtained a company in the 6th Garrison Battalion on May 5, 1808, and on August 18 was transferred to the 43rd.

[3] The officers of the Chepstow troop in 1798 were Captain Charles Lewis, Lieutenant George Buckle, and Cornet Thomas Williams. All these officers were serving in 1804, with William Morgan as chaplain and Hugh Parnell as surgeon.

[4] The officers of this troop in 1798 were Captain Richard Lewis, Lieutenant John Jones, and Cornet Peter Rigby, with Tudor Price as chaplain and Thomas Davies as surgeon. In April 1799 James Greene succeeded Peter Rigby as cornet, and in 1804 Thomas Cooke was cornet and Edmund B. Prosser surgeon.

Volunteers of that town under arms, who had previously attended in the market-place for that purpose.' The 'Hereford Journal' on January 15, 1800, announces the presentation of a standard as follows : ' The Loyal Monmouthshire Yeomanry Cavalry, commanded by Captain Lewis, are to receive their standard on Saturday next (being Her Majesty's birthday) from the hands of Mrs. Morgan, of Ruperra Castle, lady of the member for the county. The corps will march into Abergavenny on Thursday morning, where they will remain during the week. A dinner will be given to the Association, to which officers of other corps in the county have received cards of invitation. The reason for the ceremony taking place at such a season of the year arises from the fact of their having volunteered their services in any part of the district, in case of emergency; and an order having been received from the Duke of York for all those corps who have engaged to such conditions to hold themselves prepared to march at a short notice. For some time past it has been notified to the members not to leave home for any time without sending their address to the commanding officer.' The reason for this notification to the members of the corps not to absent themselves was of course the fear of invasion at the hands of France. Lord Nelson's victory at the Nile had not been forgotten, and Frenchmen were longing to attempt an invasion of England's shores. As a matter of fact, in the year 1801, preparations in this direction were undertaken by the French on a very extensive scale, camps were formed at Ostend, Dunkirk, Brest, and St. Malo, and at Boulogne a huge force was assembled, consisting of 160,000 men and 10,000 horses, together with a flotilla of 1300 vessels, carrying 17,000 hands. On October 2 Sir Sidney Smith unsuccessfully attempted to burn the flotilla with fire machines called ' catamarans.'

Lord Nelson, having taken the command of a squadron commissioned to operate between Orfordness and Beachy Head, sent a few vessels into Boulogne which succeeded in destroying two floating batteries, two gun-boats and a gun-brig.

The actual presentation of the standard above alluded to is chronicled in the 'Hereford Journal' for February 24, 1800, ' On Saturday se'nnight, being the Queen's birthday, the Monmouthshire Volunteer Cavalry were presented with a handsome standard by the lady of Charles Morgan, Esq., M.P., in Colebrook Park, the seat of Mr. Hanbury Williams, near Abergavenny. On this occasion Mrs. Morgan, in an appropriate address, delivered the standard to Captain Lewis, who made a concise and suitable acknowledgment of the honour conferred upon the corps, expressing at the same time its determination, if necessary, to die in defence of the standard. A field day followed, for which the ground was kept by a detachment of the Berkshire Fencibles.[1] At the conclusion of the drill, a sumptuous dinner was provided by the worthy member at Abergavenny.'

On October 10, 1801, the following letter, similar ones probably being addressed to other counties, was written by Lord Hobart, from Downing Street, to the Lord Lieutenant of Middlesex : ' I have received the King's Commands to signify to Your Lordship, that in consequence of the happy event of the Ratification of Preliminary Articles of Peace between His Majesty and the French Government, it is become unnecessary to proceed further in the execution of the measures directed to be taken for carrying into effect the provisions of the Act of the 38th of the King, in the event of any attempt being made by the enemy to effect a landing in Great Britain. His Majesty has directed me to add that it is impossible for him, on this occasion, not to repeat in the strongest terms the deep and lasting sense which he entertains of that steady attachment to our established Constitution, and that loyalty, spirit, and perseverance, which have been manifested by the several Corps of Yeomanry and Volunteers in every part of His Kingdom. It is therefore His Majesty's pleasure that your Lordship should forthwith communicate this letter to the Commanding Officer of each Corps of Yeomanry and Volunteers within the County of Middlesex, and direct them to read the same to their respective Corps when next assembled, and return them thanks, in His Majesty's name, for a conduct which has contributed so essentially towards maintaining the public security and enabling His Majesty to bring the contest in which he has been engaged to an honourable and advantageous conclusion. His Majesty has, at the same time, commanded me to state that there is every reason to hope that a continuance of the same disposition which has produced the Signature and Ratification of Preliminaries of Peace will speedily lead to a Definitive Treaty ; but that, until that period arrive, it is indispensably necessary that there

---

[1] The corps which did this duty is apparently wrongly described. There were no Berkshire Fencibles at this date. There was a corps of Volunteer Infantry, commanded by Major Martin Annesley at Reading, and there was the Berkshire Militia. All the troops of Yeomanry in Berkshire were raised subsequent to the year 1800 with the exception of the Windsor Cavalry, raised in October 1800, and commanded by Captain John Sturgess, and the Woodley Cavalry, raised in May 1798, and commanded by the Right Honourable H. Addington.

should be no relaxation in the preparations which have been made for the general defence. I have it, therefore, in command from His Majesty to express his firm reliance that the several Corps of Yeomanry and Volunteers will continue themselves in readiness for immediate service, and to be regularly trained and exercised as often as their circumstances will respectively admit.'

With the signing of the treaty of Amiens in 1802, the auxiliary forces were gradually reduced. Though the Monmouth troop disappeared, the Chepstow troop was retained permanently under an official letter addressed to the Duke of Beaufort on November 6, 1802. In 1803, however, the fear of invasion was again prevalent, and bodies of Yeomanry and Volunteers were speedily improvised on a most extensive scale and almost all the lately disbanded units were raised again. Included in these were the Monmouth troop. Drill and practices were carried on almost daily through many months of suspense until the arrival of October 21, 1805, when Lord Nelson by his victory at Trafalgar utterly destroyed Napoleon's sea-power.

In 1812 the Monmouth troop trained during the month of May at Newport. In 1813 the total strength of both troops was 111. Owing to riots in the neighbourhood of Abergavenny in 1816, the Monmouth troop was twice called out to enforce order.

By the year 1822 the establishment of both troops had been considerably increased, and it was in this year that the Monmouth troop was kept under arms for six days at Abergavenny for the purpose of suppressing a riot. The 'Gentleman's Magazine' states: 'On the 11th May a large party of colliers assembled at Gellyhaw Colliery, stopping by force and chaining together nineteen wagons laden with coal for the Tredegar Works. Intelligence of this outrage and complaint having been made to Mr. J. H. Moggridge, the neighbouring magistrate, he instantly repaired to the spot, accompanied by Captain Lewis's troop of Yeomanry Cavalry, who were at the time breakfasting at Woodfield. In less than twenty minutes, however, a general attack was made on the wagons in the rear, and the coals were thrown out, upon which, hoping to avoid the painful alternative of ordering the cavalry to charge, the magistrate seized one of the ringleaders; but, after some resistance, he was rescued, and the cavalry were then ordered to clear the ground, which was effected in a few minutes with equal celerity and humanity.' The wagons, being increased to the number of seventy-four, were escorted by the Yeomanry to within three miles of the Tredegar Works, where they were met by a detachment of the Scots Greys.[1] The Chepstow troop was also called out this year for the same purpose, and they had, in conjunction with the Scots Greys, then quartered at Abergavenny, a somewhat severe encounter with the rioters, the Scots Greys finding it necessary to fire on the mob, many of whom were wounded.

For the prompt assistance rendered on this occasion by the Chepstow troop, the following letter was addressed to the officer commanding, by the Lord Lieutenant.

Grosvenor Square : June 29, 1822.

Dear Sir,—I have great satisfaction in acquainting you that I have received a letter from Mr. Secretary Peel. He desires me to express to the corps who were employed during the late disturbances in the county of Monmouth in aid of the civil power His Majesty's approbation of the conduct of the officers, non-commissioned officers, and private men, and to state the high sense His Majesty entertains of the zeal and alacrity they displayed in the performance of their duty, and the great advantage that resulted from their services on that occasion.

I have the honour to be, Sir, your obedient Servant,

BEAUFORT.

To Officer Commanding, Chepstow Troop of Gentlemen and Yeomanry.

In June 1822 the Loyal Monmouthshire Yeomanry Cavalry was increased by an additional troop raised in the locality of Abergavenny by John Jones, Esq., of Llanarth Court. It recruited well, and was more than once called out on riot duty. For the sake of economy the Government, in 1828, commenced to reduce the yeomanry establishment throughout the country, and, together with the majority of the other corps, the three troops in Monmouthshire were disbanded. It was not until the year 1880 that mounted troops were again raised in the county. In this year the Monmouth troop of the Royal Gloucestershire Hussars was formed—the county has always of recent years furnished a squadron for the Gloucestershire Hussars.

As regards the other forces of the county, in the year 1801 no less than three other units can be traced. The Loyal Chepstow Volunteer Infantry was raised in July 1798 by Captain Zouch Turton, steward to the Duke of Beaufort, who was styled captain commandant, there being also in the officers' ranks a junior captain, two lieutenants, two

---

[1] The officer commanding the detachment was Captain Charles Wyndham, who succeeded to the command of the regiment on December 30, 1837. He was afterwards Keeper of the Crown Jewels at the Tower of London.

ensigns, and a surgeon. Captain Zouch Turton's proposal and scheme for raising the corps were received by the Lord Lieutenant on April 17, 1798, and he at once forwarded them to Mr. Secretary Dundas for the approbation of his Majesty. The proposed corps was to co-operate with the Volunteer Corps of Cavalry for the defence of the town and neighbourhood of Chepstow. On August 22, 1799, Colours were presented to the Chepstow Infantry by the Duchess of Beaufort, who at the same time remarked, ' I feel myself highly flattered by your obliging partiality in having permitted me the distinguished honour of presenting to you your colours ; yet it is not without some degree of diffidence and hesitation that I presume to take upon myself so interesting a task. But when I consider that I am addressing myself to men of the most liberal principles and generous conduct, who have so readily stepped forward in the hour of danger, and who have manifested so much zeal and alacrity to serve their King and their country at a very trying and critical juncture, I am encouraged to proceed, and with great pleasure deliver into your hands the ensigns of union, firmness, and fidelity, of which you are so worthy, and which I beg you will do me the honour to accept as a small testimony of my regard and goodwill to the loyal and respectable volunteers of the town of Chepstow.'

To these words Captain Turton replied : ' I most ardently wish it was in my power to express the feelings of myself and brother soldiers for the unprecedented honour this day conferred on us by your Grace in presenting to us these colours. At the time we enrolled ourselves with the rest of our loyal fellow subjects to protect our religion, our King, our laws, and our liberties from the very alarming combination of foreign enemies and deluded countrymen whose avowed object was to subvert and overthrow our happy constitution, we did not flatter ourselves that our feeble efforts could have been thus noticed and honoured. I shall therefore only presume to say that these banners will ever be considered by us the ensign of union, firmness and fidelity, and the recollection of the very noble manner in which they have been presented to us by your Grace will contribute to our determination never to lose them but with our lives. My brother soldiers, to your charge I commit these sacred banners, confident that the pledge I have made to our noble patroness that we will never lose them but with our lives will be justified on every occasion should our inveterate enemies ever call us to the trial.

On June 9, 1804, Captain Zouch Turton was appointed Lieutenant-

Colonel Commandant of the Chepstow Loyal Corps of Volunteer Infantry.[1] His commission for this rank, signed by the Duke of Beaufort as Lord-Lieutenant, was similar to the usual commission of that time, except that it bore the words ' but not to take rank in the Army except during the time of the said corps being called out into actual service.' The Loyal Chepstow Volunteers ultimately became the East Monmouthshire Local Militia, of which Thomas Molyneux was Lieutenant-Colonel Commandant, and Zouch Turton Lieutenant-Colonel. Colonel Molyneux was a most popular commandant, and on July 28, 1812, at the Beaufort Arms, Monmouth, at a public dinner, a piece of plate was presented to him, Colonel Turton remarking: 'Do not estimate it, sir, according to it's price, but as a small, yet sincere, testimony of our regard and affection for you. The friendly, gentlemanly and soldier-like conduct we have experienced from you at all times, and on all occasions, has made too deep an impression for time to obliterate; and should any external or internal foes to our country and happy constitution render our military services necessary, the first wish of our hearts would be to rally and be led (under your command) to chastise them.' The piece of plate bore an inscription as follows :—

' This piece of plate was unanimously voted by the officers of the East Monmouth Local Militia to Colonel Molyneux, their respected commandant, in public testimony of their sincere and high esteem for his official conduct as Colonel of the Regiment, which contributed in an essential degree, to that subordination and discipline, which have been the source of repeated and distinguished eulogium and honour. The officers, therefore, animated by grateful impressions, cannot but ascribe such high honour to the perseverance and indefatigable attention of their Colonel, whose personal example to his Regiment, of strict devotion to discipline, rendered the observance of it no less cheerful to his men than gratifying to himself; and they beg leave to present him with this inadequate tribute, as a permanent token of their sincere and just regard and acknowledgment, for his uniformly officer-like conduct, which so eminently qualified him to discharge his official duties.'

The Newport Volunteer Infantry was raised in 1799, and in 1801 was increased to a battalion, as the 1st Battalion of the Monmouth Volun-

---

[1] The other officers of this Corps at its formation were Major John Bowsher, Captains Robert Thompson, Thomas Benson, Thomas Jane, Anthony Gardiner, Lieutenants William Else, James Evans, Thomas Woodliffe, and Benjamin Watkins, with Edward Lewis chaplain and William Else surgeon.

OFFICERS' MESS, MONMOUTH CASTLE.
Built in 1673 from the remains of the ancient Castle.

teers, and thus made a Lieutenant-Colonel's command. In this year William Oglander was in command and Sir Robert Salisbury was Major, there being three captains, three lieutenants and three ensigns.

The Tredegar and Ruperra Volunteer Infantry was raised in June 1798 by Charles Morgan, who was Lieutenant-Colonel, there being in 1801 three captains, four lieutenants, and four ensigns. Colonel Morgan subsequently, in September 1803, became Colonel of the 1st Battalion of the Monmouth Volunteers,[1] of which Sir Robert Salisbury was Lieutenant-Colonel. There were in addition one major, eight captains, eight lieutenants, and seven ensigns.

The Loyal Abergavenny Infantry was raised in September 1803, Thomas Morgan being Captain-Commandant. The other officers were Captain Richard Williams, Lieutenants Lewis Osborne, Baker Gabb, Richard Steele, and Vere Herbert Smith; Ensigns John Harris and William Straker; with William Powell chaplain, Richard Steel surgeon, and John Phillips quartermaster. The rank and file consisted of twelve sergeants, four drummers, and 240 privates. One of the rules of the Corps was 'that the whole Corps go to church every Sunday morning, which will add much to their respectability.' Absence from roll-call entailed a fine of one shilling. Any member laughing or misbehaving when on parade was fined sixpence for each offence, and for appearing on parade in a state of intoxication a fine of five shillings was imposed. In 1805 the Corps went to Bristol for sixteen days' training, the order for the move being issued to Major Morgan in these words: ' By virtue of authority vested in Lieutenant-General Tarleton by His Majesty's Right Honourable Secretary at War; you are hereby required to cause the Loyal Abergavenny Volunteers to march on the 24th day of May, 1805, to Bristol, to remain on permanent duty sixteen days, wherein the Civil Magistrates and all others concerned will be aiding and assisting in providing quarters, impressing carriages, or otherwise as occasion may require. Given at the Headquarters of the Severn District this 17th day of May, 1805, by order of Lieutenant-General Tarleton.—(Signed) D. G. Hallyburton, Major, Assistant Quartermaster-General.' During

[1] The officers serving in the Corps in November 1803 were Colonel Charles Morgan; Lieut.-Colonel Sir Robert Salisbury, Bt.; Major Capel Leigh; Captains William Phillips, Thomas Robert Salisbury, Francis Lewis, William Williams, Anthony Hawkins, Robert Smith, William Thomas and Daniel Baker; Lieutenants Thomas Edwards, John Cobb, Charles Phillips, William Morgan, John Thomas, John Dobbins, Andrew Butler and Edmund Williams; Ensigns Edmund Jones, John Smith Phillips, Richard Haynes, George Brewer, Edward James, Robert Owen, Lewis Williams and Henry Thomas; Chaplain Thomas Leyson; Adjutant Thomas Thornley; Surgeon H. Montonier Hawkins.

this training the same officers were serving in the Corps as were in it in 1803, but the Commandant had been promoted Major.

On August 16, 1805, the Loyal Abergavenny Infantry was inspected by Brigadier-General Sir George Boughton, there being on parade seven officers and 174 rank and file. Major Morgan was absent sick. The total establishment of the Corps at the time was 228 of all ranks. In October 1807 the Battalion was at Hereford, and in May 1808 it was again at Bristol, and there still exist several of the billet-papers by which innkeepers were ordered to find accommodation for the men. The Corps was probably disbanded soon after the declaration of peace. The Usk Volunteers [1] were raised in September 1803 by Thomas Jones, who in December was appointed Major-Commandant. The other officers consisted of one captain, four lieutenants, and one ensign.

The Monmouth Infantry Association was formed in May 1798, with two captains, William Powell in command, two lieutenants, two ensigns and a chaplain. On August 19, 1799, the Duchess of Beaufort presented Colours to the Company, and the band of the Monmouth and Brecon Militia, consisting of twenty performers, was ordered by the Duke of Beaufort from Bristol to Monmouth to be present on the occasion. The Monmouth Cavalry and the Chepstow Cavalry kept the ground for the ceremony. At half-past ten o'clock the drums beat to arms, and at eleven the Volunteers were drawn up in the Market Place, in front of the Town Hall, the Chepstow Cavalry taking the right, the Monmouth Cavalry the left, which Corps united formed a line extending from Monnow Street to Church Street, and, the troops being in review order, the scene rendered most picturesque. At half-past eleven o'clock the parade advanced from the right, the band playing 'The Downfall of Paris,' until Chippenham was reached, when the Corps took their respective stations. For the accommodation of the Duchess a circular-boarded tent had been erected a few yards from the fives-court wall, and facing the tent the Volunteers were drawn up in line. The Duke of Beaufort came upon the ground attended by his aides-de-camp—Major the Marquess of Worcester and Captains Richard Jenkins and John Romsey,[2] of the Monmouth and Brecon Militia. Afterwards there followed the Duchess

---

[1] In December 1803 the officers belonging to the Usk Corps were: Major-Commandant Thomas Morgan; Captain William Adams Williams; Lieutenants Alexander Jones, Richard Reece, Stephen Williams and James Davies; Ensign Thomas Jones, jun.

[2] John Romsey was at the time Captain-Lieutenant and Captain, his appointment as such dating from May 8, 1799.

of Beaufort, accompanied by the Marchioness of Worcester, the Ladies Somerset, and others of distinction.

A party, consisting of the first twelve men on the right of the line, preceded by Captain Powell as Captain-Commandant, accompanied by Ensigns John Hoskins and Williams, advanced to the front of the tent, the band playing a grand slow march and the Volunteers shouldering arms. On arrival at the tent, the whole parade presented arms, the band playing 'God Save the King.' Captains Jenkins and Romsey, who held the Colours, then gave them to the Duchess, who presented them to Captain Powell, taking occasion to remark at the same time on the interest and connection which the House of Raglan had long held with the town and county of Monmouth, and expressing a wish that the Colours would be received as pledges of a future and lasting union. Immediately on the receipt of the Colours, Captain Powell delivered them to the Ensigns, at the same time remarking on the high honour which the Duchess of Beaufort had done the Corps, and exhorting the men, to ' consider the Colours the rallying point around which they should assemble for the maintenance of the laws, religion, and liberties of their country.' At the conclusion of Captain Powell's address, the Corps *ordered* arms, and the Reverend Charles Phillips pronounced the Consecration Prayer. A similar association to that at Monmouth, with Sir Robert Salisbury as Lieutenant-Colonel Commandant, was formed in August 1798, at Newport, with three captains, three lieutenants and three ensigns. Although these armed associations, which were formed throughout the country, cannot be classed as Volunteer Corps, they had certainly military functions of considerable importance to perform; they were only partially armed, it being considered that on invasion the unarmed portion could perform a useful function in removing to a place of safety the infirm and feeble, together with women and children. The unarmed men were also responsible for driving away to places of security for their own troops all cattle which might be of advantage to the enemy if left; they were also expected to harass the enemy by burning all buildings, stores and ambush which might be of assistance to him. These associations had been formed as early as the year 1745, but at that time they were more or less under municipal control and did not enjoy the freedom which those of the end of the century possessed. The arms and accoutrements for the associations of 1798 were provided by the Government, but the men had to find their own uniforms. The question of drill was left entirely to the commanding officer, and consequently it fluctuated in different districts.

To the present Territorial Force the county contributes three battalions, under the style of the 1st, 2nd, and 3rd Battalions of the Monmouthshire Regiment.

The 1st Battalion can be traced to May 30, 1859, when the first Monmouthshire Volunteer Corps of that period was raised at Chepstow, and when a public meeting of the inhabitants of Newport was convened by the Mayor at the Town Hall to consider the question of the formation of a Volunteer Rifle Corps. Those present unanimously approved of the formation of Rifle Corps throughout the country as a measure of national defence, and pledged themselves to further the cause by all the means in their power. The Mayor was requested to take the names of all gentlemen willing to enrol themselves as Volunteers, and also to open lists for the purpose of receiving subscriptions for the formation of a Rifle Corps in the county.

Some of the first Volunteers to be enrolled were the Hon. Godfrey Charles Morgan, M.P. (now Viscount Tredegar), Captain Hon. Frederick Morgan, Sir George Walker, Bart., and Messrs. R. B. Dowling (the owner and proprietor of the 'Merlin'), Samuel Homfray, Frank Johnstone Mitchell, and Thomas Eborall Cooke. Subscriptions towards the cause were soon forthcoming, and within a few days a sum of over a hundred pounds was received. The Hon. Godfrey Morgan originally accepted the office of Colonel of the Corps, but in an old minute book it is recorded, under date July 23, 1859. 'A letter was read by the Mayor from the Hon. Godfrey Morgan, M.P., signifying that he had sent to the Lord Lieutenant his resignation of the Colonelcy of the Monmouthshire Volunteer Rifle Corps in consequence of not having sufficient time at his disposal.' Mr. T. E. Cooke was appointed on the same date Honorary Secretary of the Corps Committee. On August 13, 1859, the Lord-Lieutenant promised to contribute a sum of 100*l.* towards a county corps and a proportionate sum towards a Newport (local) Corps. The Duke of Beaufort, not being in favour of the Volunteer movement, did not contribute. Lord Tredegar granted the use of a piece of land for practice, and also contributed a sum of 50*l.* towards the corps.

At a meeting held on October 6 of the Volunteers who had joined, it was resolved that a requisition be drawn up and signed by those who had enrolled their names as Volunteers to be forwarded by the Mayor to Captain Hon. Frederick Morgan inviting him to accept the command of the first company, and assuring him of the hearty co-operation of the Volunteers should the Lord-Lieutenant be pleased to approve of the recommendation. To this invitation Captain Morgan responded favourably. At the same meeting was read out by the Mayor an abstract of the laws then in force relating to Volunteer Corps, whether Cavalry or Infantry. Sir George Walker, Bart., was appointed Lieutenant in the 1st Newport Company, and Mr. G. B. Gething Ensign. A committee of members of the Corps was appointed to conduct its affairs, and it consisted of nine in number, five being a quorum. Mr. T. E. Cooke was appointed Honorary Secretary of the Committee. It was resolved on October 29 that the rules of the Marylebone Rifle Corps, with some slight alterations, be adopted for the Newport Corps. The Honorary Secretary was directed to write to the Lord-Lieutenant asking him, pursuant to the War Office Memorandum of July 15, 1859, to request the Colonel of the Monmouthshire Militia to provide two Drill Instructors from his regiment for the purpose of drilling the Corps. In the meantime Ensign Gething and the Honorary Secretary were authorised to make arrangements with a Sergeant of the Warwickshire Militia, then at Newport, to drill the Volunteers twice a day three times a week, between the hours of 7 and 9 A.M. and 6 and 8 P.M., at a cost of 1s. 4d. per diem. In the event of this Sergeant not being able to comply, Colonel J. F. Vaughan was to be approached to ascertain if he could allow a Drill Sergeant of the Monmouthshire Militia to be sent to Newport at once for the instruction of the Volunteers at the Government allowance of 1s. 4d. per diem.

At a meeting on December 1 it was reported that, in accordance with the authority above-mentioned, Colonel Frederick Granville,[1] of the Warwickshire Militia, then quartered at Newport Barracks, had been applied to for a Drill Sergeant. Colonel Granville had 'in the most handsome manner allowed the Sergeant-Major and a Drill Sergeant to be at the service of the corps as Drill Instructors.'

Major-General Charles C. Hay, Commandant of the School of Musketry, Hythe, visited Newport in November 1859 in order to inspect a practice ground for target shooting for the troops quartered at the barracks. Ensign Gething accompanied him, and, having inspected the marshes, he approved the site as a fit, proper, and eligible place for a range for rifle practice when it had been protected by proper defences to keep the 'balls within bounds.' On December 22 the Secretary was directed to write to Colonel Vaughan, commanding the Royal Monmouthshire Militia, to decline for the time his offer of Drill Sergeants, and

---

[1] Colonel Frederick Granville was in command of the 2nd Warwick Militia, which was embodied at the time. He had previously served as a Major in the 23rd Foot.

application was made to Colonel Granville, commanding the Warwickshire Militia, for the use of some muskets for drill instruction. The Newport Company was styled the 1st Newport Company of the 2nd Monmouthshire Rifles, a second company being subsequently formed at Newport under the command of Sir George Walker. Other companies existed at Chepstow, Tredegar, Pontymister, and Risca. The Newport companies wore a grey uniform with black facings. The ornament for the undress cap consisted of a crown, and underneath a scroll with the inscription ' 2nd Monmouthshire Rifles ' in brown.

In March 1860 Mr. Gething and Mr. Cooke waited on the Clerk to the Lieutenancy for the purpose of waiving the claim of the Newport Corps to the style of 2nd Monmouthshire, and requesting that it should be numbered 3rd Monmouthshire ' solely in order to preserve harmony among the several corps, and in consideration of the 1st Pontypool Rifle Volunteers having incurred very great expense in procuring their buttons, ornaments, and accoutrements, all numbered as the 2nd Monmouthshire (in error).'

On March 2, 1860, a communication was received from the Lord-Lieutenant forwarding several alterations made by the Secretary of State for War in the Rules proposed for the government of the Corps, among others being a prohibition to style the Committee a ' Council ' and a substitution of a ' Committee to aid the Commanding Officer in the non-military affairs of the corps.'

The Headquarters of the Newport companies were a house adjoining the Monmouthshire Railway, for which a rental of just under 15*l.* per annum was paid. A sum of money was devoted to the purpose of converting a portion of the house into a place of residence for the Drill Instructors, and a sum of about 65*l.* was expended upon making the butt for the range, the land for the purpose having been placed at the disposal of the Corps by Lord Tredegar.

In October 1860 the Pontymister Company was raised and was styled the 3rd or Pontymister Company of the 2nd Monmouthshire Rifles. This being the third company of the Corps, Captain Hon. F. C. Morgan was promoted Major and Mr. Gething was given the command of his company. In February 1861 Sergeant William Ward, late of the Rifle Brigade, was appointed Drill Sergeant to the Corps, and was paid 60*l.* per annum and given the Armoury for a house.

The 1st Monmouthshire Artillery Volunteers were granted the use of the range one day per week, in consideration of an annual payment.

A further sum was also secured annually in respect of the range by letting the land to a farmer for grazing purposes.

In 1862 the three Newport companies were united with those of Chepstow, Tredegar, and Risca, and formed a battalion styled the 1st Monmouthshire Rifle Volunteers, under the command of Lieut.-Colonel Hon. F. C. Morgan. On December 6, 1862, Sir George Walker resigned his commission, and was succeeded as Captain-Commandant of the Newport companies by Mr. Thomas Cordes. At about this time the various companies, which had hitherto been clothed differently, were, at the request of Lord Llanover,[1] the Lord-Lieutenant, given a universal uniform, the pattern of the Chepstow Company being adopted, which closely resembled that of the Rifle Brigade, the head-dress alone being different. This green uniform of the rifle pattern has been worn by the Corps ever since.

On affiliation of Volunteer with Regular regiments the Corps became the 2nd Volunteer Battalion South Wales Borderers, and it contributed a large quota to the Volunteer Company sent out to the South African War to serve under Colonel Hon. V. de R. B. Roche, commanding the 2nd Battalion South Wales Borderers. The officers who proceeded on active service were Captains L. J. Phillips and F. G. Dawson and Lieutenant Crane. Other commanding officers to succeed Colonel Morgan were Colonels Allfrey, F. J. Justice, Ingram, R. H. Mansel (formerly of the Royal Dublin Fusiliers), and J. C. Llewellin, who commanded the regiment at the time of its transfer to the Territorial Force as the 1st Battalion Monmouthshire Regiment.

The 2nd Battalion of the Monmouthshire Regiment was raised in 1859 at Pontypool and Ebbw Vale, under the name of the 2nd Monmouthshire Volunteer Rifles, the Commanding Officer being Colonel Richard Browne Roden. In 1885 the title of the Battalion was changed to that of the 3rd Volunteer Battalion South Wales Borderers. Colonel Roden having died, was succeeded in the command by Colonel Thomas Mitchell, the senior major. Colonel Mitchell resigned in 1892, and was succeeded by the present Commanding Officer, Colonel Joseph A. Bradney, who was formerly a captain in the Royal Monmouthshire Royal Engineers Militia, and who has held command of the Battalion for seventeen years. The Battalion consists of eight companies, three being at Pontypool, and one respectively at Abercorn, Blaenavon, Llanhileth,

[1] The Barony of Llanover in the United Kingdom (Hall) was created in 1859 and became extinct in 1867.

and Crumlin, while the eighth is divided between Monmouth and Usk. To the war in South Africa the Regiment sent three officers and 103 non-commissioned officers and men. The officer in command of the Company was Captain Herbert Llewelyn Rosser. Captain Harold Griffiths served in the rank of Lieutenant in the Imperial Yeomanry, while Captain Henry Charles was with the same force as a trooper. In July 1907 500 officers and men of the battalion lined the streets of Cardiff on the occasion of the visit of the King, and on June 19, 1909, his Majesty presented Colours to the regiment at Windsor. In addition to the honour 'South Africa, 1900–1902,' the regimental colour bears the motto, 'Gwell angau na gwarth,' which in English means 'Rather death than dishonour.'

The 'Court Circular' of June 19, 1909, describes the presentation in these words :—

'His Majesty the King this afternoon on the East Lawn of the Castle presented guidons and colours to the units of the Territorial Force.

'Her Majesty the Queen, accompanied by their Royal Highnesses the Princess of Wales, with Princess Mary and Prince Henry of Wales, the Crown Prince and Crown Princess of Sweden, her Royal Highness the Princess Royal and the Duke of Fife with the Princesses Alexandra and Maud, their Royal Highnesses the Princess Victoria, the Duchess of Connaught, Prince and Princess Christian of Schleswig-Holstein, Princess Victoria Patricia of Connaught, their Highnesses Princess Victoria and Princess Marie-Louise of Schleswig-Holstein, and their Serene Highnesses the Duke and Duchess of Teck were present with the King.

'General his Royal Highness the Prince of Wales, Field-Marshal his Royal Highness the Duke of Connaught, and Captain his Royal Highness Prince Arthur of Connaught, Personal Aides-de-Camp to the King, were also present with his Majesty.

'The King was attended by the Right Hon. R. B. Haldane, M.P., Minister in attendance; the Earl Beauchamp, Lord Steward; the Viscount Althorp, Lord Chamberlain; the Earl of Granard, Master of the Horse; Lieutenant-General the Earl of Dundonald, Gold Stick in Waiting; Lieutenant-Colonel F. Ponsonby and the Hon. John Ward, Equerries in Waiting; Lieutenant-Colonel G. C. Wilson, Silver Stick in Waiting; Colonel W. G. C. McGrigor, Field Officer in Brigade Waiting; and Major P. Holland-Pryor and the Indian orderly officers.

'In attendance upon the Queen were the Duchess of Buccleuch,

Mistress of the Robes; the Lady Suffield, Lady in Waiting; and the Earl Howe, Lord Chamberlain to her Majesty.

'General Sir W. B. Nicholson, Chief of the General Staff; General Sir John French, Inspector-General of the Forces; General Sir Ian Hamilton, Adjutant-General to the Forces; Major-General Sir H. S. G. Miles, Quartermaster-General to the Forces; and Major-General Sir C. F. Hadden, Master-General of the Ordnance, with their respective Staffs, and Major-General the Hon. Sir F. W. Stopford, General Officer Commanding the London District, with the London District Staff, were present.

'The Members of the Household in Waiting, the Equerries, and Military Aides-de-Camp to the King were in attendance.

'The following, some of whom were unavoidably prevented from obeying his Majesty's Command, had the honour of receiving invitations to witness the ceremony: Cabinet and ex-Cabinet Ministers, the Field-Marshals, the Lords Lieutenant of the Counties in Great Britain, and the Chairmen, Vice-Chairmen, and Secretaries of the Territorial Force Associations from which units were sent, General Officers Commanding-in-Chief and General Officers Commanding Divisions, Brigadiers and Officers Commanding Mounted Brigades, the Foreign Military Attachés, the Agents-General and Distinguished Colonial Visitors, their Highnesses the Maharao of Sirohi, the Raja of Rajpipla, and the Aga Khan, the delegates to the Imperial Press Conference, a deputation of Territorial Force Nursing Sisters, and the foreign officers who have been taking part in the International Horse Show.

'Some of the members of the House of Lords and the House of Commons were present.

'The Military Knights of Windsor were on duty on the parade ground.

'The detachments of the Territorial Force in order of precedence were formed up in three sides of a square under the command of Colonel the Hon. C. E. Bingham, 1st Life Guards, and the representatives of the Brigade of Guards attending the parade, and the colour parties of the Territorial Force, under the command of Lieutenant-Colonel G. C. Nugent, Irish Guards, received his Majesty with a royal salute.

'The consecration of the colours was performed by the Right Rev. Bishop Taylor Smith, D.D., Chaplain-General to the Forces, assisted by the following clergy and ministers: The Rev. R. L. White, M.A., and the Rev. J. G. W. Tuckey, M.A., Chaplains to the Forces, Church of England; the Rev. James Robertson, D.D., Chaplain to the Forces, retired, Church of Scotland; the Rev. A. J. Campbell, M.A., United Free Church of Scotland; the Rev. R. W. Allen, Honorary Chaplain to the Forces, Wesleyan Methodist Church; the Rev. J. E. Davies, M.A., Welsh Calvinistic Methodist Church; the Rev. J. Cairns, Presbyterian Church of England; and the Rev. Michael Adler, Jewish Church.

'The non-commissioned officers carrying the guidons or colours then moved to the saluting base, where they were halted, and handed the guidon or colour to the Officer appointed to receive them.

'The colour parties were then moved in turn from their position in mass and halted in front of the King, when the designation of the guidon or colour party was read out, and the guidons or colours were presented to his Majesty, who placed his hand upon them, and they were afterwards handed to the officers of the colour party.

'The guidons and colours then moved down the front of the representative detachments and took up position in front of their own detachments.

'On the command, the officers bearing the guidons and colours turned about and faced their detachments, when the troops saluted the colours with a general salute, the bands playing the first part of a slow march.

'The colours having been turned to the front, the troops gave a royal salute, the colours being lowered and the bands playing the National Anthem, and the detachments gave three cheers for the King.

'At the conclusion of the parade the Lords Lieutenant had the honour of being presented to their Majesties.

'The ground was kept by parties of the 1st Life Guards and the 1st Battalion Irish Guards.

'The following is a list of the Territorial units that received guidons and colours from the King: Yorkshire Dragoons, North Somerset Yeomanry, Hampshire Yeomanry, Herts Yeomanry, Montgomery Yeomanry, Lothian and Border Horse, Queen's Own Royal Glasgow Yeomanry, Sussex Yeomanry, 2nd County of London Yeomanry, Essex Yeomanry, 1st Scottish Horse, 2nd Scottish Horse, 7th Middlesex Regiment, 8th Middlesex Regiment, 5th East Surrey Regiment, 5th Nottinghamshire and Derbyshire Regiment, 6th Nottinghamshire and Derbyshire Regiment, 4th Oxfordshire and Buckinghamshire Light Infantry, 4th Cheshire Regiment, 5th Royal Sussex Regiment, 6th Royal Scots, 9th Royal Scots, 6th Essex Regiment, 5th Northumberland Fusiliers, 6th Northumberland Fusiliers, 7th Northumberland Fusiliers, 5th Argyll and Sutherland Highlanders, 6th Argyll and Sutherland Highlanders, 4th Northamptonshire Regiment, 4th Dorsetshire Regiment, 5th South Staffordshire Regiment, 6th South Staffordshire Regiment, 4th Royal Berkshire Regiment, 4th Gloucestershire Regiment, 6th Gloucestershire Regiment, Brecknock Battalion South Wales Borderers, 4th Suffolk Regiment, 5th Suffolk Regiment, 7th Argyll and Sutherland Highlanders, 8th Highland Light Infantry (Lanark), 4th East Kent Regiment, 4th Royal West Kent Regiment, 5th Royal West Kent Regiment, 5th Welsh Regiment, 6th Welsh Regiment, 7th Royal Welsh Fusiliers, 5th West Yorkshire Regiment, 6th West Yorkshire Regiment, 4th West Riding Regiment, 5th West Riding Regiment, 6th West Riding Regiment, 4th King's Own Yorkshire Light Infantry, 5th King's Own Yorkshire Light Infantry, 4th York and Lancaster Regiment, 5th York and Lancaster Regiment, 4th Leicestershire Regiment, 5th Leicestershire Regiment, 7th Royal Scots, 5th Gordon Highlanders, 4th King's Own Scottish Borderers, 2nd Monmouthshire Regiment, 3rd Monmouthshire Regiment, 4th Seaforth Highlanders, 7th Worcestershire Regiment, 8th Worcestershire Regiment, 4th Cameron Highlanders, 5th Royal Warwickshire Regiment, 6th Royal Warwickshire Regiment, 7th Royal Warwickshire Regiment, 8th Royal Warwickshire Regiment, 4th Lincolnshire Regiment, 5th Lincolnshire Regiment, 4th Royal Welsh Fusiliers, 5th Hampshire Regiment, 6th Hampshire Regiment, 7th Hampshire Regiment, 4th Somersetshire Light Infantry, 5th Somersetshire Light Infantry, 1st Cambridgeshire Regiment, 1st City of London Regiment, 2nd City of London Regiment, 3rd City of London Regiment, 4th City of London Regiment, 7th City of London Regiment, 13th County of London Regiment, 14th County of London Regiment, 19th County of London Regiment, 23rd County of London Regiment, 24th County of London Regiment, 4th East Yorkshire Regiment, 1st Hertfordshire Regiment, 5th King's Own Scottish Borderers, 6th Black Watch (Royal Highlanders), 5th Durham Light Infantry, 7th Durham Light Infantry, 8th Durham Light Infantry, 9th Durham Light Infantry, 4th Yorkshire Regiment, 5th Yorkshire Regiment, 5th Border Regiment, 1st Herefordshire Regiment, 7th Black Watch (Royal Highlanders), 6th Gordon Highlanders, 5th Royal Welsh Fusiliers, 5th Highland Light Infantry, 6th Highland Light Infantry, 7th Highland Light Infantry, 9th Highland Light Infantry.'

The 3rd Battalion Monmouthshire Regiment was formed from various corps in the county on April 1, 1861, and was styled the 2nd Administrative

Battalion Monmouthshire Volunteer Rifle Corps, and the first battalion order was issued on April 16 by Lieut.-Colonel Henry Charles Byrde. In 1861 the Corps paraded with the Royal Monmouthshire Militia at Monmouth on June 14, and acquitted itself well on this the first occasion of being brigaded with Militia troops. The Honble. James Clifford-Butler [1] succeeded to the command in March 1867, and was followed by Colonels James Pearce King, George Relph Greenhow-Relph, and Henry Burton. On June 12, 1880, it was notified that the title of the Battalion would be changed to that of the 3rd Monmouthshire Rifle Volunteers, and from July 30 to August 6 of the following year the Corps formed its first regimental camp at Llantarnam. A Horse Guards letter dated June 3, 1885, granted authority for the Battalion to be designated the 4th Volunteer Battalion South Wales Borderers, and on July 9, 1887, it took part in the great review held in the Long Valley by her Majesty Queen Victoria. Colonel Arthur Goss commanded the Corps in 1890, and on its transfer to the Territorial Force in 1908 Colonel William Dyne Steel, its present Commanding Officer, was in command. The Battalion has its headquarters at Abergavenny. Six companies of the old Corps were disbanded at the time of the transfer to the Territorial Force, and three were transferred to the 2nd Battalion Monmouthshire Regiment.

The 4th Welsh Brigade, Royal Field Artillery, composed of three Batteries, all belonging to the county of Monmouth, was in the old Volunteer Force known as the 1st Monmouth Royal Garrison Artillery (Volunteers).

In 1869 the Corps, which had been formed several years previously by the creation of two batteries at Newport, consisted of seven batteries—five at Newport, where the headquarters were, and one at Newbridge and another at Blackwood. Colonel Charles Lyne at that time commanded the Brigade, the headquarters of which were a large building close to the Newport Cattle Market, now forming part of a brewery. Early in August 1871 the Corps went into camp at Portskewett, and this was one of the first Volunteer camps held under the then new regulations. Some two years after this camp, the 1st Worcester Artillery Volunteers (then consisting of batteries at Worcester and Malvern) were amalgamated with the Monmouthshire Corps under the title of the 1st Administrative Brigade Monmouthshire Artillery Volunteers. The Worcester Corps was at the time commanded by Captain W. Stallard, of

[1] Afterwards 24th Lord Dunboyne.

Worcester, who, with the amalgamation, became a Major in the Brigade. Major C. R. Lyne, son of the Commanding Officer, was appointed junior Major in October 1876 (the senior Major being Major Stallard), in succession to Major Philip Samuel Phillips. On the resignation of the command by Colonel Charles Lyne in 1881 the Monmouthshire contingent commenced to diminish, the batteries at Newbridge and Blackwood had long previously disappeared, and those at Newport were reduced to two. The Worcestershire contingent, however (consisting not only of batteries at Worcester and Malvern, but also at Balsall Heath, near Birmingham), had greatly increased and predominated considerably over the Monmouthshire portion, and the Brigade became the 1st Worcester Artillery instead of the 1st Monmouth Artillery.

On the recommendation of Major-General Trevor Bruce Tyler, the Brigade was in 1890 converted from Royal Garrison Artillery into Mobile Artillery, the then Commanding Officer, Colonel John Roper Wright, subsequently accepting the command of the Glamorgan Royal Garrison Artillery (Militia).

The first mounted camp took place at Abergavenny in the year 1891. No. 1 Battery engaged nearly all old Artillery drivers, many of whom had settled in Newport, having retired from the Service after being stationed at the Newport Barracks. A further camp was held at Abergavenny, after which they took place at Portskewett, where targets were placed for practice similar to those at Shoeburyness.

Colonel Charles Thomas Wallis commanded the Brigade in the year 1899, and in the autumn of that year, when things looked so black in South Africa, he called a meeting of Battery Commanders and, backed up by Lord Llangattock (the Honorary Colonel of the Brigade), who guaranteed a sum of 500*l*. towards the initial expenses, Colonel Wallis was enabled to go to the War Office and arrange suitable terms for the whole Brigade to go to Aldershot for three months' training in the following year.

This was taken up keenly by all Batteries, and the months of April, May and June 1900 were spent at Aldershot and Bulford. The Batteries were at full strength (160 per Battery), and were most carefully assisted at all times by Colonel Peter Hammond, C.R.A., Aldershot. The drawback to the training was that the Brigade was armed with the 16-Pr. Muzzle Loaders, which the Staff at Aldershot called 'cast-iron soda water bottles.'

At the end of one month, notwithstanding the delay in supplying the harness, which finally was delivered in detail (not put together), the Brigade was seen to have much benefited by the training. At this period the Batteries relied entirely on their own men—*i.e.* they had no professional help, no old Service drivers or old soldiers, except the ordinary Brigade Staff, which consisted of the Adjutant, three Instructors, and two R.A. Staff Sergeants. Field-Marshal Sir Evelyn Wood inspected the Brigade twice, and Major-General Sir Alfred Turner inspected and reported on it most favourably.

The second week in June the Brigade marched by road to Bulford. Here it went through the regular course of training (six days on the range at Enford Down) under the supervision of Major Patterson, R.A., and the Okehampton Staff, and the firing and exercise were most favourably reported upon by them. Colonel Hammond, in addition to exercising constant supervision over the Brigade at Aldershot, attended the practice camp at Bulford. His report and that of Major-General Sir A. Turner were most complimentary to all ranks. The then Secretary of State for War, Mr. George Wyndham, also visited the Brigade on the occasion of a field day, and promised to equip it with some more modern guns than those then in use.

Before the end of the training the entire Brigade volunteered for service in South Africa, but the fact of the guns being the 16-Pr. R.B.L. type led to the offer being declined. However, many officers and men joined various corps at the front and did good service. During this long training the Batteries were commanded respectively by Major Clifford Phillips, Captain Hugh Watts, and Major David Ellis Williams. The last-named officer had for his Captain the Hon. John Maclean Rolls, who afterwards commanded the Battery.

In the year 1904 Colonel Clifford Phillips succeeded to the command of the Brigade. At the camp that year at Portskewett, it practised with six 15-Pr. R.B.L. guns which had been issued. The Brigade was also supplied with harness for four guns and four wagons per Battery. This remained the armament till the year 1908, when the Quick-firing (Converted) 15-Pr. was supplied.

Colonel Clifford Phillips was in command of the Brigade when it was transferred to the Territorial Force. The establishment is now twenty-two officers and 597 non-commissioned officers and men, and on April 1, 1909, the actual strength was twenty-two officers and 506 non-commissioned officers and men, and by September the full establishment had been reached with the exception of eleven.

CHAPTER II

A GENERAL GLANCE AT THE MILITIA

THERE would appear to be four methods, which, indeed, must occur to all, for the raising of a military force of a defensive character. First, the old feudal system of the land being compelled to supply, through its owners, a stipulated force. Second, the compelling of a certain portion of the population to be soldiers for a specified term by means of ballot. Third, the obligation of every male subject of military age, not incapacitated medically, to serve for a definite period. Fourth, service by voluntary enlistment.

The Anglo-Saxon military land force of the whole nation was termed the ' fyrd,' and it comprised all males able to bear arms. Green, in his ' Conquest of England,' states, ' The one national army in the time of Alfred was the Fyrd, a force which had already received in the Karolingian legislation the name of " landwehr," by which name the German knows it still. The fyrd was in fact composed of the whole mass of free landowners who formed the folk ; and to the last it could only be summoned by the voice of the " folk-moot." The head of each family commanded the other members of his particular family, and ten families constituted a tything, which was commanded by the borsholder, who was head constable. Ten tythings, being termed a hundred, constituted the command of a chief magistrate. In turn hundreds were grouped together forming a trything, under the command of the trythingman. The entire force of the country was commanded by the Dux, or Duke, who was elected by the people.'

In 827, Egbert, King of Wessex, subdued the other kingdoms of the Heptarchy, and thus was the first Saxon King of England. Up to that date, from A.D. 430, there had existed constant wars between the seven separate kingdoms, which consequently embued the people with a keen military spirit.

It was in the year 871 that Alfred the Great commenced to give his attention to the reorganisation and improvement of the fyrd, and by his diligent labours he was in eight years able to convert it into such a force that it was able to repel the Danes and afford peace within his shores. It has been generally admitted that this military organisation of King Alfred was the origin of the Militia system. In the year 1066 the fyrd, under the command of our last Saxon King, Harold II, defeated 60,000 Norsemen at Stamford Bridge, in Yorkshire. The battle was fought on September 25. The horsemen, under Harold Hardrada, were surprised by King Harold in their camp, and totally defeated; both Hardrada and Tostig were killed, and the survivors of the invading force were driven to their ships. Within a month of this victory the fyrd was seen engaged in a terrific fight against the Normans under Duke William at Hastings. The battle took place on October 14, a fortnight after the landing of the Normans. The English, under King Harold, fought entirely on the defensive, at first with considerable success, but were at last lured from their position by a feigned flight of the Normans, and were then totally routed, King Harold being amongst the slain.

The feudal system was completely adopted by the year 1088, when, according to Blackstone's 'Commentaries,' 'The King held a great council to inquire into the state of the nation, the immediate consequence of which was the compiling of the great survey called "Domesday Book,"[1] which was finished the next year; and in the latter end of that very year the King was attended by all his nobility at Sarum, where all the principal landowners submitted their lands to the yoke of military tenure, became the King's vassals, and did homage and fealty to his person.'

The special feature of the feudal system was that the bulk of the land was divided into feuds or fiefs, held by their owners on condition of the performance of certain duties, especially military services, to a superior lord, who, on default of such performance, could reclaim the land. This superior might be either the sovereign, or some subject who thus held of the sovereign, and in turn had created the fief by sub-infeudation. According to the pure feudal system, the lord was entitled to the fealty of his tenants, but not to that of their sub-tenants, every man looking only to his immediate lord. On the continent of Europe, while the system was in full operation, this principle made the great lords practically independent of their nominal sovereigns, who could

---

[1] According to Ingulphus, a contemporary writer, the book derives its name from its resembling the Last Judgment in its universality and completeness. Others, however, have stated the word to be a corruption of 'Domus Dei,' the name of the chapel in Winchester Cathedral where it was preserved.

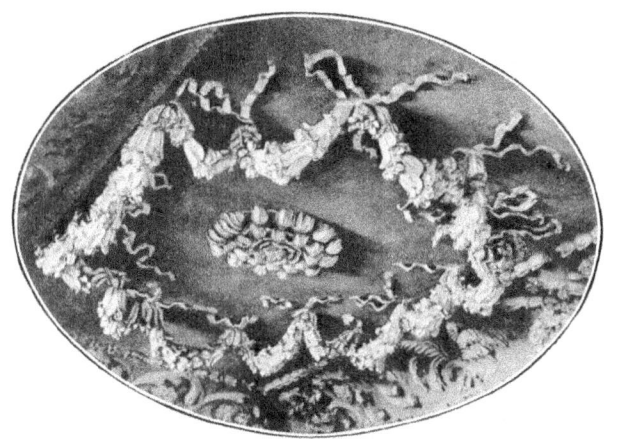

PORTION OF THE CARVED CEILING AT ONE END OF THE MESS ROOM,
NOT VISIBLE IN ILLUSTRATION BELOW.

MESS ROOM.
Royal Monmouthshire Militia, Monmouth Castle

command their allegiance only through their self-interest or by superior force; and therefore kings were often powerless against their vassals. In England, however, the sovereign was always entitled to the fealty of all his subjects. Feudal tenures were abolished in England by Act of Parliament in 1660, in Scotland in 1747, and in France at the revolution of 1789. In Germany and Austria they continued till after the revolutionary movements of 1848-50. In each case, however, they had long previously been much mitigated in their social and political effects. The feudal system of Japan was abolished in 1871, when the daimios or barons surrendered their lands to the Mikado.

The feudal laws introduced by William the Conqueror did not change the constitution of the fyrd or Militia. The whole military force of the kingdom consisted of the feudal[1] troops and the 'posse comitatus,' a new title of the Militia, which force included every free man above the age of fifteen and under sixty. The liability of the 'posse comitatus' was in a degree limited. The men could not be compelled to serve outside their own county, except in case of invasion, when they could be called upon to fight in any part of the kingdom, but not outside it. The feudal troops, however, were subject to foreign service at the King's pleasure.

King Henry II introduced certain laws in 1181 that the Militia might be kept in readiness and preparation to take the field. Everyone who held one knight's fee was required to have a coat of mail, a shield, helmet and lance; and every knight was to have as many coats of mail (lorica), helmets, shields and lances as he had knight's fees in his domain. Every free layman having in chattels or rent to the value of sixteen marks was to keep a coat of mail, a helmet, a shield, and a lance, but a free layman who was worth only ten marks was to have a habergeon (halbergellum), a chapelet of iron, and a lance. All burgesses and the whole community of freemen under the above-mentioned ranks were required to have a wambais,[2] a chapelet of iron, and a lance. Every one of the above persons was compelled to swear that he would keep his arms for the service of the King, and that he would not 'pledge, nor lend them, nor alienate them in any other manner'; nor was the lord allowed to take

---

[1] Hume thus describes the Feudal Forces: 'The military tenants, unacquainted with obedience, inexperienced in war, holding rank in the troops by birth and not merit, composed a disorderly and feeble army, and, during the few days they were obliged to remain on service under their tenures, constituted a cumbrous and dangerous machine which came gradually into disuse.'

[2] The wambais was a doublet composed of many folds of linen, stuffed with cotton, wool, or hair, and commonly covered with leather.

them from his vassal by ' forfeiture, gift, pledge, or any other manner.' Many other restrictions were imposed by King Henry II to insure a sufficient supply of arms and armour on emergency, and King Edward I,[1] in the Statute of Winchester, further corroborated the enactments of King Henry II. The Statute of Winchester was repealed in 1553, mainly consequent on the development of arms and equipments. In 1604 that portion of the Act which enforced the keeping of armour was finally abolished.

The invention of gunpowder was responsible for a total change in the manner of fighting, and consequently for the military discipline of all Europe. The Spaniards were the first who armed part of their foot with muskets and harquebuses, and mixed them with the pikes; in this they were soon imitated by most other nations, though in the reign of Queen Elizabeth the English had not entirely laid aside their favourite weapon the long-bow,[2] and generally taken to the use of fire-arms.

The first muskets were very heavy and could not be fired without a rest; they possessed matchlocks and were fitted with barrels of a wide bore that carried a large ball and charge of powder, and did execution at a considerable distance. The musketeers when on the march carried only their rests and ammunition and had boys to bear their muskets after them, for which they were allowed additional pay. The operation of

---

[1] Dugdale, in describing how the Earl Marshal Roger secured the service of Sir John Segrave, illustrates the military system of the period. He records: 'In 25 Edward I. he was by Indenture retained to serve Roger le Bigod, Earl of Norfolk, with six knights, himself accounted, as well in the time of peace as war, for the term of his whole life, in England, Wales, and Scotland, viz., in times of peace with six horses, so long as the Earl should think fit, taking bouche of court for himself and his knights, and for his esquires hay and oats, as also livery for six more horses, and wages for six grooms and their horses; likewise for himself two robes yearly, as well in times of peace as war, as for a banneret, and for his five knights the like robes as for his other bachelors, viz., two yearly. Moreover, he was by these covenants obliged to bring with him in time of war his five knights with twenty horses, and in consideration thereof to receive for himself and his company, with all those horses, forty shillings per diem, but if he should bring no more than six horses then thirty-two shillings per diem.'

[2] Sir John Smyth, in his 'Discourse on Weapons,' published in the latter half of the sixteenth century, says, 'The change effected in the military weapon of this kingdom was, owing to the youth, inexperience and vanity of some men, who were unable to offer any solid reason, and, in fact, were averse to offer any reason at all, for a conduct opposite to the opinion of soldiers, both English and foreign; and therefore for the experience, I and many others, both noblemen, gentlemen, and great captains of many nations whom I have served amongst, have had of the small effects of weapons of fire in the field, with the reasons before alleged; for my part, I will never doubt to adventure my life, or many lives if I had them, amongst eight thousand archers complete, well chosen and appointed, and therewithal provided with great store of sheaves and arrows, as also with a good overplus of bows and bowstrings, against twenty thousand of the best arquebusiers that are in Christendom.'

loading was very slow, mainly due to the length of time required for preparing and adjusting the match. The musket and rest were used in England so late as the beginning of the civil wars, as is proved by a book written by Lieut.-Colonel Bariffe for the instruction of the Militia of the City of London, addressed to Sergeant-Major-General Philip Skippon and the rest of the officers of the trained bands, and published in the year 1643; but there existed, too, at that date a lighter kind of matchlock which could be fired without a rest; a bandolier was employed for carrying the charges of powder, the balls being carried in a pouch. It was ofttimes customary for the soldier when going into action to carry a ball in his mouth to expedite the process of loading.

On the abolition of matchlocks and the introduction of flint-locks, the desirability was found for establishing regularity and uniformity in the manner of using the musket; superiority of fire was a fact soon appreciated, and collective fire was found to be more valuable than the former individual action. It was therefore found necessary to exercise the troops in quick loading and firing in bodies by word of command. From that date the Manual Exercise may be said to emanate. The Spaniards were probably the inventors of it, and their infantry was at that time the best in Europe. The original English manual was revised *circa* 1757, when the motions of the exercise were made to be performed closer to the body—this enabled troops to practise the exercises in close order; the firing and loading instructions, too, were shortened, which admitted of more rapid fire.

Botée, a French officer, writing at that period, in his 'Études Militaires,' lays down the following rules:—

1. An exercise ought to teach the soldier how to use his arms, upon all occasions whatever, with grace, quickness, and uniformity.

2. It ought, therefore, to include not only every action necessary to be performed in a day of battle, but also all such as may be useful on any other occasion or duty.

3. All useless motions and needless repetitions of such as are useful ought to be retrenched, without any regard to show; as also all motions

MATCHLOCK MUSKET, 1650

which are either tedious or attended with inconvenience or danger in the performance.

4. The origin of the several parts of the exercise is not to be considered, but only the being useful or not.

5. Each complete action ought to have its particular word of command.

6. Each word of command ought to be executed in one or more motions, which should be capable of being performed in equal time, and clearly distinguished in the explanation and in the performance.

7. When an action is too much compounded to be capable of being performed in four or five motions only, it ought to be divided into two or more words of command, not to overburthen the memory and attention of the soldier, which generally is but very moderate.

In 1759 a 'Plan of Discipline composed for the use of the Militia of the County of Norfolk' was published. It is an elaborate and detailed work compiled in three parts. In it many alterations from the corresponding Regulations of the Regular Service are found. The following interesting lines are deserving of reproduction: 'What we have been saying of the extensiveness of military science, and the difficulty of attaining to a high degree of perfection in it, ought not, however, to discourage country gentlemen from applying themselves to the knowledge of military affairs, and serving as officers in the Militia. Military science and the military art are things very different and distinct from one another. The former comprehends the great operations of war, and the business of a general or commander-in-chief; in which there is infinite variety, and room for genius and invention to exert themselves. The latter consists in the knowledge of the subaltern parts; such as the exercise, the evolutions, and the general established discipline and detail of service, which admit of little variation and are founded on certain fixed and permanent rules and principles, that are far from being difficult either to be comprehended or remembered; and we will venture to assert that so much military knowledge as is sufficient to enable a gentleman to go through the common course of duty, and be what is called a good battalion officer (which is all that is required of the militia officers who are never to command in chief), may be acquired by any man of a tolerable understanding, who will bestow a little pains and application upon it, in half a year, as well as in half a century, notwithstanding the great mystery some military pedants would make of it.'

Reverting to the general progress of the Militia, in the fifth year of the reign of Henry IV an Act was introduced describing the powers vested in the 'Commissioners of Array,' an office synonymous with that of the subsequent Lieutenant and Deputy-Lieutenants of counties. This Act provided for the preparation in case of invasion; it gave power to the Commissioners to raise and drill all 'men at arms,' and to cause all 'able-bodied men' to arm themselves according to their substance. The powers granted by this Act to the Commissioners of Array were continued through all the Tudor reigns, but in 1558 an Act was passed granting power to impress men to the service of the Militia.

Philips in his 'Civil War in Wales and the Marches' gives some interesting details as to the control of the Militia in the middle of the seventeenth century.

In 1642 an army was wanted to put down the insurrection in Ireland, and Charles I seemed anxious to obtain such an army, but the House of Commons viewed matters in a different aspect; not that they were at all less desirous to protect the Irish Protestants and to punish the perpetrators of the dreadful massacre, but because they were afraid that such a power in the hands of the King would be turned against them to their own destruction, and hence they required guarantees that this great military power should be within their control. Thus arose the question of the Militia.

1640.

The Parliament required that at least for a time, until confidence had been restored, that the command of the Militia in the various counties should be given to men to be nominated by the Parliament, such as they had confidence in, for the appointment of lords lieutenant had hitherto belonged to the sovereign. The King resisted this encroachment obstinately, and declined giving his assent to a measure depriving him of this right. The men nominated by the Commons in February 1642 were such as the King could hardly object to.

The majority of them, when the sword was actually appealed to, went over to the King, a fact which goes far to show that at this time war was not thought of by the Parliament. The names were the names of those in whom the Parliament had confidence, and they were not chosen, as some suppose, because they were inimical to the King. Of those who were nominated for the Welsh and border counties, several afterwards proved themselves most zealous Royalists—Lord Strange for Cheshire, Lord Dacres for Hereford, Lord Littleton for Shropshire and Radnor, and the Earl of Carbery for Cardigan and Carmarthen. The Lord Philip Herbert for Monmouth, Brecon and Glamorgan; the Earl of Pembroke for Carnarvon and Merioneth; the Earl of Northumberland for Pembrokeshire, Haverfordwest and Anglesey; the Lord Fielding for Denbigh and Flint, and the Earl of Essex for Montgomery, on the other hand, threw in their lot with the Parliament.

The ordinance for the Militia was presented to the King, who was on his road to York, but he refused to assent to it.

Failing to obtain the King's assent to the Militia Bill, the Parliament resolved to carry out their measure independent of him. They nominated deputy lieutenants and appointed commissioners for every county, and these were to 'settle' the Militia. Against these appointments Charles issued his declaration, maintaining that he alone had the power. This the Parliament denied. During June, July and August they issued orders to their commissioners to put their powers in execution—to assemble and train the Militia. The King, too, issued his Commissions of Array, in which he commanded certain persons nominated for each county to call out and drill the trained bands and other military forces of their several counties. The Parliament in their turn declared the Commission of Array to be against the law and the liberty and property of the subject, and denounced all who should act under them as 'betrayers of the peace of the kingdom.' Another discussion ensued; proclamation and declaration followed each other with rapidity, the King maintaining the lawfulness of the Commission, the Parliament declaring the contrary. Some of those named by the King in the Array were friends of the Parliament, and disobeyed the royal mandate; while some of those nominated by the Parliament to settle the Militia went over to the King.

About the beginning of August the King appointed the Marquis of Hertford Lieutenant-General for the western counties of England, where his influence was very great, and also for Monmouthshire, Herefordshire, and the six counties of South Wales. He was entrusted with power to order the Commissioners of Array to levy forces, to train and arm them, and to conduct and lead them against all enemies—rebels and traitors—in any of the said counties.

The year 1660 saw the institution of a regular standing army and the revision of the laws regulating the Militia, whose numbers at that time amounted to 160,000 men. An Act passed in the thirteenth year of the reign of King Charles II placed the command of the Militia solely in the hands of the Crown, this prerogative of the sovereign having been on occasions a matter of controversy. The efficiency of the Militia at the time of the Restoration was unquestionably very complete, and the pick of the force would appear to be comprised in the Militia of London. In Hume's 'History of England,' vol. iii, p. 220, it is recorded when describing the battle of Newbury, which was fought some years before the Restoration, on September 20, 1643, 'The Militia of London especially, though utterly unacquainted with action, though drawn but a few days before from their ordinary occupations, yet having learned all military exercises, and being animated with unconquerable zeal for the cause in which they were engaged, equalled on this occasion what could be expected from the most veteran forces.'

By the statute of 1673 the Militia of each county was placed under the lieutenant, who was vested with the appointment of officers, but with a reservation to the Crown in the way of commissioning and dismissal. The cost of the annual training—for fourteen days—fell upon the local authority. Offences against discipline were dealt with by the civil magistrates, but with a power to the officers of fining and of imprisoning in default. Under these conditions the Militia of England existed for nearly a century. It was a valuable force for the preservation of internal order; it was controlled and regulated in the county; it was officered by the land-owners and their relatives. While the supreme command was distinctly vested in the Crown, every practical security

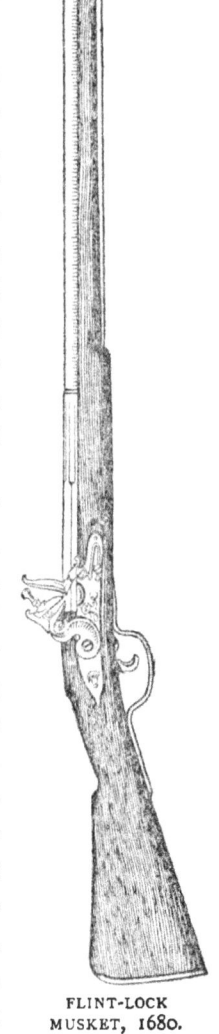

FLINT-LOCK MUSKET, 1680.

was taken against its use by the Crown for any object not constitutional or legitimate. The Regular Army was the army of the King, whereas the Militia was the army of the State. The Militia recruited from a superior class of men to that of the Regular Army, which took within its ranks vagrants and others who had sunk to the lowest ebb. Macaulay, when dealing with the battle of Sedgemoor, comments with some surprise on the fact that five or six thousand colliers and ploughmen should have been able to contend for an hour with half that number of regular troops; but it is apt to be overlooked that at that period the discipline of the Regular troops was by no means good, and that, on the other hand, the peasantry were accustomed to serve in the Militia. King James II, in an address to Parliament after Sedgemoor, does not seem to do the Militia [1] justice for their part in the fight, for they unquestionably contributed largely to the issue; and it is interesting to observe that the apprehension of Monmouth [2] himself was eventually effected by a party of the Dorsetshire Militia, who found him lying in a ditch under an ash tree in the disguise of a shepherd, awaiting his opportunity to escape from the battlefield.

In the year 1757 the reconstitution of the Militia, mainly consequent on imminent invasion at the hands of the French, was considered and brought about. Smollett, in his 'History of England,' vol. vi, p. 270, writing of events two years previous to the reconstitution, says, 'Some of the warmest friends of their country proposed a well-regulated Militia, as an institution that would effectually answer the purpose of defending a wide extended sea-coast from invasion; while, on the other hand, this proposal was ridiculed and refuted as impracticable or useless by all the retainers to the Court and all the officers of the standing army. In the meantime, as the experiment could not be immediately tried, and the present juncture demanded some instant determination, recourse was had to a foreign remedy.'

The reconstitution of the force did not deprive it of its local control, but it gave the King such powers as the appointment of the permanent staff, and a veto in the appointment and promotion of officers, of whom was required a property qualification. Each county had to supply a

[1] Fifteen hundred Militia fought for the King at Sedgemoor.
[2] Monmouth was taken under the guard of Colonel Legge, who had orders to stab him in case of disturbance, by Farnham and Guildford to Vauxhall, whence a barge conveyed him to the Tower. His execution was fixed for the next day after his committal to the Tower; on the scaffold he refused to make a dying speech and died with perfect dignity. The executioner bungled his work: according to a trustworthy eye-witness, he struck the Duke five blows and 'severed not his head from his body till he cut it off with his knife.'

stipulated number of men, to be raised by ballot of those between the ages of eighteen and forty-five. Each man, however, was permitted to provide a substitute by paying a sum of ten pounds. All serving in the Militia, both officers and men, were under the Mutiny Act and Articles of War while embodied, and their pay during embodiment was identical with that of the Regular Service. When the force was called out in case of invasion or imminent danger, it was possible for officers to be promoted for extraordinary merit, without reference to the property qualification, up to the rank of captain. At the end of every term of four years such a number of officers was discharged as was equal to the number of those who were qualified and willing to serve. The adjutants and the sergeants were appointed from the Regular Army, and retained their Army rank. Three officers were allowed to every eighty men, the men being required to serve for a term of three years. The Deputy Lieutenants and not the Commanding Officers granted discharges, which were given annually on the Tuesday before Michaelmas to those who were entitled to them. These conditions prevailed in the Militia of England for many years, and worked with success during the embodiments at the end of the eighteenth and commencement of the nineteenth century. The force contributed very considerably to the large Army engaged during the war in the Peninsula. Between the years 1803 and 1813 100,000 men, or two-fifths of those raised for the Army, came from the Militia. After the fall of Napoleon the force was unfortunately allowed to degenerate, and it was practically non-existent save for the fact that a small permanent Staff was maintained, with but few duties to perform. With the approach of the Russian War the Militia was revived, and it performed very valuable service, doing garrison duties at home and also in the Mediterranean, a course which admitted of almost the entire Regular Army being released for service at the war.

It must not be supposed that the 'calling out of the Militia' at this time was a matter easy of achievement; on the contrary, it was a process occupying many days.

From the time of the Russian War the Militia was assembled almost each year for an annual training, and its efficiency was at all times creditable. It was embodied in May 1900 on account of the war in South Africa, and 99,000 men were under arms, and 22,000 were sent abroad.

It was a matter of regret to many to see the old constitutional force, after so glorious a career, dispersed and exterminated under the Territorial

Scheme of the year 1908. Those who have served in it will be proud of their old associations, for the Militia has beyond doubt been the backbone of the military system of the country for the past thousand years and longer.

On January 15, 1908, recruiting ceased for the Militia, and its substitute, the Special Reserve, was introduced. The establishment of the Special Reserve was fixed at 80,000, and early in the year 1909 the new force had already enlisted recruits to the number of 60,000, most of whom had come from the Militia. The extended period of training for the recruit, and the reduction of the annual training to a fortnight (with one week for musketry for the infantry), at once was seen to influence the class of recruit joining, and instead of the old type of Militiaman, a new class containing younger men, almost boys, presented themselves, no doubt with the Regular Army as their ultimate goal.

The door had been opened, too, for gentlemen to enter the Regular Army through the officers' ranks of the Territorial Force—a privilege which in the past had only been extended to the Militia. This was a serious handicap on the officers' ranks of the Special Reserve, and one which was much lamented by all commanding officers.

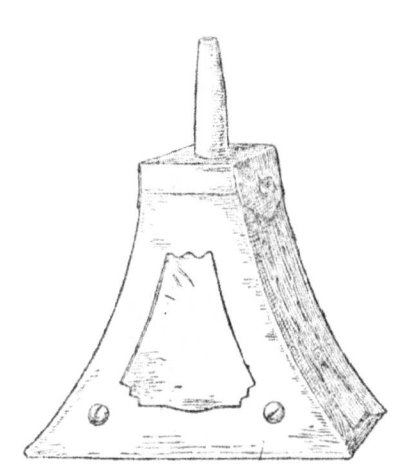

POWDER-FLASK USED BY THE MILITIA DURING THE REIGN OF JAMES I.

HENRY, 1ST DUKE OF BEAUFORT, K.G. (THIRD MARQUIS OF WORCESTER).
Inspected the Regiment in 1684 as President of the Council of Wales and Lord Warden of the Marches.

CHAPTER III

THE MONMOUTHSHIRE MILITIA AT ITS FORMATION

THE Militia of Monmouthshire was formed under Act of Parliament in the year 1660, and though no documentary record exists of the appointment of the first colonel of the Regiment, it may be taken that his commission adopted a similar form to that issued shortly before by the Council of State in respect of the Gloucestershire Militia, which was in these words :

'*To Henry Lord Herbert*,[1] *Colonel.*

'By virtue of the Authority, to us given by the Parliament of the Commonwealth of *England*, We do constitute and appoint you Henry Lord Herbert and you are hereby constituted and appointed Colonel of a Regiment of Militia foot raised or to be raised within the County of Gloucester by virtue of an Act of the late Parliament, published the 12th of March 1659, intituled " an Act for settling the Militia within England and Wales " ; for the ends and purposes expressed in the said Act, you are therefore to take into charge and care the said Regiment as Colonel thereof, and duly to exercise the inferior Officers and Soldiers of the same in Arms, and to use your best care and endeavour to keep them in good Order and Discipline, commanding them to obey you as their Colonel, and you are likewise to observe and follow such orders and directions as you shall from time to time receive from the Parliament, the Council of State appointed by Authority of Parliament, or

---

[1] In 1642 Lord Herbert, eldest son of the Earl of Worcester, was created General of South Wales and Monmouthshire and General of the King's Horse. He, in the same year, was appointed Commander-in-Chief in the absence of the Marquis of Hertford, and also raised six regiments and fortified Monmouth, Chepstow, and Raglan.

Sir William Herbert, owing to his efforts on behalf of the Duke of York at the Battle of Mortimer's Cross (February 2, 1461), was, on the Duke succeeding to the Crown as Edward IV, summoned to the King's first council and created Lord Herbert of Herbert in July of the same year. He was the eldest son of Sir William ap Thomas of Raglan by his second wife, Gwladys, daughter of Sir David Gam, one of the three brave captains said to have been knighted, after receiving mortal wounds, on the field of Agincourt.

Sir Walter Herbert, brother of the Earl of Huntingdon, was in the reign of Richard III ordered by the King to call out the Pembrokeshire Militia to oppose the Earl of Richmond's march from Milford Haven.

the Commissioners for the Militia for the said County of Gloucester, and you are also to obey your superior Officers according to the Discipline of War, in pursuance of the Trust hereby reposed in you and of your duty to the Commonwealth. Given at Whitehall the seventh day of April, 1660.

'ARTHUR ANNESLEY (President), W. PIERREPONT, J. HOLLAND, DENZELL HOLLES, WILLIAM WALLER, AN. ASHLEY COOPER, ALBT. HOWARD, EDW. HARLEY, S. CREW, JOHN TREVOR, J. POTTS, GEORGE MONCK, RICH. NORTON.'

It is probable that at its birth the Monmouthshire Militia comprised, as it did in later years, in addition to a regiment of foot, a troop of horse.[1] It was not unusual for Militia regiments at that time to have included in their strengths such troops of horse, but they were in no way connected with the various troops of Yeomanry raised at later dates in the several counties.

It is fortunate that excellent records of the Welsh Militia of so early a period as 1684 exist in a work entitled ' The Account of the Official Progress of His Grace Henry the First Duke of Beaufort through Wales in 1684.' This work was compiled in the year 1864 from the original MS. of Thomas Dineley, in the possession of the eighth Duke of Beaufort.

The first Duke of Beaufort was President of the Council of Wales and Lord Warden of the Marches. It appears that it was customary

---

[1] Of the other Welsh Militia at the end of the seventeenth century, that of Montgomery consisted of four companies of foot and one troop of horse, which possessed a Standard of damask with tassels of gold, silk, and silver, and the Standard bore the words '*pro rege.*' The Militia of Denbighshire consisted of five companies of foot and one troop of horse, as also did that of Flintshire. The Caernarvonshire Militia comprised three companies of foot and one troop of horse, while Anglesey possessed a troop of horse (whose Standard was of crimson-flowered damask, with gold and silk fringe and tassels, bearing the motto ' *nec temere nec timide* '), and four companies of foot, the Beaumaris company of which had red colours with a red cross in the canton, while the remaining companies possessed blue colours. The Merionethshire Militia also had a troop of horse, and its Standard bore in gold letters the motto ' *non palmam sine pulvere* '; this county only possessed two weak companies of foot. Radnorshire boasted a troop of horse and three companies of foot, whose colours were yellow. The Brecknockshire Militia consisted of a troop of horse, and five companies of foot.

The troop of horse belonging to the Caermarthenshire Militia carried a black Standard with fringe and tassels of gold and silver. The Cardiganshire troop had on its Standard the cipher ' C. R.' surmounted by the Royal Crown. The Pembrokeshire Militia consisted of eight companies of foot, ' all of fire-locks ' (the towns of Pembroke, Haverfordwest and Tenby each possessing its own company), together with a troop of horse, whose Standard bore the words, ' For God and the King.' Glamorganshire possessed a regiment of foot and a troop of horse. The uniform of the foot was purple, with broad cuffs and red stockings, and they wore shoulder belts and white sashes. The troop of horse was also clothed in purple.

THE MONMOUTHSHIRE MILITIA AT ITS FORMATION 47

for the Lord President so early as 1534 to make a tour of inspection of his Principality and the Marches. This tour was carried out for the purpose of seeing that the castles were in repair, properly fortified and equipped, especially as regards arms and powder. He would at the same time submit to English law all criminals who had escaped justice and sheltered in Wales. The last Lord President was the Earl of Macclesfield, who held the office for less than a year in 1689, it having been finally abolished at that date.

Henry, third Marquis of Worcester,[1] was appointed Lord President of the Council in 1672. On January 24 of that year he received a commission to raise a regiment of foot in these words:

'Charles by the Grace of God, King of England, Scotland, France and Ireland, Defender of the Faith, &c., To our Right Trusty and Right

---

[1] Henry, first Marquis of Worcester, has already been alluded to as the defender of Raglan Castle. Webb, in his 'Memorials of the Civil War in Herefordshire,' says, 'he possessed the means and spirit of a prince; he moved in a Court of his own, and in his castle of Ragland, a fortress capable of containing a garrison of 800 men, and strong and important enough to overawe a whole county, he lived in almost regal state. The officers of his household were numerous, his establishment well appointed and strictly regulated as to hours; and amongst his attendants, according to ancient custom, were to be seen, as pages, the children of gentlemen.' Edward, second Marquis of Worcester, the son of the first Marquis, was a man of liberal disposition, and was renowned as an inventor. In a speech in the House of Lords his generous qualities were eminently displayed, when he undertook 'to raise an auxiliary troop for His Majesty's life guard of an hundred horse' to be commanded by himself, with the Earl of Northampton as lieutenant; the whole troop to consist of volunteers, and not men serving for pay or gain; therefore they 'will deservedly require not to be put upon common services, and not to be tied to daily duties, but each will be at liberty to substitute some gentleman of quality, or an experienced officer, to serve for him at any time, when His Majesty requires not his personal appearance.' After this generous offer, he continued, 'My second humble offer is, at my own cost and charges, but under your Lordships' name and approbation and out of the accruing profits of my Water Commanding Engine, to cause to be erected a competent ordinary, affording as well wine as meat for one meal a day for forty indigent officers, such as the calamity of the late time has brought to so pressing necessities, and there shall be a stipend given to a person to read unto them during their meals either of military affairs or history, the better to avoid frivolous discourse.' A third offer, made at the same time, was to erect four hospitals and four houses of correction, in the principal streets of the City of London, to be endowed with a perpetuity of 500*l.* a year to each house. A further offer was a gift of '1,000*l.* a year for ten years to be allotted towards the building of Paul's according as his Grace the Lord Archbishop of Canterbury and the Bishop of London, and now Bishop of Winchester, together with the Dean and Chapter of Pauls shall set forth.'

Henry, third Marquis of Worcester, was Governor and Captain of Chepstow Castle for many years following the year 1661. In 1685, after promotion to a Dukedom in 1682, he raised 'the Duke of Beaufort's regiment of foot,' now the Devonshire Regiment. The Duke's commission as Colonel is dated June 20. His other field officers were Lieutenant-Colonel Sir John Hanmer and Major Henry Carre. The Duke retired from the Service on October 23, 1685, and was succeeded in the colonelcy by his son Charles, fourth Marquis of Worcester. The Duke refused to take the oath of allegiance to William III, and lived in retirement until his death in January 1699.

Well-beloved Cousin and Counsellor Henry Marquis of Worcester, greeting. We, reposing especial trust and confidence in your courage and good conduct, have thought fit to constitute and appoint you, as by these present we do constitute and appoint you to be Colonel of a Regiment of Foot to be raised for Our Service, the same to consist of Ten Companies and each company of Sixty men besides officers. You are carefully to discharge the Duty of a Colonel by exercising the said Regiment in Arms both Officers and Soldiers, and keeping them in good order and discipline, and we hereby command them to obey you as their Colonel, and we do further constitute and appoint you to be Captain of one of the Companies in our said Regiment, and you are from time to time to observe and follow such orders and directions as you shall receive from Us according to the Rules and Discipline of War, pursuant to the Trust we repose in you. Given at our Court at Whitehall the 24th day of January in the 24th year of our Reign. 1672-3.

'By His Majesty's Command,

'ARLINGTON.'

In return for his loyal services to the Crown he was created Duke of Beaufort in 1682, and in 1684 he undertook a detailed tour of his Principality and the adjacent Marches, commencing at Worcester on July 14. The author of the MS. already alluded to, Thomas Dineley, was present as one of the Duke's escort throughout the tour, so the more importance may be attached to his observations.

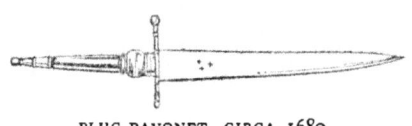

PLUG-BAYONET, CIRCA 1680

The town of Monmouth was reached at the end of the tour on the evening of Tuesday, August 19, when 'the regiment of foot of this county were drawn into line, making a guard from that town even to the walls of Troy, another magnificent place belonging to the Earl of Worcester, commander of this regiment, where not only all that accompanied his Grace through the progress, and the deputy lieutenants of the Militia here, but a numerous train of Militia officers and gentry out of other neighbouring English counties were splendidly entertained by the said noble earl.'

On August 20 his Grace inspected the Militia Regiment of the county of Monmouth, when the Earl of Worcester[1] on foot, as colonel, together

---

[1] Charles, fourth Marquis of Worcester, in 1679 was appointed a Captain in the Hereford Militia, and in 1685 commanded a troop of horse with Sir Richard Bassett, Bart., as Lieutenant, and Thomas Lloyd as Cornet. He resigned this latter command in October 1685, in

THE MONMOUTHSHIRE MILITIA AT ITS FORMATION 49

with his Staff, saluted his Grace. After the Regiment had performed several ceremonial movements, his Grace was invited by the Mayor to accept the freedom of the place, and this honour was also conferred on several gentlemen of the escort. Next, his Grace with all the gentlemen of his escort repaired to Monmouth town-hall for a repast, during which the Militia horse, led by Sir Charles Kemeys,[1] fired several volleys, and the troopers were treated with cider and 'the noted Monmouth ale.'

A commission in the Monmouthshire Militia, dated 1694, of Hopton Williams, signed by the Earl of Pembroke and Montgomery, as Lord-Lieutenant of Monmouthshire, is of interest in that it shows that at that date companies were practically independent of one another, and the colonel's duty was merely to exercise general supervision over all the companies in the county. Companies[2] were usually distinguished by the names of their commanders; thus we read, 'Francis Lewis, gent, to be ensign in the company of foot whereof George Lewis, of St. Pierre, esquire, is captain.'

The commission alluded to runs :

[3] 'Thomas Earl of Pembroke and Montgomery,' &c.
'*To my loving friend Hopton Williams, Esq.*

'Whereas the King and Queen Majesties according to an Act of Parliament intituled " an Act for Ordering the Forces in the several

---

favour of his brother, Lord Arthur Somerset. During the same month the troop was incorporated into Sir John Lanier's regiment of horse. Lord Worcester in 1685 was appointed 'Colonel of that regiment whereof Henry, Duke of Beaufort, was late Colonel'; his commission is dated 'Whitehall, October 26.' The list of King James's Army, as it lay encamped on Hounslow Heath in 1686, shows Lord Worcester's regiment as possessing ten companies of fifty men each. The uniform was red lined with tawny, and tawny breeches and stockings. Lord Worcester predeceased his father on July 13, 1698. His death was caused by jumping from his coach ' to avoid the danger he was exposed to by the unruliness of the horses running down a steep hill with him.'

[1] Sir Charles Kemeys, 3rd Baronet (son of Sir Charles Kemeys, 2nd Baronet), was M.P. for the County of Monmouth 1685-7 and 1695-8; M.P. for Monmouth Boroughs 1690-5; died 1702-3.

[2] This training by companies dates from the time of the Romans, when the centurion's command was the recognised military unit. In England the regimental organisation was not introduced until early in the seventeenth century, and even in 1625 Sir John Oglander, Lieutenant of the Isle of Wight, in a return states : ' the names of Captains as they are to take place and be ranked when they shall appear in the field with their companies and in all meetings on martial business.' The development of the powers of the rifle in recent years has again rendered the company the fighting unit in the field.

[3] Thomas Herbert, 8th Earl of Pembroke, K.G. (son of Philip Herbert, 7th Earl), Lord High Admiral of Great Britain, Lord-Lieutenant of the counties of Pembroke, Carmarthen and Brecon; died January 1732-3.

Counties of this Kingdom " have by Commission under the Great Seal of England nominated and appointed me the said Earl, &c., Lieutenant for and in the said County of Monmouth and for and in the Cities, boroughs, liberties, corporated and privileged places and other places whatsoever within the said Counties or the limits or precincts thereof, And whereas by the said Act of Parliament the respective Lieutenants of Counties, Cities and Places so nominated by their Majesties have power and authority (amongst other things) from time to time to constitute Officers and give Commissions to such Persons as they shall think fit to be Colonels, Majors, Captains, and other commission Officers of Regiments, Troops, and Companies, as in and by the said Act of Parliament is enacted and declared, in pursuance of the Power and Authority Given to me the said Earl, &c., by force and virtue of the said Act and Commission aforesaid, I do hereby constitute and appoint you the said Hopton Williams, Lieutenant of a company of Militia of Foot raised or to be raised for their Majesties' service within the said County of Monmouth, belonging to the regiment whereof Sir John Williams, Bart., is colonel, and of which Company Charles Price, Esq., is Captain. You are therefore to take into your charge and care the said Company as Lieutenant thereof and duly to exercise the inferior Officers of the same in arms and also to use your best care and endeavour to keep them in good order and discipline, commanding them to observe you as their Lieutenant; and you are from time to time to observe and follow such orders and directions as you shall receive from their Majesties, myself or the Deputy Lieutenants of the said County, or any two or more of them, and you are to obey the Superior Officers of the said regiment and company in pursuance of the trust hereby reposed in you, and of your duty to their Majesties. Given under my hand and seal the thirtieth day of May, in the sixth year of the reign of our Sovereign Lord and Lady William and Mary, by the Grace of God, of England, Scotland, France and Ireland, King and Queen, Defender of the Faith, Anno Domini 1694.

' PEMBROKE.'

The officers serving in the Monmouthshire Militia in 1697 were:

Sir John Williams, Baronet . . Colonel . . 68 men
Henry Probert, Esq.[1] . . . Lieut.-Colonel . 72 ,,

---

[1] Henry Probert, of Argoed, Penalt (son of Sir George Probert, Knt., M.P.), M.P. for the Monmouth Boroughs 1698-1700; sheriff 1690; died circa 1719.

THE MONMOUTHSHIRE MILITIA AT ITS FORMATION

John Arnold, Esq.[1]	Major	66 men
Charles Price, Esq.[2]	Captain	74 ,,
George Lewis, Esq.[3]	Captain	70 ,,
Edward Perkins, Esq.[4]	Captain	64 ,,
Henry Morgan, Esq.[5]	Captain	76 ,,

There were therefore seven companies, with a total strength of 490 men, and, in addition, the Regiment possessed a troop of horse consisting of fifty-five sabres, commanded by Nicholas Arnold[6] as captain.

Sir John Williams (the son of Sir Trevor Williams, of Llangibby Castle, who was created a baronet on September 14, 1642, on account of his eminent services to the cause of Charles I) was Lord of the Manors of Ewyas Lacy, Waterslow, and Trescaillon, and proprietor of other lands in Herefordshire; he was also Lord of the Manor of Caerwent, Monmouthshire, which estate he obtained an Act of Parliament in the reign of William III to sell for the discharge of debts contracted in the public service. From 1698 until 1704 he represented the county of Monmouth in Parliament. He lived until the year 1704, when, having died without issue, he was succeeded by his brother, Hopton, who is mentioned in the commission above quoted. Sir Hopton Williams was member of Parliament for Monmouthshire from 1705 to 1708. He was the third son of Sir Trevor Williams, and was born in 1663.

RING BAYONET, CIRCA 1689.

In the year 1707, in company with his colleague in Parliament, John Morgan, he presented an address of congratulation from the county to Queen Anne on the legislative union of England and Scotland taking place. He died on November 20, 1723.

Sir Hopton Williams, having succeeded to the baronetcy, was colonel of the Monmouth Militia in 1704; for a commission dated March 1 of that year, also signed by the Earl of Pembroke and Montgomery as

---

[1] John Arnold, of Llanfihangel Crucorney (son of John Arnold, Esq., of Llanfihangel, M.P.), M.P. for the Monmouth Boroughs 1681–98; sheriff 1669.

[2] Charles Price, of Llanfoist (son of Thomas Price, Esq., of Llanfoist), sheriff 1690.

[3] George Lewis, of Penhow (second son of Thomas Lewis, Esq., of St. Pierre), sheriff 1698; died circa 1705.

[4] Edward Perkins, of Pilston (son of Christopher Perkins, Esq., of Pilston), sheriff 1696; died March 1702–3.

[5] Probably Henry Morgan, of Caerleon (3rd son of Thomas Morgan, Esq., of Lansor Fawr).

[6] Nicholas Arnold (son of John Arnold mentioned above) was one of the band of gentlemen pensioners.

Lord-Lieutenant, appoints an officer as 'Lieutenant in the Company of Militia in the County of Monmouth, whereof Thomas Lewis, Esquire, is Captain, and Sir Hopton Williams, Bart., is Colonel.'

The address presented by Sir Hopton Williams and Mr. Morgan to Queen Anne on August 12, 1707, was worded :

'*To the Queen's Most Excellent Majesty.*

'The General advantage we reap with the rest of our fellow-subjects from the happy union of both your Majesty's kingdoms of England and Scotland (a work in vain attempted for the preceding Century and by Heaven reserved for your most prudent completion) extracts from us the deepest marks of our acknowledgment and congratulation, but being a reminder of the ancient Britons we deem ourselves farther obliged than others to a grateful return of this blessing since we find the name of Britain prefixed to your royal titles. It is a Balm that must heal the wounds of your British nation and make them value themselves that they once more assume their ancient name ; our forefathers in their greatest glory were confined on this Side the Humber, but by this happy union we find ourselves extended (and that without the expense of blood or treasure) with the conquering Romans to the Utmost Thule. We find your Majesty's most prudent administration hath hereby obviated the subtle designs of our enemies in making us one people, whom the God of nature seems not to divide. May that divine light which inspires your most Sacred Majesty and your counsels in this great and glorious work still guide us in the way of Peace, preserve us in that Unity we are commanded by your Majesty to promote, and continue us one till no longer a people. These are the real and Incessant prayers of your Majesty's most loyal and dutiful subjects.

'Windsor, August the 12th day, 1707.'

Again further allusion is found to Sir Hopton Williams in another document :

'We John Francklyn, Clerk of the Church of Langibby in this County of Monmouth, and Griffith Edwards and Phillip Powell, Churchwardens of the parish of Langibby in the said County, do certify that Sir Hopton Williams of Langibby in the said County, Baronet, upon the Lord's day, commonly called Sunday, the second day of November instant, immediately after Divine Service and Sermon did in the Parish Church of Langibby aforesaid receive the Sacrament of the Lord's Supper, according

SIR JOHN WILLIAMS, BARONET
Colonel,
1690-1704

SIR HOPTON WILLIAMS, BARONET.
Colonel,
1704-1725.

to the Usage of the Church of England, In witness whereof we have hereunto subscribed our hands the second day of November Anno Domini 1707.

'(Signed)   JOHN FRANCKLYN, *Clerk*.
GRIFFITH EDWARDS } *Churchwardens.*
PHILLIP POWELL

'Trevor Williams of Langibby in the above-said County, Esq., and Lewis Roberts, of the same Parish and County aforesaid, do hereby make oath that they do know Sir Hopton Williams, Baronet, in the above written certificate named, and who now present has delivered the same into Court, and do farther severally make oath that they did see the said Sir Hopton Williams receive the Sacrament of the Lord's Supper in the Parish Church in the said certificate mentioned, and upon the day, and at the time in the said certificate in that behalf certified and expressed, and that they did see the said certificate above written subscribed by the said John Francklyn, Minister of the Church of Langibby aforesaid, and Griffith Edwards, and Phillip Powell, Churchwardens, of the Parish of Langibby. And farther that the said Trevor Williams, and Lewis Roberts, do say upon their respective oaths that all other matters and things in the said certificate recited, mentioned or expressed are true, as they verily believe.

'(Signed)   TREVOR WILLIAMS } *Witnesses.*'
LEWIS ROBERTS

At the end of the seventeenth century the troopers were armed with carbines and pistols, while the infantry carried the musket and pike, which latter weapon took the part of the bayonet. The pike found its way into France and England by way of Switzerland. Markham, in his 'Soldiers' Accidence,' published in 1648, says pikemen should have strong, straight, yet nimble pikes of ash wood, well headed with steel and armed with plates downward from the head at least four feet, and the full size or length of every pike should be fifteen feet besides the head. In the year 1645 the length of the pike was fifteen feet besides the head; in 1670 it was eighteen feet, including the head; and in 1680 it was fifteen feet exclusive of the head and foot; the head at this date was four inches in length. Lord Orrery, in his 'Treatise on the Art of War,' disagrees with the custom of the time of having the pikes of a regiment of miscellaneous lengths; he advocates all pikes being made of ash, and of sixteen and a half feet in length, with thin iron plates running down the shaft to the extent of four feet to prevent damage by the sword.

The musket of this period was a cumbrous weapon, and the heavier ones were fired with the assistance of rests. It is probable that the musketeer's drill had not changed much during the latter half of the seventeenth century. In 1643 there were no less than forty 'postures' for the musket,[1] which were 'only for Military Instruction in time of Trayning, and to make the Souldier most exquisite and perfect. But in the time of present Service before the face of the enemy, or in fight, then all this great number of postures the Captain shall reduce into three only, and no more. The three postures or words of command which are used for the musket in the face of the enemy, in Fight, or in Skirmish, are these: (1) Make Ready, (2) Present, (3) Give Fire.'

Thirty years before the close of the seventeenth century the bayonet was beginning to assume a recognised position in the vocabulary of arms. At this time it was constructed so that it fixed into the bore of the musket, a system which did not admit of the piece being discharged while the bayonet was fixed. On April 2, 1672, a warrant was issued by King Charles II establishing a regiment of Dragoons, which was to be armed with a match-lock musket, with a collar of bandoliers, and also a bayonet or great knife. In 1689 a bayonet was in existence which allowed of the musket being discharged while it was still fixed. The

---

[1] The first weapons fired from the hand were called hand-cannons, coulouverines, and hand-guns. The hand-gun used in England was a short piece, as appears from the statute of the 33rd of Henry VIII, whereby it was enacted that no hand-gun should be used of less dimensions than one yard in length, gun and stock included. The haquebut, a shorter weapon, under the same statute, was not permitted to be less than three-quarters of a yard in length, gun and stock included. It is probable that this weapon derived the name from the fact that it possessed a curved or hooked butt. The first introduction of hand-guns into England was in the year 1471, when King Edward IV, landing on the Yorkshire coast, disembarked three hundred Flemings, armed with 'Hange-Gunnes.'

The name harquebus was given to a gun fitted with a match-holder which came down upon the priming pan when a trigger was pulled. After the musket had been introduced into the French Army (circa 1575) the harquebus remained the favourite weapon of private persons, because it was lighter and was supposed to possess greater precision. It was not a heavy arm, and was seldom fired from a rest, except by horsemen, who had a light rest secured to the saddle-bow.

The harquebus, as well as the hand-gun, haquebut and dag, were at first fired with a match, and afterwards with the wheel-lock, a contrivance for creating sparks by the friction of a notched wheel, wound up by means of a spanner, being brought into contact with a flint. The balls were carried in a bag or purse, the powder in a horn or flask, and the priming, which was an exceedingly fine species of powder, termed 'serpentine powder' from the portion of the lock which held the match.

The petronel, or poitrinal, was a heavier weapon, fired from the breast of the soldier with a rest to support it.

invention consisted of the attachment of two rings to the handle of the bayonet, which were placed over the muzzle of the musket. In the year 1690 this contrivance was further improved upon by the invention of the socket mode of fixture.

The musket was a heavy species of harquebus, carrying also a larger ball, and it was necessary in its early days to fire it from a rest, which was sometimes fitted with a spiked head for defence while loading, thus fulfilling in a degree the functions of the more modern invention of the bayonet. The Duke of Albemarle, in 1671, strongly recommended this contrivance both for musketeers and dragoons. In the reign of James I the musketeer carried his powder in a bandolier, which consisted of twelve small boxes tied together and carried over the shoulder, each box containing a charge.

The caliver was a lighter kind of musket with a matchlock, and was fired without a rest.

The pistol came into use early in the sixteenth century, for by 1520 it was common as a weapon of the German mercenary cavalry, who were called pistoleers from its use. The early pistol was fitted with the wheel-lock, which was superseded by the flint-lock, and the latter by the percussion-lock. Pistols with more than one barrel have been in use even from the introduction of the weapon, those with two having the barrels sometimes side by side and sometimes one over the other. The stock of the pistol has been made of many forms, the old cavalry weapon having it only slightly curved, so that it was held, when pointed at an object, by the right hand, with the lock uppermost, the barrel to the left, the trigger to the right.

CHAPTER IV

THE EMBODIMENTS OF 1696, 1760, AND 1778

In the year 1696 the Lords Lieutenants of counties received an intimation from the Privy Council, instructing them to embody the Militia in their respective counties. On the receipt of these instructions the Lord Lieutenant of the county communicated with the Deputy Lieutenants thus :

'The Lords of the Privy Council having thought it necessary at this time of public danger by the intended Invasion from France and the horrid conspiracy against his Majesty's Life, to raise the Militia in the several counties of this Kingdom, and to secure the persons and arms of all Papists and others whom you have reason to suspect to be disaffected to the Government, and Directions being sent to me for this purpose, I herewith transmit the same to you, and desire and require you upon Receipt hereof forthwith to meet together and to give all such orders as you shall judge proper for putting the same in speedy and effectual execution.'

It has already been mentioned that the various companies at this date were usually distinguished by the name of the captain, but it also occurred that some were named as belonging to a certain district or place : thus there is a commission dated November 15, 1715, signed by John Morgan, of Tredegar, Lord Lieutenant, appointing Thomas Lewis, of St. Pierre, Esquire, to be captain of the company of Militia for the hundred of Caldicot, in the county of Monmouth, under the command of Sir Hopton Williams, of Llangibby, Bart.

Hostilities with the French in the year 1756 were the cause of the reorganisation of the Militia. During the seventy years preceding that date the force throughout the country, though it had been embodied on three occasions—namely, in 1696, 1715, and 1745—had remained dormant, and but little was done to render it efficient, it being only occasionally called out for training. Up to 1756 the Militia was provided by owners of property, not of land exclusively, in proportions set out in

COMMISSION OF LIEUT.-COLONEL HENRY PROBERT.
Dated August 14, 1702.

the Act of 1662. No person was bound to provide a horse, horseman and arms unless he had a real estate of 500*l.* a year or a personalty of 6,000*l.*, nor a foot soldier and arms unless he had 50*l.* a year in land or a personal estate of 600*l.* in goods or money; but a joint obligation of providing a horseman and arms might be imposed on two or three individuals. Mainly the result of the deficiencies of the 1745 embodiment, the Act of December 1757 caused the exercise of the ballot for the first time; and from that date the expenses of the force no longer came as a charge upon property, but each county was required to furnish a fixed quota of men. The quota for the whole country was originally fixed at upwards of 60,000 men, but it was subsequently reduced by the House of Lords to 32,040. The force consisted of infantry only, and not of horse and foot as hitherto. The Lords Lieutenants were empowered to assemble and arm the Militia and to grant commissions to the proper number of officers, who were required to have a property qualification, one half of which property had to be within the county for which they served. A deputy lieutenant or colonel was required to have an estate of the yearly value of 400*l.*, or be heir-apparent to a person possessing one of the yearly value of 800*l.* The qualification of a lieutenant-colonel or major was an estate of the value of 300*l.* yearly, or be the heir-apparent of one of 600*l.*; that of a captain an estate of 200*l.*, or be the heir to double the amount; while a lieutenant was required to have either an estate of 100*l.* yearly or be the son of a person possessed of one of 200*l.*, and an ensign's qualification was half this latter amount. Officers, on special occasions, were allowed to be promoted up to the rank of captain on account of merit. The acceptance of a commission did not entail the relinquishment of a seat in Parliament; also at the end of every term of four years such a number of officers had to be discharged as equalled the number of those who were qualified and willing to serve. Adjutants were appointed from the Regular Army, who still preserved their Army rank, and sergeants of the Army, too, were appointed to the force, and were allowed to return after their Militia service on producing certificates of good behaviour. Ale-house keepers and sellers of spirituous liquors were disqualified from being sergeants. The number of privates to be raised in Monmouthshire was 240, and in Brecon 160. Three officers were allowed to eighty men. Regiments consisted of from seven to twelve companies of forty men each, and were trained in half companies on the first Monday in the months of March, April, May, June, July, August, September, and October; and in companies on the third Monday of the same months; and as regiments or battalions on the Tuesday, Wednesday, Thursday, and Friday in Whitsun week in every year. The Lord Lieutenant was required to appoint a clerk and also a sergeant-major out of the sergeants, and also a drum-major out of the drummers, of each regiment or battalion. The drills above mentioned consisted of six hours per diem, but the men were not allowed to be under arms for more than two hours at a time. They were enlisted for three years, and were not liable to serve outside the United Kingdom, and could not be compelled to go more than six miles from their homes to perform their company drills. Discharges were granted by deputy lieutenants, and not by commanding officers, and breaches of discipline were punished by justices of the peace. If a man was drunk on duty he might be fined ten shillings, or be put in the stocks for an hour.

STOCKS AT MITCHEL TROY, NEAR MONMOUTH.

The punishment of confinement to the stocks[1] was sometimes meted out for minor offences at this time. It differed from the restraint by fetters in

FINGER-STOCKS PRESERVED IN THE PARISH CHURCH, ASHBY-DE-LA-ZOUCH, LEICESTERSHIRE.

[1] Militiamen for absence or disobedience were usually fined for the first offence two shillings, or were kept in the stocks for an hour. For the second offence they would be fined four shillings, or four days in the House of Correction; and for the third and subsequent offences fines of six shillings were inflicted, or confinement for one month in the House of Correction was allowed as the alternative.

that the latter punishment would be carried out within a prison, whereas the person sentenced to the stocks underwent the ignominy of public exposure. The use of the stocks was not resorted to to any extent as a military punishment in England, but it was practised in Scotland, and in the regulations issued in the year 1700 to the Edinburgh Town Guard (or trained bands) the stocks are ordered as a lighter penalty than the 'wooden horse,' which was the most common of the punishments for minor offences. It consisted of an imitation of a horse, made of wood, the legs being either fixed to the ground or fastened to a moveable truck; the planks forming the back of the animal were joined so as to make a most acute angle. Upon this uncomfortable angle the sentenced man had to sit, sometimes with his hands tied. His feet would be weighted according to the enormity of his crime, and sometimes so much as 60 lb. would be suspended. For purely military offences the criminal would be limited, as regards exposure, to the barrack square; but in the case of injury to a civilian the soldier would be perambulated around the market-place, and frequently with the cause for this torture posted in large letters on his back. Thus at a court-martial at Tangier a man was sentenced to half an hour on the 'wooden horse' ' for giving a Jew a box on the ear.' It appears that artillerymen were not sentenced to the 'wooden horse,' but were ordered to 'ride the gun.' Thus at Tangier on June 25, 1664, a gunner for insubordinate conduct was ordered 'in face of the parade for the space of an hour to ride the gun with a 12-pound ball at each heel.'

Punishment drill existed even in these early days. At St. Helena in 1706 a man was ordered to carry three muskets on each shoulder for a distance of about a mile and a half. Grose, in his 'Military Antiquities,' published in 1786, alludes to a curious form of punishment termed the 'whirligig.' In describing it he states, ' In garrisons where martial law prevails, the followers of an army are liable to military punishments. One formerly very common for trifling offences committed by petit sutlers, Jews, brawling women, and suchlike persons, was the whirligig. This was a kind of circular wooden cage which turned on a pivot, and when set in motion whirled round with such amazing velocity that the delinquent became extremely sick, and commonly emptied his or her body through every aperture.'

The punishment of degrading a man to the position of a pioneer is mentioned by Markham in 1622. He says: 'When any common soldier shall commit a slight offence, savouring either of carelessness, slothfulness, or baseness, then presently[1] to take away his sword and make him a pioneer; which in times past I have known so hateful and intolerable to every quick and understanding spirit, that they would with more alacrity have run to the rack, the bolts, or strappado, nay even to death itself, rather than to the mortal degradation.'

Of those more severe punishments at the end of the seventeenth century, death, of course, came first. Sir James Turner points out that the death penalty could be inflicted in four ways: by beheading, by two different ways of shooting, and by hanging. To be beheaded was considered a more aristocratic death than execution by the other methods, and it was generally employed in the case of officers of distinction. Thus a court-martial held on October 19, 1695, sentenced Major-General Ellenberg to be beheaded for the surrender of Dixmunde.

In the case of a man sentenced to be shot, it was not infrequent that the sentence was carried out with the prisoner's grave before his eyes, the whole regiment being paraded for the occasion. Having been pinioned, the condemned man would be led before the regiment, and after the sentence had been carried out, his corpse would sometimes be carried three times round the parade. Cavalry soldiers usually suffered death at the hands of the pistol, while the musket was employed in the case of infantrymen. Death by hanging was as a rule only meted out for the basest of crimes; though before the first Mutiny Act of 1689 it was more frequently resorted to.

The Mutiny Act introduced shooting for many crimes formerly punished by hanging. The severity of the punishment of hanging was sometimes even more accentuated by the body being ordered to be left hanging. Thus on May 14, 1664, a soldier, for desertion to the enemy, was ordered to be hanged, ' and there continue hanging until he rot off.'

The punishment of whipping, which was inflicted by means of stout switches, was not regarded as one of great severity, and it was certainly not so extreme as that of flogging, a process of flagellation by cords introduced towards the middle of the eighteenth century. As a rule, the number of strokes ordered for a sentence of whipping was thirty-nine or less, but records exist of excessive administration; for instance, two men of the Fourth Foot, in Flanders, were sentenced for desertion ' to be whipped by the hangman with a rope about his neck at the head of every regiment of his Majesty's subjects, and to have twenty-one lashes at each regiment.' Twenty-six regiments being present, this

---

[1] The word ' presently ' is here used in its strict sense of ' immediately.'

punishment entailed over 500 lashes. Dealing with flogging in later years, at a regimental court-martial held at Newbury on April 29, 1793, a private of the Monmouth and Brecon Militia, for absenting himself from quarters and for theft, was sentenced to 400 lashes, whereof 100 were subsequently remitted. On June 24 of the same year another private of the regiment, for getting drunk frequently on detachment, and otherwise misbehaving, was sentenced to 300 lashes, and received 200 of the number. A third court-martial, held at Wells, sentenced a private of Captain Morgan's company for not returning at the expiration of his furlough, and for obtaining it by false pretences, to 300 lashes, 75 of which number were remitted.

On August 23, 1810, the Sergeant-Major of the South Gloucester Militia was sentenced by court-martial at Brighton to be degraded to the ranks and to receive 300 lashes for 'abrupt and improper conduct' to a subaltern officer of the Regiment. At the same time the Guard, consisting of one sergeant, two corporals, and eighteen privates, for refusing to arrest the Sergeant-Major by direction of the Subaltern, were sentenced to 200 lashes each, the non-commissioned officers being reduced at the same time. A portion of these sentences was subsequently remitted.

The gatloup, gantelope, or gantlet was a form of whipping of less disgrace than that inflicted by the provost alone. The word, being derived from the German *gasse*, a street, and *laufen*, to run, indicates that the sentenced man had to run between lines of his own comrades, who would chastise him with switches as he passed. No doubt the expression 'to run the gauntlet' had its origin in this punishment of the gatloup, which was even known in the Roman army.

When the office of regimental provost was abolished towards the end of the seventeenth century it fell to the lot of the drummers to ac as executioners. Thus the sentence of a court-martial of January 13, 1696-7, runs: 'to receive twenty stripes apiece from a drum-beater upon the naked back.'

The cat-o'-nine-tails, consisting of a short rod with nine knotted cords, was in use in the Navy at the end of the seventeenth century; for it is recorded that on September 16, 1678, for theft, ' a seaman had twenty-nine lashes with a cat of nine tails, and was then washed with salt water.'

The punishment of having the tongue bored with a hot iron was meted out for blasphemy, and it was given alike to officer and man. Other punishments in the form of mutilation of the body were the cutting off of the ear, or the nose, and branding with a hot iron.

In the year 1756 the French, having augmented their navy very considerably, ordered all British subjects in France to leave the country, published an edict for the encouragement of privateers, seized every British vessel in their ports, and sent their crews to prison. They then began to threaten England with invasion, and, in order to give this project an air of probability, were extremely busy in their military preparations on the coast of the English Channel. But the design of these preparations was merely to divert attention from the armaments in the Mediterranean, where the blow was really intended. The King, the Ministry, and their adherents in Parliament were, however, so completely duped by the French manœuvre that Hessian and Hanoverian troops were sent for to protect England. At length the destination of the armament at Toulon was so certain and universally known that the British Government suddenly, with too great speed and lack of intelligence, commenced to act. It was known to all Europe that the French squadron at Toulon consisted of thirteen ships of the line, and that 15,000 land forces were there ready for embarkation; nevertheless, only ten British ships were sent out, and the command was given to Admiral Byng, a man whose courage and abilities had until then been untried. With this squadron not completely manned, without either hospital or fireship, he sailed from Spithead on April 7. He had on board Major-General Stuart, Lord Effingham, Colonel Cornwallis, and about forty inferior officers whose regiments were in garrison at Minorca; also a regiment to be landed at Gibraltar, and about a hundred recruits. On April 18 a French fleet of twelve ships of the line and transports, carrying 16,000 troops, appeared off Minorca and threatened Mahon. The castle of St. Philip, which commands the town and harbour, was a strong fortress; but the garrison had been reduced to 3,000 men, and Lord Tyrawley, the Governor, as well as a great many officers, were absent. The defence of the place therefore fell upon General Blakeney, a brave officer, but old and

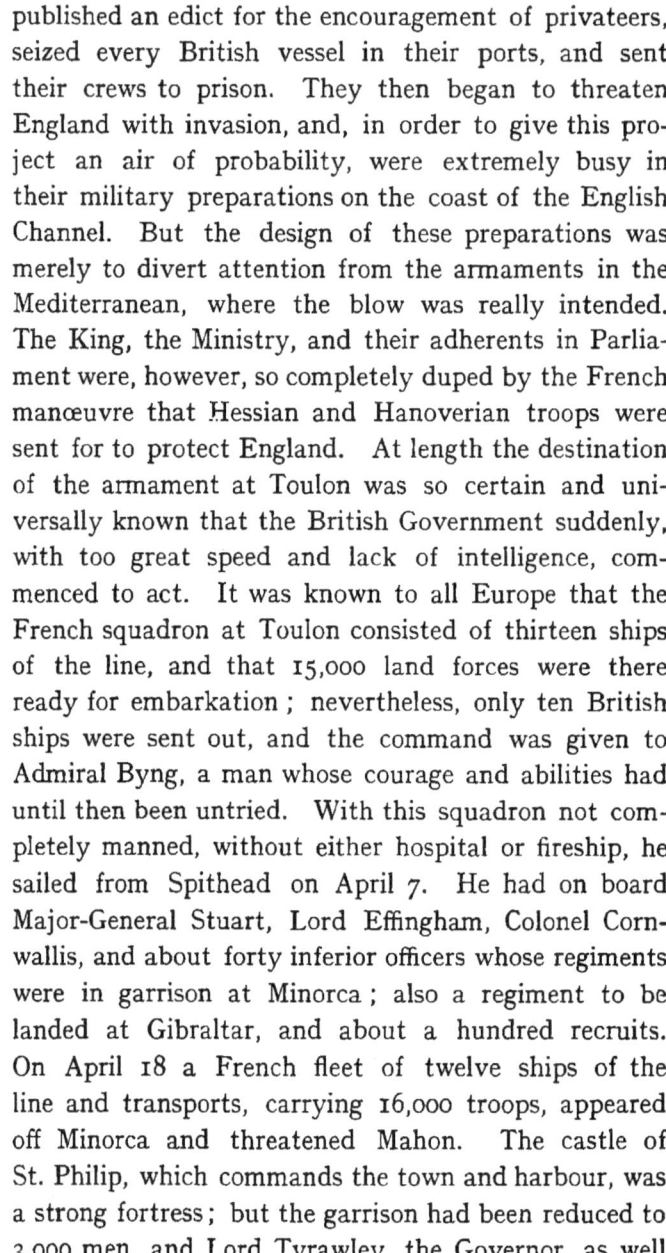

HEAVY FLINT-LOCK MUSKET, 1744.

invalided. Byng hove in sight of St. Philip's on May 19. On the following day the French admiral, De la Galissonière, bore down with his whole force. Byng ranged his ships in line of battle, and Admiral West, the second in command, engaged with his division and dispersed the ships opposed to him; but Byng kept aloof. On the following morning the French were out of sight. Byng then called a council of war, expressed his determination to retreat, as his force was so inferior to that of the enemy, and, sailing to Gibraltar, left Minorca to its fate. Nevertheless, St. Philip's held out till June 27, when, some of the outworks having been carried, the garrison was obliged to capitulate. Byng in December of the same year was tried by court-martial on charges of treachery and cowardice; of these accusations he was found by the court to be innocent, but condemned, by the twelfth article of war, of not having done all in his power to relieve St. Philip's and defeat the French fleet. Though recommended to mercy, public clamour was too great, and he was shot on the quarterdeck of the *Monarque*, March 14, 1757.

The Seven Years' War kept England busily engaged, and in 1758 war raged in all quarters of the globe, which necessitated the forces of England being strained to the utmost. Further plans of invasion on the part of the French were made at Havre and Toulon, but Rodney and Hawke frustrated these efforts. In 1759, in consequence of the military demands owing to further threats of invasion, the Militia was embodied; but towards the close of the year 1762 was disembodied, and for the following fifteen years was assembled annually for twenty-eight days' training and exercise, the old system of training having been abolished.

Previous to the embodiment of 1759 an official letter was addressed to the Lieutenants of counties in the following terms:

Whitehall, June 5, 1759.

'MY LORD,—The King having, by a most gracious message, acquainted His Parliament with His having received repeated intelligence of the actual Preparations making in the French Ports to invade This Kingdom, and of the imminent Danger of such Invasion being attempted, to the end that His Majesty may (if He shall think proper) cause the Militia, or such part thereof as shall be necessary, to be drawn out and embodied, and to march as Occasion shall require; I am commanded to signify the King's Pleasure to your Grace (your Lordship, or You), that you do forthwith transmit to One of His Principal Secretaries of State, for His Majesty's Information, an Account of what Progress has been made in the County of —— in the Execution of the Acts[1] of Parliament, past in the 30th and 31st years of His Majesty's Reign for the better Ordering of the Militia Forces in the several Counties of that Part of Great Britain called England, and also an exact Return of the actual State and Condition of the Militia in the County above-mentioned under Your Direction, in order that the King may be fully informed how soon the whole, or any part, of the Militia of the said County may be in readiness to be drawn out and embodied, if His Majesty shall think proper, and to march as Occasion shall require.

'I am, &c.,
'W. PITT.'

A MONMOUTH MILITIAMAN, 1750.

At the same time an appeal was made to Lieutenants of counties, urging them to 'use their utmost diligence and attention to carry into execution the several Acts of Parliament made for the better ordering the Militia Forces of that Part of Great Britain, called England.'

A reply to this appeal was communicated by Thomas Morgan, his Majesty's Lieutenant for the two counties of Monmouth and Brecon, in two letters, as under :

Brickendonberry in Hertfordshire, Jun 19, 1759.

'HOND. SIR,—I take the Liberty of sending you the inclosed account of the several Gentlemen who have lately offered to accept Commissions

---

[1] In 1756, owing to hostilities with the French, the question of the Militia was discussed seriously in Parliament, and in that year the force was first organised in its more familiar form as a permanent provision for the defence of the realm. It ceased to be a charge on property, each county being required to furnish a fixed quota of men, and this was the first occasion of the introduction of the ballot clauses. The Royal Assent on June 28, 1757, to the organisation introduced by the Pitt Ministry did not affect the Irish Militia, which was not organised until the year 1793, or the Scotch regiments until 1797.

in the Militia for the county of Brecon, and I beg you will be pleased to lay it before His Majesty for his approbation of them, and I will make no delay in issuing Commissions to such of them as His Majesty is pleased to approve of. My Deputy Lieutenants and self in person have had several meetings for executing the Militia Laws in the said county, and have sworn in and inrolled several of the Militia men, and hope shortly to complete the Rest.

'I do assure you, Sir, that I shall in obedience to His Majesty's Commands use my utmost Diligence and attention in the execution of the Militia Laws within the County of Brecon, and am with the greatest respect,

'Honoured Sir,
'Your most obedient and most humble servant,
'THOS. MORGAN.'

The following are the names of the gentlemen who offered to accept commissions in the Militia of the county of Brecon:

Sir Edward Williams of Llangoed Castle, Baronet, Colonel.
Penry Williams of Penpont, Esq., Lieut.-Colonel.
Charles Powell of Castlemaddock, Esq., Major.
Owen Evans, Esq., Captain.
John Meredith of Brecon, Esq., Capt.-Lieutenant.
Hugh Penry of Llwynkyntofyn, Esq., Lieutenant.
John Powell, Junr., of Llangewy, Esq., Lieutenant.
Thomas Phillips, Junr., of Brecon, Gent., Lieutenant.
John Foster of Llangorse, Gent., Ensign.
Richard Williams, of Aberbrane, Gent., Ensign.
William Powell of Brecon, Gent., Ensign.
Henry Williams of Llanspithill, Gent., Ensign.

The list of the gentlemen who offered themselves for commissions in the Monmouthshire Militia, unfortunately, has not been traced.

Towards the close of the year 1759 the Lieutenant for Brecon[1] addressed a letter to the King concerning the Militia of the county.

'*To the King's most Excellent Majesty.*

'I, Thomas Morgan, Esquire, your Majesty's Lieutenant for and in the County of Brecknock, do hereby humbly Certify and Return to your

[1] The 3rd Battalion South Wales Borderers, named as such in the year 1881, consists of the old Brecon and Radnor Regiment of Militia. The first records of the Brecon

Majesty, that in pursuance of Two several Acts of Parliament made and passed in the Thirtieth and Thirty-first years of your Majesty's Reign, the one Intituled " an Act for the better Ordering the Militia Forces in the several Counties of that part of Great Britain called England " and the other Intituled " an Act to Explain, Amend and Enforce the said first-mentioned Act," Three Fifths of the Militia men of the said County of Brecknock have been chosen, sworn and Inrolled, and that Three Fifths of the Commission Officers of the Militia Forces

Militia refer to the year 1684, when the Duke of Beaufort, as Lord Marcher, made a progress through Wales. In an account of that progress it is found that the county Militia at that time consisted of a troop of horse and five companies of foot. On Wednesday, August 6, 1684, ' His Grace the Duke of Beaufort, accompanied by the Earl of Worcester and other persons of quality, took a view of the Militia of this county in a meadow near the town, where they were drawn up to exercise, and made several close and laudable fireings. It (the Militia) consists of one troop, commanded by a captain, lieutenant, cornet and quartermaster ; and of five companies of foot, with green colours flying. The regiment is commanded by a colonel, captains, lieutenants and ensigns.' The foot were clad in new hats, blue cassocks, white sashes with blue worsted fringe, broad buff-coloured shoulder-belts, and short red-yarn stockings. The horse appeared well accoutred with buff coats, carbines, pistols, back and breast-plates, potts, bridles and collars, cuisses with great coats strapped behind them. It is further related that on the following day the Duke of Beaufort parted with Colonel Jeffreys, the officer commanding, ' well satisfied with the good order he found the Militia in, both horse and foot of this county, and his receptions, not only through, but in the town of Brecon, which were very noble.' The Duke was attended to the confines of the county by the high sheriff, gentry and Militia troop, and on the borders of Carmarthenshire he was met by the dignitaries and Militia of that county.

In the year 1746 the well-known evangelist, Howell Harris, of Trevecca, was in command of a company, and it is said that it was no uncommon sight to see the reverend gentleman preaching in his regimentals. The next reference to the Brecon regiment of Militia is found on a tablet in the Priory Church, near the tomb of Sir David Williams, of Gwernyfed, which is inscribed, ' To the Memory of Edward Williams, Esq., for some time Major Commandant of the Brecknock Militia, son of Sir Edward Williams, Bart., who died at Brecon 1 Dec., 1779.'

In 1803 the sixth Duke of Beaufort commanded the Brecon and Monmouth Militia, and from the incorporation into one regiment of the forces of the two counties the name of ' The Brecon and Monmouthshire ' was given to the regiment, but in the year 1793 it was changed to ' The Monmouth and Brecon.'

In the year 1820 the regiment was separated into ' The Royal Monmouthshire Militia,' of which the Duke of Beaufort was colonel, and ' The Royal Brecon Militia,' of which Francis Chambre was major commandant. The succeeding commandants of the Royal Brecon Militia were Colonels J. F. Vaughan Watkins, Douglas John Dickinson, William Bridgwater, and Major David Edward Jones, of Velindre, Llandovery. In 1876 the ' Royal Brecon ' and the ' Royal Radnor ' were amalgamated under the command of Colonel W. Jones-Thomas, who resigned in 1898, and was succeeded by Colonel C. Healey, C.M.G.

During the Crimean War the Brecon, Radnor and Cardigan Militia regiments were embodied, but were not called upon for active service. When the Brecon and Radnor battalions were amalgamated, Colonel Jones-Thomas and Captain Farquhar presented the old colours of the Radnor local Militia to Presteign Church, where they remain to this day.

raised and to be raised in and for the said County have been appointed, taken out, and accepted their several Commissions, and Entered their several Qualifications, as by the said several Acts of Parliament, in that case made, they are directed, viz. :

Colonel	*Lieutenants*
Sir Edward Williams, Bt.	Hugh Penry, Esq.
	Thomas Phillips, Esq.
Lieut.-Colonel	John Meredith, Esq.
Penry Williams, Esq.	Samuel Evans, Esq.
Major	*Ensigns*
Charles Powell, Esq.	Richard Williams, Esq.
	Henry Williams, Gent.
Captain	William Winstone, Gent.
Owen Evans, Esq.	Howell Harris, Gent.

'Dated the Fifth Day of December 1759.

'THOMAS MORGAN.'

The Lieutenant of Monmouthshire wrote to the Home Office from Ruperra on February 20, 1760, 'As our Monmouthshire Militia cannot raise seven companies we are only entitled to one field officer, so Mr. Hanbury, who was appointed Lieutenant-Colonel to it has resigned up the commission he had, and I take the liberty to recommend John Chambre, Esquire,[1] an experienced officer, to succeed Mr. Hanbury in that Commission.'

Again, on March 20, 1760, he wrote to the same Office, 'Sir,—I have this day been favoured with your letter enclosing His Majesty's Sign Manual to draw out and embody the Militia of the County of Monmouth, and likewise his Majesty's Commission appointing me Brigadier-General of the Militia for the Counties of Brecknock and Monmouth.—I am, Sir, with great respect, your most obedient humble servant,

THOMAS MORGAN.'

On November 25, 1760, his Majesty King George III was proclaimed at Newport in Monmouthshire with every mark of respect and demonstration. A stage was erected in the market-place, to which proceeded the Mayor and Corporation, accompanied by town constables and mace-

---

[1] The family of Chambre, spelled also Chambré, Chambres, Chamber and Chambers, originally owned property in Middlesex and Herefordshire. Lieutenant-Colonel John Chambere, of Llanfoyst, Monmouthshire, died on January 17, 1777.

bearers and attended by some officers of the Glamorganshire Militia. Many of the neighbouring gentlemen and clergy walked in the procession from the King's Head inn.

The warrant under the new Act to supply the Monmouthshire Militia with arms,[1] accoutrements, and colours was dated December 10, 1759, when the strength was 240 men.[2] Thomas Morgan, Lieutenant of the county, was commandant; and the facings were green. It was the first regiment raised by ballot in 1757 to comply with the new requirements imposed on county Militia.

The regiment was embodied in March, 1760, and disembodied by royal warrant of December 15, 1762. In 1760 John Chambre was appointed Lieut.-Colonel.

The officers serving in 1761 were as follows:

Lieut.-Colonel
John Chambre

Captains
Charles Van
Thomas Morgan
Paul Morgan

Lieutenants
Roger Edwards
Samuel Rosser

Ensigns
Charles Heylin
George Fryer

Adjutant and Q.M.
Charles Heylin

Surgeon
George Fryer

Agent
Mr. Richardson, Downing Street, Westminster.

The corresponding warrant for the arms and accoutrements of the Brecon Militia bears the same date as that for the Monmouthshire. The facings of this regiment were also green. It was embodied on

---

[1] Under the Act of 1757 the Lieutenants of Counties were empowered to assemble and arm the Militia, and to grant commissions to the proper number of officers, submitting their names to the King within one month after appointment. The property qualification for officers, which varied in different counties, required that half should be situated within the county of the regiment. In 1760 the qualifications for the County of Monmouthshire were:—

	An estate of the yearly value of	Or heir-apparent to one of
Deputy Lieutenant or Colonel	£300	£500
Lieut.-Colonel or Major	200	400
Captain	150	300
Lieutenant	100	200
Ensign	50	100

[2] This was the contribution required of Monmouthshire towards the quota of the whole of England, which amounted to 32,040 men. Breconshire contributed 160 men.

January 25, 1760, and consisted of 160 men, the Lieut.-Colonel being Sir Edward Williams, Baronet.

Warrants concerning the Militia of the counties of Monmouth and Brecon were issued on March 21, 1760, and January 29, 1760, respectively, in the following words:

'It is his Majesty's Pleasure that you cause the Militia of the County of Monmouth to assemble with convenient speed at such Place or Places as you shall think proper, and march from thence by such Routes and in such Divisions as you shall think most convenient to Cardiff and Cowbridge, where they are to be Quartered, and follow such orders as they shall receive from Lieutenant-General the Earl of Ancram [1]; Wherein, &c.

'Given at the War Office this 21st day of March, 1760.
  'By His Majesty's Command,
            'BARRINGTON.
'To Thomas Morgan, Esq., His Majesty's Lieutenant of
  the County of Monmouth.'

'It is His Majesty's Pleasure that you cause the Militia for the County of Brecknock to assemble with all convenient speed at Brecknock and march from thence by such Routes and in such Divisions as you shall think most convenient to Abergavenny, where they are to be quartered and remain and follow such orders as they shall receive from Lieut.-General the Earl of Ancram, Wherein &c.

'Given at the War Office this 29th day of January, 1760.
  'By His Majesty's Command,
            'BARRINGTON.
'To Thomas Morgan, Esq., His Majesty's Lieutenant for
  the County of Brecknock.'

On October 21, 1760, the Monmouthshire Militia was ordered to proceed from Monmouth, where it was then quartered, by the shortest and most convenient route to Bristol, to relieve the Rutlandshire Militia in guarding French prisoners of war. A detachment of the regiment had previously, on July 23, been sent from Cardiff to Bristol for quarantine duty.

It having been represented to His Majesty in Council, by the Mayor and Aldermen of the city of Bristol, that from the situation of the port

---

[1] William Earl of Ancram was Colonel in 1745, Major-General in 1755, and Lieutenant-General in 1758.

and channel of Bristol the quarantine ordered to be observed there during the danger of the plague could not even with the utmost vigilance of the officers of the Customs there, be properly carried into execution, unless assisted by a military force by land, a detachment of one captain, two subalterns, three sergeants, three corporals, two drummers, and fifty private men of the Monmouthshire Militia was ordered to march from Cardiff forthwith by the shortest and most convenient route to Bristol, to relieve the Rutlandshire Militia upon that duty. A detachment consisting of twelve men with proper non-commissioned officers was ordered to be detailed from the main detachment from time to time, to keep guard, and to assist the officers of the Customs in opposing any person or persons who might attempt to break the quarantine; but they were not to repel force with force unless in case of absolute necessity, or in the event of being required to do so by the civil magistrates. It appears that while the detachment was doing quarantine duty it was quartered at Portishead.

The Brecon Militia, in July 1760, were marched from Abergavenny to Yarmouth to relieve the Norfolk Militia in guarding French prisoners of war at that place. The march occupied twenty days, Yarmouth being reached on August 20. The route taken was *via* Monmouth, Gloucester, Buckingham, Bedford, Cambridge, Newmarket, Bury, and Beccles. In November 1760 the regiment returned to its own county, having been relieved at Yarmouth by the 2nd Battalion of the Norfolk Militia.

In those days the marching orders reached regiments by means of the attachment of the following instructions to the letter:

'War Office.
' All Postmasters and others whom it doth or may concern are hereby required to forward these by Express from Stage to Stage until they shall arrive as directed, as they tender His Majesty Service.
' By His Majesty's Command.'

The Brecon Militia, having returned to its own county, were ordered on May 19, 1761, to proceed to Bristol to relieve the Monmouth Militia, which returned to Monmouth.

Amongst the Monmouth Corporation vouchers is preserved one dated September 12, 1761 : ' Thomas Thomas, for drink for the soldiers when the King was married, seven shillings and ten pence.'

The regiments of embodied Militia in 1762 were :—

Regiment	Colonel	Lieut.-Colonel	Date of Embodiment
			1759
Wiltshire	Thomas Lord Bruce	William Northey	June 20
Dorsetshire	George Pitt	William Hanham	,,
Devonshire, 1st Batt.	Duke of Bedford	Sir Richard Warwick Bampfylde, Bt.	,, 21
Devonshire, 2nd Batt.	Sir John Prideaux, Bt.	John Duke	,,
Devonshire, 3rd Batt.	Sir Bourchier Wrey, Bt.	George Buck	,,
Devonshire, 4th Batt.	Sir John Rogers, Bt.	Charles Hayne	,,
Norfolk (W.), Batt.	Rt. Hon. Major-General George Townshend	William Windham	,,
Norfolk (E.), Batt.	Sir Armine Wodehouse, Bt.	Henry W. Wilson	,,
Kent (W.), Batt.	Robert Lord Romney	Robert Fairfax	,, 22
Richmondshire	Sir Ralph Milbanke, Bt.	Sir B. Graham, Bt.	July 2
Cleveland	Thomas Duncombe	Charles Turner	,, 2
Somerset, 1st Batt.	Earl Poulet	C. Warre Bamfylde	,, 3
Somerset, 2nd Batt.	—	Sir Charles Kemeys Tynte, Bt.	,, 3
Surrey, 1st Batt.	William Beaumont	Jeremiah Hodges	,, 3
Surrey, 2nd Batt.	George Onslow	—	,, 3
Warwickshire	Earl of Denbigh	Hon. George Shirley	,, 6
Berkshire	Arthur Vansittart	John Dodd	,, 25
Gloucester (S.), Batt.	Norborne Berkeley	Sir William Codrington, Bt.	,, 25
Yorkshire (W. Riding), 1st Batt.	Savill Finch	John Lister	Sept. 5
Yorkshire (W. Riding), 2nd Batt.	Sir George Saville, Bt.	Sir George Dalston, Bt.	,, 5
Yorkshire, (W. Riding), 3rd Batt.	William Thornton	Daniel Lascelles	,, 5
Rutlandshire	Geo. Bridges Brudenell	—	,, 30
Hertfordshire	John Sabine	Jacob Houblon	Oct. 8
Suffolk (W.), Batt.	Duke of Grafton	John Affleck	,, 8
Suffolk (E.), Batt.	Lord Orwell	William Wollaston	,, 8
Huntingdonshire	Duke of Manchester	Richard Astell	,, 8
Lincolnshire (N.), Batt.	Earl of Scarbrough	Robert Viner	,, 27
Lincolnshire (S.), Batt.	William Welby	Philips Glover	,, 27
Essex (W.), Batt.	William Harvey	John Conyers	,, 27
Essex (E.), Batt.	Isaac Martin Rebow	John Bullock	,, 27
Cheshire	Viscount Malpas	John Lord Grey	,, 27
Caermarthenshire	George Rice	—	Dec. 7
Flintshire	—	Sir Roger Mostyn, Bt.	,, 7
Pembrokeshire	Hugh Owen	—	,, 11
Hampshire (N.), Batt.	Sir John M. Cope, Bt.	Bernard Brocas	,, 11
Westmoreland	Sir James Lowther	R. Lowther	,, 24
			1760
York (E. Riding)	Sir Digby Legard, Bt.	Henry Willoughby	Jan. 1
Northumberland	Sir Edward Blackett, Bt.	Abraham Dixon	,, 25
Brecknockshire	Sir Ed. Williams, Bt.	—	,, 25
Durham	Earl of Darlington	Robert Shafto	Feb. 22
Bedfordshire	Marquis of Tavistock	—	Mar. 4
Monmouthshire	Thomas Morgan	John Chambre	,, 17
Cornwall	John Molesworth	Francis Basset	April 23
Hampshire (S.), Batt.	—	Sir Thomas Worsley, Bt.	May 10
Buckinghamshire	Lord Le Despenser	Sambrooke Freeman	,, 13
Leicestershire	John Grey	Thomas Boothby	July 3
Denbighshire	Richard Myddelton	Watkin Wynne	,, 14
Cumberland	—	Sir Wilfrid Lawson, Bt.	,, 26
Lancashire	Lord Strange	— Townley	Dec. 19
			1761
Glamorganshire	Earl Talbot	Sir Edmund Thomas, Bt.	Jan. 14
Gloucestershire (N.), Batt.	Norborne Berkeley	Lord Tracy	April 4
Carnarvonshire	Thomas Wynn	—	1762.
Middlesex (E.), Batt.	Sir W. B. Procter, Bt.	— Ashurst	,,
Middlesex (W.), Batt.	George Cooke	—	,,
Westminster, Batt.	Sir Thomas Frederick	Sir John Gibbons	,,

Instructions awaited the Brecon Militia on its arrival at Bristol, ordering the regiment to proceed immediately to Bideford to guard French prisoners. In October 1761, having been relieved at Bideford by the northern battalion of Militia for the county of Gloucester from Winchester, the Brecon regiment returned home.

In June 1762 both the Monmouth and the Brecon Militia were quartered at Pilmouth, Barnstaple, guarding French prisoners. In August of that year the Brecon Militia marched into quarters at Plymouth, and on the 26th of the month the officer commanding the Monmouth Militia received the following order :

'It is His Majesty's Pleasure that you cause His Majesty's Battalion of Militia for the county of Monmouth under your command at Barnstaple to march from thence three days before the Fair begins there (after leaving a sufficient Detachment on the French Prisoners at Pilmouth) to the next adjacent Place or Places, where they are to be quartered and remain until the Fair at Barnstaple is over and then return to their present Quarters.

'26th August, 1762.
> 'By His Majesty's Command,
> > 'TOWNSHEND.

'To the Officer Commanding His Majesty's Battalion of
  Militia for the County of Monmouth at Barnstaple.'

In September 1762 the Brecon Militia returned to their county from Plymouth, and in October the Monmouth Militia returned to Monmouthshire, being relieved at Pilmouth by four companies of the 74th Foot. Previous to the orders for disembodiment being received by the Militia of Monmouth, Brecon, and thirty-four other regiments, instructions as below were circulated to the commanding officers :

'As the time is now drawing near when it may probably be thought expedient to disembody the corps of Militia under your command, I am to signify His Majesty's Pleasure, that if the Battalion under your command should not, in its present distribution, happen to be so conveniently quartered as it might be for the return of the non-commissioned officers and private men to their respective Divisions of the County of Monmouth from which they were ballotted, you are hereby empowered to march any Companies, Parties, or Detachments belonging to the Battalion under your command from their present quarters to any place or places within the said county, for the greater convenience of the said Companies, Parties, or Detachments at the time of their being disembodied, in doing which you will follow your own discretion, and be governed by the good of the service and the convenience of the men, and all civil magistrates.

4th December, 1762.

'By His Majesty's Command,

'TOWNSHEND.

'To the Officer Commanding Monmouth Militia
    at Monmouth.'

As to the few years preceding 1778, in which year the Militia was again embodied, several records of events have been found. On May 9, 1763, a notice was issued to deputy lieutenants and justices of the peace for the county of Monmouth, requiring them to meet at the 'dwelling-house of Richard Shepard, Inn-holder, situated in the town of Usk in the said County, on Tuesday the 31st May, in order to put the Militia laws in execution.' On August 15 of the same year it is recorded that 'several corps of Lord Robert Manners's Regiment passed through the City of Gloucester on their route to Monmouth, Ross, etc.,' part of the regiment being quartered at Gloucester. On May 7, 1764, a notice was issued concerning the Monmouth Militia as follows:

'The Militia for the County of Monmouth are hereby to take notice that they are to meet at the town of Abergavenny in the said County on Monday the 21st May to be exercised for one month according to Act of Parliament; where all men sworn and enrolled as Militiamen for the county aforesaid, either in their own right or as [1] substitutes, are required to attend at that time, and they must answer the contrary at their peril.'

On May 21, 1764, the annual meeting of the Lieutenants and Justices, for carrying out the Militia Laws, took place at the Angel Inn, Abergavenny. On this occasion a notice was circulated to the effect that, 'there being one lieutenant and two ensigns wanting in the said Militia, such gentlemen as are inclined to accept Commissions are desired to give in their names at the said General Meeting, and to signify in which of those ranks they are willing to serve.'

---

[1] Fortescue, in his 'History of the British Army,' when alluding to the matter of exemption fines, points out that in the year 1807 the sum of 14,958l. was paid into the Treasury as exemption fines, the result of the ballot. Of this amount 2500l. came from Durham alone, but Monmouthshire was the lowest contributor with a sum of only 10l. The average prices of substitutes ranged from 10l. in the Isle of Wight to 45l. in Monmouthshire, where they were highest.

On June 11, 1764, three companies of Lord Robert Bertie's regiment of English Fusiliers went into quarters at Monmouth. The following year the Monmouthshire Militia assembled for its annual training of twenty-eight days on October 1 at Abergavenny, and in 1767 the place of assembly was Monmouth, as it was in the subsequent years. The penalty for the failure of a Militiaman to appear for training was at this time a fine of 20*l*. or six months' imprisonment in the common gaol. In October 1769 Mr. Thomas Bryan died at Tredegar. He had been for many years steward of the Tredegar estates and clerk of the Lieutenancy, and his signature appeared on the notices each year ordering the Militia up for its annual training. He was succeeded in the office by Mr. J. A. Bowen. On May 20, 1771, died in London Mr. Thomas Morgan, the Lieutenant for the counties of Monmouth and Brecon, who was buried on May 26 at Machen, in Monmouthshire. In addition to being at his death the Lieutenant for the counties referred to, he also represented Monmouthshire in Parliament, and was Colonel of the Monmouthshire Militia. A contemporary biography records: 'The life of this gentleman from his early youth was uniformly regulated by a modest and ingenuous, a mild, humble and benevolent turn of mind. Under the constant influence of this amiable disposition he enjoyed an ample fortune and distinguished station, without excess, without vice, and without pride or ostentation. He was liberal to the poor, kind and serviceable to his friends, affable, obliging and hospitable to all. In his domestic relations he proved himself an eminently dutiful son, affectionate brother, and indulgent master. He will ever live in the hearts and affections of those who knew him, who at present by their sincere regret for his death bear the most exceptional testimony of his real worth.' He was succeeded as His Majesty's Lieutenant by the Duke of Beaufort, who also became Colonel of the Monmouthshire Militia on December 23, 1771.

On April 13,[1] 1778, the Monmouthshire Militia was again embodied,

[1] The officers serving at the commencement of the American War embodiment were:—

Colonel the Duke of Beaufort	December 23, 1771
Major Hon. S. H. Neville	June 22, 1778
Captain R. Lucas	April 29, 1772
,, R. Morgan	March 26, 1778
,, C. W. Coxe	July 25, 1780
,, T. Stepney	October 24, 1780
Captain-Lieut. J. Rudhall	July 7, 1779
Lieutenant W. King	July 10, 1778
,, T. Roberts	July 25, 1778

THE EMBODIMENTS OF 1696, 1760, AND 1778

consequent on the large number of regular troops required in America. The order for the embodiment of the Regiment ran thus:

'The Lord Lieutenant, having this day received His Majesty's Commands to draw out and embody the Militia of the said County of Monmouth, gives this public notice that the said Militia is hereby required to assemble for that purpose at the Town Hall in the town of Monmouth on Monday the 13th April next at ten o'clock in the forenoon, instead of the 31st May as before advertised.

'BEAUFORT, Lord Lieutenant.'

The order is dated March 27, 1778, at Grosvenor Square, and a footnote is added to the effect that 'Any Militiaman not joining his corps at the above appointed time will be punished as the law directs.' On May 13 General Hope reviewed the regiment at Tetbury, where it was quartered, and paid the Duke of Beaufort and the rest of the officers the highest compliments on the appearance and steadiness of their men.

Much jealousy existed at this time between the Regular Army and the Militia in the matter of recruiting, and the Commanding Officer of the Monmouthshire Militia was instructed to refrain from issuing advertisements which might compete with the recruiting for the line.[1]

Monday, June 22, 1778, was an eventful day in the annals of the regiment. His Majesty the King, accompanied by the Queen, reviewed the regiment in Windsor Park. His Majesty complimented the Duke of Beaufort very highly on the 'handsome appearance of the men.' He particularly remarked on the neatness of their uniform and their great steadiness and activity. The King thanked the officers for the pains they had taken in training the regiment so admirably, which, he said,

Lieutenant F. Davies	March 26, 1780
,, J. Haswell	October 24, 1778
Ensign E. Oxnard	February 24, 1779
,, L. Hollester	February 25, 1779
,, A. Lloyd	July 18, 1779
,, T. J. Phillips	April 27, 1780
,, J. Roward	October 24, 1780
Adjutant John Haswell	July 9, 1778
Quartermaster J. Rudhall	June 25, 1778
Surgeon F. Davies	March 26, 1778

[1] Note the subsequent change of this condition. On June 14, 1860, an order was circulated from the War Office prohibiting line recruiting parties picking up Militiamen, and directed Commanding Officers of Militia only to consent to such men enlisting in the Army as were of unsettled habits and over whom they had little control out of the training. Militia Commanding Officers were in turn instructed not to enlist men who might be likely recruits for the Army.

was shown in every manœuvre. The Duchess of Beaufort was present, dressed in the uniform of the regiment. This review took place on the occasion of the regiment marching through Windsor to Warley Common, where it was to be quartered.

On May 24, 1779, a meeting of the Lieutenants of the counties of England was held at the St. Alban's Tavern, London, for the purpose of determining the seniority of the Militia regiments. It was agreed to draw lots, and the number drawn for Monmouthshire was twenty-three. On June 18 of the same year, the regiment being stationed at Coxheath Camp, the following notice was circulated by the Duke of Beaufort, as Lord Lieutenant of Monmouthshire :

' Whereas by an Act of Parliament passed the third day of the month, entitled " An Act for augmenting the Militia," it is enacted that from and after the passing thereof, if any person or persons, properly qualified according to the Laws now in force, shall offer to His Majesty's Lieutenant of any County to raise one or more company or companies to be added to the regiment or battalion of any County or Riding, that it shall and may be lawful for His Majesty's Lieutenant to accept such offers and appoint officers accordingly. In pursuance thereof of the said Act of Parliament, any person or persons properly qualified and desirous of raising one or more company or companies to be added to the Battalion of the Militia for the County of Monmouth, are desired to give notice to His Majesty's Lieutenant of the said County. And whereas it may be expedient to appoint a general meeting of the said county of Monmouth in order to consult what measures may be proper to be taken for the service of the public in the very critical situation[1] of this country, I do hereby appoint a general meeting to be held at the King's Head in the Town of Monmouth at twelve o'clock in the forenoon on the 6th of August, and I do earnestly request the gentlemen, clergy, and freeholders of the said county to attend the said meeting.

'BEAUFORT.'

At this time the regiment appears to have been considerably below its establishment, and the Lord Lieutenant ordered a meeting of the deputy lieutenants to be held at the King's Head Tavern in Monmouth on August 6, at ten o'clock, for carrying into execution the several Acts

---

[1] In the summer of the year 1779 the French began to threaten an invasion, and 50,000 men were spread along the coast of France from Havre to St. Malo. Spain having joined France in the war against England, manifestoes were published both at Paris and Madrid, containing long statements of alleged grievances.

of Parliament relative to the Militia, and especially for issuing orders for balloting to fill up the vacancies in the regiment. The regiment was still at Coxheath Camp, and the meeting referred to was called in compliance with a letter from the Secretary for War ordering the Monmouthshire Militia to be completed to its establishment. At this time the regiment was known as the 'Monmouthshire Fuzileers,' and the uniform was red, faced with blue and gold.

Coxheath Camp was the scene of one or two stirring events. On August 18, 1779, a captain of the Buckinghamshire Militia was shot dead by the Provost's guard. He was challenged by the guard, and answered angrily, 'I'm an officer; let me pass, or I'll shoot you,' and actually did shoot and wound the sentry dangerously, but, endeavouring to escape, was shot dead himself. On August 24 a lieutenant [1] of the Monmouth Militia was tried for disobedience of orders and for actually inciting the men of the company to which he belonged to mutiny and desertion. The evidence against the prisoner was so very contradictory that the court, without the least hesitation, honourably acquitted him. Whereupon the lieutenant immediately challenged his adversary (a lieut.-colonel) to a duel, and in rear of the ground of the Northamptonshire Militia settled the dispute. The lieutenant, having received the colonel's first and second shots, fired his last pistol with a deadly aim which, unfortunately, hit the colonel in his left breast, of which wound he died in about seven minutes, much to the intense grief of his adversary, who was related to him. The lieutenant was immediately put under arrest in his own tent until handed over to the civil authorities. During the very time when this affair occurred preparations were being expedited for the reception of His Majesty the following week, and a large marquee was being erected for the use of the King.

At the same place a sergeant-major was tried by court-martial for buying base and counterfeit [2] halfpence at the rate of 28s. worth for 1l. sterling, and paying the soldiers therewith. The case being clearly proved

[1] It is impossible to decide with any precision the names of the subaltern or lieut.-colonel in question. The 'Gentleman's Magazine,' referring to the affair, records: 'A duel was fought at Coxheath between a lieutenant in the Militia and a lieut.-colonel, when the latter was shot in the left breast and expired immediately. The deceased had charged the lieutenant with exciting his men to mutiny, of which he was honourably acquitted by a court-martial.'

[2] On April 23, 1810, the following Order was read to the men: 'The Commanding Officer orders that no Pay Sergeant under any pretence whatever tenders to the men as their pay any halfpence otherwise than those which are good current coin of the realm called Mint Halfpence.'

against him, the court sentenced him to be reduced to the ranks and to receive 900 lashes. Having had 400 of the lashes from a drummer, the usual administrator of chastisement, he was sent to the hospital as a prisoner, and was further chastised with 500 lashes on his release from that establishment as a sick person.

In May 1780 the Monmouthshire Militia arrived at Bristol, where it relieved the Glamorganshire Militia, which proceeded to Preston in Lancashire. At a meeting of the Common Council at Bristol on September 16 of that year, a letter was read from the Duke of Beaufort and the officers of the Monmouthshire Militia expressing their satisfaction at having received the thanks of the corporation for their late services to the city, and for the city having made a present of a hundred guineas to the non-commissioned officers and private men of the battalion.

In February 1781 the regiment returned to Monmouth, but in March it was ordered to Bristol again, *viâ* Chepstow, where it remained only a few days; for, though on the 30th of the month it received orders to proceed to Beccles and Lowestoft, in Suffolk, these orders were countermanded later, and in April the battalion returned to Monmouth. After having been quartered at its home for two months, the regiment proceeded in two divisions, *viâ* Gloucester, Cirencester, Farringdon, Abingdon, Wallingford, Henley, Maidenhead, Hounslow, Greenwich, and Deptford, to (1) Rochester, Stroud, Chatham, and Brompton, and (2) Gravesend, Northfleet, and Chalk Street.

On July 5 the whole proceeded to Coxheath Camp, Kent, where the regiment had been previously quartered; and in November four companies went to Deal, one company to Sandwich, and one to Margate and Ramsgate. The route from Coxheath was *viâ* Ashford, Charing, Lenham, and Canterbury. After the recruits from Monmouth had joined at Deal in May 1782, the regiment marched in July of that year from Deal to Lenham Heath *viâ* Canterbury, Faversham, Ospringe, and Lenham; and in November four companies proceeded to Uxbridge, Hillingdon, and Cowley, while the remainder went to Beaconsfield, Gerrard's Cross, and Chalfont St. Peter's, in Buckinghamshire.

Having started on February 28, 1783, in two divisions from Uxbridge for Monmouth, *viâ* High and West Wycombe, Oxford, Witney, Gloucester, and Newnham, the regiment was disembodied in March of the same year.

CHAPTER V

THE REGIMENT AT THE CLOSE OF THE EIGHTEENTH CENTURY

From the conclusion of peace in 1783, resulting in the disembodiment of the Militia, but little is to be said of the Regiment of Monmouthshire until the year 1793, when it was again embodied for a very long period. At the end of the eighteenth century desertions from the regiment seem to have been very numerous, and rewards exceeding the Government sums were usually offered to persons instrumental in obtaining the arrest of deserters[1]; thus on February 16, 1784, the following notice was issued. 'Deserted from his Majesty's Battalion of Monmouthshire Militia from Captain Morgan's Company, Frederick Meredith, fifer, aged twenty-one years, five feet ten inches high, dark complexion, black hair, grey eyes : had on when he deserted a light coloured coat, white regimental waistcoat, and black breeches : was born in the parish of Skenfrith in the aforesaid county and is by trade a shoemaker. Whoever secures the said deserter, so that he may be brought to justice, shall receive one guinea reward, over and above what is allowed by Act of Parliament for apprehending deserters, by applying to Mr. John Haswell, Adjutant to the said regiment, St. Mary Street, Monmouth.' In the year 1796 desertions were so numerous that the following notice was circulated by the Duke of Beaufort :

DESERTERS

FROM HIS MAJESTY'S INCORPORATED BATTALION

OF

MONMOUTH AND BRECON MILITIA

Commanded by

COLONEL THE DUKE OF BEAUFORT.

---

[1] In 1768 men for not joining their regiments were punished by a fine of 20*l.*, or a sentence of six months' imprisonment. The penalty for desertion after receiving the Militia Bounty was the same. In 1787, by the King's Command, it was read at the head of each Militia regiment that 'all the Deserters from the Militia would be sent to the East Indies or Coast of Africa for life.'

Whereas several Men have deserted from the above Regiment, since it was Embodied in January 1793;

COLONEL THE DUKE OF BEAUFORT

Hereby gives notice

That if any of the said Deserters will surrender themselves at the Head Quarters of the Regiment, at Lewes, in the County of Sussex; or to Sergeant Potter, of the said Regiment, now quartered at Monmouth, on or before the First Day of December next, they shall be received into the Regiment again without Punishment.

But if after this Notice, these Deserters should not surrender themselves within the above mentioned Time, any Person apprehending any One of them, will be intitled to a

REWARD OF ONE GUINEA,

over and above what is allowed by Act of Parliament, by applying to

MESSRS. ROSS AND OGILVIE, AGENTS,

Argyle Street, Westminster, or to

Mr. John Pearce, Paymaster to the said Regiment.

** The said Deserters are hereby informed, That they are liable to be taken up at any Time hereafter, *even after the Regiment is Disembodied;* are liable to Punishment and Imprisonment, and to serve in the said Regiment for the space of Five Years.

October 31, 1796.

The general unrest on the Continent in the year 1792 followed by the execution of the French king on January 21, 1793, occasioned great ferment in London. The Militia was embodied and the Tower was fortified and guarded. The French ambassador was dismissed and immediate hostilities were anticipated. Nearly the whole of Europe was arrayed against the French, who had not a single ally, but who, nevertheless, were able to put eight armies on foot. In the spring of 1793 ten thousand British troops, under the Duke of York, landed at Ostend, and having joined the imperial army under the Prince of Coburg, assisted to defeat the French at St. Amand.

In the year 1793[1] the Monmouthshire Militia was amalgamated with

---

[1] The officers serving at this time in the Brecon and Monmouth Militia were:—

Colonel the Duke of Beaufort	December 23, 1771
Lieut.-Colonel the Earl of Abergavenny	April 5, 1793
Major the Marquis of Worcester	February 1, 1793
Captain Richard Morgan	March 26, 1778

THE REGIMENT AT CLOSE OF EIGHTEENTH CENTURY

that of the County of Brecon, which, since the year 1760, had been known as the Brecon Rifles.

The strength of the Brecon and Monmouth Regiment at the time of the amalgamation was 240, but in 1799 it increased to 896. The Militia of Brecon and of Monmouth having been embodied, together with the rest of the Force, were ordered on February 21 and 19 respectively to be in readiness to march to Newbury on March 4 and February 25, there to be amalgamated and quartered. The Marquis of Worcester, writing to his wife under date February 1, 1793,[1] from Monmouth, says: 'I got here to-day and was much disappointed at not finding here his Majesty's approbation of my appointment, though Mr. Nepean promised faithfully to send it by the post two days ago. However, my father and I intend setting off early to-morrow morning to Brecon, as they will not be in the secret whether my commission is signed or not.' The commission referred to was that of Major. He also remarks, 'We have got several new officers in the Monmouth and want but two to complete, but I am afraid the Brecon want several.'

Later in the day he writes: 'The post is just delivered. My father has received Dundas' letter, approving my appointment, but the order for joining the two Regiments has not yet arrived.'

A further letter dated 'Brecon, February 2, 1793,' runs: 'I think the

Captain Jacob Rudhall	February 1, 1793
,, Matthew Gwyn	February 25, 1793
Captain-Lieut. Thomas Jones	April 5, 1793
Lieutenant Thomas Bellamy	May 15, 1788
,, John Haswell	March 7, 1792
,, Clement Brigges	February 1, 1793
,, A. Harvest Isaacson	April 5, 1793
,, Aythan Lewis	April 5, 1793
Ensign Robert Wright	February 1, 1793
,, James Pidding	February 2, 1793
,, David Williams	February 26, 1793
,, David Price	March 4, 1793
,, William Price	April 5, 1793
Adjutant John Haswell	July 9, 1778
,, A. Harvest Isaacson	
Quartermaster Thomas Jones	January 11, 1793
,, A. Harvest Isaacson	

Surgeons, William Price and James Pidding.

After the amalgamation the regiment was for a time known as the Brecon and Monmouth Militia until 1794, when it was regularly styled the Monmouth and Brecon Militia. In this latter year the Duke of Beaufort was granted the rank of colonel in the Army.

[1] These letters in 1895 were in the possession of Lady Mary Farquhar, daughter of the Marquis, who was afterwards sixth Duke of Beaufort. They subsequently became the property of his granddaughter, who in 1909 was the Dowager Lady Raglan.

Regiment seems in better order than I expected, and the Adjutant has very much the appearance of a gentleman and seems as if he understood his business; but I am very glad I came here, as the quantity of things that are wanting is inconceivable, as the former Major does not seem to have taken much care of the stores, &c. It is very necessary that I should stay here the greatest part of next week.'

In a letter written on the Sunday following he remarks :

' I have been to Church with the soldiers, much to the surprise of the people here ; for amongst the various things the officers *never* did, that was one.'

The next day's letter records :

' All yesterday evening we had the most violent hail storms there could be, and the same this morning, so that we could hardly exercise the men; but, however, we employ ourselves in buying them clothes, and in putting the accounts into a system, so I hope at last we shall do pretty well ; though there is not a single article in store. I should not think of staying here, if I did not think it proper, for there is but one officer, besides the Adjutant and myself, so it is necessary for the appearance of things that I should stay on, and next week I fancy the new Captain will join, so then I may be absent some time.'

Later, after adverting to his stay at Brecon being longer than had been expected, he writes :

' Many of the men come to me to be let off because they are married and so forth, but I always tell them that is no reason, for that *I* am in the same situation. I assure you the men behave uncommonly well, and I am confident my being here contributes not a little to it, as they are more in awe of me than they used to be of the former little Major. The Adjutant seems to do extremely well ; he is very young, only twenty-three.'

Lord Worcester left Brecon soon after he wrote the above, but returned there on February 24, 1793, and on his arrival found by orders from the War Office that the Regiment was to march, on March 4, by Abergavenny, Chepstow, Newnham, Tetbury, Chippenham, and Marlborough to Newbury, which (with two halts of two nights each at Newnham and Chippenham) they were to reach on March 12.

On February 28, 1793, Lord Worcester writes from Brecon :

' The Pembroke Militia halted here to-day, so by dint of a little lecturing our Regiment looked very clean and well, and did their exercise very steadily, indeed much better than ever I saw them.'

TYPES OF MILITIA UNIFORM 1793.
1. Light Infantry Company. 2. Battalion Company.
3. Grenadier Company. 4. Battalion Company.

From the original drawings by E. Scott, engraved and published at 31 Old Bond Street, August 12, 1793.

THE REGIMENT AT CLOSE OF EIGHTEENTH CENTURY

On March 2 he observes:

'To-morrow I think I shall be able to decide about going to town; I say I *think*, because the men have had a mind to make a *row* about some money. If they do not seem perfectly quiet on Monday when we march out, I shall not like to leave them, but I hope by making a pretty strong speech to them to-day, and reading the Act of Parliament, that it will come to an end.'

Later that day he writes:

'I shall be heartily glad when we are gone from here, for since writing the above the men have again had a mind to show symptoms of restiveness, but by the spirit of Mr. Isaacson and Captain Gwyn[1] (for I was doing some other business at the instant) it is quelled for the evening; when we get out of the county it will be all very well again.'

With reference to going to London he adds: 'Placed where I am, it is both my duty and for my credit to be with the Regiment as much as possible. I do not dislike the thoughts of going to Chatham, but I had rather stay at Newbury till we are in pretty good order.'

He mentions he had given orders that the Regiment should start on their march at half-past five on Monday morning, March 4.

Some extracts from the private diary of Mrs. Isaacson, wife of the Adjutant of the Brecon Militia, describing the march to Newbury, are worth recording. Captain Isaacson was the Adjutant of the Brecon and Monmouth Militia, until 1802. Mrs. Isaacson writes: 'On March 4, 1793, I took my final leave of Brecon and arrived with my servant in a chaise at Abergavenny in time for dinner. On the 5th I began my journey to Monmouth, dragging up hill and down dale, until I reached the Beaufort Arms, where we stayed two nights. On my rising the first morning after my arrival I thought the view of Chippenham beautiful, and Monmouth seemed cheerful. I saw everything here with delight. On the 7th the regiment continued its route, and marched into the small but pleasant little town of Newnham. After a tedious ride up hill and down, over dreadful roads, I arrived in good time to join the party for dinner. On the 8th we crossed the Severn much to my delight. Now, thought I, we are near at home. We had a bitter cold ride over the downs of Tetbury. Captain Gwyn, of the Regiment, found the cold so severe that he asked that I would take him in my chaise. I could

---

[1] This officer was first appointed captain in the Glamorganshire Militia on October 22, 1780, before serving in the Brecon and Monmouth.

not refuse him. As soon as he was seated, turning to me he said : " Will you have a little brandy, madam ? " " No, I thank you, sir." " Then I will," said he, and put the bottle to his mouth. We arrived at Tetbury in good time for dinner and I may say with a good appetite for it. On March 9 we left Tetbury on our route through Malmesbury to Chippenham, a very neat, healthy-looking place with most beautiful roads and fertile country. There Captain Gwyn insisted on playing the drum after dinner, to the great annoyance of the corps. They took him into another room, where he and others played in concert till late at night. On the 10th our next day's march was to Devizes, a severe cold place, being nearly surrounded by Salisbury Plain and Marlborough Downs. On the 11th, from Devizes we continued our route to Marlborough, making our headquarters at the Castle Inn, a most spacious building and everything being in good style. I believe it belonged to the noble Duke of Marlborough. On the 12th, about two o'clock, I overtook the Regiment on its march to Hungerford, and well I might, though it had started early, for I had a pair of blood horses with a knowing driver that took me at the rate of ten miles an hour. On the 13th my next and last day's journey was to Newbury, and Speenhamland in the county of Berks, where the Monmouth and Brecon Regiment met, commanded by His Grace the Duke of Beaufort, the Earl of Abergavenny, and the Marquis of Worcester, and there were about twenty more most respectable officers, none more so than my own dear Captain.'

In April 1793 two companies of the Herefordshire Militia, quartered at Bristol, were ordered to Bath to quell riots. Shortly afterwards the Brecon and Monmouth Militia were ordered to proceed from Newbury to Wells (Somerset). On May 30 two companies of the Regiment were ordered to Shepton Mallet, the officer in command receiving the following instructions from the War Office. ' It is his Majesty's Pleasure that you cause the companies of the Monmouth and Brecon Militia under your command at Shepton Mallet to be aiding and assisting to the Civil Magistrates, upon their requisition, in preserving the public peace, in quelling any riots or disturbances that may happen at that place or in the vicinity thereof, and in apprehending and securing the Offenders ; but not to repel force by force, unless in case of absolute necessity.' An additional two companies at least seem to have been sent to Shepton Mallet at a later date, for an order issued from the War Office to the Officer Commanding the Monmouth and Brecon Militia at Shepton Mallet and dated

THE REGIMENT AT CLOSE OF EIGHTEENTH CENTURY

June 15, 1793, runs: 'It is his Majesty's Pleasure that you cause four companies of the Monmouth and Brecon Militia, under your Command at Shepton Mallet, to march from thence, on the second day after the receipt of this order, to Warminster, where they are to be quartered and furnish escorts for four successive Divisions of Prisoners of War (each supposed to consist of 250 men) from thence to Bath, where they are to be delivered over to a detachment of the Herefordshire Militia; each escort is to consist of one captain, two subalterns, and sixty private men, with proper non-commissioned officers, who, after performance of this service, are to return to their present quarters and remain until further orders.'

Towards the end of June a company of the Regiment was sent from Wells to Taunton for suppressing riots there, and on the completion of the escort duty above referred to an additional company was ordered to reinforce it. On July 11 these two companies proceeded to Shepton Mallet, being relieved at Taunton by the Montgomeryshire Militia. On August 8, 1793, the distribution of the Militia throughout the country was as follows:

Regiment	Companies	Where quartered
Anglesea	1	Portsmouth.
Bedford	6	Harwich Camp.
Berks	9	Ashdown Camp.
Buckingham	7	Winchester, 1 Waltham.
Cambridge	8	Warley Camp.
Carmarthen	2	Swansea, 1 Pembroke.
Carnarvon	1	Eastbourne Barracks.
Cardigan	2	Aberystwith; under orders for Gloucester, on their way to the coast of Sussex.
Cheshire	9	Lincoln.
Cornish	6	Exeter by 9th inst., 1 Topsham, 1 Ottery St. Mary, 1 Tiverton, 1 Axminster.
Cumberland	3	Chester, 2 Northwich.
Denbigh	5	Whitehaven.
Derby	9	Warley Camp.
Devon { East	10	Dover Castle.
Devon { North	8	Ashdown Camp.
Devon { South	8	Ashdown Camp.
Dorset	10	Ashdown Camp.
Durham	4	Whitby, 2 Scarborough Barracks.
Essex { East	5	Deal, 2 Sandwich, 1 Ramsgate.
Essex { West	8	Ashdown Camp.
Flintshire	2	Woolwich.
Glamorgan	6	Maker Camp.

86 ROYAL MONMOUTHSHIRE MILITIA

Regiment		Companies	Where quartered
Gloucester	South	9	Portsmouth Barracks.
	North	7	Roboro' Camp.
Hants	North	8	Ashdown Camp.
	South	7	Gosport Barracks.
	I. of Wight.	1	Isle of Wight.
Hereford		8	Bristol.
Hertford		9	Warley Camp.
Kent	West	10	Harwich Camp.
	East	5	Lexden Camp.
Lancashire		4	Doncaster, 3 Rotherham, 2 Retford.
Leicester		8	Gorleston Camp.
Lincoln	North	10	Warley Camp.
	South	10	Lexden Camp.
Merionethshire		1	Plymouth Barracks.
Middlesex	East	8	Ashdown Camp.
	West	8	Gorleston Camp.
	Westmr.	8	Ashdown Camp.
Monmouth & Brecon		4	Wells, 2 Shepton Mallet.
Montgomeryshire		4	Taunton.
Norfolk	West	8	Lexden Camp.
	East	8	Ashdown Camp.
Northampton		8	Weymouth, 1 Dorchester, 1 Poole. Wareham, 1 Abbotts, 1 Bridport, 1 Lyme.
Northumberland		6	Hull, 1 Bridlington, 2 Dunham.
Nottingham		4	Lynn, 2 Spalding, 2 Boston.
Oxfordshire		9	Ashdown Camp.
Pembroke		2	Warley Camp.
Radnorshire		2	Canterbury Barracks
Rutland		2	Dover.
Shropshire		10	Roboro' Camp.
Somerset		12	Maker Camp.
Stafford		9	Plymouth Barracks.
Suffolk	West	8	Ashdown Camp.
	East	8	Harwich Camp.
Surrey		10	Brighton, 3 Eastbourne, 1 Seaford Brrks. Watling, 4 Chichester.
Sussex		12	Ashdown Camp.
Warwick		10	Liverpool.
Westmoreland		3	Holywell and Mold.
Wilts		8	Hastings, 2 Winchester, 1 Rye, 1 Dungeness. Hythe, 1 Folkestone, 1 Dover Town. Hythe Battery.
Worcester		9	Roboro' Camp.
York W. Rid. (1st)		7	Tynemouth, 3 Sunderland.
York W. Rid. (2nd)		10	Manchester.
York, N. Riding		10	Newcastle.
York, E. Riding		6	Caister Camp.

THE REGIMENT AT CLOSE OF EIGHTEENTH CENTURY

On September 30, 1793, the four companies of the Monmouth and Brecon Militia stationed at Wells were ordered to proceed at once to Bristol to assist the civil power in suppressing riots and disturbances. They remained there until the middle of October when, having been relieved by the Cornwall Militia, they returned to Wells. On October 16 one company was ordered to Glastonbury.

In May 1794[1] the whole Regiment proceeded in two divisions from Wells to Maker Height, near Plymouth. The routes adopted were as follows:

			1st Division, 3 Cos.	2nd Division, 3 Cos.
Saturday,	Mar.	10	Somerton, Langford and Huish.	
Sunday,	,,	11	Halt.	
Monday,	May	12	Taunton	Somerton, Langford and Huish.
Tuesday,	,,	13	Wellington	Taunton.
Wednesday,	,,	14	Bradwich and Collumpton.	Wellington.
Thursday,	,,	15	Halt	Halt.
Friday,	,,	16	Exeter and St. Thomas	Bradwich and Collumpton.
Saturday,	,,	17	Chudleigh, Bovey Tracey and adjacents	Exeter and St. Thomas.
Sunday,	,,	18	Halt	Halt.
Monday,	,,	19	Ashburton, Buckfastleigh and adjacents	Chudleigh, Bovey Tracey and adjacents.

[1] The officers serving in 1794 were:—

Colonel the Duke of Beaufort	December 23, 1771
Lieut.-Colonel the Earl of Abergavenny	April 5, 1793
Major the Marquis of Worcester	February 1, 1793
Captain Jacob Rudhall	February 1, 1793
,, Mathew Gwyn	February 1, 1793
,, Thomas Jones	April 5, 1793
Captain-Lieut. Thomas Bellamy	July 15, 1793
Lieutenant John Haswell	March 7, 1792
,, Clement Brigges	February 1, 1793
,, A. Harvest Isaacson	April 5, 1793
,, Aythan Lewis	April 6, 1793
,, Robert Wright	July 15, 1793
Ensign David Williams	February 26, 1793
,, William Price	April 5, 1793
,, John Hodges	June 16, 1793
,, Miles Lowley	September 23, 1793
,, William Jones Fry	December 11, 1793
Adjutant John Haswell	July 9, 1778
,, A. Harvest Isaacson	
Quartermaster A. Harvest Isaacson	
Surgeon William Price	April 5, 1778

		1st Division, 3 Cos.	2nd Division, 3 Cos.
Tuesday,	May 20 .	Brent, Ivy Bridge, and adjacents	Ashburton, Buckfastleigh, and adjacents.
Wednesday,	,, 21 .	Plymouth	Brent, Ivy Bridge, and adjacents.
Thursday,	,, 22 .	Halt	Plymouth.
Friday,	,, 23 .	Maker Camp . . .	Maker Camp.

Mrs. Isaacson, after proceeding to Southampton for a time, joined the Regiment at Maker Camp. Her husband met her at Exeter and in her diary she describes their arrival at Plymouth thus: 'We arrived just in time for him (Captain Isaacson) to change his dress and mount his charger. It being the King's Birthday all the Regiments were under arms, bands playing and colours flying. At one o'clock the Royal Salute was fired by five thousand men. When all was over I returned to my lodgings, a very short distance from the camp, to dress, as we were to dine with the General (Morrice) and his family. There I met my old acquaintance Captain Skinner, who was Brigade-Major to the General and brother to Lady Nugent, with whom I was very intimate. Also Mrs. Wynot, my old schoolfellow, both recognising me at the same time. Her husband was Major in the Worcester, then in camp on the same ground with us, together with the South Devon, West York and Northampton.'

Early in November the Regiment left Plymouth, two companies went to Honiton, two to Ottery and two to Topsham. They proceeded by two routes; the first division of four companies going to Honiton and Ottery by way of Modbury, Totnes, Newton Bushell and Exeter, the march occupying six days; the second division of two companies reached Topsham in the same number of days. Mrs. Isaacson says: 'On the 4th from hence (Modbury) we proceeded to Newton Bushell, where the Regiment halted for one day. There I remember, it being November 5, the boys were busy firing off squibs, to the great danger of the Town, the market place having hundreds of pounds of cartridge powder belonging to the Regimental Store there. From this place I was persuaded to take a journey of about five miles to view the Channel Fleet, consisting of more than a hundred sail riding in Tor Bay. We were within a short distance when the Captain said, " I shall be too late for parade," and we returned home.'

The list showing the quarters of the Militia on March 19, 1795, gives the six Companies of the Monmouth and Brecon at the following stations: Honiton 2, Exmouth 1, Topsham 1, Sidmouth 1, and Ottery 1. One of

THE REGIMENT AT CLOSE OF EIGHTEENTH CENTURY

the two companies at Honiton was ordered to Axminster and Kilmington on April 7, 1795, and did not return to Honiton until after the 17th of the month. Early in May the whole Regiment marched to Maker Heights, Plymouth, where it encamped on the same ground as before. Mrs. Isaacson's Diary records : 'We had elegant balls in the Monmouth Reading Room, where Lord and Lady Worcester attended. I went with the General's Lady and her Niece, Miss Urquhart. In September, the weather now getting cold for Camp, I took my Anthony (her baby) and servant to Plymouth Dock, now called Devonport, where we remained until the Regiment moved into winter quarters. They were in November ordered to Devizes in Wiltshire, a miserably cold place. Here we experienced great civility from some few families. Lady Abergavenny being with us, took me to a Ball which was given to the Officers of the Regiment. She sent me in her carriage both there and home. Our stay was short in Devizes, as Lord Abergavenny did not like the situation for his Lady, and the Regiment was removed to Lymington in Hampshire, where I soon followed with my little family. We had good lodgings here, and a charming little town it is. We had many troops near—Welsh, Dutch, French, Scotch, and a Hulan Regiment, composed of all nations, people and languages.'

The march from Plymouth to Devizes occupied seventeen days, and was by way of Tavistock, Okehampton, Crediton, Tiverton, Wellington, Taunton, Bridgewater, Wells, Frome, and Trowbridge. The route from Devizes to Lymington was not so long and only took four days. The whole Regiment was quartered at Lymington Barracks. Some slight disturbances seem to have occurred on March 1, 1796, while the Regiment was there, the foreign troops quarrelling amongst themselves. A French Regiment meeting one day the guard of the Monmouth and Brecon, the French Adjutant reported that Lieutenant Philip Rawlings of the Monmouth and Brecon had pushed him uncivilly in the crowd. In consequence a duel was determined on by the two officers in question, but just before the appointed hour the affair was settled amicably.

On May 19 the Officer Commanding the Monmouth and Brecon received the following order from the War Office. ' It is His Majesty's Pleasure that you cause the Monmouth and Brecon Militia under your command at Lymington Barracks, when they leave that place on account of the ensuing election, to be marched to and be quartered at Eling Barracks until three days after the said election is over, when they are to return to their present quarters.' Later in the year the Regiment was ordered to proceed to Barham Downs and encamp. The route occupied sixteen days and was by way of Southampton, Alresford, Farnham, Guildford, Reigate, Sevenoaks, Maidstone and Canterbury. In the autumn of this year the whole Battalion went into winter quarters at Lewes in Sussex. It remained there until June 1797, when it was ordered to Brighton, though as late as August two companies appear to have still been quartered at Lewes. This year the Prince of Wales reviewed the Regiment together with four others; on the conclusion of the review, as the Regiment was marching back, a waterspout burst over it, utterly spoiling many of the officers' coats. Later in the year the men of the Regiment seem to have mutinied and demanded money in place of the bread and meat served out to them, so that they could buy for themselves. The General commanding the District had several of the ringleaders tried by Court Martial, and after fifteen had been publicly chastised the others became peaceful. In October the Regiment was moved to Eastbourne. While there it was one night alarmed by the firing of a gun, it being supposed that the French were approaching, for Eastbourne was considered a likely place for a landing. The gun, however, transpired to have been fired by a ship in distress not far from the shore. Several men of the Monmouth and Brecon swam to the wreck on the following day to see what they could find.

From Eastbourne the Regiment went to Worthing. Here a practical joke was played one day by Mr. Baring, son of Sir Francis Baring, and a friend, Mr. Dalton. Being on an excursion round the coast, they came to Worthing late at night. They were strangers to the persons who kept the inn, and were questioned by the Commanding Officer of the Regiment as to their identity, to which they would not answer. A guard was immediately set on their apartment, and seals on their luggage. Still persisting in not giving their names, they were next morning conveyed in a chaise guarded by an officer (Lieutenant William Brown) to Brighton, there to be examined by Lord Charles Somerset, the General of the District. The General, however, at once recognised Sir Francis Baring's son, and so any further amusement from the incident was frustrated.

Fear of French landings and suspicions of all foreigners and unknown persons being spies were most prevalent in 1797; but, as a matter of fact, an exploit by the French resulting in a descent on the Welsh coast, was an actual reality. In the month of February of that year, a small armament consisting of two French frigates, a corvette, and a

THE REGIMENT AT CLOSE OF EIGHTEENTH CENTURY 91

lugger carrying a force of 1400 sailed towards the Bristol Channel, and, after a vain attempt to destroy the shipping in the harbour of Ilfracombe, which they were prevented from doing, by the spirited conduct of the North Devon Regiment of Volunteers, the Frenchmen arrived on the coast of South Wales, and were descried from the heights above St. Bride's Bay on Wednesday the 23rd, steering round St. David's Head. After sailing a few miles to the northward in Cardigan Bay they drew near the shore, and cast single anchor to the north of a small promontory, under Llanwannwr. They remained but a short time at that place, moving very soon half a league nearer to Fishguard, and finally anchoring in a small bay near Lanonda Church. They immediately hoisted French colours, and put out their boats. The country people were greatly alarmed, and instantly abandoned their houses. The cliff at this point is very steep and rugged, and such was the difficulty of ascent, that they climbed up the side of it on their hands and knees, throwing their muskets before them. As soon as they had got to the top of the hill they set the furze, and what combustibles they could get, on fire, to apprize their comrades of their success. It has been said that they were directed either by Irishmen or Welshmen, who were perfectly acquainted with the coast, but the difficulty of the spot they fixed upon renders that theory highly improbable, especially when it is considered that at the distance of three miles to the southward and two to the northward there are very convenient landing-places; and moreover this spot is at least four or five miles from a good road, the country being extremely mountainous, rocky and uneven.

Their debarkation was completed before Thursday morning, when numbers of them dispersed over the country to procure provisions and wearing-apparel, or, in other words, to plunder. In those houses wherein they found inhabitants, they took but few things, but entirely ransacked and gutted those that were abandoned.

The number of troops landed from the enemy's ships was about 1400, and the most prompt measures were taken by the chief men of the county to check their progress. A force of about 700 men, commanded by Earl Cawdor, was collected, and arrived at Fishguard in the evening; this consisted of 200 men of the Cardigan Militia, 100 of the Pembroke Fencibles, 300 of the Fishguard and Newport Fencibles, and Lord Cawdor's troops of Yeoman Cavalry. These men, though properly trained to the use of the musket, had never seen active service, but many of the officers had been long in the service, and were experienced in war. Lord Cawdor's official despatch describes the terms of the surrender which he demanded :

> 'London Gazette Extraordinary.
> 'Monday, February 27, 1797.
> 'Whitehall.

'A letter, of which the following is a copy, has been this day received from the Right Honourable Lord Cawdor, by His Grace the Duke of Portland, His Majesty's Principal Secretary of State for the Home Department.

> 'Fishguard, Friday, February 24, 1797.

'My Lord,—In consequence of having received information on Wednesday night at eleven o'clock, that three large ships of war and a lugger had anchored in a small roadstead upon the coast in the neighbourhood of this town, I proceeded immediately, with a detachment of the Cardigan Militia and all the provincial force I could collect, to that place. I soon gained positive intelligence they had disembarked about 1200 men, but no cannon. Upon the night's setting in, a French officer, whom I found to be the Second-in-Command, came in with a letter, a copy of which I have the honour to enclose to your Grace, together with my answer ; in consequence of which they determined to surrender themselves prisoners of war, and accordingly laid down their arms this day at two o'clock.

'I cannot at this moment inform your Grace of the exact number of prisoners, but I believe it to be their whole force ; it is my intention to march them this night to Haverfordwest, where I shall make the best distribution in my power. The frigates, corvette, and lugger, got under weigh yesterday evening, and were this morning entirely out of sight. The fatigue we have experienced will, I trust, excuse me to your Grace for not giving a more particular detail ; but my anxiety to do justice to the officers and men I had the honour to command, will induce me to attend your Grace, with as little delay as possible, to state their merits, and at the same time to give you every information in my power upon this subject.

'The spirit of loyalty which has pervaded all ranks throughout this country, is infinitely beyond what I can express.

> 'I am, etc.,
> CAWDOR.'

> 'Cardigan Bay, 5th of Ventose, 5th year of the Republic.

'Sir,—The circumstances under which the body of the French troops under my command were landed at this place renders it unnecessary to attend any military operations, as they would tend only to bloodshed and pillage.

THE REGIMENT AT CLOSE OF EIGHTEENTH CENTURY 93

'The officers of the whole corps have therefore intimated their desire of entering into a negotiation, upon principles of humanity, for a surrender. If you are influenced by similar considerations, you may signify the same by the bearer, and in the meantime hostilities shall cease.

'TATE, Chef de Brigade.

'To the Officer Commanding,
  His Britannic Majesty's Troops.'

'Fishguard, February 23, 1797.

'Sir,—The superiority of the force under my command, which is hourly increasing, must prevent my treating upon any terms short of your surrendering your whole force as prisoners of war. I enter fully into your wish of preventing an unnecessary effusion of blood, which your speedy surrender can alone prevent, and which will entitle you to that consideration it is ever the wish of the British troops to show an enemy whose numbers are inferior.

'My Major will deliver you this letter, and I expect your determination by 10 o'clock by your officer, whom I have furnished with an escort that will conduct him to me without molestation.

'I am, etc.,
'CAWDOR.

'To the Officer Commanding the French Corps.'

The surrender was soon determined on, and fixed for the following day (Friday) at noon. From the place of their first encampment, if it may be so called, they marched with Lord Cawdor at their head to Goodwick Sands, under Fishguard, where they gave up their arms. The prisoners displayed the constitutional levity of Frenchmen on the occasion; as soon as they had surrendered their arms some began to sing, some to smoke, and some to dance and leap, others resorted to eating bread and cheese, but a few exhibited dark and indignant countenances.

They were marched on Friday night to Haverfordwest, and confined in different places, some in the castles, some in churches, and some in storehouses. They were soon afterwards removed to Milford and put on prison ships. Two of the ships which had brought them over were captured on their return to Brest; and thus ended this singular expedition.

The Monmouth and Brecon Militia, in June 1798, proceeded to Bristol, and remained there for three years. In the spring of the year the Supplementary Militia for the County of Monmouth had been sent to Eastbourne to join the Regiment, the march occupying nineteen days; the detachment from the county of Brecon also marched to Eastbourne. The Marquis of Worcester writing from Monmouth on March 12,[1] 1798, where he and his father had arrived the previous day, says: 'All this morning we have been employed in examining the men; many of them are very stout fellows, but owing to the great hurry in which Government have pressed this business on, many men, from want of proper notice, are still absent, and I am afraid they will not all arrive before the order for our march reaches us. To-morrow I am to go to Brecon and shall ride there (about thirty-five miles), and my father will follow me on Thursday.'

Writing from Brecon on March 14, 1798, he remarks: 'The gentlemen of this county have sent us all the men they ought, and upon the whole I think they are better than those in Monmouthshire; Captain Lewis seems to have arranged the business very well, and to have spared no pains either last year or this in putting things in good order. The men do not seem at all unwilling to go from here, and I think we might have as many as we liked, for they seem to dislike it less than when we marched from here before.'

On March 16, 1798, he writes from Monmouth: 'My father and I arrived here yesterday evening. I think our journey, both to Brecon and this place, has been of use, as our officers would not have ventured to reject so many men as unfit for service as we have, and at the same time I believe our coming has pleased the people both great and small, and kept them in good spirits and good humour. Lewis[2] and Jenkins[3] are to be captains of the two new companies; and we have enlisted three very good-looking young men as lieutenants and ensigns, and I am not without hopes we shall get another before we go away next Monday.'

General orders had been issued by the War Office on April 24 to the officers commanding Militia Regiments, on the subject of the Supplementary Militia. The instructions contained in them ran as follows:

'His Majesty having deemed it expedient that the whole Supplementary Militia of —— should be embodied as soon as possible (that part only excepted as may voluntarily engage to serve in His Majesty's Forces), I have the honour to signify to you the Commander-in-Chief's Orders,

---

[1] On this same date the Corporation of Monmouth agreed to subscribe one hundred pounds for the support of the war.
[2] Aythan Lewis promoted Captain, February 25, 1798.
[3] Richard Jenkins promoted Captain, April 25, 1798.

THE REGIMENT AT CLOSE OF EIGHTEENTH CENTURY

that you cause a detachment from the —— regiment of Militia, consisting of one Field Officer, two Captains, and four Subalterns, with as many non-commissioned Officers and Drummers as can be spared from the duty of the Regiment, to proceed without loss of time, agreeable to the route transmitted herewith, to ——, the place appointed for the assembling of the Supplementary Militia of ——, there to receive and take charge of —— Supplementary Militia men. It is essential that this detachment should reach —— on or before May 3, but as the distance is too great to allow them to arrive in time, by the usual mode of marching, you are hereby authorised to direct the officers to proceed in carriages, and the non-commissioned officers on the outside of coaches, or other vehicles, for which the necessary expense will be allowed by the War Office.

'For the information of Officers employed on this duty, I have the honour to acquaint you that the quota of Supplementary Militia men allowed by Act of Parliament to enlist into His Majesty's regular forces is far from being completed; the Supplementary Men assembled at —— are for four days after their assembling to have the option of enlisting into the —— Regiment of Foot; and His Royal Highness, the Commander-in-Chief hopes that the officers will be actuated by a zeal for the good of His Majesty's Service, to use their influence with the men and will persuade them to enter as Volunteers into the above Regiment, by explaining to them the following terms under which they will enlist, viz., "That they will receive seven guineas bounty, and are to serve during the war, and six months after the conclusion of a general peace, and no longer; and that they shall not be liable to serve out of Europe."

'As it is probable that circumstances may prevent any officers of the —— (regular) regiment attending at ——, for the purpose of receiving such men as may choose to enlist in the Regiment, His Majesty has declared his pleasure that they shall be invited thereto by any Deputy-Lieutenant, or other magistrate, that may be present at the time of their assembling, and that the Chief Constable, or the Peace Officers of ——, shall be empowered to receive and take charge of any men that may offer to serve in the —— (regular) regiment, to which measure you will please very strongly to recommend it to the officers of your Regiment, to give all the assistance in their power. At the expiration of four days, or as soon after as possible, the officer commanding the detachment will receive a route, by which he will march the Supplementary Militia men whom he will have received (such only excepted as may have engaged to serve in the —— regiment of foot) to your headquarters. The men will march with their supplementary clothing, arms, and accoutrements, and are entitled to their marching guineas, and on their arrival at the headquarters of the —— Regiment of Militia, must be furnished with the necessities mentioned in the margin.*

	* For Sergeants.	For Corporals and Privates.
1 shirt	6/6	5/9
1 pair stockings	3/–	1/6
1 pair shoes	6/–	6/–
1 pair long gaiters	4/–	4/–

'Knapsacks will be supplied by Government. You will direct the officer commanding this detachment to report to the Secretary-at-War his arrival at ——, the day fixed for assembling the Supplementary Militia, and likewise the day on which he shall be prepared to march on his return to your headquarters, in order that the necessary route may be sent him. You will also instruct him to make the same communication to me for the information of His Royal Highness the Commander-in-Chief.—W. FAWCETT, A.-G.'

The Marquis of Worcester, writing from Eastbourne on April 17, 1798, remarks :—

' Our Recruits seem to be improving very fast, and everything appears in good order.'

Again on April 24 he observes :—

' To-day being the 24th of the month, the Regiment is to be mustered, according to the new Regulations. I have plenty to do daily, and I should be sorry to be away for more than a day or two, the only time I have to myself is after dinner. Isaacson,[1] the Sergeant-Major, and I are at work the whole day, and have not time enough for all we have to do.'

He writes from Lymington in Hampshire: ' It is absolutely necessary that either I or my father should be with the Regiment, so that proper order and discipline should be maintained, composed as it is *of men of so many different nations* ; besides English, Welsh, Scotch, and Irish,—Germans, Dutch, and even *Frenchmen*. It is curious to hear in the streets of Lymington French spoken by some of the Militiamen.'

The march of the Monmouth and Brecon Militia from Worthing to

---

[1] Captain Anthony Harvest Isaacson.

THE REGIMENT AT CLOSE OF EIGHTEENTH CENTURY

Bristol occupied thirteen days. It was made in three divisions of three companies each, the Regiment's strength having been augmented by five companies in this year. The remaining two companies had been left at Bexhill and Canterbury respectively. That at Bexhill was the Light Infantry Company, and that at Canterbury the Grenadier Company. Both these companies having met at Petworth, followed the Regiment to Bristol. At this time the Colonel, the Lieutenant-Colonel, and the Major each commanded a company, and there were eight captains for the remaining ones. The establishment provided for thirteen lieutenants, one per company, with a second to each flank company, and nine ensigns. There were fifty sergeants and twenty-four drummers. At the end of the year 1799 the Regiment was reduced to six[1] companies; of these, three were commanded by the field officers, and the others by Captains Thomas W. Davis, Aythan Lewis, and Sir Samuel Fludyer.[2] Captain Thomas Jones was subsequently appointed second Major, and assumed command on the senior officers going on leave and not rejoining. The establishment now became twenty-four sergeants, thirteen drummers, and 387 rank and file.

Before the Regiment was reduced to six companies the following circular letter from the War Office was received, which no doubt was responsible for securing many men of the Regiment for the Regular Service.

'Horse Guards: July 13, 1799.

'His Royal Highness the Commander-in-Chief directs it to be declared to the Militia Forces at large that an Act of Parliament has passed with a view to enable His Majesty to provide for the vigorous prosecution of the war, in which, among other provisions, it is enacted, that it shall be lawful for one-fourth of the private men of the embodied Militia to enter as Volunteers into such of His Majesty's Regular Regiments of Infantry as His Majesty shall by any Order, under his royal sign manual,

---

[1] The strength of the six companies was:

	Sergeants	Corporals	Drummers	Privates
Colonel's company	4	4	3	61
Lieut.-Colonel's company	4	4	2	60
Major's company	4	4	2	61
Captain T. W. Davis' company	4	4	2	60
Captain A. Lewis' company	4	4	2	61
Captain Sir S. Fludyer's company	4	4	2	60
	24	24	13	363

[2] Second baronet; died 1833; succeeded in the baronetcy Sir Samuel Fludyer, Bt., who was Lord Mayor of London in 1762.

think proper to appoint, and that His Majesty has in consequence been graciously pleased to assign the following Regiments for the reception of Volunteers from the Militia Forces :—

'The 4th (or King's Own) Regiment of Foot, whose headquarters are at Salisbury, commanded by General Morrison.

'The 5th (or Northumberland), whose headquarters are at Boston in Lincolnshire, commanded by General Sir A. Clarke, K.B.

'The 9th (or East Norfolk), whose headquarters are in the Tower of London, and a detachment at Faversham, in Kent, commanded by Lieut.-General Bertie.

'The 15th (or East York), whose headquarters are at Newcastle-upon-Tyne, commanded by Lieut.-General Powell.

'The 16th (or Buckinghamshire), whose headquarters are at Margate, commanded by Major-General Bowyer.

'The 17th (or Leicestershire), whose headquarters are at Norwich, commanded by Lieut.-General Garth.

'The 20th (or East Devonshire), whose headquarters are at Preston in Lancashire, commanded by Lieut.-General Leigh.

'The 31st (or Huntingdonshire), whose headquarters are at York, commanded by Major-General Lord Mulgrave.

'The 35th (or Dorsetshire), whose headquarters are at Beverley, commanded by General Fletcher.

'The 40th (or 2nd Somersetshire), whose headquarters are at Taunton, commanded by General Sir G. Osborne, Bt.

'The 46th (or South Devonshire), whose headquarters are at Poole, commanded by Major-General Sir J. H. Craig, K.B.

'The 52nd (or Oxfordshire), whose headquarters are at Canterbury, commanded by General Trapaud.

'The 56th (or West Essex), whose headquarters are at Gloucester, commanded by Lieut.-General Hon. C. Norton.

'The 62nd (or Wiltshire), whose headquarters are at Helstone, commanded by General Matthews.

'The 63rd (or West Suffolk), whose headquarters are at Landguard Fort in Essex, commanded by Lieut.-General the Earl of Balcarres.

'The 82nd (or Prince of Wales's), whose headquarters are at Blandford in Dorsetshire, commanded by Major-General Pigot.

'The Commander-in-Chief is well acquainted with the spirit which universally pervades every part of His Majesty's Forces ; and from the frequent opportunities he has had of observing the zeal and honourable

THE REGIMENT AT CLOSE OF EIGHTEENTH CENTURY

exertions, which have particularly characterised the Militia during this war, His Royal Highness entertains no doubt that many will embrace this opportunity of extending their services, and of adding fresh lustre to the British Arms by aiding the efforts of our Allies, sharing their glory, and by improving their late successes of contributing with them to secure the first object of His Majesty's paternal anxiety, a speedy restoration of peace, on terms secure and honourable to this country.

'The Commander-in-Chief is persuaded few arguments will be necessary to animate the men to whom he is addressing himself; but His Royal Highness has directed that it should be explained to the Militia Forces that the Legislature has not been unmindful of the interest of those who may choose to become Volunteers for the Regular Service; for the Act of Parliament expressly declares that every Volunteer who shall enter from the Militia into any of the above-mentioned regiments shall be enlisted to serve for five years, or during the continuance of the present war and for six months after the expiration thereof, and no longer; and shall not be liable to be sent or to serve out of Europe; and that every such person shall, in addition to the usual and accustomed oaths to be taken by every person enlisting as a soldier in His Majesty's Forces, take the following Oath, that is to say :—

'"I, A.B., do sincerely promise and swear, that I will be faithful and bear true Allegiance to His Majesty King George, and I do swear, that I will faithfully serve in the —— Regiment of His Majesty's Regular Forces, within any part of Europe, during the term of five years, or for the continuance of the war, and for six months after the expiration thereof, unless I shall be sooner discharged."

'The Act of Parliament declares likewise, that every such Volunteer shall serve in the Regiment of which he may make choice, and that he shall not, on any account whatever, be drafted to serve in any other regiment. It further provides that every Volunteer so entering into any of the above-mentioned regiments, shall receive a bounty of ten guineas, one-third of this bounty to be paid to him, or to such person or such of his family as he may direct, on his being attested; and one guinea to be laid out in providing immediate necessaries if it shall be thought requisite by the magistrate before whom he may be attested. The remainder of this sum of ten guineas to be paid to him on his joining the regiment of which he may have made choice, or on his arrival at the place of assembly fixed on for the rendezvous of the Volunteers from the Militia of the district; where he will be received by proper officers of the Regiment in which he has chosen to serve, and by them will be conducted to the headquarters.

'Every Volunteer will be entitled to pay, subsistence, and clothing, as a private soldier in the regiment of which he may make choice, according to the regulations of the service, from the instant of his obtaining his discharge from the Militia. No man is to be allowed to claim the benefit of a Volunteer under this said Act, unless he shall be at least five feet four inches high, and free from bodily infirmity.'

As a result of the above-quoted General Orders, the Royal Buckinghamshire Militia in two days sent 320 men, being one-fourth of the Regiment, and consequently the whole number that could be allowed to take service in the Regulars, to the 4th Regiment, and were attested and enlisted for it by their Colonel, the Marquis of Buckingham.

Throughout the year 1800 the Monmouth and Brecon Militia remained at Bristol. In April 1801 two companies were at Shrewsbury, two at Kidderminster, one at Wenlock, and one at Bridgnorth. On May 11, 1801, the Bridgnorth Company was ordered to march to Kidderminster to join the two companies already there, and proceed with them to Fort Monckton, Southampton, which march occupied fifteen days. The two Shrewsbury companies joined the Wenlock Company at Bridgnorth and the whole proceeded to Fort Monckton as a second division of three companies. In July the Regiment was at Colchester Barracks; on November 12 three companies were ordered to Monmouth, one to Abergavenny, and two to Brecon; but on arrival at Henley-on-Thames the company under orders for Abergavenny was ordered to Monmouth.

On February 18, 1802, a concert was given in the Town Hall, Monmouth, by the band of the Monmouth and Brecon Militia for the benefit of Drum-Major Graham of the Regiment. A copy of the bill for this concert is preserved in the Rolls Hall, Monmouth; it states that the concert was given 'Under the sanction of the Officers of the Monmouth and Brecon Militia and by desire of the Ladies and Gentlemen of Monmouth and its vicinity.' The bill concludes with the statement, 'the Hall will be well aired for several days previous.'

On April 12, 1802, the general instructions for disembodiment were circulated and the various companies of the Monmouth and Brecon Militia were accordingly disembodied, having been on continuous service for nine years.

THE REGIMENT AT CLOSE OF EIGHTEENTH CENTURY

Under the Militia Act of 42 Geo. III. cap. 90 (1802), the qualifications for officers were changed. They were as follows:—

Rank	Estate of yearly value of	Or heir to estate of yearly value of
	£	£
Deputy Lieutenant	150	300
Colonel	600	1200
Lieut.-Colonel	400	800
Major Commandant	400	800
Major	200	400
Captain	150	or son of person who was or who died worth £300.
Lieutenant	30 (one of several qualifications)	60 (one of several qualifications).
Ensign	20 (one of several qualifications)	30 (one of several qualifications).

With the exception of those of the Lieutenants and Ensigns, the estates were required to be situated half within the county of the Regiment.

Under this same Act the quota of privates to be raised in the county of Monmouth was 280, and that in the county of Brecon 204.

GORGET—1800-1830.

CHAPTER VI

THE EMBODIMENTS DURING THE PENINSULA AND WATERLOO CAMPAIGNS

The peace treaty signed at Amiens on March 28, 1802, which admitted of the disembodiment of the Militia, was hardly expected to secure a permanent peace. It was just the means of giving the country a brief rest from hostilities, and many of those fighting England's wars must have been indeed glad of it. Lord Nelson, who had by his great exertions but a short time before been victorious at Copenhagen against the Danish fleet, and whose father died on April 26 at Bath, determined, in company with Sir William and Lady Hamilton, to recruit his health in the months of July and August by making a tour into Wales. Passing through Oxford (where he was admitted to the degree of LL.D.) and Gloucester, he visited Ross, Monmouth, Brecon, and Milford; and afterwards journeyed to Swansea, Haverfordwest, Hereford, and Ludlow; he then proceeded through Worcester, Birmingham, and Warwick to Coventry. The freedom of the cities of Monmouth,[1] Hereford, and Worcester was presented to him in the most complimentary manner, and the gratitude of his countrymen was publicly displayed throughout the whole excursion.

Heath's 'History of the Town of Monmouth,' published in 1804, records that Lord Nelson visited the place on Thursday, August 19, 1802. His lordship, accompanied by Sir William and Lady Hamilton and Doctor and Mrs. Nelson, made the excursion down the Wye Valley from Ross in a pleasure boat, and he was received by the townsfolk with every degree of respect due to his exalted merit. At three o'clock in the afternoon the corporation in their robes, attended by the band of the Monmouth and Brecon Militia, proceeded to the riverside to await his lordship's arrival, and on his approach the band played 'See the Conquering Hero Comes,' and then, on his landing, 'Rule Britannia.' It then headed the procession to the Beaufort Arms, playing all the time until Lord Nelson retired for dinner.

[1] The resolution for according the freedom of Monmouth to Lord Nelson is dated January 14, 1802, and runs: 'Ordered that the freedom of this borough be presented to Lord Nelson and Lord St. Vincent as a compliment due to their services.'

On March 8, 1803, scarcely one year after the signing of the treaty at Amiens, King George III., in a message to Parliament, adverted to the necessity for being prepared, and it was resolved to call out the Militia and augment the naval force. On May 12, in consequence of imminent war, the British Ambassador, Lord Whitworth, quitted Paris, and the French Ambassador was directed to leave London.

By July a huge army had been assembled at Boulogne for the invasion of England, but the British fleet was too formidable an opponent for such a force to attempt to cross the Channel. The result of this threat of invasion, however, was the enrolment in England alone of no fewer than 300,000[1] men in volunteer corps and associations.

The Monmouth and Brecon Militia, on embodiment in 1803, consisted of seven companies. The Royal Warrant for the embodiment was dated March 18, 1803. Four companies came from Monmouthshire and three from Brecon, and on the Brecon companies arriving at the town of Monmouth the whole Regiment proceeded to Winchester. The facings of the uniform at this date were blue, and the officers wore gold lace and gold epaulettes. The strength was 461 non-commissioned officers and men. The Duke of Beaufort was still the Colonel, and the Earl of Abergavenny and the Marquis of Worcester were the Lieutenant-Colonel and Major respectively. On June 24 Lord Arthur[2] Somerset received a captain's commission *vice* Captain Thomas Jones. He had for subordinates Lieutenant Charles Bygrave and Lieutenant John Sargeaunt,[3] the latter of whom joined the 61st, or South Gloucestershire Regiment of foot, as Ensign, on July 31, 1806.

Companies were now each commanded by a captain, the field officers being relieved of that work. Each company possessed one lieutenant and one ensign, with the exception of the two flank companies, which had two lieutenants and no ensign.

The Regiment remained at Winchester for six weeks, and on July 17 marched into camp at Stokes Bay, where it was quartered under canvas till November 13, on which date it went into winter quarters at Haslar Barracks, Portsmouth. Preparatory to a field day, it was constantly customary at this time to issue the warning, 'Every man will parade

---

[1] The returns for the County of Monmouth for the year 1804 as to the strength of the Yeomanry and Volunteers give the numbers as 125 cavalry, and 1624 infantry, not including officers. In this year the total strength of these forces in England, Scotland, and Wales amounted to 379,943.   [2] Fifth son of Henry, fifth Duke of Beaufort.

[3] This officer, like several others who have been in the regiment, resided in Herefordshire. He was promoted Lieutenant in the 61st Foot on May 20, 1807.

with his firelock well flinted,' and another very common order was 'Every man will see that his hair is well tied.'

At Haslar the Regiment was quartered with the Militia Regiments of Glamorgan, Merioneth, and Hereford, and guard duty was divided between the four regiments, the guard consisting of three officers and 131 non-commissioned officers and men. The district in which Haslar Barracks were situated was the South-Western District, commanded by Lieutenant-General His Royal Highness the Duke of Cumberland, with headquarters at Winchester, the sub-district being commanded by Major-General Whitelocke. In February the 2nd Battalion of the 48th Regiment came to Haslar, and took its share of guard duty.

A guard consisting of one sergeant, one corporal, and six privates was, from February 24, mounted at Block House Fort to furnish one sentry over the guns there; and another about twenty paces outside the gate leading to Haslar, for the purpose of protecting the boats lying in Haslar lake. It was ordered that the Regiment was always to appear on the evening parade with 'flints properly fixed, the flints to be put in flat side upwards and fixed in with lead, and not to be taken out until the morning parade.' One officer per company was required always to be present to turn out with the Regiment at a moment's notice if necessary. Until February 27 the guard had been composed of men of the various regiments at the station, each furnishing a section; after that date it was a battalion duty, and the regiment furnishing it was also required to detail a picquet consisting of one subaltern and twenty non-commissioned officers and men.

On February 29 the Monmouth and Brecon Militia paraded in marching order for inspection by Brigadier-General Whitham, and was drawn up as follows:—

Advanced Guard.
Camp Colour Men.
Pioneers.
Cart with Intrenching Tools.
Battalion Guns.
The Regiment in column of companies.
Bât Horses with Ammunition, under the charge of
the Quartermaster-Sergeant.
Bât Horses with Surgeon's Medicines.
Ditto Adjutant with Military Stores.
Ditto for Battalion Companies.
Rear Guard.

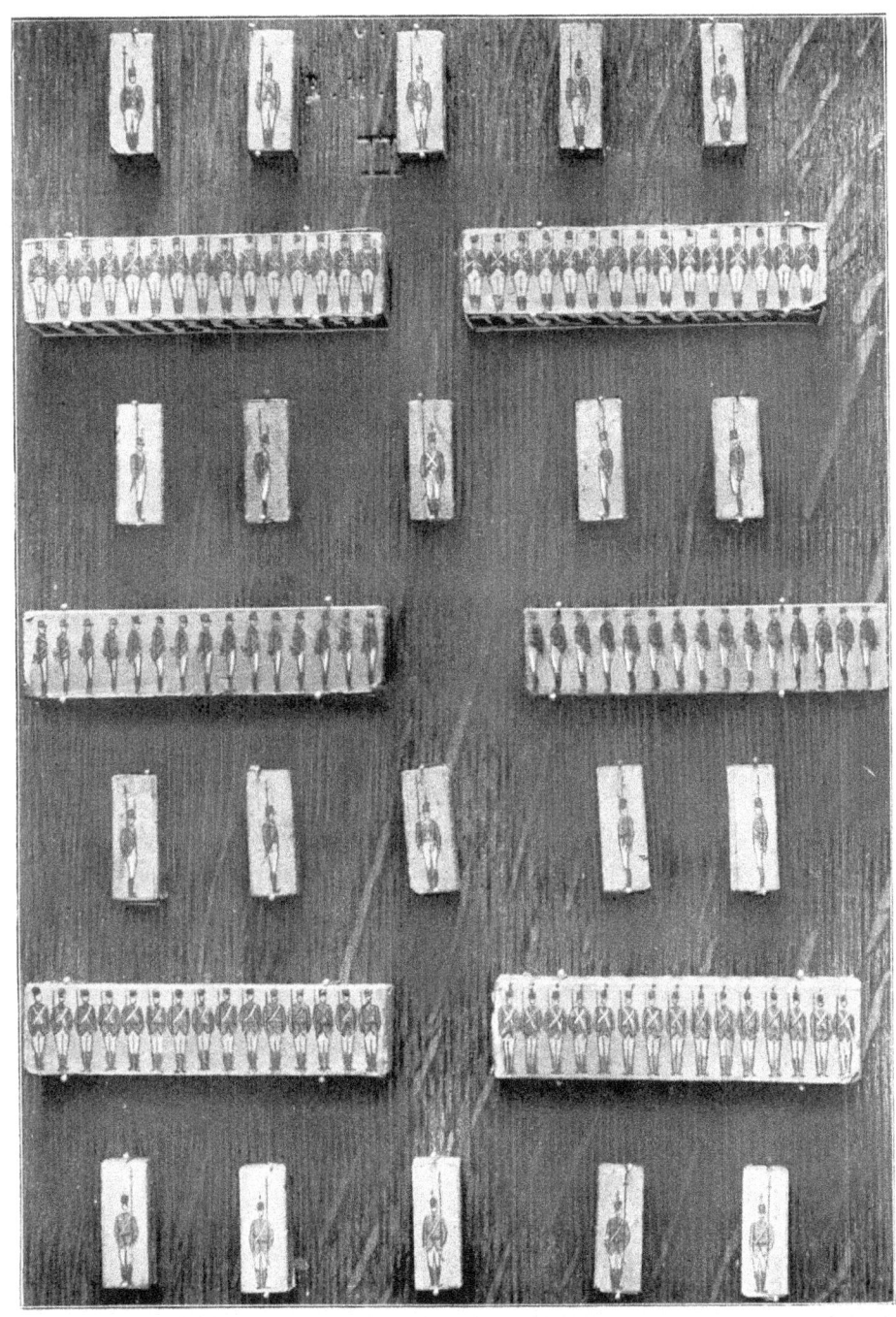

SET OF DRILL BLOCKS, CIRCA 1800, WHICH HAVE BEEN IN THE POSSESSION OF THE REGIMENTAL SERGEANT-MAJOR SINCE THAT TIME.

On March 11, being relieved at Haslar by the 2nd Battalion of the King's German Legion, the Monmouth and Brecon Militia crossed over from Gosport to Portsmouth and occupied Portsea Barracks, detaching one captain, one subaltern, and 105 non-commissioned officers and men for duty at Cumberland Fort.

In Orders for April 27 appeared:—

'Without any interference as to the particular mode of uniform worn by the regiments of Militia in this garrison and its dependencies, Major-General Whitelocke assuredly expects that all officers belonging to a regiment will at all times be precisely uniformly dress'd. The stock or silk handkerchief should be neatly worn about the neck without any extravagant exercise of fancy. No part of the shirt to be seen over the stock. The hat should be worn in conformity to the established regulations, and in this particular it will always be more desirable to witness an endeavour to be military and uniform than an inclination to deviate from what is correct.'

The officers were reminded that it was contrary to the Order of the Regiment to appear on parade without queues, without powder in the hair, or in any other respect improperly or unregimentally dressed. Again, on May 15, is found:—

'The frequent blunders and unmilitary conduct witness'd on the part of non-commissioned officers commanding guards and of sentries in this garrison are become not only discreditable, but also bring a degree of disgrace upon the military profession. To obviate which in as great a degree as possible the Field Officer of the day, with the aid of the officers on duty under him, as soon as the guards are mounted, is expected to ascertain that all orders of the guards and of every sentinel are correctly understood as required by his report upon honour.'

On May 24 the Monmouth and Brecon Militia paraded at 3.30 A.M. in marching order and proceeded to Chichester in three divisions. The Caermarthen Militia also left Portsmouth for Winchester. It was notified: 'Major-General Whitelocke has infinite satisfaction in returning his best thanks to both these Corps for their orderly and military conduct during the time he has had the honour to command them.' During a portion of the time that the Monmouth and Brecon Militia was at Portsmouth it was commanded by Major T. W. Davis, but later Lord Arthur Somerset returned to duty and assumed command as the senior Major, he having received his majority on August 25, 1803.

The strength on leaving Portsmouth for Chichester was twenty-three officers, thirty-six sergeants, and 747 rank and file. After having been quartered at Blatchington for a time, the Regiment proceeded to Lewes, where it remained for a year. At Blatchington the Duke of Beaufort, who had been absent for some time, rejoined, and held many inspections of the arms, which were by no means in a satisfactory condition, many of the bayonets and ramrods having been lost and many locks being defective. On October 20 the Regiment was inspected by Brigadier-General Lord Craven, and on the 26th of the same month it proceeded to Lewes, where it was in garrison with other troops. The orders for September 25, 1805, contain: ' The Duke is happy to say that he approved of the conduct of the Regiment in the field on Wednesday last, and he flatters himself that to-morrow he shall have the satisfaction of seeing that every man is steady and attentive to his duty in the field, and that the Regiment may so conduct itself as to meet the approbation of His Royal Highness the Commander-in-Chief.'

During the year 1805 a large number of officers and men volunteered for the Regular Army, a detachment of no less than 111 leaving in April alone. Of that number three officers and eighty-one men went to the 35th Regiment. In this same year Sir Samuel Fludyer[1] succeeded the Earl of Abergavenny as Lieutenant-Colonel, the latter officer having resigned on account of ill-health. On October 12, the Regiment left Lewes and returned to its old quarters at Blatchington, where it remained until Christmas, when it went to Horsham. On February 3, 1806, it left Horsham and proceeded to Steyning, where, with the exception of a break of a further few days at Horsham, it was quartered for some time.

In January 1806 it was announced that the two days' pay voted by the Monmouth Volunteers to the Patriotic Fund, with the addition of the officers' subscription, had amounted to the respectable sum of 61*l*. In addition the inhabitants of Usk had subscribed 25*l*. and the Royal Usk Volunteers[2] contributed nearly 17*l*. Brigadier-General Sir G. B. Boughton, on promotion, vacated the Severn Command early in the year. He had done much to assist the Volunteer movement, and was generally popular. His district included Radnor, Brecon, Monmouth, and Glamorgan.

---

[1] ' 5 July, 1805.—The Duke of Beaufort, having received His Majesty's approbation, has appointed Sir Samuel Fludyer, Bt., to be Lieutenant-Colonel of the Regiment in the room of Lord Abergavenny, who has resigned on account of the indifferent state of his health. Commission dated July 1, 1805.'

[2] The Royal Usk Volunteers were raised in September 1803, with Thomas Jones as Major Commandant.

The regimental order-book of the Monmouth and Brecon Militia for March 23, 1806, while the Regiment was at Steyning, records : ' The Regiment will parade for muster to-morrow morning at the usual hour of parade, at which time an Examination of Arms and Necessaries will take place, and the Articles of War will be read. The Servants will attend with their hair properly cut.' On April 24 the Corps was inspected by Major-General Alexander Mackenzie, who expressed his satisfaction on its appearance. June 4 was the King's birthday, and the Regiment paraded at 12 o'clock in new clothing, with three rounds of blank ammunition, to fire a salute. After four months at Steyning, on June 24 it proceeded to Chichester by way of Arundel.

On August 29, 1806, a general meeting of the Lieutenancy was held at the ' Three Salmons,' Usk, for the purpose of carrying into execution an Act of Parliament passed on July 16 of that year, entitled ' An Act for the return of correct lists of persons liable to serve in the Militia under an Act passed in the 42nd year of His present Majesty, and to suspend the ballot for the Militia in England two years.'

A further meeting of the Lieutenancy was held at Usk on March 6, 1807, to consider the steps to be taken for carrying into execution the provisions of ' An Act to enable His Majesty annually to train and exercise a proportion of his subjects and to provide for the defence of the realm,' and also an order of His Majesty's Most Honourable Privy Council directing 1353 men to be raised in the county of Monmouth.

The Monmouth and Brecon Militia left Chichester on September 17, 1807, four companies going to Bognor, and the other three to Aldewick. Owing to the weakness of the Regiment recruiting parties were detached under a major ; a captain, two lieutenants and ten non-commissioned officers and men going to Monmouth ; and a captain, a lieutenant, and six non-commissioned officers to Brecon. After a month at Bognor the three companies at Aldewick rejoined headquarters, and on October 16 the Regiment marched to Arundel, and next day to Steyning, arriving at Horsham again on the 18th. A letter dated ' Horse Guards, 12th October, 1807,' on the subject of leave, was the cause of each officer in rotation being allowed six weeks' leave at this time. The regimental orders for October 20 refer to this letter as follows :—

' In consequence of the Circular Letter dated Horse Guards, 12th October, 1807, Capt. Jenkins has got leave of Absence from the 14th inst. for six weeks, and on his return the next Senior Captain may avail himself of Leave for the same time—by this Order no Subaltern can have leave of Absence until those now on Duty in the County return to the Regiment. On the 25th inst. four private men per company may be indulged with leave of Absence for six weeks. Officers of companies will give in the names of those men on the morning parade of the 24th inst., and the Duke desires that the officers will only recommend men of good character, and such as have conducted themselves in a proper manner, for this indulgence. If any men of the above number who have obtained this indulgence do not return on the day their furlough expires no other man will be allowed to go on furlough, and those who are absent will be considered as deserters and punished accordingly.'

During the same month new greatcoats were issued, and an order of October 28 runs: 'The pay sergeants of companies will see that the men's new greatcoats are immediately marked with paint in the same manner the old ones were.' An order of December 5 substituted blue pantaloons for officers on Sundays for church parade for the white ones hitherto worn. The Regiment did not leave Horsham until May 27, 1808, when it proceeded to Bristol.

Desertions were numerous again at this time, and the notices circulated for the recovery of men who had thus left the Regiment were of frequent appearance. A specimen is provided by one dated April 6, 1807:—

'DESCRIPTION OF TWO DESERTERS FROM THE
ROYAL MONMOUTH AND BRECON MILITIA

'Hugh Williams, born in the parish of Llangwny, county of Anglesea, North Wales, 33 years of age; 5 feet 9½ inches high; stout-made, dark complexion, black hair, blue eyes, very much marked with the smallpox; by trade a labourer; deserted when on furlough in March last.

'David Powell, born in the parish of Llangattock, near Crickhowell, Breconshire, 21 years of age; 5 feet 9 inches high; stout, well-made, grey eyes, dark hair, ruddy complexion; by trade a mariner and navigator; deserted from Chichester on the 24th day of March in regimentals.

'Twenty shillings over and above what is allowed by Act of Parliament will be paid for the apprehending either of the above deserters on application to the paymaster at the Headquarters of the regiment.'

On May 1, 1807, the Monmouth Volunteers[1] assembled for

[1] This corps, the 2nd Battalion of Monmouth Volunteers, was raised in August 1803, and the officers on its formation were Lieutenant-Colonel Commandant Thomas Molyneux,

THE PENINSULA AND WATERLOO EMBODIMENTS 109

the purpose of completing their establishment, and for undergoing a term of training of thirteen days in conformity with the new regulations. Thomas Molyneux[1] was Lieutenant-Colonel Commandant. The weather was intensely wet, but notwithstanding, much useful work was got through and the musters had never been greater than on this occasion.

On July 20 Colonel Molyneux inspected the Chepstow and Caldecot Volunteer Infantry at Chepstow, and he was very pleased with their appearance. The bad weather, however, prevented the men from going through the whole of their evolutions 'for which they were so distinguished.'

A meeting of the Lieutenancy took place at the 'Three Salmons' at Usk, on August 27, 'to carry into execution an Act lately passed for speedily completing the Militia of Great Britain, and for increasing the same under certain limitations and restrictions.'

In September the Chepstow Volunteers were assembled for permanent duty at Chepstow for fourteen days, and the 1st Battalion of the Monmouth Volunteers, commanded by Sir Charles Morgan, were on similar duty at Brecon. In October the 2nd Battalion, commanded by Colonel Molyneux, not having performed the number of days duty required by Act of Parliament, assembled at Monmouth for ten days' successive training. The orders to the men stated, 'Those men not attending will be subject to the ballot for the new Militia which takes place on the 12th October.'

On October 19 a meeting of the Lieutenancy took place at the 'Three Salmons' at Usk, 'to apportion the number of men to be raised under the last Militia Act between the several sub-divisions of the county and to fix days for sub-division meetings in order to carry the said Act finally into execution.' The names of persons required to serve in the Militia were posted on the church door of each parish, and all men claiming any kind of exemption had to appeal to the deputy-lieutenants on a specified date, in order to get their names struck off the list. On January 28, 1808,

---

Major Robert Willis, Captains Robert Williams, Joseph Evans, Stephen Attlay, Thomas Phillips, Lieutenants Richard Blakemore, George Palmer, Thomas Davies, Thomas Wancklyn, Ensigns Thomas Evans, William Dawe, Charles Tyler, Richard Powles, with Charles Phillips chaplain, John Lorymer paymaster, Edward Lucas quartermaster, and James Powell surgeon. The Minutes of the Corporation of Monmouth record, under date September 20, 1803: 'Ordered that the Steward pay twenty guineas to the subscription for raising a corps of Volunteers at Monmouth.' The first Battalion of Monmouth Volunteers was raised in September 1803, and succeeded the Newport Infantry. It was commanded by Colonel Charles Morgan.

[1] Afterwards Sir Thomas Molyneux, Bart.

terminated the period allowed for raising the men under the recent Act of Parliament. Those parishes which had not furnished their proper quota became liable on that date to a fine of 60*l*. for each man deficient, subject to the following provisions : If the quota were completed within one month from January 28, three-quarters of the fine was returned to the parish. If completed within two months, one-half of the fine was returnable, and if within three months, one-fourth.

On May 20 the second battalion of Monmouth Volunteers marched to Bristol, to enter upon permanent duty; previous to the march the Regiment was encamped for nine days at Monmouth with the Hereford and Archenfield [1] Volunteers, each of which Regiments in succession marched to Monmouth for fourteen days' training. On September 23, the second battalion of Monmouth Volunteers assembled to finish the twenty-six days of training required by Act of Parliament for that year, it being the last training previous to the Regiment being converted into local Militia. Colonel Molyneux took the opportunity of complimenting the Corps on its soldier-like conduct on all occasions since he had had the honour of commanding it, and said he did not doubt but that the men would continue to act in a manner so worthy of their character. The Regiment assembled at eight o'clock on the morning of October 28, 1808, at the Town Hall, Monmouth, for the purpose of being attested as local Militia. The training in 1809 was at Monmouth and lasted for fourteen days. As many as 800 men assembled, Lieut.-Colonel Thomas Molyneux being in command.

The local Militia force was authorised to be raised by the Act 48 Geo. III. cap. 111, for England, and 48 Geo. III. cap. 150, for Scotland. Lord Hawkesbury, on the introduction of the Local Militia Bill, gave as a reason for establishing the new force, which was intended in a large measure to replace the Volunteers, that, although the Volunteer system was not objected to so far as it went, it could not altogether be depended on because its efficiency entirely rested upon the spirit which might prevail at the time, and which might dwindle and evaporate. The local Militia, being a more permanent and compulsory force, would remedy this defect. The quota was fixed at 213,609 men, who were to

---

[1] Preserved in the Royal United Service Museum are the coattee, breeches, sash, and sword of Lieutenant W. Brown, of the Light Company of the Archenfield (Hereford) Local Militia (disbanded 1816). This uniform shows the distinction between the Light Company and the ordinary Battalion Companies of a Regiment at that time. The Battalion Companies wore long instead of short tails to the coattee, aigulets instead of wings, and a straight instead of a curved sword.

be raised by ballot of those between the ages of eighteen and thirty; no substitutes were allowed, and the period of service was four years. The service was at first intended to be strictly local, but in 1813, by 54 Geo. III. cap. 10, the men's voluntary services were made available for any part of the United Kingdom until March 25, 1815. In point of numbers this new force did not add so much to the national defence as at first sight it might appear, for the greater part of the men were obtained from the existing Volunteer force by a mere transfer; in fact, in many cases whole regiments went over to the new force. The local Militia force was only in existence for a period of eight years, it having been raised in 1808 and disbanded in 1816. There were 179 regiments in England, comprising 151,370 men. The East Monmouth Regiment, consisting of ten companies with headquarters at Monmouth, was raised on September 24, 1808, Lieutenant-Colonel Thomas Molyneux being Commandant. The West Monmouth Regiment had its headquarters at Newport and was raised on the same date, and also consisted of ten companies, under the command of Colonel Sir C. Morgan, Bt. There were twenty-four local Militia regiments in Wales, with a strength of 16,368 men. Both the East and West Brecon Regiments had their headquarters at Brecon, and both possessed eight companies. The East Regiment was raised on September 24, 1808, and the West on March 23, 1809. Scotland contributed sixty-seven regiments, with a strength of 45,871.

On arrival at Bristol on June 6, 1808, the Monmouth and Brecon Militia was 689 strong, having recruited no fewer than 400 men in six months. On June 7 the daily orders contained: 'The parades of the Regiment are at half-past ten o'clock in the morning, and at half-past seven in the evening. When the first drum beats (which will be at ten o'clock in the morning, and seven in the evening) an officer per company will inspect their respective companies; the officers that inspect the companies are requested to be punctual to the hour, as the companies must march to the public parade when the second drum beats. The Commanding Officer directs that the soldiers are never to appear out of their quarters without being in every respect regimentally dressed, and officers are requested to notice any soldier they may see offending against this order, and report him to the Commanding Officer. Any soldier confined by an officer or non-commissioned officer to be sent to the regimental guard-room.

'The duty of the officer of the day will be to visit the regimental guard, and to make the non-commissioned officers acquainted with his residence, that they may (should it be necessary) know where to find him. The pay sergeants to be provided with a list of the men's names to whom bounties are due with the sums due to each, and also the names of the men that have died, with the state of their accounts.'

The orders for the following day state that 'The Regiment will in future parade three deep, and the sergeants must be careful that the men are properly sized.' At this period the men still wore white breeches and gaiters, but the officers seem to have generally worn blue pantaloons. On June 11 the daily orders contain the words, 'Officers will have the goodness to recollect that they are always to appear with powder in their hair.'

The orderly room of the Regiment at Bristol was in Lower College Street, and the officers' mess was at the 'White Lion' in Broad Street. The officers were in lodgings and the men in billets. One company was always on detachment at Wells.

In the orders for July 17, 1808, appears: 'The sergeant of the guard is upon no account to allow any man near or in the guard to smoke a pipe.'

The Regiment seems to have degenerated very considerably this year, both in appearance and general behaviour. The Commanding Officer constantly complained of it, and on September 1 he ordered, 'In consequence of the drunken and disorderly and unsoldierlike conduct of the men, and particularly the frequent and almost daily desertion that takes place in the Regiment, the Duke positively forbids any soldier having liberty from any parades of the Regiment till further orders, and unless the men conduct themselves better for the future, the Duke is determined not to allow them any indulgence whatever.' Again on September 10 he remarked, 'The Commanding Officer is ashamed to find the disgraceful crime of desertion so prevalent in the Regiment, and he assures the men that every deserter brought to the Regiment shall be punished in the most severe manner, and Thomas Jephtha Jenkins received so small a part of his punishment this morning, that the Commanding Officer assures the Regiment that the whole of the punishment awarded by the Court Martial shall be inflicted as soon as the surgeon reports the man fit to receive it.'

On July 16 new knapsacks were issued to the men at a cost to each man of 6s. 6d. At this time new portions of uniform were constantly

THE PENINSULA AND WATERLOO EMBODIMENTS 113

being introduced, which must have been a serious tax on the men, since they had to defray the cost themselves for these innovations. Each man was provided with two pairs of shoes and three shirts. In October 1808, when the new clothing was issued, black leggings were ordered for the whole Regiment, each man being charged 4s. 3d. per pair for their provision. Leather gloves were issued at the same time, at a cost of 1s. 5d. These gloves were ordered to be discontinued in March 1809 for all purposes except guard duty. During May long trousers and short gaiters were issued to the men for summer use. An order received from the Commander-in-Chief in June, however, resulted in this extra dress being put aside for a time.

At the end of October 1808 the Duke of Gloucester reviewed the Somerset, Carmarthen, and Monmouth and Brecon Regiments of Militia on Clifton Downs. He afterwards inspected Sir John Jervis's[1] Rifle Corps. Shortly after this review two companies of the Monmouth and Brecon Militia left headquarters for Milford.

In January 1809, owing to constant complaints on the part of the townsfolk of improper behaviour by men of the Regiments in the streets after tattoo, a picquet was mounted each evening to patrol the streets, and all men of the Regiments found about the town after tattoo were at once arrested and punished severely.

On February 18 Sergeant-Major Davis was appointed to the Local Militia. He had been with the Monmouth and Brecon Militia for many years. Sergeant Adams was also promoted Sergeant-Major and transferred to the same Force, and in April Captain Aythan Lewis was appointed an Adjutant in the Local Militia.

About this time a letter was received by the Commanding Officer from the Secretary of State for War on the subject of men of the Militia being invited to volunteer for regular service in the Line. Under the authority of the letter from Whitehall, 169 men could avail themselves of this procedure; they were allowed to join any Regiment, with the exception of the 1st, 27th, 30th, 48th, 53rd, 60th, 87th, 98th, 99th, 100th, 101st, 102nd, and 103rd. Men taking on unlimited service received a bounty of fourteen guineas, while those enlisting for seven years received ten guineas. The full quota, 169 men, volunteered from the Monmouth and Brecon. Of the other Militia Regiments at Bristol

[1] Sir John Jervis raised in 1796 a corps of Volunteers which he equipped at his own expense. He again raised and equipped a corps in Somerset in 1803, the one alluded to above, of which he was appointed Captain Commandant on December 13.

over a hundred volunteered from the Somersetshire, and about twenty from the Carmarthenshire.

As a result of this transfer the ranks became much depleted, and in June recruiting parties had to be sent out to Monmouth and to Brecon. These parties consisted of one captain, three sergeants, four corporals, and four privates, with one drummer and fifer.

The powdering of officers' hair at this time was carried out with much precision. In July 1809 an order appeared, ' The Duke is sorry to observe that some of the Officers do not wear Powder, or at least they wear so little it is hardly observable, but he begs that when in Regimentals they will constantly wear it. He also recommends that they should wear it shorter, both as being convenient as also looking better.' The men of the band, too, wore their hair powdered.

While at Bristol the principal duty of the Regiment was the guarding of the French prisoners at Stapleton. A certain amount of promiscuous traffic went on between the prisoners and the men of the Regiment, which had to be dealt with very severely whenever detected. The Duke of Beaufort in orders for October 4, 1809, assured the men that if in future any man was discovered disobeying the orders on this subject, which had been so repeatedly issued, he would be under the necessity of making a most severe example of him. He also stated that it would be necessary for him to apply to the Commander-in-Chief for the immediate removal of the Regiment from their quarters, if such unsoldierlike conduct continued.

On October 25, 1809, his Majesty's birthday, the Duke of Beaufort directed that one shilling should be given to each corporal, private, and drummer, and two shillings to each sergeant for the purpose of drinking his Majesty's health.

Whenever the Regiment was ordered to appear in marching order the men wore white trousers and gaiters, the officers when in marching order wore gorgets.[1] In February 1810 an order was issued to the effect that greatcoats properly slung were to be worn at all parades.

On October 25, 1810, when the Regiment paraded for inspection by General George Warde, in review order, the officers wore white cloth

[1] In the days when complete armour was worn, each portion of the body had its proper protection ; that for the neck and collar-bone being a piece of armour termed a ' gorget,' which was fitted over the cuirass or corselet. After the Restoration in 1660, when armour gradually came into disuse, the ' gorget ' was worn alone in place of the cuirass, and it at length became the last and only surviving remnant of armour in the Infantry. It remained in use in the Army and Militia until 1830, being worn by officers as a badge of rank, and as a sign of their being on duty.

breeches and black gaiters. The inspecting officer was much pleased with the steadiness and general appearance of the Regiment. As it was daily expected at this time that the Regiment would be leaving Bristol, the men were reminded that only five married women per company could be allowed in accordance with former orders. As a result of the General's very satisfactory report after the inspection on October 25, and having regard to the general good conduct of the Regiment since it had been in the garrison of Bristol, the Duke of Beaufort intimated that he would give to the non-commissioned officers and old soldiers a pair of breeches each, ' to be delivered as soon after Christmas as they can be got ready.'

On November 6 the Regiment commenced its march in two divisions to Berry Head. On the preceding day the orders contained the following words : ' The Lieutenant-Colonel takes this opportunity of expressing to the non-commissioned officers and men of the Regiment, his conviction that they will by their steadiness and soldierlike conduct both at the time of assembling and on the march from the garrison, deserve the very high compliment paid to them by General Warde, in the general order of the 2nd instant. Should to-morrow any individual so far forget what is due to himself and to the Regiment, as to appear intoxicated, or in any other improper manner, it is the determination of the Lieut.-Colonel to punish him in the most exemplary manner.'

The first day's march was to Wells, the second to Somerton, the third to Chard, the fourth to Honiton, the fifth to Exeter, where a day's halt was allowed, owing to the arduous march from Honiton, and the seventh to Newton Bushell, arriving on the eighth day at Berry Head. Soon after arrival a Court of Inquiry was appointed, consisting of the captain of the day and two subalterns, to examine the accounts of Captain Lewis's Company, and to report to the Commanding Officer the cause of the irregularity of the payment of the men which the Commanding Officer witnessed on the march. At an inspection on November 10 nine greatcoats were found to be missing, which were ordered to be replaced at once, the defaulting men being put under stoppages. On December 5 the Duke of Beaufort acquainted the non-commissioned officers and old soldiers, that in place of the breeches already alluded to, he intended giving to them grey trousers and spats. Many men of the Regiment at this time were unacquainted with the English language, and when the Articles of War were read to the Regiment it was necessary to interpret them in Welsh.

On March 25, 1811, it was ordered, ' In future the non-commissioned officers and men of the Regiment will at all times wear breeches and gaiters, except when the Regiment is ordered to parade in marching order, when the grey pantaloons and gaiters will be worn.' On Sundays the officers wore either white pantaloons or breeches.

In April it was intimated by the Commander-in-Chief that men of the Royal Monmouth and Brecon Regiment of Militia to the number of sixty-nine would be allowed to extend their service into the Line, of whom those who enlisted for seven years would receive a bounty of ten guineas, and those who chose to extend their service for life would receive a bounty of fourteen guineas. They might make choice of any Regiment of the Line, with the exception of the 43rd, 51st, 52nd, 68th, 71st, 85th and the Rifle Corps, into which Regiments only the Light Infantry Companies of the Militia could extend their service. The 60th, 98th, 99th, 100th, and 101st Regiments were also excepted. One sergeant and one corporal were able to be received into the Line, according to their rank, for every twenty men volunteering, but those sergeants and corporals had to be attested as private soldiers.

The men were required to give in their names before May 1, the day appointed for the volunteering, and they were also required to name the Regiment selected by each. On April 28 the Commanding Officer issued the following order concerning the volunteering :—

'The Commanding Officer having this day received an order from the Commander-in-Chief, that men from 5 feet 7 inches to 5 feet 10 inches will be allowed to Volunteer into the 43rd, 51st, 52nd, 68th, 71st, 85th and 95th Regiments, the Commanding Officer, wishing to give every encouragement and every fair chance to those men who propose to show their spirit by Volunteering into the Line, purposes to-morrow after the Field day, in his presence, that the men who have given in their names to the Adjutant by this evening parade, should all draw lots to decide which of them to the number of 69 should be allowed to Volunteer.'

The men selected were required to parade on May 1 at 6 A.M.

This event was evidently the cause of the circulation of much drink in the Regiment, each man toasting his comrade before his departure. The Commanding Officer in consequence made allowance for any small irregularities during the next day or two, but on May 6 he cautioned them of the 'necessity of their immediately returning to their former habits of sobriety and regularity.'

Up to July 1811 the Regiment had only been liable to serve in Great Britain, but in that month men were all re-sworn so that their service could be extended to Ireland. The Regiment accepted the additional

THE PENINSULA AND WATERLOO EMBODIMENTS

liability with a true spirit, and the Commanding Officer was much gratified at the zeal which the men evinced in extending their service to Ireland, 'which conduct does them the highest honour and which cannot but in the fullest manner meet the approbation and wishes of his Highness the Prince Regent, when the noble determination is laid before his Royal Highness.'

On July 18, 1811, there appeared in Daily Orders:

'The Duke of Beaufort has this day received a letter from Mr. Secretary Ryder, transmitting to him an order of his Royal Highness the Prince Regent in Council directing, in Conformity with the Provisions of the 23rd Sect. of the 51st George 3rd, Cap. 20, to raise by Beat of Drum or otherwise in the Counties of Monmouth and Brecon, and the Adjoining Counties, such a number of Volunteers for the Regiment as will complete it to 484 Private Men, being the original Quota fixed for the Counties under the 42 Geo. 3rd, Cap. 90, Sect. 19; and also in addition to the number of men required under the endorsed Order in Council a proportion of Supernumeraries to be raised equal to one-seventh of the original quota and a proportion of Boys of the Age of Fourteen years and upwards may be enlisted not exceeding one-fourth of the number that are required to join.

'The Distribution of the Levy Money for Recruits raised for the Militia under the 51 George 3rd, Cap. 20 was—

	Men £ s. d.	Boys £ s. d.
On being attested in money	£5 5 0	£2 2 0
Do., in necessaries	5 5 0	1 12 0
On joining the Headquarters of the Regiment in Great Britain—		
In money	5 5 0	2 2 0
In necessaries	5 5 0	1 15 6
Total bounty to recruit	£21 0 0	£7 11 6
Reward to the Officers and Party to cover all expenses, to be distributed in such manner as the Colonel or other Commandant of the Regiment shall direct	2 2 0	2 2 0
Total for Levy Money	£23 2 0	£9 13 6

Captain Chambre and Captain Bridgwater being the first Officers for this Duty will proceed immediately on this service, the former to Monmouth and the latter to Brecon. Those officers will receive the necessary instructions for the Duty prior to their leaving Head-quarters from July 25.'

In July of this year ten men per company were granted leave for the purpose of assisting at the harvest.

The arms at this time were a cause of much trouble, and in August the Officer Commanding had to draw attention to the fact that many of the locks were out of repair, the cock and hammer being so close together as to render it impossible to fix a flint; so much so that, out of a party of a hundred men told off for a particular duty which might have involved the use of their arms, thirty of the muskets were found to be defective.

In August an epidemic affecting the men's eyes ran through the Regiment, and precautions had to be taken as to special towels and washing utensils being allotted to the men afflicted; also many of the women in the barracks had to quit to make additional room for the sick men. On the 29th of the month the Regiment commenced its march to Pendennis Castle in two divisions. The first division consisted of four companies with the band, drums and colours; the second, comprising three companies, left on the following day. The first day's march was to Ashburton, the second to Tavistock, and the third to Launceston, where there was a halt of two days, one day being Sunday. At the Church Parade on that day the men wore breeches and gaiters, and the officers blue pantaloons.

From Launceston the route was to Bodmin and thence to Truro, where the Regiment was quartered for a fortnight. The daily orders of September 5 state, 'As the Regiment may be detained here (Truro) some days the Commanding Officer will dispense with the Officers wearing their gorgets on the Parade until the order for Marching is put in Orders, except such Officers as may be upon Duty,' while on the following day there appeared, ' To-morrow being the Market Day, the Soldiers will no longer be dieted by the Innkeepers but must provide their own Messes.' Pendennis was reached on September 14, the baggage having gone to Falmouth by water. At this time the clothing seems to have been most complete; on one day a parade was ordered with the men in 'grey trousers,' and the following day they were to appear in their ' best breeches and gaiters,' which indicated that each man had more than one pair of breeches. Soon after arrival at Pendennis an inspection was held by Major-General William Thomas, and the arms of the Regiment were thoroughly overhauled for the purpose, many having been found to still possess defective locks.

The gardens around the garrison having been plundered by the men for potatoes and other vegetables, it was found necessary to place a patrol on duty for their protection, and orders were given that any man found in a 'suspicious situation' was to be taken up. Only a few days after the placing of the patrol three men of the Regiment were caught stealing turnips and potatoes and were made prisoners. They were confined to barracks for a month, and ordered to mount four extra guards.

On October 14 some of the men on guard had to be confined owing to neglect of duty, a crime punishable with death. The Officer Commanding, however, wishing to treat the cases leniently, ordered one man to be confined to barracks for two months, and to mount eight extra guards and attend all the drills of the Regiment; another was confined to barracks for one month and ordered to mount four extra guards and attend all drills, while other men had similar but more lenient punishments meted out.

Many men of the Regiment, on leave, not having rejoined on the proper date, it was found necessary to grant no further general leave of absence while the Regiment was at Pendennis. The Guard was required to 'turn out' and present arms whenever the Governor or Lieut.-Governor of Pendennis Castle approached, no matter whether he was in uniform or not, but at this date, beyond members of the Royal Family, no person was entitled to military compliments who was not in uniform. When reliefs passed an officer in uniform they 'carried arms' instead of the command 'Eyes right' or 'Eyes left' being given. As now, sentries were not allowed to quit their arms or walk more than ten yards on each side of their posts, nor were they permitted to converse, loiter or lounge upon their posts. They were not allowed to remain in their sentry boxes in good or even moderate weather.

From December 27, 1811, whenever the Wet Drum beat, the men for guard paraded with their greatcoats open over their accoutrements. In 1812 the men still wore trousers in marching order, and breeches and gaiters in review order; stocks were also still worn at that time. While at Pendennis the men were frequently cautioned on the subject of being absent from barracks at night, and such breaches of discipline were frequent; on January 18, 1812, two men for this offence were ordered ' to be confined in the Black Hole upon bread and water until further orders, and when released to be confined to the barrack yard for two months, mounting one extra guard each week, and attending all drills.' A drummer was also consigned to the Black Hole on February 20 for ' most improper behaviour to the Sergeant of the Guard.'

On the first week in April the officers appeared in new jackets and caps in compliance with an order of the Duke of Beaufort of January 29. In May 1812 many volunteers for the Line were forthcoming; some went to the 5th Regiment and proceeded to Plymouth, but the remainder were ordered first to Exeter. No soldier in confinement or under the sentence of a Court Martial, by order of the Commander-in-Chief, was allowed to volunteer without the express permission of the Commanding Officer of the Regiment.

On June 24, 1812, the Monmouth and Brecon Militia commenced the march back to Bristol, the baggage being taken by water. The first day's march was to Mitchell, the second to Bodmin, and the third to Launceston, when Sunday intervened. On the fourth day's march Okehampton was made, then in turn Crediton, Tiverton and Wellington, until Bridgwater was reached, where the Regiment remained a fortnight; on July 17 it proceeded to Wells, reaching Bristol on the 18th. There were also quartered at Bristol the Royal North British Dragoons (Scots Greys) and the Militia Regiments of Oxfordshire, Leitrim and East Middlesex.

On July 19, 1812, Major-General John Oswald,[1] commanding the Severn District, called the attention of the Regiment to a recent order respecting the prompt assembling of the corps in case of alarm, and the adjutants of the various Regiments at the Station were ordered to meet at the Brigade Office 'every morning until further orders, immediately after guard mounting.' On July 19 General Oswald also made an inspection of the Regiment in marching order on Durdham Downs; the officers wore blue pantaloons, and feathers in their shakos.

At this time several escorts were furnished by the Regiment to take charge of deserters and prisoners of war. A deserter from the Second Foot, for instance, had to be escorted to the Isle of Wight, and a few days afterwards a French prisoner of war was taken from Abergavenny to Stapleton Prison.

In August of this year the Duke of Beaufort received a complaint from the Dean[2] of Bristol to the effect that the drums interrupted the service in the cathedral on Sunday mornings, and, as a result, the Duke ordered that all music and drums should be discontinued during the

---

[1] Colonel, Greek Light Infantry Corps, February 25, 1811.

[2] On January 6, 1813, in consequence of further correspondence from the Dean, it was notified 'Major-General Gordon Cuming having received an application from the Dean relative to the men drilling in front of the Cathedral, directs that no drilling may take place in the street or pathway, but be wholly confined to the Green, and all drums are forbidden between the hours of parade.'

hours of Divine service, both morning and evening, and an order of August 7 forbade all music and drums within the City of Bristol.

On the occasion of the anniversary of the Prince Regent's birthday on August 10 the troops in the garrison fired a *feu-de-joie*. The line was formed as follows: Oxfordshire Militia, Royal East Middlesex Militia, Royal Bristol Volunteers, Leitrim Militia, Monmouth and Brecon Militia. The Regiment assembled on College Green, in three columns, at eleven o'clock, and then marched to Durdham Downs. The field-pieces of the Royal Bristol Volunteers were on the right of the line. The *feu-de-joie* was given as follows: seven guns from the artillery followed by a running fire from the right of the front rank to the left of the line, and back again from the left of the rear rank to the right of the line, when seven more guns were fired. The troops then gave a Royal Salute, the bands playing God save the King, upon the termination of which the whole line gave a vociferous cheer, and then marched past the General.

In August 1812 Lieut.-Colonel Sir Samuel Fludyer resigned his commission. In orders there appeared, 'Sir Samuel Fludyer in taking leave of the Regiment begs to express the sense he entertains of the uniformly good conduct of the soldiers during the many years he has had the honour of serving with them. The officers, he hopes, accept his sentiments of acknowledgment and gratitude for the assistance they have afforded him in his command, and for the kindness with which it has pleased them to receive his efforts to maintain the discipline of the Regiment. With hearty good wishes for their welfare, he bids them farewell.' He was succeeded as Lieut.-Colonel by Thomas Lewis.[1] On August 20 Major-General Oswald announced that he was about to be transferred to the staff of the Army, serving under General the Marquis of Wellington, and until his successor Major-General John Gordon Cuming[2] was appointed, Colonel the Duke of Beaufort[3] commanded the Severn district.

---

[1] Promoted Lieutenant-Colonel, August 25, 1812; the son of Charles Lewis of St. Pierre, and a Deputy-Lieutenant of Monmouthshire; died in 1847.

[2] Half-pay, Inverness Fencible Infantry.

[3] Sir,—I have had the honour to lay before the Commander-in-Chief your letter of the 16th inst., and am directed to acquaint you, that His Royal Highness approves of your delivering over the command of the Severn District to Colonel the Duke of Beaufort, until the arrival of a General Officer at Bristol, who will be appointed to succeed you in the command of the Severn district.

I have, etc.,
Harry Calvert,
A. G.

Horse Guards: August 19, 1812.

General Oswald, in relinquishing his command, spoke in high praise of the general behaviour of the troops of the district. Major-General Gordon Cuming, having assumed command, addressed the officers and men of his district on September 23, 1812, as follows: ' Major-General Gordon Cuming cannot assume the command of the Severn district without expressing to the troops the very high satisfaction he feels in having under his command, Regiments and detachments that have conducted themselves in so orderly a manner, such as has been represented to him to have been the case for so considerable a time past. To the commanding officers and also to all the officers of the several corps, much praise is due; and it is the Major-General's desire that the non-commissioned officers and soldiers may be made acquainted with the favourable opinion he has formed of them for their past conduct, and the few punishments that have been found necessary and unavoidable. He confidently trusts therefore that a continuation of the same demeanour will mark the character of the troops in Bristol garrison in every situation in which they may be placed, to enable him to report them according to their merits, which will give him the highest satisfaction. As the Major-General believes that every soldier and officer is perfectly aware of the responsibility of the troops in this quarter, more particularly in that of the principal guard at Stapleton, he begs most earnestly to call the attention of every individual to that point, to which too much attention cannot be paid. The reasons are too obvious to require further explanation, and he trusts the officers will very strongly impress them on the minds of the respective guards under their command. The Major-General observes by the reports of the field officer of the day that he makes his rounds during the day for Stapleton guard. It is highly necessary to visit this guard during the night, which will be made between the hours of ten at night and four in the morning, but varying the hour of visiting, and which he will at all times specify in his report. The field officer will also communicate with the depôt guard on his way to and from Stapleton.'

The manual exercise at this time is perhaps worth alluding to. On the command ' Rear ranks, take open order,' at the word ' order ' the officers brought the sword to the recover, keeping it perpendicular and the guard of the hilt in line with the eye.

At ' March ' the officers took three paces obliquely to the left so as to cover the second file from the right of the division (if but one officer with the division; if two, the junior in like manner covered the second file from the left, and if three, the junior covered the centre file of the division), where they remained until the officer on the right of the battalion gave a signal to bring the sword to the 'post,' for which purpose that officer took four paces to the front, and faced to his left, and after giving the signal stepped back in his proper position.

When the word of command was given, 'Rear ranks, take close order,' at the word ' order ' the officers recovered their swords and faced to the right, at 'March' they resumed their places in battalion and brought the sword to the advance.

When the officers were ordered to take post in the rear for the manual exercise, they marched three paces beyond the rear rank and halted of their own accord; and at the word ' front ' faced to the ' right-about ' and bringing the sword to the 'post' remained steady in that position during the performance of the manual.

In October 1812 the Regiment, during the election in that month, was marched to Tetbury and Wotton-under-Edge, but such men as were freemen of the City of Bristol were allowed to return to record their votes. While at Tetbury, no man was allowed to proceed more than a mile from the town. The election over, the Regiment returned to Bristol on October 20, and soon afterwards Major-General Cuming held an inspection of it, when he expressed some dissatisfaction at the unsteadiness in the ranks.

In the year 1813 the rank of ' colour-sergeant ' was first created. The general orders from the Horse Guards on the subject, issued on July 6, were:—

'The Commander-in-Chief commands it to be declared in general orders, that his Royal Highness the Prince Regent, in consideration of the meritorious services of the non-commissioned officers of the Army, and with a view of extending encouragement and advantages to those of the infantry, corresponding to the benefit which the appointment of troop sergeant-major offers in the cavalry, has been most graciously pleased, in the name and on the behalf of his Majesty, to direct, that in all regiments of the infantry, whose services are not subject to limitations, the pay of sergeant-major shall henceforth be raised to three shillings per day, and that the pay of one sergeant in each company of battalions of the above description, viz., of those serving without limitations, shall be raised to two shillings and fourpence per day, and that the said sergeant shall be distinguished by an honourable badge, of which, however, and of the advantages attending it, they will, in case of misconduct, be liable to be deprived at the discretion of the Colonel, or Commanding Officer of the regiment, or by the sentence of a court martial.

'In consequence of the above most gracious intimation of his Royal Highness the Prince Regent's pleasure, the Commander-in-Chief directs that the sergeants selected for this distinction shall be called the "colour sergeants," and that they shall bear above their chevron the honourable badge of a regimental colour supported by two cross swords.

'It is his Royal Highness's pleasure that the duty of attending the colours in the field shall at all times be performed by these sergeants, but that these distinctions shall in no wise interfere with the regular performance of their regimental and company duties.'

On February 4 was celebrated the King's birthday. A review was held by Major-General Gordon Cuming of all the troops in the Bristol Garrison, followed by the firing of a *feu-de-joie* in honour of his Majesty. The battalions formed up on College Green in order of seniority, and the whole column, preceded by artillery, moved off at 12.30 P.M.; on arrival on Durdham Downs, near Redland, the column formed into close column of companies, and in its next formation opened to wheeling distance, afterwards forming into line. The ground on the occasion was kept by Dragoons.

Later in February the officers were required to provide themselves with overalls, to be worn both as the morning dress of the Regiment and also for marching and drill order, blue pantaloons being kept for afternoon dress and for dinner.

A regimental court-martial assembled on February 19 to try a private of the Regiment for (1) quitting his guard without leave on the road to Stapleton on January 30, 1813, and (2) deserting from the Regiment on or about January 30 and not returning until February 7. The prisoner was found guilty and sentenced to four months' solitary confinement in Lawford's Gate Prison. On April 14 a court-martial was held on two privates of the Regiment for being absent from the guard at Stapleton without leave and for selling spirits to the French prisoners; the first portion of the charge being proved against them, they were each sentenced to one month's solitary confinement and to mount four extra guards.

On July 17, 1813, the Monmouth and Brecon Militia embarked in six transports for Ireland; an intimation of the likelihood of this move had been made earlier in the year. Other regiments in the Severn district had received similar orders, the Royal East Middlesex, the 2nd Somersetshire, the Royal North Gloucester, and the Leitrim having been already

THE PENINSULA AND WATERLOO EMBODIMENTS 125

warned. The Bristol Garrison was consequently in a state of perpetual change, and amongst the military events in this ancient city during May 1813 and the following months were—

May 17, Brunswick Hussars disembarked at Bristol.
May 22, Sligo Militia marched in and embarked for Ireland.
June 17, Longford Militia succeeded the Royal North Gloucester.
June 25, 2nd Somersetshire Militia embarked for Ireland.
July 10, Royal East Middlesex Militia embarked for Ireland.
July 10, Anglesea Militia marched in.
July 10, South Gloucester Militia marched in.
July 10, 2nd Surrey Militia marched in.
July 10, Warwickshire Militia from Ireland disembarked.
July 14, Bedfordshire Militia embarked for Ireland.

In April 1813 a detachment of seventy-two men from the Monmouth and Brecon Militia joined the Army in the Peninsula, and many Militia uniforms figured at the Battle of Vittoria (June 21, 1813), the wearers having only just joined the line.

The Duke of Beaufort did not accompany the Regiment to Ireland, owing to his Parliamentary duties. On July 13 he wrote:

'The Regiment being about to embark for Ireland in a very few days, the Duke of Beaufort laments that, owing to some particular business, it will not be in his power to accompany it; at the same time he flatters himself he shall be able to pay some little time with the Regiment in the course of a few months, and cannot but avail himself of this opportunity of assuring both the officers and men that, whether present with or absent from the Regiment, he is always most anxious for its welfare and for everything that may contribute to its comfort and convenience. The Duke is extremely happy to hear of the general good conduct of the men, and trusts that at the time of embarkation they will behave in a sober, steady manner, and that upon their arrival in Ireland they will continue to conduct themselves properly and sustain the high character he flatters himself the Regiment has always had for good order and discipline. The Duke begs the officers will accept his best thanks for their attention to their duty, and as an encouragement to the men to behave properly he has directed a supper to be given to the sergeants this evening, and to each corporal, drummer, and private soldier one shilling to drink the King's health.'

The diary of Captain Thomas Morgan contains much concerning the regiment during the time that it was in Ireland. He commences by saying that he, in company with two other officers, embarked at Bristol on board the 'Harmony' at 7 A.M. on July 17. At 2 P.M., he remarks, 'I began to be ill.' On the 19th, 'Captain Williams[1] as white as a clout and very sick, frequently putting out his tongue.' On the 21st, 'All well.' The voyage to Dublin occupied six days, and on arrival Captain Morgan saw a man who had been apprehended for passing forged notes rescued by the mob. On the 23rd, the Regiment left Dublin; the first division reaching Naas on the evening of the 23rd, and Kildare on the 24th, where there was a halt for Sunday, it being St. James's Sunday. Portarlington was reached on the 26th and Tullamore on the 27th, where, on August 12, the Regiment was inspected by Major-General Sir William Ayllett,[2] and a *feu-de-joie* was fired, in conjunction with the Inniskilling Dragoons and Yeomanry, in honour of the Prince Regent's birthday. From Tullamore small detachments consisting of one sub-altern, one sergeant and thirty-five rank and file were quartered for three months at Clara, Kilbeggan, and Phillipstown, all small places about seven miles distant. Captain Morgan, on October 5, went to a fair at Ballinasloe, and saw sold 76,218 sheep, 6,604 oxen, and 2,098 cows; he also saw a pony 12½ hands leap a wall of 5½ feet with a boy up, and without the boy it cleared a wall of six feet.

On November 7 was received the news of Bonaparte's defeat in Russia, and as a result Tullamore was illuminated. On the 29th the Regiment fired a *feu-de-joie* in consequence of the insurrection in Holland and Lord Wellington's victory, and there were grand illuminations in the evening.

On December 20 the 1st division of the West Suffolk Militia marched into Tullamore and the 2nd division arrived on the following day, when all the officers dined with those of the Monmouth and Brecon Militia.

Large numbers of volunteers were still required for the regular service, and the Regiment sent fifty-four men to the Royal Wagon Train, thirty-one to the 1st Foot Guards, sixty to the 51st Regiment, and four to other regiments, making a total of 149. They left the Regiment on January 8, 1814; four officers also joined the Regular Army. Special instructions were issued from the War Office in December 1813 to the following effect:

'The non-commissioned officers and private men will be permitted to volunteer as hitherto, for any of the regiments of Foot Guards, or

---

[1] Captain William Williams; appointed Captain, October 26, 1803.
[2] Half-pay, 6th Garrison Battalion.

THE PENINSULA AND WATERLOO EMBODIMENTS

infantry of the line (with the exception of the 60th), and must be attested accordingly, and not for any particular battalion of the regiment.

' Men may enter generally into his Majesty's regular forces, and will be received and appointed to regiments now serving in Europe. With every hundred men of this description, a captain, lieutenant, and ensign will be transferred from the Militia to the line, and non-commissioned officers in the proportion of five sergeants, six corporals, and two drummers.

' General officers commanding districts will appoint general or field officers of the line, who are to be assisted by competent medical officers, to inspect the volunteers. They will be careful in rejecting every man who is not conformable to the regulations, according to the corps for which he is intended, or who is considered surgically unfit for active service.

' Volunteers for the Foot Guards and the line generally, or for particular regiments, will receive a bounty of sixteen guineas if enlisting for an unlimited period of service, and twelve guineas if for a limited period.

' The age and standard for the respective corps are fixed as follows, viz. :

	Age not exceeding	Height not under
Foot Guards	35	5 feet 5 inches.
Line	35	5 feet 4 inches.

' The standard for the light infantry and rifle corps to be the same as that for the other regiments of infantry. The Royal Wagon Train will also be allowed to receive volunteers from the British Militia. No man under eighteen years of age is to be approved for this corps, or who exceeds five feet four inches in height, or is less than five feet two inches.

' Volunteers for the Royal Wagon Train, for an unlimited period, will receive a bounty of twelve guineas, and those enlisting for limited service a bounty of eight guineas.

' No Militia man who may be in confinement or under the sentence of a Court Martial, no person employed as adjutant's clerk, regimental clerk, drummer, musician in the band, armourer, or who shall have been trained as an artilleryman or matross, and as such shall be attached to any artillery belonging to any regiment of Militia, not exceeding twenty men in each battalion, is to volunteer without the consent of the Officer commanding the Regiment.

'In case the Colonel or Officer commanding should refuse to discharge any private who should be desirous of volunteering into the regular service, the approving General or Field Officers are to inquire in writing the reasons for such refusal, and transmit the same for the decision of the General Officer commanding the District.

'The approving General and Field Officers will take care that the volunteers are regularly discharged from the Militia, and that their accounts are closed, and every just claim satisfied; they will also be careful that they are immediately reattested for the regiment into which they have volunteered, or for general service in the line, according to the forms of attestation prescribed by the present Mutiny Act.

'Men volunteering for regiments stationed in the same garrison, or in the immediate neighbourhood, are to be delivered over as attested, and the Officers commanding regiments of Militia will be responsible that the attestations are duly forwarded.

'The General Officers Commanding Districts will take the necessary steps for forwarding the men who may volunteer for particular regiments and will transmit to the Adjutant-General returns of the numbers from each corps. Returns of the numbers of men who volunteer from the respective regiments of Militia for general service in the line are also to be transmitted without delay to the Adjutant-General, and the men are to remain with the Militia until the orders shall be received for their transfer to the regular service.

'The General Officers Commanding Districts will communicate with the Quartermaster-General, with respect to marching the volunteers to their destination.

'The volunteers are to take with them the clothing of the present year, and are to leave with the Militia their greatcoats, and other regimental appointments.

'The sub-division Officers and parties employed on the recruiting service are not to be called to assist in this duty, as the volunteering must not be permitted to interfere with the regular recruiting.

'No Officer or party is to be sent to the quarters of any Militia regiment during the volunteering, without the concurrence of the Officer Commanding the regiment of Militia; and those allowed to attend are strictly enjoined from interfering further than may be sanctioned by the Colonel or Commanding Officer of the Militia Regiment.

'Furloughs are not to be granted to the volunteers previous to their joining the headquarters of their corps, or the regimental depot—after which the Officers Commanding will be at liberty to apply to the General Officer of the district for short furloughs, provided the service will admit of this indulgence.

' An allowance will be made to the Officers appointed to take charge of the volunteers; viz., 6d. per mile when proceeding from the quarters of their regiment, and 4d. per mile when returning, and they will further receive a daily allowance during the time they are so employed, according to their rank, as follows : Captains, 10s.; Subalterns, 5s.

' The General Officers commanding Districts will make arrangements with respect to the volunteering of the Militia for the regular service, under the aforegoing Regulations. The volunteering of corps of Militia for extended service in Europe will be carried into effect by the Colonels or Officers commanding the respective regiments, under the instructions of the Secretary of State.'

A heavy snowstorm fell during the month of December 1813, and detachments of the Regiment were engaged in clearing the Kilbeggan Road, so that the people could go to market.

Captain Morgan's diary states that he visited the seat of Lord Sunderlin[1] on April 1, and that he saw in the plantation a monument erected to Catherine Malone—a figure resting on an urn, with the following inscription round the brim :

> Tho' lost for ever, still a friend is dear,
> The heart still pays ye tributary tear
> To Mrs. Cathe. Malone, &c., &c.,

In testimony of ye many excellent qualities she possessed. For in the liberality and cultivation of her understanding, she was equalled but by few. In the unbounded generosity, in the warmth, sincerity, and benevolence of her heart surpassed perhaps by none ; yet did humility add lustre to those virtues to which it rendered her in appearance a stranger. Let this marble then be raised and let this spot be sacred to unassuming worth.
A.D. 1765.

On April 7 an officer and 27[2] additional volunteers for the Line set out for Dublin. The 10th of the same month was Easter Day, and the Regiment fired a *feu-de-joie* at the news of the Allies entering Paris. The Inniskilling Dragoons and the West Suffolk Militia also took part in the ceremony.

---

[1] The Barony of Sunderlin (Malone) in the Peerage of Ireland was created in 1785 and became extinct in 1816.
[2] Seventeen of these went to the 51st Regiment.

Ireland was in a very disturbed state in this year, and sentries were more than once fired at when at their posts. Sir William Aylett, the Officer commanding the Cork district, ordered in consequence, that every sentry should load at 'retreat,' and 'cause himself and his duties to be respected.' If necessary, sentries were to be doubled, and it even became necessary for all guards to load at 'retreat.'

On April 1, 1814, the strength of the Regiment was 387. On the 13th news of peace arrived at Tullamore, and on the 18th the garrison fired a *feu-de-joie* on account of the good news of Bonaparte's dethronement. There was also a general illumination at night. As a result of peace having been declared, recruiting for the Militia ceased under an order of April 16, and on the 21st General Orders issued from the Horse Guards contained:

'The re-establishment of peace, having enabled his Royal Highness, the Prince Regent, in the name and on the behalf of his Majesty, to direct the disembodying of the Militia forces, the Commander-in-Chief, previous to their return to their respective countries and counties, desires thus publicly to offer to them his best acknowledgments for the zeal and perseverance with which they have during a long and eventful war shared with the Regular Army in every military duty which has fallen within their province.

'From the gallant and patriotic spirit displayed by the Militia were derived, at the most critical periods of the war, the means of reinforcing the disposable force of the country, a measure which most essentially contributed to its military renown, by placing the British Army foremost in those confederate bands, which resisted the unbounded ambition and overwhelming power of the late Ruler of France, and by their bravery and discipline, under the direction of Divine providence, rescued that country from tyranny and oppression, and restored to Europe the blessing of peace.

'The Commander-in-Chief feels personally indebted to the Militia forces for the ready and cheerful obedience with which they have, at all times, received his commands, and he requests that with these heartfelt expressions of approbation they will collectively and individually accept his warmest wishes for their welfare and happiness.

'FREDERICK. Commander-in-Chief.'

As each Regiment was disembodied Generals commanding districts conveyed their personal thanks for the valuable services of the Militia.

Monmouth Militia.
SUB-DIVISION.

Hundred of *Penfret Forest Division*

To *Joseph Coates Castle Bayby Ward Ironmonger*

Notice is hereby given unto you,

That you are chosen, by Lot, to serve in the Militia of the County of Monmouth, and that you are to appear at the House of *Charles Russell* Victualler, at *Sun Inn Crossway* in the said County, on *Thursday* the *Twentieth* Day of *March instant* next, before the Deputy Lieutenants and Justices of the Peace, to be then and there assembled, to take the Oath in that behalf required; and to be Enrolled to serve in the Militia of the said County, as a Private Militia Man, for the space of Five Years; or otherwise to provide a fit Person, to be then and there approved by the Deputy Lieutenants and Justices, who shall take the said Oath, and be then and there Enrolled as aforesaid.

Given under my Hand the 10th Day of *March* in the Year of our Lord 1817 *John Charles*

Constable of *Castle Bayby Ward*

For instance, a General Order dated Edinburgh, February 6, 1815, runs as follows:

'Major General Hope will be on parade to-morrow afternoon at three o'clock to see the Royal Cumberland Regiment of Militia, for the last time previous to its march to their own county, for the purpose of being disembodied. The Major-General takes this opportunity of expressing his satisfaction and entire approbation of the good conduct of the Regiment, and of its orderly and regular behaviour in quarters and in garrison during the time it has been under his command, and wishes every happiness to the Officers, non-commissioned officers and men, who no doubt must be anxious to return to their families and friends after so long a period of absence for the good of their country; and they must ever feel a sincere satisfaction in their own minds at having, by their extended services to the sister kingdom of Ireland, enabled Government to avail itself of every disposable man for foreign service, by which this long war has at last been brought to so glorious a termination.'

The Monmouth and Brecon Militia remained at Tullamore until September 12, 1815, but the men were allowed to go to their homes as their service expired. Of the other Militia in Ireland the Shropshire, Waterford, Sligo and 3rd Lancashire were at Limerick; the Derbyshire, Tipperary and City of Limerick at Cork, with the Oxfordshire at Spike Island, Carlisle and Counden forts.

At Fermoy were the Renfrew and County of Limerick Regiments with detachments of three Regular Regiments, and at Clonmel were the Tyrone and Queen's County Militia, while at Carlow was stationed the Clare Militia.

July 7, 1814, was the day of Thanksgiving for Peace at Tullamore and the Regiment went to church. Constant troubles were encountered by the outlying detachments, and several men were killed in small scuffles. There is but little to record of the Regiment's doings up to its departure from Tullamore. On August 16, 1814, the 61st Regiment marched into the place, and the West Suffolk Militia, which had been quartered all the time at Tullamore, left for England on August 29, and the North Mayo Militia marched into the place. On September 13 the 50th Regiment marched in and the North Mayo left, but the Tyrone Militia arrived on the following day. The 45th Regiment also arrived.

Captain Morgan's diary for May 13, 1815, records: 'Gave Lieutenant Nicholson[1] one guinea to return six guineas if Boney is the head of the French Government May 13, 1816,' and again on June 5: 'The 4th Royal

[1] Lieutenant William Nicholson; appointed Lieutenant November 19, 1807.

Irish Dragoon Guards and the Royal Monmouth and Brecon Regiment fired three rounds in the barrack field, commanded by Captain Powell.[1] Captain Chambre[2] carried the King's Colour in consequence of Nicholson being ill. Betted Isaacson[3] half a crown that the Regiment would not be in Ireland this day two months.'

The news of Napoleon's defeat at Waterloo reached Tullamore on June 26, and on the 28th the 4th Royal Irish Dragoon Guards and the Monmouth and Brecon Militia fired a *feu-de-joie* in honour of the occasion. On August 12 the same two Regiments, in company with the Tullamore Volunteers, fired a further three rounds. There was a ball at Tullamore on August 16, which resulted in a great tumult, and on the following day a man was hanged for stealing and opening a letter. On the 22nd a subaltern, sergeant, corporal and eighteen privates escorted six prisoners to Naas, and on the same day a detachment of the 27th Fusiliers marched in to Tullamore. On September 10, 1815, the route arrived for the Regiment to march to Carrick-on-Suir on the 12th. The General Officer Commanding circulated on September 10: 'Major-General Kemmis cannot suffer the Royal Monmouth and Brecon Regiment to move without expressing his high opinion of its good order and discipline, the gentlemanly conduct of its officers, and correctness of the non-commissioned officers and men, both in their quarters and in their duty. For their future welfare he offers his best wish.'

The Regiment was at Maryborough on the 14th *en route* for Ballinakill, where it arrived in the evening. Captain Morgan's diary records, ' Infernal beds at Inn, lice, &c.; passed in morning through Lord De Vesci's beautiful grounds at Abbeyleix. Saw sheep tethered by chains, and capital mangel wurzel,' and he also noted down the following lines, which evidently he had seen engraved on some stone :

> To smooth the lawn, to decorate the dale,
> To raise the summit or to scoope the vale,
> To mark each distance through each op'ning glade,
> Mass kindred tints or vary shade from shade,
> To bend the arch, to ornament the cot,
> In all let Nature never be forgot,
> Her varied gifts with sparing hand combine,
> Paint as you plant, and as you work design.

---

[1] Captain Charles Harrison Powell; appointed Captain June 16, 1807; son of William Powell of Monmouth, surgeon; died 1848.

[2] Captain Christopher Chambre; appointed Captain March 25, 1813; son of Christopher Chambre of Llanfrist; died 1847.

[3] Anthony Allett Isaacson; appointed Lieutenant March 25, 1813; son of Captain Anthony Harvest Isaacson. Became vicar of a parish of Newport, Monmouthshire.

THE PENINSULA AND WATERLOO EMBODIMENTS

On the evening of September 16 the Regiment reached Kilkenny and Callen, whence it proceeded to Carrick-on-Suir on the 18th. On the 19th the 97th Regiment marched in and one of its men was flogged. The next day the 20th Regiment arrived on its way to Templemore, and a man belonging to it was court-martialled for shooting Private John Green of the Monmouth and Brecon Militia. In November the Regiment proceeded to England, and arrived at Bristol after having been two years and four months in Ireland; the last muster was on Christmas Eve 1815, when the strength was 321 of all ranks. On the 26th the Regiment started for Chepstow, *en route* to Monmouth, and on January 6, 1816, it was disembodied, the Colonel, the Sergeant-Major and others being carried round the town.

This long embodiment had extended over a period of nearly thirteen years, throughout which time the Regiment had shown itself on all occasions to possess a very high standard of efficiency. The Militia had been the means of liberating the Regular Army for service in Spain, and at Waterloo, where its services were so sorely required. In addition to having contributed this great service to the country, the Militia had sent direct to the wars many thousands of men, and the Monmouth and Brecon Regiment had alone contributed over three thousand during the thirteen years of embodiment, and no doubt it was well represented at such victories as Vimiera, Talavera, Salamanca, Albuera, Vittoria and Waterloo.

After peace had been declared the triumphs of the nation were succeeded by internal distress and discontent. It was not until then that the people began to feel the burthens which the war had occasioned. The price of wheat rose before the end of 1816 from fifty-two shillings a quarter to double that amount. A multitude of persons were thrown out of employment through the depressed state of trade, and their numbers were swelled by the soldiers and sailors discharged at the termination of the war.

FLINT-LOCK MUSKET, 1820

CHAPTER VII

FROM 1816 TO THE END OF THE CRIMEAN WAR EMBODIMENT

THE success of the British Arms both in the Peninsula and at Waterloo, coupled with glorious victories at sea, resulted in that state of stupor and inertness on the part of the British people which has been so conspicuous amongst other nations suddenly elevated to a position of serene supremacy. A successful war seems to demoralise a national military spirit, and military inactivity is usually the sequence; such was certainly the case after the battle of Waterloo. The Militia having been disbanded was given no further thought; the law ordering it to be trained annually was rescinded under an Act of Parliament of the year 1817, and an Act for the suspension of training was yearly submitted to Parliament formulated thus; 'Whereas by an Act, passed in the last session of Parliament, cap. 57, intituled "An Act to empower His Majesty to suspend training, and to regulate the quotas of the Militia," it is enacted that it shall be lawful for His Majesty, by any Order or Orders in Council, to suspend the calling out of the Militia of the United Kingdom, or any part of the United Kingdom, or of any county, shire, stewartry, city, town, or place, for the purpose of being trained and exercised in any year, and to order and direct that no training or exercising of the Militia of the United Kingdom, or of any county or counties, riding or ridings, shire or shires, stewartry or stewartries, city or cities, town or towns, or place or places, specified in any such Order or Orders in Council, shall take place in any year, anything contained in any Act or Acts of Parliament relating to the Militia to the contrary notwithstanding; and whereas it is deemed expedient that such training and exercising should be dispensed with in the present year, it is ordered by His Royal Highness the Prince Regent, in the name and on the behalf of His Majesty, and by and with the advice of His Majesty's Privy Council, that the calling out of the Militia of that part of the United Kingdom called Great Britain, for the purpose of being trained and exercised in the present year, be suspended, and that no training or exercising of the said Militia do take place in the present year.'

The Act for suspending the ballot or enrolment for the Local Militia was similarly presented to Parliament each year in the following words, 'Whereas an Act, passed in the last session of Parliament, cap. 38, intituled "An Act to empower His Majesty to suspend the ballot or enrolment for the Local Militia," it is enacted that it shall be lawful for His Majesty, by any Order in Council, to direct that no ballot or enrolment for the Local Militia shall take place; but that such ballot and enrolment shall remain and continue suspended for the period specified in any such Order in Council, and from time to time, by any like Order or Orders in Council, to continue such suspension so long as His Majesty shall deem the same expedient, anything in any Act or Acts of Parliament to the contrary notwithstanding; and whereas by an Order in Council, made the twenty-seventh of June one thousand eight hundred and sixteen, it was ordered by His Royal Highness the Prince Regent, in the name and on behalf of His Majesty, and by and with the advice of His Majesty's Privy Council, that no ballot or enrolment for the Local Militia should take place from and after the date of the said Order for the space of one year, but that the ballot and enrolment for the Local Militia should remain and continue suspended for the space of one year from the date of the said Order: and whereas it is deemed expedient to continue such suspension of the ballot and enrolment for the Local Militia for the space of one year from and after the twenty-seventh day of June next; it is therefore ordered by His Royal Highness the Prince Regent, in the name and on the behalf of His Majesty, and by and with the advice of His Majesty's Privy Council, that no ballot or enrolment for the Local Militia do take place for the space of one year from and after the twenty-seventh day of June next, but that the Ballot and Enrolment for the Local Militia do remain and continue suspended for the space of one year, from and after the said twenty-seventh day of June next.'

In 1832 this annual Local Militia Act was repealed, but the force has never since been raised.

In 1816, in addition to the Brecon Local Militia, of which Captain Aythan Lewis,[1] formerly an officer of the Monmouth and Brecon Militia, had been appointed adjutant in 1809, and Captain John Meredith,[2] another

---

[1] Appointed Captain in the Monmouth and Brecon Militia, February 25, 1798.
[2] Appointed Captain in the Monmouth and Brecon Militia, May 25, 1809.

ROYAL MONMOUTHSHIRE MILITIA

officer from the same Militia Regiment, in 1813, there also existed the East Monmouth Local Militia and the West Monmouth Local Militia; both these Regiments had as adjutants officers from the Monmouth and Brecon Militia, Captain Thomas W. Davis,[1] whose monument stands at the west end of St. Mary's Church, Monmouth, being Adjutant of the former Regiment, and Captain A. H. Isaacson of the latter.

The Royal Monmouth Militia[2] came out for training for twenty-one days in September 1821, and again in 1825. It consisted of only four companies with a total strength of 260 non-commissioned officers and men, the Duke of Beaufort being Colonel on each occasion and Thomas Lewis Lieutenant-Colonel.

In 1829 an Act of Parliament was passed greatly curtailing the permanent staff of the Militia throughout the country. One staff-sergeant was allowed for every forty men, and in addition there were an Adjutant and a sergeant-major.

It is recorded that in 1831 a detachment of the Royal Monmouth Militia, improperly armed and without uniform, proceeded hurriedly, under command of Captain John J. Kane,[3] the Adjutant, to the Forest of Dean, to assist in suppressing a riot. The detachment, however, was no match for the rioters, who were very numerous, and it was compelled to retire before them. The next day the 3rd Dragoons arrived at Coleford and soon settled the affair, the leader of the rioters, Warren James, being taken. Captain Kane, however, received a letter of thanks for his efforts on the occasion—

'The Magistrates assembled at Coleford cannot allow Captain Kane and Captain Mitchell,[4] with the men under their command, to return home without begging these officers to accept of their best thanks for the ready manner in which they complied with the wishes of the Magistrates to attend at Coleford in aid of the Civil Power, and for the active and attentive manner in which they have performed the duty imposed upon them, and they request the officers will be so good as to explain to the

---

[1] Appointed Captain in the Monmouth and Brecon Militia, May 25, 1796.

[2] In the year 1820 the Monmouth and Brecon Militia had been divided into the Royal Monmouth Militia and the Royal Brecknock Militia. Major Francis Chambre, Captains Thomas Bridgwater and Christopher Chambre, Lieutenants William Nicholson and Richard Smith, with Quartermaster George Burley, all went with the latter corps.

[3] John Joseph Kane was gazetted Ensign in the King's Own Regiment on October 21, 1813, and was present with his Regiment in the action at New Orleans on January 8, 1815. He also served as Aide-de-Camp to Brigadier-General Brooke with the Army of Occupation in France.

[4] An officer of the Royal Marines on recruiting duty at Monmouth.

COLOURS PRESENTED BY THE 6TH DUKE OF BEAUFORT, 1813.
(Now hanging in the Officers' Mess at Monmouth Castle.)

non-commissioned officers and men under their command how highly the Magistrates approve of their conduct.

'(Signed)   BEAUFORT.
WORCESTER.
GEORGE ROOKE.
P. J. DUCAREL.
MAYNARD COLCHESTER.
CHARLES CRAWLEY.
EDWARD MACHEN.'

In 1831 the Regiment came out for training for the last time until 1852; its strength was much the same as it had been during the two previous trainings. For the subsequent twenty years, until 1852, the Militia was allowed to fall to pieces in a most disgraceful manner. The permanent staff was further reduced, and even the arms and stores were recalled. Those of the Royal Monmouth Militia were returned to London in 1831, and consisted of 282 muskets, with flints, bayonets, and ball cartridge, 16 halberds, together with uniform and equipment. The Colours[1] were left at Monmouth, they having been presented by the Duke of Beaufort at a cost of fifty pounds in 1813; beyond them, only the big drum and the arms for the permanent staff, then reduced to five, were not removed.

On November 23, 1835, the Duke of Beaufort died, having been in the Regiment for forty-two years, and having been in command of it for thirty-two years. He was succeeded in the command by Colonel Thomas Lewis of St. Pierre.

In 1848 the political situation compelled the Government to consider the Militia question, and it would seem that the Government, after four years of deliberation, had come to a decision in the matter.

On February 16, 1852, Lord John Russell, in a Committee of the whole House of Commons on the Local Militia Acts, explained the ministerial proposition. Having enumerated the reasons which had induced the Government to strengthen, at that juncture, the defences of the country, he stated that the Government had carefully considered whether it should establish the Militia on the plan of the old Regular Militia, or on that of the Local Militia, and it had decided on the latter course. The scheme included that two-thirds of the officers should be appointed

---

[1] These Colours may now be seen hanging in the Officers' Mess at Monmouth. The Regimental Colour bears the Arms of the Duke of Beaufort on a blue field.

by the Lord Lieutenants, one field officer in each corps, and one-third of the others, being appointed by the Crown. The qualification for officers of a certain amount of landed property was to be dispensed with. With regard to the men it was proposed that, instead of the limitation of eighteen and thirty years of age, as under the old Local Militia Act, the limits subjecting parties to the ballot should in the first year be from twenty to twenty-three years of age, in the second year from twenty to twenty-five; but any person between twenty and thirty might volunteer, and he would serve one year less than those balloted for, whose period of service was to be four years, which could be extended by six months by Order in Council, and six months further still by Act of Parliament. It was proposed that the men should be formed into battalions and assemble for training twenty-eight days in the first year, and fourteen days in each subsequent year. In the event of a danger of invasion the force might be embodied and sent to any part of the country where its services might be required. In the first year it was intended that the number raised should not be less than 70,000 at a cost somewhat under 200,000*l*. In the second year the number raised was to be 100,000, and in the year after 130,000, and there was a chance of the Force attaining as large a figure as 150,000. Mr. Cobden contended that the country might be abundantly protected by the Navy if the ships were not sent abroad, but Lord Palmerston pointed out that our insular position was in some respects our strength, in others our weakness. Our shores were exposed on so many points that it was impossible to provide for all. Our Navy was as efficient at that time as it had ever been, but that, said Lord Palmerston, was no reason why other precautions should be neglected. It would be madness, he stated, to rely entirely upon the fleet, which could not prevent the landing of a hostile force. It was absolutely necessary to have a land force, and he considered a force of the nature of that proposed by the Government to be the best—one trained to arms, dormant in time of peace, but ready to act with the Regular Troops in war; but he gave preference to the old Regular Militia system to that of the Local Militia. What the country wanted was a Regular Militia, whereas a Local Militia was an occasional force for a particular exigency.

In the end the Government was defeated on its proposals by a minority of eleven votes. Lord John Russell said he considered that the vote showed that Ministers had no longer the confidence of the House, and the result necessarily followed—the termination of the Russell Administration.

The first important measure initiated by the new Government was the Bill for the organisation of the Militia, the introduction of which devolved on the Home Secretary, Mr. Spencer Walpole, who stated that it was impossible at that time to bring on any one point 25,000 men in case of emergency, such was the military situation of the country. In urging the House to his utmost to support his Bill, he quoted the words of Edmund Burke, ' Early and provident fear is the mother of safety ; for in that state of things the mind is firm and collected and the judgment unembarrassed ; but when fear and the thing feared come on together and press upon us at once, even deliberation, which at other times saves, becomes one's ruin, because it delays decision ; and when the peril is instant the decision should be instant too.'

The proposition of the Government was first to raise, if possible, without abandoning the ballot, a force of 80,000 men, to be drilled and trained under the regulations of the 43rd George III. ; 50,000 only to be raised the first year, and 30,000 the second year, the period of service being five years. Secondly, it was proposed to raise these men by bounties of 3*l*. or 4*l*., either to be paid down at the time or at the rate of 2*s*. or 2*s*. 6*d*. per month, the man being at liberty to take it in one way or the other. Thirdly, with respect to the officers, it was proposed to dispense with the qualifications required by the 43rd George III. in regard to all officers below the rank of Major, and generally to consider the having been in the Army equivalent to qualification. Fourthly, the Bill provided that the number of days' training required in the year should be twenty-one, the Crown having the power to extend the period to seven weeks, or to reduce it to three days. Lastly, with regard to the embodiment of the men, it was not proposed to make any alteration in the then existing law. The expense for bounty and equipment under the Bill was to be approximately 1,200,000*l*., but if spread over five years it was to be about 240,000*l*. a year, except in the first year, when the cost of the equipment, including clothing, would increase the expense to 400,000*l*.

The threat of invasion at the time of the introduction of the Bill was indeed acute ; yet, as at the present day, there were the numerous objectors to the scheme both on the ground of expense and of inconvenience to the nation. Mr. Hobhouse, in opposing the Bill, said he thought that the measure was ' disproportionately large, costly, and inconvenient to the people.' He thought the Navy was amply sufficient to repel any danger to the country.

The second reading of the Militia Bill was moved on April 23, when a debate of two nights took place, resulting in a Government majority of 190. Upon the Bill being committed several amendments were proposed, one being moved by Mr. Bright to the effect that ' notwithstanding the Militia Act, no Militiaman should be subject to flogging or other corporal punishment,' which was ultimately negatived by a majority of 105. The third reading was passed by a majority of 45, and the House of Lords having received it favourably, the Bill soon afterwards became law. An Order in Council, dated June 30, 1852, fixed the number of men to be raised in each county under the Act of Parliament. Monmouthshire was required to furnish 467 men in 1852, and 283 in 1853, making a total of 750.

OFFICER'S CROSS-BELT BADGE,
1852–1877

The county furnishing the largest number was Lancashire, where 9,046 men were raised, and the smallest number was in Rutlandshire, which county only contributed 109.

The Act gave power to the Secretary of State to make regulations from time to time limiting the ages at which gentlemen might be appointed officers of the several ranks, and to secure the appointment of persons as officers. It also rendered any officer who had served in the rank of Captain, or in a senior rank, in the Regular Army, eligible to be appointed a Captain or Major of Militia without any property qualification, and a retired Major of the Regular Army, or a regular officer of more senior rank, was eligible, without any property qualification, to be appointed a Lieutenant-Colonel or Colonel of Militia. The Act empowered the Sovereign in Council to apply the ballot in all districts where voluntary enlistment was not satisfactory; it also enabled the ballot to be resorted to in all districts in case of ' Actual invasion or imminent danger thereof.' Men over the age of thirty-five were not liable to be balloted for. The training amounted to twenty-one days per annum, and the Sovereign was empowered to call out any Regiments for training more than once in the year, provided the aggregate duration of the trainings of each Regiment did not exceed twenty-one days.

In 1852 the Royal Monmouth Militia trained in the autumn for twenty-

SKETCHES BY LIEUTENANT J. M. ZAMOISKI DURING THE CRIMEAN WAR EMBODIMENT.

THE CRIMEAN WAR EMBODIMENT

one days, the strength being 330 men, all recruits. The Battalion consisted of six companies. The Sergeant-Major did the duties of pay and quarter-master sergeants, and there were only three permanent staff sergeants, but some non-commissioned officers of the 48th Regiment were attached as instructors. In 1853 the training took place in the spring, 22 officers and 648 men being present; in the autumn of that year the full establishment of 750 privates was secured.

The question of the precedence of the numerous Militia Regiments was, after much deliberation, determined by a Board of Officers at Aldershot in 1855. The Artillery Regiments took their seniority alphabetically, the Infantry Battalions selected their precedence by lot. The Monmouth and Brecon Militia at the beginning of the century had the number thirty-one, and this same number was again drawn for the Royal Monmouth Militia, the Brecon Regiment securing the number 132.

LIGHT INFANTRY BUTTON, 1852-1877

It was notified in February 1854 that the Secretary at War had approved certain regulations for the Colours of the Regiments of Militia, and Officers Commanding regiments were requested, prior to having any Colours made, to apply to Albert W. Woods, Esq., the Inspector of Regimental Colours, for drawings, in order that all the Colours might conform to the regulations mentioned.

On May 25, 1854, the Commanding Officer of the Royal Monmouth Militia received His Majesty's Warrant for the embodiment of the Regiment consequent on the war in the Crimea, and four days afterwards it received orders to proceed to Newport on May 31. The Lieutenant of the County communicated the reception of the Warrant to the Commanding Officer in a letter dated 'Pontypool Park, May 24, 1854. Sir,—I have had the honour of receiving from Viscount Palmerston, Secretary of State, His Majesty's Warrant and Command immediately to draw out and embody the Royal Monmouth (Light Infantry)[1] Regiment of Militia, under your command, and to take such steps as may be necessary in order to be ready to march, as occasion may require, to such posts within the kingdom as may be judged proper,

---

[1] The Regiment had been created a Royal Regiment under the name of the Royal Monmouth and Brecon Militia in the year 1804, when most of the Welsh Regiments had the same honour conferred on them. It was constituted a Light Infantry Regiment with the reorganisation of 1852.

to assign them under the command of such General Officer or Officers as shall be appointed over them, and to obey such further orders as shall be judged necessary for the safety and defence of the kingdom.' The Royal Monmouth Light Infantry marched out of Monmouth for Newport, by way of Chepstow, early on May 31. From Chepstow the journey was completed by train, Newport being reached at about half-past one. The Regiment consisted of 26 officers and 679 non-commissioned officers and men. It was the first Militia Regiment to volunteer for active service, the officers offering five thousand pounds to equip it for the purpose. This offer was made on January 28, 1854, and repeated in 1857, but on each occasion was declined by the Government.

On December 12, 1854, Officers Commanding Companies were ordered to requisition for twenty rounds of service ammunition per man, to be kept constantly in the men's pouches and to be inspected daily. Each packet had to be marked thus:

R.M.M.
1 Co.
160. Robt. Price.

The Scale of Parades and Drills at Newport was:—

Day	Forenoon	Afternoon
Sunday	Divine Service at 10 A.M.	—
Monday	Adjutant's drill with arms and accoutrements; dress, drill order.	Firelock drill under the Sergt.-Major, all persons to attend except Servants.
Tuesday	Marching out in H.M.O., at 10 o'clock, Arms.	Roll call at 3.
Wednesday	Commanding Officer's Parade.	Battalion drill under the Sergt.-Major, commanded by Junior Sergeants.
Thursday	Setting-up drill without arms under the Adjutant.	Setting-up drill under the Sergt.-Major. Servants to attend this parade.
Friday	Companies drill under the Commanding Officer.	Coal Fatigue.
Saturday	Parade in H.M.O. and Inspection of Necessities in Barrack Rooms.	Medical Inspection.

School for Recruits from 1.45 to 2.45 o'clock P.M. School for Recruits and Voluntary, 5.45 to 8 o'clock P.M.

N.B.—If Tuesday was wet the marching out was on Wednesday. If Wednesday was wet, it did not take place in that week.

On December 18, 1854, thirteen men of the Regiment, under the command of a sergeant, proceeded to Winchester, having volunteered into the 23rd Royal Welsh Fusiliers. The same sergeant on December 28 proceeded to Usk Prison to receive over from the civil authority a deserter from the Regiment. By the end of the Crimean Embodiment 1603 men had passed through the ranks of the Regiment, of whom nearly 300 had gone to the Regular Army, chiefly to the Royal Welsh Fusiliers and the Guards.

The Orders for January 14, 1855, state: ' The Reverend G. R. Gleig, Chaplain-General to the Forces, being expected in the course of to-morrow to inspect the school, the volunteers, recruits and children attending will not leave the barracks to-morrow in order to their meeting him on the shortest notice,' and after the inspection of the school by the Chaplain-General the Commanding Officer circulated:

' The Lieutenant-Colonel takes this opportunity of informing all the men, the non-commissioned officers more especially, that their promotions will depend very much upon their attainments in writing, reading, and arithmetic, and he hopes to find in future the school well attended. Such non-commissioned officers who are not sufficiently advanced will be required to attend until dismissed.

' The Lieutenant-Colonel is much gratified to notify that the Chaplain-General to the Forces, who inspected the School this day, has expressed himself *very much* pleased with the progress hitherto made, and he has promised to make a most favourable Report to the Right Honourable The Secretary of War.'

On January 16 there appeared in Orders, ' New forage caps of the Light Infantry pattern having been received, Officers Commanding Companies will send in requisitions for the full number of their Companies to-morrow.'

On January 22, Lieutenant Thomas Freke Lewis[1] joined the 23rd Royal Welsh Fusiliers, and the same day appeared an order that the men were to wear their coatees on all parades. Towards the end of January Lieut.-Colonel Henry Morgan Clifford[2] left the Regiment for a time to attend to his Parliamentary duties, and the command devolved upon Major Edmund P. Herbert,[3] who on the 31st of the month was cautioned to be in readiness to move at the shortest notice to Pembroke Dock; consequently on February 3, 200 men, besides officers and non-commissioned officers, proceeded thither and the headquarters of the Regiment were transferred to that place. Colonel Clifford having returned to the

[1] Son of the Reverend Francis Lewis of St. Pierre. Died 1908.
[2] Son of Morgan Morgan-Clifford of Perrystone in Herefordshire.
[3] Son of John Jones of Llanarth; assumed the name of Herbert by Royal Licence; was Chief Constable of the county of Monmouth.

command, the men for Pembroke Dock paraded at 2.30 A.M. in heavy marching order, with colours and band. They proceeded to Haverfordwest by rail, where the officers were entertained at breakfast by the Royal Pembroke Artillery, and marched thence to Pembroke Dock. The snow was so deep that the mounted officers had to walk. Arriving at their destination that evening (Saturday) the men went into billets till Monday, when they went into barracks, relieving the 31st Regiment, which had been ordered to the Crimea.

The 31st Regiment vacated the fort at 11 A.M. and the Royal Monmouth Militia took up the same quarters at 11.30 A.M., parading near the Victoria Hotel with loose coats at 11.15 A.M. The surplus men who could not be quartered in the fort were billeted. On the Sunday following, the Regiment paraded for Divine Service, with loose coats over coatees, and shakos which possessed a worsted tuft. When loose coats were to be worn, four G's were sounded after the Dressing Bugle.

SOCKET BAYONET, 1853

On February 14, the orders ran, ' In consequence of the Royal Artillery being unable to furnish more than twelve men to-morrow for Guard, the Main Dock will be reinforced six men by the Royal Monmouth Militia.' The middle of February saw the introduction into the Regiment of tailors' and shoemakers' shops, and from that time private tradesmen in these trades were excluded from the barracks. On February 23, the orders stated, ' The forenoon parade to-morrow will be in Barracks, and each man will parade with pouch and belt and sling-belt in hand, the pouch to be clean inside and out, the ammunition in the centre compartment, and each packet marked with the number and name of the man entrusted with it.'

Colonel John Francis Vaughan[1] and Captain George Griffin Tyler[2] during this time were serving in the Crimea,[3] attached to the 23rd Royal Welsh Fusiliers, then forming part of the Light Division, and the former officer wrote :

---

[1] Son of William Vaughan of Courtfield, Monmouthshire.

[2] Son of the Reverend James Endell Tyler, rector of St. Giles'-in-the-Fields ; assumed by Royal Licence in 1877 the name of Griffin in lieu of Tyler.

[3] Colonel Wood, of the Grenadier Guards, wrote regarding the draft in the Crimea to Colonel Clifford on November 9, 1854, from the Horse Guards : ' I wish that all the Militia colonels would act in the same spirit that you do ; and I shall send your letter on to Windsor, in order that your spirit may be held up as an example to others.'

'Light Division Camp, before Sebastopol : February 25, 1855.

'SIR,—I have the honour to report that Lieut.-Colonel Lysons, commanding the 23rd Royal Welsh Fusiliers, directed me, as supernumerary Lieut.-Colonel, temporarily attached to his Regiment, to proceed on the 24th instant to Balaclava to take command of a draft recently arrived from England, and to march them to the headquarters of the Regiment in front of Sebastopol. This draft consisted of two officers, two non-commissioned officers and 102 rank and file. To the latter, nearly all volunteers from the Royal Monmouth Militia, this report has reference. The march from Balaclava to the camp of the Light Division, especially to young soldiers in order and heavily accoutred, is an arduous one, and drafts have often, especially in unfavourable weather, reached their quarters but late at night, or straggled in exhausted the following morning. I have pleasure in stating that the volunteers of the Royal Monmouth Militia performed this march to my entire satisfaction. They evinced the same buoyant cheerfulness and the same excellent spirit within sound of the enemy's cannon as they showed when they marched from Newport. They arrived at the hour appointed and without having a straggler. The band of the 23rd met us at the limits of the Light Division camp. We fixed bayonets, and amidst encomiums for their steadiness and soldier-like bearing, your volunteers marched by the numerous officers and men who had turned out to see them. On their regimental parade they were inspected by Major-General William John Codrington and their commanding officer, Colonel Lysons, and the manner in which they expressed themselves was such as to be highly flattering and gratifying. General Sir G. Brown has also signified his entire approbation. I am directed by Colonel Lysons to convey to you, Sir, his high approval of the volunteers which the Royal Monmouth have given to the Royal Welsh Fusiliers, and from among the first trophies which this gallant Regiment may win he has been good enough to promise me that he will send some Russian arms to deck the mess-room of the Royal Monmouth. I beg to state that any men who may be permitted to volunteer from the Royal Monmouth Militia for active service will be 'welcomed in the ranks of the Royal Welsh and received with open arms by their old comrades.

'I have the honour to be, Sir, your obedient servant,
'J. F. VAUGHAN, Lieut.-Colonel R.M.M.
'Attached to the 23rd R.W.F.

'Lieut.-Colonel Clifford, M.P.,
'Commanding R.M.M., Pater Barracks, Pembroke.'

ROYAL MONMOUTHSHIRE MILITIA

The draft alluded to was taken out by Lieutenant Freke Lewis, who afterwards obtained his company in the Royal Welsh Fusiliers,[1] and served with distinction throughout the campaign.

On March 6, 1855, at a meeting of the Town Council of Newport, it was resolved unanimously ' That the Council desire to record their sense of the exemplary conduct of the Royal Monmouthshire Militia during its sojourn at the Newport Barracks, and to express their gratification that the county possesses a Regiment of Militia which is universally admitted to be one of the best disciplined in the Kingdom.'

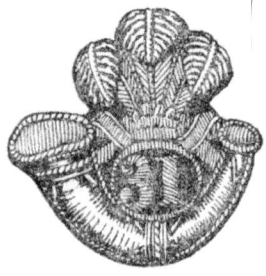

OFFICER'S CAP BADGE,
1852-1877

Lieutenant-Colonel J. F. Vaughan's leave of absence from the Regiment for service in the Crimea was in March extended by the General Officer Commanding from March 10 to May 1.

A letter was circulated to the various Militia Regiments by Lord Panmure, Secretary of State for War, on March 23, in these words :

' SIR,—A case having been submitted to the law officers of the Crown to ascertain whether Militia men enrolled under the 15th and 16th Victoria, Cap. 50, can be required to serve beyond fifty-six days with a Regiment embodied under the 17th Victoria, Cap. 13, I have the honour to acquaint you that the result of the submission is to confirm me in my opinion that Militia men enrolled under 15th and 16th Victoria, Cap. 50, can be required to serve beyond fifty-six days with a Regiment embodied under the 17th Victoria, Cap. 13, and that the late Statute applies as well to Militia men enrolled before as to those enrolled after the passing of the same.

' I have the, &c.,

' (Signed) PANMURE.

' The Officer Commanding, Monmouthshire Militia.'

The Regiment paraded on April 18, 1855, and again on June 5, for inspection by Colonel Sir A. Cloete, C.B., K.H., Commanding the Monmouth and South Wales District, and on May 19 to each man was issued three rounds of blank ammunition and the Regiment was paraded at 10.30 A.M., to celebrate Her Majesty's birthday. Sir A. Cloete after the

---

[1] Many of the men were intended for the Grenadier Guards, but were rejected on account of not coming up to the standard of height. The Royal Monmouth Militia sent large numbers of men to the Grenadier Guards.

inspection of June 5 highly complimented the Regiment both for drill and discipline; he said the battalion movements were 'very good,' the manual and platoon 'excellent,' and the Light Infantry evolutions 'really admirable'; as a result of this very satisfactory report, the Commanding Officer dispensed with the evening parade on the following day and released the defaulters.

From June 24, one company was kept off duty each day for the purpose of firing ten rounds of ball per man, and each shot was registered. Firing commenced at 2 P.M.; the first two shots were fired at 50 yards, the next four at a hundred yards, and the last four at 150 yards.

In July a reading and news room was instituted for the garrison in the town in Pembroke Street. No payment was required of the men to make use of it. A lance-corporal was appointed Reading Room Clerk, and the room was open to the men from 11.30 A.M. The journals and periodicals supplied were: *The Times, The Globe, The News of the World, The Star of Gwent, The Monmouth Beacon, The Hereford Times, The Illustrated London News, Cassell's Illustrated Family Paper, The United Service Gazette, Potter's Electric News, Punch, The London Journal* and *The Family Herald*.

Summer trousers were issued to the men this month, for which they were required to pay 7s. 6d. per pair. They were worn for all parades and duties.

The Garrison Orders for August 16, 1855, contain:

'The Lieutenant-Colonel Commanding regrets being again under the necessity of directing a private of the Royal Monmouth Militia to be tried by a Court Martial for disobedience of the Garrison Order prohibiting soldiers proceeding to the town of Pembroke without a pass. He cautions the troops in Garrison against a repetition of a breach of that order, which will on detection be followed by a Court Martial.'

By order of the Officer Commanding the Regiment, the above was read to the men at every parade for a week.

On October 4 there appeared in Orders:

'Lieut.-Colonel Clifford very much regrets to inform the men, that he has received this day reports from several respectable persons residing in the town, that a gang of men who had been in the "Duke of Wellington" public-house last night behaved themselves most recklessly in the streets, by throwing large stones into the windows. Lieut.-Colonel Clifford therefore directs that no man shall henceforth enter the "Duke of Wellington" public-house; the picquet will parade the town from 7.30 to 9.30 o'clock to preserve order. From this evening and until further orders the picquet will be increased to four non-commissioned officers, and twelve rank and file, it will be divided in two divisions and patrol the town at uncertain hours between 7 and 10 o'clock as may be ordered.'

In the winter of the year 1855 a severe storm arose, preventing all communication between Thorn Island, where was quartered a detachment of seventy-five men of the Pembroke Artillery Militia,[1] and the mainland.

On Christmas Eve the men on Thorn Island signalled that their resources were at an end, whereupon Colonel Vaughan, commanding the Royal Monmouth at the time, chartered a steamer in the Dockyard and proceeded as near to the island as was practicable. He then, in company with Surgeon George Wilson, attempted to land in a boat, taking with him provisions. This, however, was found to be impossible, but he succeeded in throwing beef, biscuits and materials for plum puddings ashore, and it is recorded that the officer in command of the detachment caught, with much dexterity, a pair of fowls thrown by Surgeon Wilson, and also a leg of mutton thrown by Colonel Vaughan.

The Royal Monmouth Militia left Pembroke Dock on July 22, 1856, and entrained for Chepstow, where the Regiment was entertained and billeted for the night, proceeding on the following day to Monmouth, where, after being quartered for eight days, it was disembodied on July 31, 1856, after having been on permanent duty for over two years.

[1] The Pembrokeshire Militia can be traced to the year 1588, when the county contributed '800 Trayned and Armed Ablemen, 396 Pyoners and 30 Patronelles' to the national force. In 1684 it comprised a troop of horse and eight companies of Infantry armed with muskets, and their motto was 'For God and for King.' The Regiment has been embodied on six occasions. During the embodiment at the time of the Seven Years' War it was for a time quartered at Monmouth and Chepstow, and in the American War embodiment it was again at Chepstow, subsequently doing duty in London during the Gordon riots. It was created a Royal Regiment in 1804 and in 1807 was named 'The Royal Pembroke Fuzileers,' becoming subsequently in turn 'The Royal Pembroke Light Infantry,' 'The Royal Pembroke Militia (Rifle Corps),' and 'The Pembroke Artillery.' The Colours of the Regiment, which were received from King George III. in 1808, were laid up in the Parish Church of St. Mary's, Haverfordwest, in June 1909. The party handing them over included Earl Cawdor, Lord Lieutenant of Pembrokeshire, Colonel F. P. Edwardes (Hon. Colonel), and Lieutenant Colonel Willis (the Commanding Officer). The Archdeacon of St. Davids received the Colours, and at the conclusion of the ceremony the trumpeters sounded the 'Last Post.'

THE ROYAL MONMOUTHSHIRE LIGHT INFANTRY AT PEMBROKE DOCK.
1855.
(From a Painting by Lieutenant Houghton Forrest)

CHAPTER VIII

THE REGIMENT BETWEEN 1857 AND 1876

THE services rendered to the nation by the Militia during the campaign in the Crimea were indeed great. In addition to furnishing many thousands of volunteers for the Regular Service it had taken up garrison duties both in the Mediterranean and at home, and had thus enabled the Regular Army to proceed *en masse* to the war. On the conclusion of the campaign and the disembodiment of the Militia much the same state of things prevailed in the country as had been the case in 1816; only this time the neglect of the military forces of the Crown was checked by an incident of extreme gravity. Though symptoms of a discontented and rebellious spirit had been observed in India as early as 1844 it was not until the invention of the Enfield rifle and its issue to the troops in 1857 that a climax was reached. The cartridges issued for the new rifle were greased, and the discontented natives maintained that the fat used was that of swine and cows, whereas in reality it was mutton fat, and they asserted that the intention was to deprive the Brahmin Sepoys of their caste, for the fat of pigs and cows would be an abomination both to the Hindoo and to the Mahomedan. The seizure of Delhi in May 1857 by the insurgents commenced the long list of struggles which obtained throughout the Mutiny. British troops were hurried to India, and in December 1857 special volunteering from the Militia to the Regular Army took place. Indeed, the weakness of our land forces at the time may be appreciated after reading a Royal Warrant dated September 1857, which states : ' We, considering that the military operations in which we are engaged in India render it necessary to send a large part of our regular forces abroad, deem it proper to provide without delay additional means for the military service at home.'

In 1858 a Royal Commission was appointed for the purpose of inquiring into ' The establishment and organisation of the Militia, with a view of rendering it more efficient for military purposes.' The members of the Commission comprised six peers and ten Militia officers.

They drew attention to the undesirability of the continuance of the system of the Militia volunteering to the Line, since, in their opinion, it was calculated to militate against discipline and was a perpetual source of inconvenience. The Commission also recommended that the training should be extended to twenty-eight days, that the permanent staff should be increased, that promotion should be by seniority, and that preliminary drill and a recognised musketry course should be established.

In 1858 the Royal Monmouth Militia under Colonel J. F. Vaughan trained for twenty-one days from September 9. Colonel Clifford, the former Commanding Officer, in that year became Honorary Colonel, and Major E. O. Herbert, the next senior officer, resigned on his appointment as Chief Constable of Monmouthshire. In 1859 one of the recommendations of the Royal Commission was attempted, for in that year the Royal Monmouth Militia trained for twenty-eight days, from June 22. Not long after the training a quartermaster was sanctioned for the Regiment, and the first to be given the appointment was Sergeant-Major John Finnerty. Other additions to the staff at the same time included an instructor of musketry, a drum-major, an orderly-room clerk, and an acting hospital-sergeant.

OFFICER'S BELT BUCKLE, 1852-1877

The next year saw the fulfilment of a further recommendation of the Royal Commission—the establishment of a preliminary drill. The Regiment's training of twenty-seven days in May was preceded by a preliminary drill of seven days. During this year's training an inspection of the Regiment was made by Colonel Henry Phipps Raymond, of the 85th Regiment, commanding the troops at Pembroke Dock. The training of 1861 was held from April 22 until May 18. In 1862 the preliminary drill was extended to fourteen days, and it was maintained in like duration until 1865, when the Regiment assembled about 600 strong at Monmouth on May 4 for twenty-seven days' training. The conduct of the men in this year was exceedingly good, and it was remarked that 'they wheeled and marched like a wall.' The officers' mess was at the Beaufort Arms Hotel, and those present at the training were Colonel Vaughan, Majors John Selwyn Payne and Francis

THE REGIMENT BETWEEN 1857 AND 1876

McDonnell; Captains Wheeley, Tyler, Brook, Russell, Davies, and Sheehy; Lieutenants Allaway, Wheeley, Williamson, Zamoiski, Metcalfe, Segrave, Steward, and Capper; with the Adjutant Lieut.-Colonel J. M. Carter, Quartermaster J. Finnerty, Surgeon G. Wilson, and Assistant-Surgeon G. Willis. On the 29th of the month the Regiment was reviewed by Colonel Roberts, commanding the 28th Regiment, who in conclusion addressed the men thus:

'After the close inspection I have made I am happy to say that I am much pleased with what I have seen. Several of the movements you have gone through with great precision. Your advance in line was as good as I ever saw in my life. There were several things you were not perfect in—in fact, I could not expect you to be. On the whole, however, I am very pleased with your movements. Your marching past at quarter distance was very good in quick time, but not so good in slow time; still, it was good when I take into consideration that you are only out twenty-seven days in the year, and when I say that I have seen a Regiment of the Line not do it so well, I certainly could not expect better from you, especially on ground like this. But I am not surprised at your efficiency when I see you commanded by such a gallant officer as Colonel Vaughan, of whose gallant exploits in the Crimea I had heard before I was aware I was appointed to inspect you, and I should be surprised to find any regiment commanded by him not in a state of efficiency.'

OFFICER'S SHAKO PLATE, 1852-1877.

In 1866 the preliminary drill lasted for seven days only, the Regiment assembling for training on May 10. The inspection took place on June 4, when Colonel James Kennard Pipon, the Inspector-General of Militia, was the inspecting officer, and in 1867 the preliminary drill was again for seven days only. Captain Robert John Hickman, the newly appointed adjutant, was with the Regiment on this occasion.

In this year, too, there was held at Montagu House, Whitehall, under the presidency of the Duke of Buccleuch, a meeting of the commanding officers of Militia, to consider suggestions to be made to the Secretary of State for War with regard to proposed alterations in the organisation of the Militia force. Colonel Vaughan did not attend the meeting, the Regiment being out for training at the time, but he submitted to His Grace the President a letter containing expressions which he requested to be brought to the notice of the meeting.

'Lieutenant-Colonel Vaughan assumes that an army of reserve is desirable, and that any fact which throws light on the question of the fitness of Militia for that purpose is, at the present moment, very valuable. It has been suggested that Militia Regiments should be attached to given Line Regiments, whose county name they bear, as reserve Battalions; that men from the reserve (Militia) Battalions should be free to join the Service (Line) Battalions when wanted; that men, after a given number of years in the Line Battalions, should complete their service in the Reserve, and that a certain number of officers and men should enter as volunteers for active service in time of war.'

Colonel Vaughan corroborated the above proposals by means of his personal experience during the Crimean Campaign. He pointed out that in 1854 the Royal Monmouth Militia sent two officers (Lieutenant Freke Lewis and Ensign John Lawrence) and a very considerable number of men to the 23rd Royal Welsh Fusiliers in the Crimea, and that he himself, in 1855, when attached to the same Regiment, marched a draft of one hundred men, who had joined from the Royal Monmouth Militia, from Balaclava to the front. Colonel Vaughan stated that in March 1855 half the duty men in the 23rd were from the Royal Monmouth Militia, a state of things which created a very great sympathy between the two Regiments, so much so that on June 11 of that year the Royal Monmouth Light Infantry contributed a day's pay of the entire Regiment to their old comrades serving with the 23rd at the war. The subscription was forwarded by Colonel Vaughan (then back with the Royal Monmouth Militia at home) to Colonel D. Lysons, C.B., commanding the 23rd, who, in reply to this generous act, wrote from Sebastopol on July 8, 1855:

'With the most heartfelt pleasure I received your welcome letter of the 11th ultimo. I hastened to call around me the sturdy little mountaineers who a few months ago left their native hills to fight the battles of their country, and as I read to them paragraph after paragraph, replete

THE REGIMENT BETWEEN 1857 AND 1876

with warm feeling and kind sympathy, their brightened countenances exhibited more strongly than their lips could express or my feeble pen can describe how truly they appreciated the generous manner in which their old comrades of the Royal Monmouth Light Infantry have subscribed to their comfort. Your old followers are still preserving their high character in our ranks. You have good reason to be proud of having commanded such a gallant set of fellows. I feel confident that the name of the Royal Welsh Fusiliers will never suffer while supported by such stout hearts, and if our old corps should have the fortune to gain fresh laurels many a leaf in the garland will be due to the Royal Monmouth Light Infantry. I assure you many a word of regret has been spoken since you left our camp; the interest you took in everything connected with the Regiment I have the honour to command, and the kind feeling you have shown towards myself and my companions, will ever be held in warmest remembrance by us. We all most heartily re-echo the sentiment expressed by your brave soldiers, who proposed " to join us as a body," and why not ? Come, bring your gallant fellows with you, and a hearty soldier's welcome will await your arrival.'

In October 1867 the permanent staff of the Royal Monmouth Militia was ordered to be placed on active duty as a precaution against any surprise at the stores from Fenians or Fenian fire.

The Regiment assembled for training in 1868 on April 27. Parades were held daily at 6.30 A.M., 10.20 A.M., and 3 P.M., and the 'Last Post' was sounded at 10 P.M. With regard to clothing, dress clothing at this time was required to last for five trainings, and fatigue clothing three years and two years. When the clothing of the enrolled men had been worn the prescribed period it could be taken away at the end of the training by the non-commissioned officer or man wearing it. Part-worn articles of men who had become non-effective were required to be reissued so as to last the prescribed period.

MINIE RIFLE, 1856

On May 17 there appeared in orders, ' a number of men, not exceeding one-fourth of the effectives, may, with the permission of their commanding officers, enlist in the Militia Reserve.' There were privileges offered to, and duties required of, men so enlisting. The enlistment was for five years, and men received, in addition to the ordinary Militia bounty and gratuity, 1*l*. for every yearly training. The training could be performed with a Line Regiment; and, with the approval of the Secretary of State and the concurrence of their Commanding Officers, men electing to be so trained were conveyed at the public cost to the station where the Line Regiment was quartered. The men were required to serve five years in the Militia from the time of their enrolment into the Militia Reserve, and should Her Majesty be at war with a foreign Power, or should the kingdom be in danger of invasion, they could be required to serve in the Regular Army, though in no case for a longer period than six months after peace had been proclaimed.

On May 21 the Regiment paraded in heavy marching order for inspection by Lieut.-Colonel Sir Edward Campbell. Six rounds of blank ammunition were issued to each man. Major J. S. Payne commanded the Regiment in the absence of Colonel Vaughan, sick. The inspecting officer again spoke highly of the Regiment.

During the training of 1868 was celebrated the coming of age of the Marquis of Worcester, which occurred on May 19. In addition to a very large ball, at which most of the officers of the Regiment acted as stewards or took a prominent part, an ox with gilded horns was roasted whole in St. James's Square, and was then paraded through the town (the regimental band playing 'The Roast Beef of Old England'), and eventually cut up in Agincourt Square. Other events were the distribution of a ton and a half of beef and 2,500 loaves amongst the poor of the town, athletic sports, boat races, a public dinner, and a display of fireworks which concluded the festivities.

In 1869 the annual training, which was preceded by a preliminary drill of fourteen days, commenced on May 24. The eight companies were commanded by Captains G. G. Tyler, J. Davies, B. Sheehy, and R. R. Williamson, and Lieutenants W. H. Wheeley, F. B. Vaughan, J. A. Metcalfe, and W. A. H. K. Allaway, the last of whom was promoted Captain on May 28, Captain T. Brook having resigned. On June 15 a board of officers consisting of Major J. S. Payne, president, and the officers commanding companies as members, assembled to carry out the 105th Article of the Militia Regulations, respecting the forfeiture of bounty owing to misconduct. The shooting results during this training were good, 479 men being classified in the first period, while over 51 per cent. became second-class shots, and nine obtained the good shooting prize of 25*s*. The physical requirements of the

THE REGIMENT BETWEEN 1857 AND 1876

men who joined the Militia Reserve were this year fixed at: chest, 33 inches; age, under 30; height, 5 feet 4 inches. The inspection took place on June 16, Lieut.-Colonel Sir Edward Campbell again being the inspecting officer. Ten rounds of blank ammunition were issued to each man for the occasion; and the Duke of Beaufort witnessed the ceremony and addressed the men. On the conclusion of the training the usual charges were made against the men in respect of dirty clothing, or wilful damage to it. The charges inflicted for the various articles were: dress tunic, 6d.; trousers, 6d.; shell jacket, 3d.; summer trousers, 6d. ; towel, 1d. ; holdall, 1d.

The preliminary drill in the year 1870 was extended to twenty-one days, but was reduced again to fourteen in the following year. The Regiment came out for training on May 16. On the 18th two new officers were posted to the Battalion, Lieutenants J. M. Bannerman[1] and T. J. Buchanan, the latter of whom on May 25 was appointed acting-adjutant. On the second day of the training, while Bugler Helps (the big drummer), two other men of the Regiment, and A. H. Goss, son of the quartermaster-sergeant, were on the river in a boat, an accident occurred, resulting in the capsizing of the boat at Boys Rocks, and Williams and Goss were drowned. The funeral of Williams took place with military honours on May 20. A kit inspection was held on May 28, at which each man was required to produce the following items: one forage cap, one shell jacket, one shirt, one pair socks, one holdall, one blacking, four brushes, one sponge, and one towel, and punishment was meted out to those who failed to bring them. On May 28 two privates of the Regiment, for breaking out of their billets and for theft, were sentenced in the civil court to three months' imprisonment with hard labour. The nine best shots of the Regiment were this year again awarded prizes of 25s. each, and the nine men shot amongst themselves for the honour of being ' best shot of the Regiment,' in respect of which honour an additional sovereign was granted. Private John Jenkins was the successful competitor, making the remarkably high score of eighty points, as compared with fifty-seven, the score of the best shot of the previous year. The inspection this year was made by the Honble. J. J. Bourke, commanding the 88th Regiment, who, though finding a few faults, expressed himself as generally satisfied. The Duke of Beaufort was present, and in orders on June 11 there appeared:

'His Grace the Lord-Lieutenant has communicated to Lieut.-Colonel

---

[1] Son of John Bannerman, of Byaston Leys; subsequently joined the 4th Regiment.

Vaughan the gratification which he experienced at seeing how smartly and well the Regiment worked, and how thoroughly soldierlike and steady it was under arms on the day of inspection. His Grace has been pleased to express his approbation of all ranks, and Lieut.-Colonel Vaughan has much satisfaction in making this known by Regimental Order.'

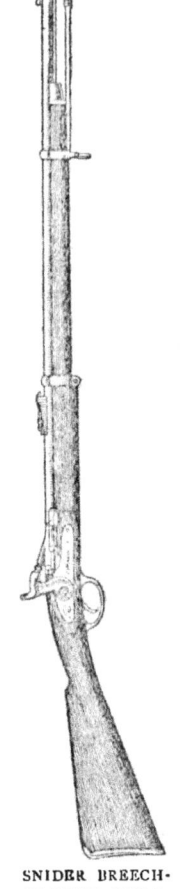

SNIDER BREECH-LOADING RIFLE, 1870

In 1871 the preliminary drill consisted of twenty-seven days and commenced on April 10, there being 136 recruits. The Regiment assembled at Monmouth on May 8, and was 719 of all ranks. Six new officers were appointed on March 30, T. M. Reid (late Lancashire Militia), B. J. Salvin, Lord H. E. B. Somerset,[1] J. Thirkill, J. A. Nunn, and J. C. Partridge, the last of whom was placed supernumerary. Lieutenant Dashwood resigned this year, he having joined the Regiment in 1867. The parades during this training were at 6.30 A.M., 9.30 A.M., 11.30 A.M., and 3 P.M. From May 13 the first parade was daily on the racecourse, the next two on Castle Hill, while that at 3 P.M. was on the racecourse. The subaltern officers who had not passed for their companies for a few days attended drill under the adjutant at 6.15 A.M. Subalterns were examined for promotion by a Regimental Board, consisting usually of two field-officers and a senior captain.

The band played at mess on Tuesdays and Thursdays, and from 2 P.M. to 3 P.M. on Mondays, Wednesdays, and Fridays it played in Agincourt Square.

All officers were required to have in their possession at the annual inspection copies of the Queen's Regulations, Field Exercise, and Rifle Exercise. On May 26 fourteen non-commissioned officers and men shot amongst themselves for the honour of being best shot of the Battalion. The laurels went to Private Charles Thomas, of D Company, who obtained eighty-seven points: the money prizes were allotted as usual. There being so much irregularity at this time in the direction of the men absenting themselves from parade, the Commanding Officer warned the Regiment that all future offences would be dealt with by a Regimental Board. On June 2 the Battalion paraded on Castle Square at 10.15 A.M. in heavy

[1] Lord Henry Edward Brudenall Somerset, fourth son of the eighth Duke of Beaufort.

marching order for inspection again by Colonel Bourke. He complimented the Regiment after the parade on its drill, but was not altogether satisfied with the appearance of the men, no allowance apparently being made by him for the fact that they were mostly pitmen, and therefore different in appearance to men with other pursuits. In spite of the inspecting officer's remarks, on June 12 there appeared in orders, ' His Grace the Lord Lieutenant has been pleased to notify to the Commanding Officer his entire satisfaction with the report of the very high state of efficiency of the Regiment as made to him by Colonel Honble. J. J. Bourke, Assistant Adjutant-General of the Western District.' As a matter of fact the inspecting officer had reported the Regiment to be ' second to no regiment of Militia in the kingdom.'

In 1872 fear was entertained by the Town Council that the Regiment would be moved away to Brecon for training, and consequently the Mayor (Major A. Rolls [1]) proceeded to the War Office and held an interview with Mr. Cardwell and Sir John Ramsden, the result of which was favourable to the Town Council. Since the last inspection a new supernumerary subaltern had been appointed—V. F. J. Somerset [2]—in March. The training commenced at Monmouth on April 21, and the credit of the Regiment was forthwith cried down through the town as usual. The inspection took place on the Castle Square on May 17, at 9.45 A.M., the men parading in heavy marching order.

The books required to be in the possession of officers this year were the Queen's Regulations, Field Exercise, Manual and Rifle Exercise, and Regulations and Instructions for Encampment. The inspecting officer was again Colonel Bourke, who appeared to be well satisfied with the Regiment, though under a new regulation he was not permitted to address the men. The regimental dinner was held at Willis's Rooms, King Street, St. James's, on May 30, Colonel Vaughan presiding. On December 19 there was buried at Monmouth with military honours Quartermaster John Finnerty, who had joined in 1852, having been previously twenty-three years in the 47th Regiment. His appointment as Quartermaster dated from October 10, 1859.

In 1873 the recruits were given eighty-three days' preliminary drill, and the Regiment assembled on May 19 for training in the Forest of

---

[1] Son of John Rolls, of The Hendre, Monmouth, and resided at Croft-y-bwla. He was appointed Major in the Royal Monmouth Light Infantry, April 26, 1853.

[2] Vere Francis John Somerset, son of Poulett George Henry Somerset, M.P., and great-grandson of Henry, fifth Duke of Beaufort.

Dean. Since the previous training, Captain W. A. Allaway, Lieutenant J. Thirkill, and Assistant-Surgeon Willis had retired, and Lieutenant T. R. Oakley and Assistant-Surgeon Norman had joined. The Regiment marched out of the Castle for its camp, with the band playing ' The Girl I left behind me ' and ' Auld Lang Syne.' It had been anticipated that a welcome reception would not be awaiting it in its new quarters, but this was soon found to be erroneous, for the men were received with every kindness, the villages through which the Regiment passed were decorated in its honour, and Colonel Vaughan stated in his official report, ' The Regiment received a perfect ovation all along the line of march.' The inspection was held by Colonel E. Wodehouse at Coleford Meend, where the Regiment was encamped, on June 11, and he appeared to be well satisfied, judging from the words he addressed to the Commanding Officer. As the men marched back to Monmouth on the conclusion of the training they again met with much cordiality, and at Coleford the following address, bearing 200 signatures of the principal residents in the place, was presented to Colonel Vaughan :

' We, the undersigned, inhabitants of Coleford and its immediate neighbourhood, have great pleasure in testifying to the general good conduct of the Royal Monmouthshire Light Infantry during its term of encampment in Dean Forest, under command of Colonel Vaughan. The harmony and good feeling existing from the first between the soldiers and the civilians has been maintained without any interruption ; and to Colonel Vaughan, as the officer in command, we think great praise is due for the admirable and impartial manner in which he has ordered the habits of the camp and its relations to the town and district. We hope the residence in camp has answered the expectations of those who promoted its appointment, and that the general efficiency of the Regiment under camp training has been secured. June 11, 1873.'

Colonel Vaughan replied to the address in these words : ' Gentlemen, on behalf of the officers, non-commissioned officers, and men of the Royal Monmouthshire Light Infantry, whom I have the honour to command, I beg to return you my warmest thanks and acknowledgment for the cordial reception you gave us in marching through Coleford on our way to camp, and I now thank you for this handsome compliment, so numerously and so influentially signed. It is a practical and conclusive refutation of the character imputed to the Royal Foresters and to the Regiment under my command. I acknowledge that I felt indignant that such timid and unfounded apprehensions and sinister auguries should have existed amongst a very small number of people—indignant, because it not only reflected upon the Regiment I command, but upon the Foresters, with whom I have always lived, and respecting whom I have never had any reproach to make. Gentlemen, it is not usual for the Service to make long speeches, but we will express our thanks, as soldiers are wont to do, with three hearty cheers.' The Regiment then proceeded on its route to Monmouth, the day being very wet. On arrival, the townsfolk turned out in large numbers to greet it, the band playing ' When Johnny comes marching home ' and ' Home, Sweet Home.' On the following day the men left for their homes.

The year 1874 saw several changes in the officers' ranks when the Regiment came out for training at Monmouth on June 8. Captain W. A. Allaway, Captain J. A. Metcalfe (who had joined the Durham Militia), Lieutenants B. Salvin, Lord H. E. B. Somerset, and T. R. Oakley [1] had all resigned. The two vacancies in the Captains' list were filled by the promotion of Lieutenants W. J. Steward and F. B. Vaughan, while the officers joining the Regiment were W. C. St. I. Partridge,[2] R. L. Payne,[3] G. F. Walker, W. E. C. Curre,[4] and W. F. H. Beevor.[5] During this year no less than sixty-seven men deserted between April 13 and June 8, and there are frequently recorded such orders as ' Sergeant Gregory will proceed to Cork, Ireland, for the purpose of identifying a deserter from the Royal Monmouth Militia.' The permanent staff was kept busy throughout the year recruiting in the various towns of the county, Pontypool in particular sending several recruits to the Regiment.

The preliminary drill in 1874 commenced on April 13, the parades being at 9.15 A.M., 11.30 A.M., 2.30 P.M. and 4 P.M. A board of officers, with Major F. C. D. Barclay, 24th Regiment, as president, assembled at Monmouth on June 4, to examine such officers of the Royal Monmouth Militia as were brought before it in accordance with clause 23, Auxiliary and Reserve Forces Circular, 1874.

The inspection this year was made on July 3 by Colonel E. Wodehouse, who commanded the 25th Brigade Depot, as a result of

[1] Thomas Robert Oakley, son of Thomas William Oakley, of Lydart, in Monmouthshire.
[2] Son of Joseph Partridge, of Llanddeir Scyrrid.
[3] Son of Colonel John Selwyn Payne. Subsequently joined the Tower Hamlets Militia, and then entered the Army.
[4] William Edward Carne Curre, son of Edward Matthew Curre, of Itton.
[5] William Frederick Holt Beevor, son of the Reverend William Holt Beevor, Canon of Llandaff.

which the following letter was issued from the War Office on August 20:

'His Royal Highness the Field-Marshal Commanding-in-Chief is pleased to observe that the report of the inspecting officer is satisfactory and shows that the Regiment has much improved in the several points remarked upon at the inspection last year.

'The men turned out in marching order very clean and the kits were laid out very well and uniformly. The drill and discipline of the Battalion were good, and the behaviour of the men was very good. The young officers are reported as especially well drilled.

'(Signed) GARNET WOLSELEY, Major-General.'

By the training of 1875, which commenced on May 8, under Colonel Vaughan, Lieutenants Vere Somerset, R. L. Page,[1] and G. F. Walker had retired, and W. E. Wiseman-Clarke and H. T. Smith had been given commissions in the Regiment. Several recruits were obtained this year at Tredegar, Pontypool, Newport, and Abergavenny, in addition to a large number at Monmouth itself, and several men of the Regiment enlisted into the Royal Artillery.

The recruits assembled for preliminary drill on March 8, the men being billeted as usual. The landladies of houses in which men were billeted were required to attend at the Orderly Room between 11 A.M. and 12 noon on certain specified dates to receive their money. Private John Brian, *alias* John Murphy, was sentenced on March 11 by the civil power to three months' imprisonment for fraudulent enlistment into the Regiment whilst belonging to the North Durham Militia. On April 13, Private T. Butler was deprived of four days' pay and sentenced to 168 hours' imprisonment with solitary confinement for absence and making away with necessaries. On May 19 thirty-eight men were deprived of pay by the Commanding Officer for absence and drunkenness, and on the following day thirty-five more lost their bounties by order of a Regimental Board. At this training the men were ordered to appear always in kerseys and best trousers when outside their billets. The inspection took place on May 27 by Colonel J. P. Redmond, C.B., commanding the Brigade Depot at Pembroke. The ordinary movements having been performed, the Regiment was divided into two Battalions, under Colonel Payne and Colonel McDonnell, and some brigade movements were carried out.

When the Regiment came out for training on May 8, 1876, several

[1] Joined the Tower Hamlets Militia.

changes had taken place amongst the officers. Lieutenant W. C. St. I. Partridge had transferred to the 108th Foot, Lieutenant W. F. H. Beevor had resigned, and E. C. P. Curzon, R. Hyde-Clarke and E. H. V. Haldane had joined. Several recruits were enrolled at Tredegar early in 1876, and other places specially recruited were Newport, Pontypool, Abergavenny, and Coleford. On April 20 instructions as to the wearing of medals appeared in orders :

'The attention of the permanent staff sergeants is called to the following extracts from General Orders 51 of 1875 :

' " I.—Military decorations and medals are to be worn with the tunic only, and on the left breast. They are to be worn in a straight horizontal line, suspended from a single bar of which the buckle is not to be seen. The riband is not to exceed one inch in length unless the number of clasps requires it to be longer; when the decorations and medals cannot on account of number be suspended from the bar, so as to be fully seen, they are to overlap; they are to be worn over the sash and under the pouch belt.

' " II.—Military medals will be worn in the order of the dates of the campaigns for which they have been conferred, the first decoration or medal obtained being placed furthest from the left shoulder.

' " III.—Military medals granted to non-commissioned officers and men may also be worn as indicated in the foregoing paragraphs, or may be stitched in a straight horizontal line on the tunic. In undress uniform the ribands only are to be worn by soldiers; they should be stitched on the jacket and should be half an inch in length." '

In this same month instructions were issued concerning the Regimental picquet.

'The Regimental picquet will in future remain in the Castle Square and not parade the streets. Two policemen are to be on night duty, who will in case of any disturbance immediately warn the picquet, when, according to the requirements of the case, a portion of them will be marched out under a non-commissioned officer. Should the disturbance be of any serious nature the officer on duty (who will leave his address with the sergeant of the picquet) will be immediately sent for.'

At this time soldiers were not allowed to smoke in the streets and non-commissioned officers were ordered ' to be most particular on all occasions to check men smoking in the streets, taking their names and bringing them up before the captains of their companies.' On May 24 a board of survey, with Lieut.-Colonel J. S. Payne president, was appointed to report upon the condition of eight iron targets, forty-one knapsacks and straps, forty-one mess tins and covers, twenty-six great coats, and 517 mess-tin covers.

The inspection in 1876 was made by Colonel F. E. Drewe, who remarked that over a hundred men of the Royal Monmouth Light Infantry had served under him in the ranks of the 23rd Foot during the Crimean War. He also added that the Regiment was likely to be converted into Engineers.

PENINSULA MEDAL. STRUCK 1848 BY QUEEN VICTORIA.

This particular specimen was issued to James Talbot (45th Regiment).

CHAPTER IX

EVENTS BETWEEN 1877 AND 1881

On January 9, 1877, Colonel J. F. Vaughan relinquished the command of the regiment, and on December 17 of the following year died at Biarritz. The *Army and Navy Gazette*, in alluding to the resignation, makes comment thus :—

'The services of Colonel Vaughan are worthy of record. Colonel Vaughan joined the Regiment as captain in April 1836, was promoted major in July 1847, lieut.-colonel in July 1853, and hon. colonel in 1858, so that he had been in actual command of the Regiment for more than twenty years, during which time the Regiment deservedly acquired the reputation of being one of the best drilled and disciplined in the Service. The Colonel also saw active service, although only as an amateur, he having gone to the Crimea at the latter end of 1854, and remained some three months in the camp of the Royal Welsh Fusiliers, in which regiment he had many personal friends among the officers, and for which some 300 of his men had volunteered. This Militia regiment, we hear, on account of its great efficiency has been selected by the authorities as one to be converted into an Engineer corps, and is likely soon to change its Light Infantry character.'

Colonel Vaughan was succeeded in the command by Lieut.-Colonel John Selwyn Payne,[1] under date February 23, 1877. Colonel Payne had seen ten years' service in the 14th Foot, and had been in the Royal Monmouth Militia for twenty-four years. On April 6 he was granted the honorary rank of Colonel.

Other changes in the Regiment at this time were caused by the death of Captain C. G. Kane on October 1, 1876, and by the transfer to the adjutancy of the Antrim Rifles of Captain R. J. Hickman, who had been Adjutant of the Royal Monmouth Militia for ten years. The transfer

---

[1] Colonel Payne's son subsequently joined the Regiment as a Second-Lieutenant, and was afterwards appointed to the Regular Army. In 1909, as Major-General R. L. Payne, C.B., D.S.O., he commanded the Nowshera Brigade of the Northern Army in India.

was officially effected on February 15, 1877, and was the means of eliciting from Captain Hickman these words:

' On leaving the Regiment, after ten years as your Adjutant, I cannot help placing on record my appreciation of the able and cheerful manner

> App.^d
>
> Victoria R.
>
> Most humbly submitted to Your Majesty that, with a view to the convenience of the Service, as well as to the advisability of raising Corps of Engineer Militia, the Royal Monmouth (Light Infantry) Militia be converted into an Engineer Corps, and that the change take effect from the 1st April 1877
>
> By Your Majesty's most humble and most devoted Servant,
>
> Gathorne Hardy
>
> A / Monmouth / 418
>
> War Office
> 20. March. 1877

in which I have always been supported in the duties by all members of the Permanent Staff during my command, and also to bearing testimony to the general good conduct of every individual member of the Staff. I wish you all farewell, and shall often look back with feelings of pleasure

EVENTS BETWEEN 1877 AND 1881

to my old associations.' In accordance with a Horse Guards letter of February 20, 1877, Captain Sir Arthur Mackworth, Bt., R.E., was appointed Adjutant of the Regiment, which was converted into Royal Engineers on March 27 of the same year. The *London Gazette* of that date records: 'The Queen has been graciously pleased to approve of the conversion of the undermentioned Militia Regiment as follows: The "Royal Monmouth" from "Light Infantry" into "Engineers."' Again in the *London Gazette* of November 23, 1877, there appears: 'Her Majesty has been graciously pleased to approve of the Royal Monmouth Engineer Militia being in future designated "The Royal Monmouthshire Engineer Militia."'

In 1877 the recruits assembled on March 12 for eight weeks' preliminary training. Parades were held daily at 9.30 A.M., 11.30 A.M., 2.30 P.M., and 4 P.M., and the Band played regularly each day in the Barrack Square from 3.30 to 4 P.M.; 'Retreat' was sounded by all the Buglers in Agincourt Square at 6 P.M., after which the Band played for a quarter of an hour, marching up and down the square. The picquet was mounted at the same hour and posted in the square, so as to prevent the crowd closing in on the Band.

On March 20 Captain and Honorary Major J. Davies,[1] who had been twenty-five years in the Regiment, was promoted major, and was granted the honorary rank of lieut.-colonel on April 27. Lieutenant J. M. Bannerman was on the same date promoted captain.

The conduct of the recruits seems to have been very good this year, and the regimental guard was for a time reduced in consequence. The picquet consisted of eight men (one per company), and was paraded at 6 P.M. daily. The orders issued to the sergeant of the picquet were: 'At 11 P.M. he will report to the orderly officer whether the men are all in their billets or not, and will receive his orders as to dismissing the picquet. He will communicate his address to the Superintendent of the Police, and will also note down the names and addresses of the men of his picquet when he parades them at 6 P.M. In the event of any disturbance during the night the sergeant will at once proceed to the scene of the disturbance and render every assistance to the civil police, taking with him as many men of his picquet as he considers necessary.'

On Saturdays the picquet was increased to two non-commissioned officers and sixteen men, and it was not broken off until midnight, and not then unless the men were all in their billets and quiet.

---

[1] James Davies, son of Henry Davies of The Garth, Monmouth.

Further changes in the officers' ranks in April were: Surgeon George Wilson under Royal Warrant was styled surgeon-major, Assistant Surgeon George Norman was styled surgeon, and Lieutenant Joshua Arthur Nunn was transferred to the Army Veterinary Department as veterinary-surgeon on probation.

The Regiment assembled for twenty-seven days' training on May 7, and nothing exceptional took place during the period. The inspection was made on June 1 by Colonel W. Phillpotts, the Commanding Royal Engineer in South Wales. He expressed his approval of the state of discipline and efficiency of the Regiment, and directed that it might be published in Regimental Orders that he would report to the War Office that he considered the drill and general appearance of the Regiment to be highly satisfactory, and that the conduct of the men during the training had been very good.

The pay and allowance of Engineer Militia was fixed at the following rates by Clause 91, Auxiliary and Reserve Forces Circular, 1877, dating from October 1, 1877:—

STAFF.

	s.	d.	
Sergeant-Major	3	5	Not being soldiers serving on their Army engagements.
Quartermaster-Sergeant	2	9	
Paymaster-Sergeant	2	5	
Orderly-room Clerk	2	5	During non-training period, 3d. a day in lieu of rations in addition to these rates.
Bugle-Major	2	5	
Sergeants	2	5	
Buglers	1	1	
Buglers (under sixteen)	0	9	

Sergeants acting as Company Sergeants-Major received during preliminary drill and training extra duty pay of 6d. a day.

NON-COMMISSIONED OFFICERS AND MEN OF THE MILITIA.

	s.	d.			s.	d.
Sergeants	2	6	Sappers		1	1
Corporals	1	$4\frac{1}{4}$	Boys (under sixteen)		0	8

Every non-commissioned officer and man drawing pay as above received whilst out for preliminary drill or training a ration of bread and meat free from all stoppage, or an allowance of 6d. in lieu, except for the day during which he was in receipt of a hot meal, or an allowance in lieu thereof, or marching money.

The year 1878 saw the Regiment at practical engineering work at

COLONEL JOHN FRANCIS VAUGHAN.
Commanded the Regiment 1853-1877.

Pwll-Holm, which had been purchased by the War Department for the purpose; and the officers' mess was for the first time established at the Castle, where, on June 13, the Duke of Beaufort dined with Colonel Payne and the officers. Pwll-Holm is about a mile and a quarter from the Castle, and is a piece of land some twenty-seven acres in extent, of which the level part occupies seventeen acres. It has a frontage to the river Monnow of 700 yards, and the river has an average width of 100 feet, and a depth of 15 feet in places.

Before the training took place Major J. G. Wheeley[1] had resigned his commission, and Lieutenant T. M. Reid was promoted to command the vacant company. Other officers who resigned were Lieutenants J. C. Partridge, H. S. Smith, R. Hyde-Clarke, E. H. V. Haldane, and Surgeon G. A. Norman; and those gazetted to Second Lieutenants' commissions were T. P. Price,[2] J. A. Moggridge, A. B. Elton, A. J. Pardoe, H. F. N. Hopkins, K. W. Hedges, and G. L. Morris. Lieutenant H. S. Goodlake also joined from the South Gloucester Militia.

The recruits assembled for four weeks' preliminary drill on April 8. They were not clothed until they had been inspected by the medical officer, who inserted on each man's card as to his fitness or otherwise. During this month the Staff sergeants were ordered to discontinue the pouch belt except when swords were worn, since at this time the sword-belt was worn outside the scarlet frock. The blue frock was not worn on duty under arms, but only in the offices and as a working dress. From April 19, 1878, the Militia Reserve non-commissioned officers and men received Army pay as sappers at the Royal Engineer rate— 1s. 1½d. per diem. On April 22 the whole of the Reserve men paraded with arms, accoutrements and complete kits, knapsacks, and mess tins, and on the 25th proceeded by the 9.40 A.M. train to Chatham, one hundred in number, and did great credit to the Regiment while there, a mobilisation of the Army and Militia Reserves having taken place.

The distribution of the officers throughout the eight companies at this training was:

A Company	B Company
Captain T. M. Reid.	Captain F. B. Vaughan.
Second Lieutenant T. P. Price.	Lieutenant W. E. C. Curre.
	Second Lieutenant G. L. Morris.

---

[1] John Griffiths Wheeley, son of Robert Wheeley, of The Pentre, Abergavenny.

[2] Thomas Phillips Price, son of the Reverend William Price, vicar of Llanarth; was M.P. for North Monmouthshire, 1880-1886.

C COMPANY

Hon. Major R. R. Williamson.
Second Lieutenant H. F. N. Hopkins.

D COMPANY

Captain W. H. Wheeley.
Lieutenant W. E. Wiseman-Clarke.

E COMPANY

Hon. Major J. M. Z. Gray.
Second Lieutenant C. S. Foote.
Second Lieutenant A. B. Elton.

F COMPANY

Captain W. J. Steward.
Second Lieutenant K. W. Hedges.

G COMPANY

Captain J. M. Bannerman.
Second Lieutenant A. J. Pardoe.

H COMPANY

Hon. Major B. Sheehy.
Lieutenant H. S. Goodlake.
Second Lieutenant J. A. Moggridge.

The Adjutant, Captain Sir A. W. Mackworth, was absent on leave during a portion of the training, and his duties were performed by Captain W. J. Steward. The trained men of the battalion were put through their annual course of ball practice, under the instruction of Lieutenant Curteis, of the 24th Regiment, and the whole of the company officers attended with their respective companies. On May 25, in honour of Her Majesty's birthday, a *feu-de-joie* was fired at 12 noon by the Regiment, three rounds of blank ammunition being issued to each man for the purpose. On the 26th the Regiment commenced a course of instruction in field works at Pwll-Holm, which was continued daily. The men were marched to the ground from the 10 A.M. parade in the Castle Square, and remained there during the day. Officers commanding companies paid their men at Pwll-Holm, and had their dinners kept back until 5 P.M., Saturdays excepted, a canteen being provided on the ground.

Colonel Phillpotts made the annual inspection of the Regiment on June 18, commencing with a visit to the field works at Pwll-Holm. On the 19th he inspected the books, kits, hospital, and barracks, and on the 20th the Regiment paraded in new clothing for inspection in drill. Colonel Phillpotts directed that it should be made known to the Regiment that he was satisfied with the result of his inspection. The field works were executed under somewhat exceptional difficulties in consequence of the bad weather, and were satisfactory to the extent that they were carried out. The interior economy and discipline of the corps he considered to be also satisfactory, and the drill was steady and creditable to the Regiment.

In September 153 men were struck off the strength as deserters, and in the same month permission was granted by the Lieutenant-General Commanding the Western District for the non-commissioned officers and drummers of the Permanent Staff of the Militia to wear plain clothes during the non-training period when not on duty, with certain restrictions applicable to Militia quartered with Regular troops in barracks.

The training of 1879, as in the subsequent years, lasted for forty-one days, under a letter from the War Office dated March 16, 1879. Colonel J. S. Payne having retired, Colonel F. McDonnell succeeded to the command. He had been in the regiment for twenty-six years, and had previously served in the Highland Light Infantry. Captain and Honorary Major B. Sheehy was promoted to the vacant majority, and Lieutenant W. E. C. Curre received his company; Major and Honorary Lieut.-Colonel J. Davies was absent abroad from the training. Lieutenant T. P. Price was later promoted, as Major J. M. Z. Gray had been appointed to the command of the Hampshire Submarine Miners Engineer Militia. Lieutenant H. S. Goodlake was granted leave of absence from the training, as he was studying for a Line commission, and Lieutenant W. E. Wiseman-Clarke was also absent with leave. Lieutenant C. S. Foote had joined the 40th Regiment, and Lieutenant K. W. Hedges resigned during the training. The new officers were E. L. Lister and A. D. Homfray.

On March 24 the companies ceased to be distinguished by letters of the alphabet, and were in future identified by means of numerals; thus A Company became No. 1, and H Company No. 8.

On April 21 the Regiment assembled, and men were invited to volunteer for the Militia Reserve under the following conditions :

They had to be not less than 5 feet 5 inches in height, with 33 inches chest measurement; they were required to have attained the age of nineteen years, but to be under thirty-four years. They were also required to have served two trainings (the current one included), and to have been of good character.

The terms of enlistment were as under :

If the man had *not* less than twelve months to serve in the Militia he would be engaged for the remaining portion of his current engagement.

If a man had less than twelve months to serve in the Militia he would be engaged for the unexpired portion of the period of such engagement and for four years in addition, and at the same time would be re-enrolled for the same period in the Militia.

A bounty of 1*l*. (in addition to the Militia bounty) was paid at the termination of the training for each complete year of service in the Reserve, and for any remaining portion, provided it was one of not less than six months.

Volunteers were required this year for eight regiments which were first on the roster for foreign service, and for the depots of those battalions then engaged in active operations against the enemy. The following conditions had to be observed:

Age 20 to 31 years.

Chest measurement 34 inches and upwards.
Height not under 5 feet 5 inches.
No married men to be taken.

A bounty of 1*l*. was given to Militiamen on such enlistment, and a bounty of 2*l*. to Militia Reserve men who were so enlisted, and who were enrolled during or before 1878, but the latter did not receive their Reserve bounty for the current year.

The following were the Brigades for which volunteers were required:

1st Brigade,	Berwick-on-Tweed.	29th Brigade,	Northampton.
7th ,,	Pontefract.	36th ,,	Taunton.
11th ,,	Preston.	38th ,,	Devizes.
12th ,,	Preston.	45th ,,	Canterbury.
15th ,,	Burnley.	50th ,,	Hounslow.
16th ,,	Ashton-under-Lyne.	58th ,,	Stirling.
19th ,,	Lichfield.	60th ,,	Hamilton.
24th ,,	Cardiff.	63rd ,,	Belfast.
25th ,,	Brecon.	65th ,,	Armagh.
26th ,,	Derby.	68th ,,	Galway.

On Saturday, May 24, 1879, the Regiment paraded in review order at 10 A.M., to fire a *feu-de-joie* in honour of Her Majesty's birthday. Colonel W. Phillpotts, R.E., C.R.E. South Wales district, inspected the Regiment, commencing with the field works at Pwll-Holm on May 27; and after examining the books on the 28th, on the 29th he inspected the Regiment at 11.30 A.M. in marching order in new clothing.

The Inspecting Officer desired that it should be made known to the officers, non-commissioned officers, and men of the Regiment that he considered the progress made by them that training had been very satisfactory, that the field works executed were highly creditable, and also the steadiness, general appearance, and drill of the battalion.

By the training of 1880, which commenced on May 31, the following changes had taken place: Lieutenant W. E. Wiseman-Clarke had resigned, Lieutenant H. S. Goodlake had joined the 41st Regiment, Lieutenant J. A. Moggridge the 40th, and Lieutenant A. B. Elton the 19th. The new officers were W. F. H. Morgan, R. C. Hanbury-Williams,[1] E. A. Kennedy, H. M. Worsley, H. W. Strachan, E. Oakes, and H. R. Blakeney.

On February 28, 1880, the whole of the non-commissioned officers and buglers of the Permanent Staff paraded as a funeral party at 3.30 P.M. to attend the funeral of Sergeant Thomas James, of the Regiment. The recruits assembled on April 5 for eight weeks' preliminary drill, and non-commissioned officers were cautioned to be most particular in seeing that the men were properly dressed outside their billets, and that they did not smoke in the streets when in uniform. After April 10 passes for the men to the extent of five per company were granted by the Commanding Officer from 5 P.M. on Saturday until 9 A.M. on Monday; men who had been brought up for misconduct during the week were deprived of the privilege. In consequence of the general good conduct of the men the hour of tattoo from April 26 was extended to 10.30 P.M.

Seven non-commissioned officers of the Regiment were attached this year to the 25th Brigade Depot for instruction. In reporting on them, the Officer Commanding the depot stated: 'I have much pleasure in saying that during the time they have been attached they have conducted themselves most satisfactorily, and have paid strict attention to their duties.'

The battalion commenced its annual course of musketry on June 3, under the instruction of Lieutenant Edward Poynton, of the 13th Light Infantry. The first parade of each company for ball practice was attended by all the officers of the company, and one officer of each company was always required to be present at the practices.

The Commanding Officer made it known to the men on June 2 that there had been established for their use a free reading and recreation room at the house known as the 'British Workman' in Monnow Street. The room was open daily until tattoo, and was inspected by the captain of the day. Regimental sports were also held this year at May Hill.

Colonel Phillpotts, R.E., made the annual inspection of the Regiment

[1] Richard Capel Hanbury-Williams, son of Ferdinand Capel Hanbury-Williams, of Nant-Oer; died 1891.

on June 24, commencing with the Barrack Yard; and afterwards the regimental, company, and officers' books were all laid out in the Armoury at 10 A.M. Officers commanding companies were required to ascertain previous to the inspection, in accordance with Paragraph 90 of the Militia Orders of 1878, whether any man had any complaint to bring before the inspecting officer. On June 25 the Regiment paraded at 10 A.M., in marching order without knapsacks, greatcoats, and leggings, for inspection by Colonel Phillpotts. The Inspecting Officer had great pleasure in intimating his approval of the way in which the Regiment turned out at his inspection, and he was much gratified to receive the report of the Regiment's very good conduct during the training.

Some of the members of the Permanent Staff having been found to have accepted civil employment, their attention was called to Paragraph 398 of the 'Regulations for the Militia, 1880,' which stated: 'All Members of the Permanent Staff of the Militia, whether serving on their Army engagement or not, will be liable to perform any military duties which may be required of them. They will not be allowed to engage in any civil occupation which would not be permitted to a soldier with his regiment.'

In the year 1881 the military forces of the Crown underwent a considerable change by the Territorial scheme then introduced.

CHAPTER X

THE REORGANISATION OF THE ARMY AND MILITIA IN 1881

'I WILL first ask the House to recall to their recollection our military condition in 1867, fourteen years ago, when General Peel, standing at this table, moved the Army Estimates.' So spake Mr. Childers in March 1881 when introducing in the House of Commons his scheme of reorganisation. The organisation of our military forces, he continued, was far less efficient then than it was in 1881. The Militia at the earlier date was practically separated from the Army, and less than 2,000 Militiamen annually enlisted into the Army. The Volunteers had only about 150,000 efficients in 1867 against about 200,000 in 1881, were hardly at all connected with the Army, and were still regarded with little favour in many quarters. In the Army itself the system which was known as 'long service' had in two respects entirely broken down. It held out insufficient inducements to recruits, so much so that from 28,000 a year in 1859, the number annually recruited had fallen in 1865 to about 13,000, against above 20,000 stated by Lord William Poulet, the Adjutant-General, to be required; and it had entirely failed to produce any Reserve. Almost the whole body of the older officers disapproved the system, and favoured that which before 1847 had been known as 'life service,' and which had in that year been abolished, against the general sense of the officers, by the personal influence of the Duke of Wellington. Indeed, it is most instructive to read on this question the evidence taken by the Recruiting Commissions of 1860 and 1866. The Commission of 1860 was appointed because, to use the words of the report, 'even when, after the Mutiny, the bounty was increased and the standard lowered to such an extent as to bring boys instead of men into the ranks, the required establishment was not complete.' But the remedies proposed failed; and then the second Commission was appointed, in 1866, because the number of recruits had fallen to the extent just described. Then, as before and since, the most varied opinions were given as to every detail of Army service; but the great majority condemned the then existing length of service (ten or twelve years) as too short. The Adjutant-General in 1866 especially complained of the youth of non-commissioned officers, and urged the increase of pensions as a means of filling the Army with older men. The Commander-in-Chief was anxious for enlistment for twenty-one years, and did not consider any army of reserve necessary. Lord Grey thought the Militia a gigantic mistake, and that the failure of the plan for a Reserve was due to the manner of its administration. There was a minority who advocated still shorter service; so that every view, from life enlistment to a colour service like that which prevailed in foreign armies, was represented by witnesses before the Commissions. On the question of the adequacy of recruiting for a ten or twelve years' service, the second Commission was hopeful, if large additions were made to the pay and prospects of the soldier; but as to the formation of a Reserve, they practically despaired. For a solid Reserve they said they must look to the Militia; and for two or three years after their report nothing in this respect was done, and, meanwhile, the country was dissatisfied. The Crimean War had indeed shown, some years before, that without a Reserve of men who had passed through the Army the military force of the country would soon be exhausted; but it was the two great wars in which Germany was concerned which had occasioned the deepest anxiety in the public mind. In 1866 Prussia, with an army consisting of men between twenty and twenty-three years of age, enlisted for three years with the colours, and supported by reserves, had, in seven weeks, totally defeated the more veteran troops of Austria; and in 1870 the French Army, which had only then recently been re-formed on the basis of containing a much larger proportion of old soldiers, received a still more crushing defeat at the hands of Germany. Is it to be wondered at that the difficulty in obtaining recruits and the impossibility of forming a Reserve with long service, taken in connection with the evidence of what a short service system could do on the Continent, made public opinion all but unanimous in favour of such a system being tried in England? Lord Cardwell did not, however, effect this change all at once. In the Artillery and Cavalry it commenced in 1874, and as the period with the colours was fixed at eight years, it was only in the financial year 1881–2 that the Reserve began to be fed from these arms. In the Infantry it began in 1870, and for some time recruits were accepted both for long service (that is to say, twelve years with the colours) and for short service (or six years with the colours and six in the Reserve). But it was soon found that both systems would not work together. Men would not enlist for long service if they could enter the Army for the shorter period; and in 1881 the only term of Infantry service, with unimportant exceptions, was six years. Lord Cardwell's second reform, the first in point of date, was to recall from the Colonies a large number of Battalions serving there, until the numbers of the home Battalions, and of those serving in India and the Colonies, were just equal. He then took advantage of this equality to combine the Battalions in pairs, a system which he found in existence with respect to the first twenty-five Regiments, and for this purpose adopted a plan proposed by the Commander-in-Chief for linking, as it was called, a pair of Battalions, so that each Battalion abroad was mainly fed by drafts from the one at home, which, when low on the roster, was little more than a recruiting machine. With the two Line Regiments he linked two county Militia Regiments, establishing depot centres for the four Battalions; and to this depot he appointed a Colonel and other officers, both for the recruits to the two Regiments and for training the Militia. Lord Cardwell's third reform was the abolition of purchase. The disadvantages of that system were manifest; but it had one great merit, inasmuch as it enabled officers who did not care to make the Army their profession, or saw little chance of advancement, to retire by the sale of their commissions, and thus secured a most unequal, but still large flow of regimental promotion. It remained, however, to be seen how this promotion could be secured in a professional service. In 1881 there had been from eight to ten years' experience of these changes, and the time had arrived for reviewing them, and, if any defects had appeared, for applying the necessary remedies.

The changes in 1881, which particularly concerned the Auxiliary Forces, were not many in number. Her Majesty was graciously pleased to increase the number of her aides-de-camp by four, and these much prized though honorary distinctions were conferred on Volunteer officers.

Her Majesty also approved an alteration in the regulations of the Order of the Bath, under which five Knight Commanderships and twenty-five Companionships of the Civil Branch of that Order were to be conferred upon officers of the Auxiliary and Reserve Forces who might, while in command of a Regiment, have contributed in a marked degree to its efficiency. The regulations under which Militia and Volunteer Officers were allowed to retain their rank or to obtain steps of honorary rank after long service or on retirement were amended. It was decided that after fifteen years' commissioned service in any of the Auxiliary Forces, or in combination with Army Service, an officer would be allowed, if duly recommended, to retain his rank and wear his uniform; that after twenty-five years' similar service in the Militia or Yeomanry, or thirty years in the Volunteers, a Lieutenant-Colonel or a Major would be allowed a step of honorary rank, and a Captain after twenty years in the Militia or Yeomanry, or twenty-five in the Volunteers.

With respect to the Militia, the arrangements for bringing the old Constitutional Force into closer connection with the Regular Army were brought about by means of making county Militia Regiments the third and fourth Battalions of the new Territorial Line Regiments. Up to this time the bulk of the Regular Regiments had been identified merely by numbers, but in 1881 was introduced the system of linking two Battalions together under a Territorial designation—thus what were formerly known as the 35th and 107th Foot became the Royal Sussex Regiment, and the 3rd Battalion of the Royal Sussex Regiment was the new title given to the Sussex Militia. At the same time were introduced revised regulations for the retirement of Militia Officers. Hitherto frequent instances had existed of officers being in command of their Regiments when past the age of seventy, and many of the Majors had attained that age as well. From 1881 no Colonel or Lieutenant-Colonel was to retain his appointment after fifty-five, or, in special circumstances, sixty years of age; and all future Majors and Captains were to retire at fifty.

The object of the linking of two Regular Battalions was to give such a name as would imply a distinctive local association, likely to infuse into the corps a feeling of comradeship and pride in the place from which it was recruited. In some instances the task was easy enough. Where the two Battalions constituted the same Regiment, the old designation was retained in most instances. Thus the 9th Norfolk, the 16th Bedfordshire, the 22nd Cheshire, and others simply lost their numerical distinctions, and were henceforth known only by the name of the county with which they had long been associated. In some others, where the recruiting ground had been changed, there was no difficulty. The 20th Regiment, for instance, which had been transferred from Devonshire to Bury, was transformed from the 'East Devonshire' to the 'Lancashire Fusiliers' without any trouble or any sensible injury to susceptibilities. Even in the case of some of the Regiments whose constitutional parts had hitherto been only *linked*, a solution readily presented itself. Thus, the 28th North Gloucestershire and the 61st South Gloucestershire, and the 44th East Essex and the 56th West Essex, inevitably became the Gloucestershire and the Essex Regiments respectively. In these instances the process was almost self-adjusting. But in many cases the task of the christening committee must have been delicate and troublesome. The manifestation of feeling upon the subject of the Highland tartans was only one peculiarly prominent illustration of the many susceptibilities aroused by the projected changes of name and equipment.

One of the happiest features of the new plan of nomenclature was the association of certain Regiments with some of the great towns of the United Kingdom. Thus, the 7th Fusiliers became the 'City of London Regiment,' the 8th Regiment the 'Liverpool,' the 63rd and 96th the 'Manchester,' and the 102nd and 103rd the 'Dublin.' This is the best kind of association, for it rests upon a basis well defined, and locally understood by means of the word itself, and in process of time it was doubtless found that a reciprocity of pride and healthful association was established in each case between the great town and its own special Regiment.

The Militia battalions of each Territorial Regiment, although having no additional liability imposed upon them in respect of the duration or character of their service, were in every other way thoroughly identified with the Line battalions. The permanent staff of the Militia battalions consisted of so many men from the Line battalions, and the uniforms of officers and men were made the same with the exception that the Militia battalions had the letter 'M' upon their appointments. The Militia officers wore gold lace like the Line. As regards the assimilation of uniforms between the Line and the Militia, several Militia battalions had to abandon the rifle green for the red, while in order to affiliate, for purposes of mobilisation, similarly clad Militia regiments to the 60th Rifles and the Rifle Brigade, it was necessary to change the uniform of the Royal London and the two regiments of Tower Hamlets Militia from red to green.

MARTINI-HENRY RIFLE, 1880

CHAPTER XI

THE ROYAL MONMOUTHSHIRE MILITIA BETWEEN 1881 AND 1889

THE Royal Monmouthshire, retaining its old title, trained in 1881 from May 16 to June 25. Since the last training Captain W. J. Steward and Captain J. M. Bannerman had resigned, as had also Lieutenants G. L. Morris, W. F. H. Morgan, and E. Oakes. This training was also Sir Arthur Mackworth's last, he being the first Adjutant of the Regiment to come under the new regulations by which adjutants held office for a term of five years. He had also been promoted Major on June 25. Of the new officers, Lieutenant J. A. Bradney[1] came from the Shropshire Militia, while W. F. Batt,[2] E. Feetham,[3] R. H. O. Capper,[4] and E. W. Croker held commissions for the first time.

Lieutenant A. J. Pardoe was promoted Captain on February 22 and Lieutenant E. L. Lister on May 31. The recruits assembled on Monday, April 4, for six weeks' preliminary training. Pay-Sergeants were required to send into the Orderly Room by 9 A.M. daily parade states of their respective companies, showing the recruits separately from the old soldiers. Absentees were shown as 'absent without leave,' and men temporarily absent were accounted for as 'on pass.' Men temporarily discharged were shown in the company parade states as 'absent with leave.'

A room known as the Skating Rink and situate in Monnow Street was provided as a reading and recreation room for the men on April 6. It was open daily from 6.30 A.M. to 9.30 P.M. on week-days, and from 8 A.M. to 10 A.M. and again from 12 NOON to 9.30 P.M. on Sundays. A corporal was placed in charge of the establishment.

---

[1] Joseph Alfred Bradney (son of the Reverend Joseph Christopher Bradney, rector of Greet, Salop), and afterwards Colonel Commanding 2nd Battalion Monmouthshire Regiment.

[2] William Ferdinand Batt, son of William Forster Batt, of Abergavenny; died unmarried.

[3] Edward Feetham, son of the Reverend William Feetham.

[4] Richard Harcourt Ord Capper, son of Richard Harcourt Capper, who was a Lieutenant in the Regiment, and who afterwards became Major in the Herefordshire Volunteers.

During this training the Regimental Band played at Pwll-Holm on Sundays between the hours of 4 and 5 P.M. Officers and soldiers in uniform were admitted free to the concert, but all persons in plain clothes, whether accompanying an officer or soldier or not, were required to pay one penny as admission fee. A sergeant was stationed at the entrance gates to receive the money, which was devoted to regimental purposes as directed by the Officer Commanding. The military police were present to prevent anyone entering the ground except through the main entrance gate, and they had instructions to turn off the War Department ground any person behaving in a disorderly manner or doing any damage to Government property.

Five passes per company were granted for leave of absence from after the dinner hour on Saturdays until the dinner hour on the following Monday. Company sergeant-majors were required to initial the passes and to exercise great vigilance that only deserving men obtained them. Those who had been before the Commanding Officer during the year were not eligible for them.

The recruits' musketry course commenced on May 3 under the instruction of Lieutenant G. Dease, Royal Fusiliers. Company Sergeant-Major Rees acted as Sergeant Instructor of Musketry, and a fatigue party of twelve men was detailed daily for range purposes.

Standing orders were framed on May 4 for the guidance of company orderly sergeants. They consisted of :—

1. He will parade and inspect all men of his company who are for duty whether with or without arms.

2. He will attend for orders daily, and will communicate the details of men required for duty to his company sergeant-major from whom he will receive the names of the men to be warned for duty.

3. He will warn all men of his company required for duty or fatigue.

4. He will ascertain the names of men marked for extra drill and men confined to barracks, parade them for drill and furnish a list of men confined to barracks to the non-commissioned officer commanding the Regimental Guard.

5. He is responsible that prisoners confined in the Guard Room are supplied from their billets with the means of washing, shaving, and cleaning themselves previous to appearing before the Commanding Officer.

6. He will show the orders to the officers of his company, and warn all employed men for any parade or duties that may concern them.

Certain of the non-commissioned officers were attached this year for instruction to the 1st Battalion Royal Fusiliers at Pembroke Dock. On their leaving to rejoin the regiment the officer commanding the Fusiliers reported 'the behaviour of these non-commissioned officers has been most exemplary during the period they have been attached to my Regiment.'

The distribution of the officers this year was :—

No. 1 Company.—Captain W. E. C. Curre, 2nd Lieut. R. C. Hanbury-Williams.

No. 2 Company.—Captain F. Vaughan and 2nd Lieut. E. A. Kennedy.

No. 3 Company.—Capt. and Hon. Major R. R. Williamson, Lieut. J. A. Bradney, and 2nd Lieut. E. W. Croker.

No. 4 Company.—Lieut. E. L. Lister and 2nd Lieut. W. F. Batt.

No. 5 Company.—Captain T. M. Reid and 2nd Lieut. H. W. Strachan.

No. 6 Company.—Captain A. J. Pardoe and 2nd Lieut. E. Feetham.

No. 7 Company.—Captain and Hon. Major H. W. Wheeley and 2nd Lieut. H. A. M. Worsley.

No. 8 Company.—Captain T. P. Price, 2nd Lieut. H. R. Blakeney, and 2nd Lieut. R. H. O. Capper.

On May 24, it being her Majesty's birthday, a Royal Salute was fired at twelve noon. The Regiment paraded in Review Order, officers wearing lace trousers and mounted officers saddle-cloths. The men wore their best clothing. Busbies were worn by the Royal Engineers at this time.

On May 31 a sapper who had been absent from the training for over fourteen days was sentenced to make good the training by another year's service, in accordance with the Militia Regulations.

It was announced during the training that officers, non-commissioned officers, and men of the Regiment were invited to compete in the National Rifle Match for the United Service Challenge Cup to be held at Wimbledon. The names of those desirous of competing, together with authenticated registers of scores made by them since January 1880, had to be in the Orderly Room by June 25. The team from each of the various services consisted of eight men.

Colonel Phillpotts was this year Inspecting Officer again. He commenced his inspection on June 21 by an examination of the Field Works at Pwll-Holm, after which he expressed himself much gratified with the work done and recorded his approbation of the prompt and orderly manner in which a bridge of casks was thrown across the river Monnow. On the two following days the other usual routine of the inspection was

COLOURS WORKED BY THE LADIES OF MONMOUTHSHIRE AND PRESENTED DURING THE CRIMEAN WAR EMBODIMENT.

(Now hanging in the Officers' Mess at Monmouth Castle.)

carried out, the Review Parade taking place at 10.15 on June 23. The Inspecting Officer directed that a Regimental Order be published recording his satisfaction at the clean and smart appearance of the Regiment, their steadiness on parade, and the reports he had received of their good conduct throughout the training.

During the year 1881 the designations of Trumpet-Major, Drum-Major, Bugle-Major, and Pipe-Major were abolished, and those of Sergeant-Trumpeter, Sergeant-Drummer, Sergeant-Bugler, and Sergeant-Piper substituted. These non-commissioned officers were in future accounted for in Returns in the column for Sergeants and not in that for Drummers.

Lieutenant W. F. N. Noel, on October 1, 1881, succeeded Major Sir Arthur Mackworth, who had relinquished the Adjutancy on September 7, between which dates Quartermaster Perkins had commanded the Permanent Staff. Lieutenant Noel was promoted Captain in the Royal Engineers on July 22, 1882.

By the end of the year 1882 many resignations had taken place among the officers. Major and Honorary Lieutenant-Colonel J. Davies after having been twenty-nine years in the Regiment resigned; he was for nineteen of those years Senior Captain owing to the slowness of promotion. Honorary Major R. R. Williamson succeeded him and was granted the honorary rank of Lieutenant-Colonel, but he too retired on March 14. Honorary Major W. H. Wheeley was then promoted Major and Lieutenant R. C. Hanbury-Williams became Captain. Lieutenant J. A. Bradney had also been promoted Captain earlier in the year. Other resignations were those of Major and Honorary Lieutenant-Colonel B. Sheehy, Surgeon-Major G. Wilson, Lieutenant E. A. Kennedy, and Lieutenant H. F. N. Hopkins, the last of whom had joined the Essex Regiment. The gentlemen joining as Second Lieutenants were S. W. E. Gilliat, H. C. Moffatt,[1] and W. A. M. Pollock-Gore.

The recruits trained from April 3. Non-commissioned officers and sappers were always required, when parading with arms, to fall in with sight protectors on the muzzles of the rifles and jags inside the breeches. Company sergeant-majors had to inspect the arms and see that these articles were carried, after which they would be put in the pouches until the end of the parade, when they would be reinstated.

In orders for March 16, 1882, appears 'The non-commissioned officers of the Permanent Staff will read up and acquaint themselves with the Martini-Henry Rifle Exercise, a pamphlet upon which may be had

[1] Son of George Moffatt, of Goodrich Court, Herefordshire.

from the Orderly Room. The drill for this Regiment will be as for Rifle Battalions.'

On the issue of the Martini-Henry rifle to the Permanent Staff, the following sections of the Manual and Firing Exercises had to be amended to read thus :—

Fix Swords.—Place the rifle between the knees, guard to the front, at the same time seize the scabbard with the left hand, turning the handle of the sword to the right front ; then seize the handle with the right hand, knuckles upwards, and draw the sword halfway out until the wrist and elbow are in line.

Two.—Draw the sword to the front, turning the point upwards when it is clear of the body and seize the rifle with the left hand under the upper band. Place the back part of the handle against the right side of the barrel, knuckles to the right, arm close to the body, and slide the spring on to the catch and ring on to the muzzle ; drop the left hand to the side, and seize the rifle with the right hand between the bands.

Three.—Return to the ' Order.'

When performing the above in quick time, the time for each motion was taken from the right.

Unfix Swords.—Place the rifle between the knees, guard to the front, grasp the handle with the right hand, knuckles to the front ; seize the rifle with the left hand below the upper band, knuckles to the front, thumb against the upper band, forefinger on the spring bolt, tighten the knees on the rifle, and press the spring raising the sword about one inch.

Two.—Raise the sword off the muzzle, drop the point to the left side, edge to the front ; place it in the scabbard, raising the right hand, seize the scabbard with the left hand and guide the sword into the scabbard ; drop the left hand to the side and seize the rifle with the right hand between the bands.

Three.—Return to the ' Order.'

When performing the above in quick time, the time for each motion was taken from the right.

On May 8 a Regimental Board, with Captain R. C. Hanbury-Williams as President, assembled at 11 A.M. to examine and report on the condition of 857 Snider rifles and sword-bayonets about to be sent to Weedon.

The Regiment assembled for forty-one days' training on May 15, when the distribution of the officers was :—

No. 1 Company.—Captain W. E. C. Curre, Lieut. S. W. E. Gilliat, and Lieut. H. F. N. Hopkins.

No. 2 Company.—Captain F. B. Vaughan and Lieuts. R. H. O. Capper and A. G. M. Tozer.

No. 3 Company.—Captain J. A. Bradney and Lieut. E. Feetham.

No. 4 Company.—Captain E. L. Lister and Lieut. W. F. Batt.

No. 5 Company.—Captain T. M. Reid and Lieut. H. W. Strachan.

No. 6 Company.—Captain A. J. Pardoe and Lieut. E. W. Croker.

No. 7 Company.—Captain R. C. Hanbury-Williams and Lieut. Gore.

No. 8 Company.—Captain T. P. Price and Lieuts. H. A. M. Worsley and H. C. Moffatt.

A reading and recreation room was provided for the men during this training at a room known as the 'Henry Lodge' Room at the corner of Monnow Street and St. John Street. It was open daily from 7 A.M. till 9.30 P.M. on week-days, and from 12 NOON till 9.30 P.M. on Sundays.

On June 3 the Regiment paraded in Review Order for the celebration of the anniversary of her Majesty's birthday, and on June 21 Colonel A. T. Storer, R.E., C.R.E., Pembroke Dock, commenced the annual inspection of the Regiment with an examination of the Field Works at Pwll-Holm. He expressed his high approval of the manner in which the Military Engineering was carried out. On June 21, Captain Hoskyns, R.E., gave a lecture on 'The Afghan War.'

No less than seven officers resigned in 1883. They were Captains A. J. Pardoe and T. P. Price, Lieutenants H. W. Strachan, H. C. Moffatt, S. W. E. Gilliat, H. A. M. Worsley, and E. W. Croker. Captain F. B. Vaughan was promoted Major, and the gentlemen receiving commissions in the Regiment were the Honble. R. FitzR. Somerset,[1] F. H. V. Henry, L. C. V. Henry, W. B. M. Jackson,[2] E. L. J. Murphy, and H. H. Clay,[3] while Captain W. H. H. W. Wilson transferred from the 3rd Battalion of the Welsh Regiment.

The recruits assembled on April 9, and the Regiment on May 14. Colonel A. T. Storer was again the Inspecting Officer, and he was satisfied with all that he saw.

In 1884 W. C. St. I. Partridge rejoined the Regiment as a Captain. He had left in 1875 to join the 61st Regiment, of which he had been Adjutant. Early in the year Lieutenant W. F. Batt was promoted Captain, and Lieutenant A. G. M. Tozer joined the Northumberland

---

[1] Honble. Richard FitzRoy Somerset, youngest son of the second Lord Raglan.

[2] William Birkenhead Mather Jackson, son of Sir Henry Mather Jackson, second baronet.

[3] Henry Hastings Clay, son of Henry Clay of Piercefield.

Fusiliers. The only new officer was C. C. E. Morgan.[1] In January a Report was called for from the Horse Guards to give information as to whether (in the event of it being decided to proceed with the scheme) each Militia battalion could furnish ten men belonging to, or prepared to join, the Militia Reserve who would be willing to perform Army Hospital duties on the following conditions :—

1. Volunteers for the Militia Hospital Corps to enlist into the Militia Reserve for service with the Hospital Corps for six years.

To be men of good character, able to read and write, and be at least twenty years of age and have served not less than two trainings.

2. The men to be available for training in nursing and ambulance duties at the Depôt Army Hospital Corps, Aldershot, or in any District in which the means of training exists.

3. To be available to be called out for duty in Hospitals at home on the mobilisation of an Army Corps for active service, whether the Militia were embodied or not.

4. When called up for training annually to do duty in the station or Camp Hospitals of the Division in which their Corps is embodied, or in such other Hospitals as may be determined upon at the time of their being called out.

5. The men to receive the same rates of pay and Departmental Pay when embodied as if they were serving in the Army Hospital Corps and be subject to the same rules of discipline.

In the District Orders of March 12 appears :—

'The officer commanding 1st Royal Munster Fusiliers will detail four non-commissioned officers from the Battalion under his command to assist in drilling the recruits and men of the Royal Monmouthshire Engineer Militia from 7 April to 28 June 1884. The non-commissioned officers detailed to report themselves to the Commanding Officer Royal Monmouthshire Engineers Militia, Monmouth, on the 6th prox.'

Intimation having been received from the Horse Guards on March 25 that the letters 'R.E.' on the collars of greatcoats of warrant, non-commissioned officers, and men of the Corps be immediately removed, the Permanent Staff were ordered to conform at once to the regulation.

The recruits assembled on April 7, and on the same date the officers serving at the Preliminary Drill received the following instructions :—

'His Royal Highness the Field-Marshal Commanding-in-Chief has

---

[1] Charles Courtenay Evan Morgan, son of Colonel Honble. Frederick Courtenay Morgan, M.P., and grandson of the first Lord Tredegar.

received her Majesty's commands to direct on the present melancholy occasion of the death of Colonel H.R.H. Prince Leopold, Duke of Albany, K.G., fourth son of her Majesty the Queen, that the officers of the Army be required to wear when in uniform a band of black crape round the left arm as prescribed by the Regulations. The mourning will commence from the 30th March and be continued until the 11th May next.'

Captain W. C. St. I. Partridge was officer Instructor of Musketry, and Sergeant William Sullivan, Royal Munster Fusiliers, Sergeant Instructor, both during the recruits course and also during the training of the Regiment. Officers going through their musketry course paraded in red frocks with rifles and side-arms.

The Regiment came up on May 19, and Colonel A. T. Storer, C.R.E., South Wales, was the Inspecting Officer. In December it was communicated that 'The Field-Marshal Commanding-in-Chief considers the Report on this Regiment very satisfactory.'

In 1885 Lord Tredegar, who had served in the 17th Lancers in the Crimea and who had been present at the battles of Alma, Balaclava, and Inkerman, was gazetted on December 9 Honorary Colonel of the Regiment in succession to Colonel H. M. Clifford, who had died on February 12, 1884. During the year Lieutenant W. A. M. Pollock-Gore joined the Royal Scots and Lieutenant R. H. O. Capper went to the Prince of Wales' North Staffordshire Regiment. The gentlemen joining were the Hon. G. W. R. Somerset,[1] late R.N., E. A. Herbert,[2] C. M. Crompton-Roberts,[3] E. J. B. Buckley,[4] and T. R. Symons.[5]

. . . .

The undermentioned officers of the Regiment were employed with the Depôt Companies Royal Engineers at Chatham during the absence on special duty of officers of the Corps in the Soudan and in South Africa, viz. :—

    Captain W. E. C. Curre . . . . . . 1.1.'85
    Lieutenant W. A. M. Pollock-Gore . . . . 1.1.'85

---

[1] Honble. Granville William Richard Somerset, third son of the second Lord Raglan.

[2] Edmund Arthur Herbert, son of Major Edmund Philip Herbert of Llansantffraid, Monmouthshire.

[3] Charles Montagu Crompton-Roberts, son of Charles Henry Crompton-Roberts, of Drybridge, Monmouthshire.

[4] Egerton John Bulkeley Buckley, son of the Reverend Joseph Buckley, rector of Sopworth, Gloucestershire.

[5] Thomas Raymond Symons, son of Thomas George Symons, of The Mynde, Herefordshire.

Lieutenant F. H. V. Henry	1.1.'85
Captain T. M. Reid	28.2.'85
Captain R. C. Hanbury-Williams	11.3.'85
Lieutenant E. L. J. Murphy	11.3.'85

Officers commanding Corps and Regimental Districts were informed that it was intended that all Militia officers attached to Line battalions or Regimental depôts should attend the training of their own battalions and be summoned in the ordinary way, returning at the conclusion of the training to the battalion or depôt to which they were temporarily attached.

It was notified, too, for general information that the instructions contained in Paragraphs 205, 208, and 209 of the Militia Regulations regarding the discharge of Militiamen by purchase would be suspended until further orders, and that in future men belonging to the Militia or Militia Reserve, whether embodied, called out for training or not, would not be permitted to purchase their discharge.

It was intimated from Army Headquarters on April 4 that an association had been established of which General Sir D. Lysons, K.C.B., was Chairman, which had for its object the furtherance of a scheme initiated in 1884 for assisting discharged soldiers and Army Reserve men of good character in obtaining employment, and that His Royal Highness had approved of the Committee of the Association communicating with officers commanding Regimental Districts and with other military authorities in order to further the objects of the society.'

On April 6 the recruits assembled for fifty-six days' preliminary drill, and the Regiment trained as usual for forty-one days, but the scene this year was changed to Chatham, where the men underwent special instruction in Military Engineering. An advance party, under command of Captain W. C. St. I. Partridge, proceeded in marching order from Monmouth to Chatham by train on May 27. The Regiment left Troy Station by special train on the evening of the 29th.

The District Orders of May 29 contain :—

' The Queen's Birthday will be celebrated by the Troops on Saturday, 6th June.

' The Royal Standard will be hoisted at 8 A.M. at the following places : Fort Amherst, Chatham, Sheerness, Tilbury Fort.

' A Royal Salute will be fired at noon from Tilbury Fort and Sheerness.

' The whole of the Troops in Garrison as strong as possible will be formed on the Great Lines at 11.45 A.M. in the following order from the right :

D 3rd Bde. R.A. } In line at full intervals.
R.E. Field Co.

Royal Engineer Battalion
2nd Berkshire Regiment
Royal Marine Light Infantry
Royal Monmouth Engineer Militia
3rd East Kent Regiment
} Deployed in line at "open order" twelve paces between battalions.

'*Dress.*—Review order.

' Each Infantry soldier to carry three rounds of blank ammunition.

' Troops to move in " Quarter Column " and at once deploy on their marker.

' The order of procedure will be as follows :

' (a) At noon the Field Battery will fire seven guns. The Infantry will fire a *feu-de-joie* (each Battalion coming to the " ready " on the word of its own Commanding Officer immediately the Artillery commences firing). The word " present " will be given by commanding officers on a signal from the Major-General.

' The Infantry bands massed in rear of the centre will play six bars of " God save the Queen." The men will remain with their rifles at the " present " until the bands have ceased playing. They will then " load " and remain at the " ready " position.

' (b) The Field Battery will fire seven guns. The Infantry will fire a second round as before. The bands will play six bars of " God save the Queen " as before.

' (c) The Field Battery will fire seven guns. The Infantry will fire a third round as before ; the bands will play " God save the Queen " and the Infantry will then " Order Arms," " fix bayonets," and " shoulder " by order of commanding officers on a signal given by the Major-General.

' (d) The caution " Royal Salute " will be repeated by all commanding officers and passed by all mounted officers.

' The order " present arms " will be given by commanding officers on a signal from the Major-General ; the bands will play " God save the Queen." On a signal from the Major-General officers commanding will order Battalions to " shoulder " and " Order Arms." The Troops will give three cheers for Her Majesty by a signal from the Major-General.

' (e) The Infantry will form quarter column on right companies of Battalions, these closing to line of quarter columns with thirty paces interval on the right Battalion. The Troops will march past; Infantry in column in double companies.

'The Field Battery will then trot past.

'The Infantry will march past in mass of quarter columns, at thirty paces distance, in line of quarter columns of thirty paces interval.'

On June 5 the Regiment paraded for the inspection of the Commandant, School of Military Engineering, at 9.45 A.M., in Field Day Order, and it acquitted itself well. Companies were exercised almost daily in such work as Blockhouses, Shelter Trenches, Mine-shafts and Galleries, Redoubts, Railways, Batteries, and Water Supply. Each was marched off separately to its own particular work at 9 A.M. The companies employed on the Chatham side returned to camp for dinner at 1 P.M. and paraded for work again at 2 P.M. Those companies which crossed the river to Upnor took their dinners with them and cooked them there. The weather was exceptionally fine, there being only two wet days. A further inspection was held on June 29 by General Monck and Colonel E. C. Gordon, Commandant S.M.E., and Sir John Stokes and General Elkington (Inspector-General of Auxiliary Forces) came down for the occasion, and all were most pleased at what they saw. The result of the inspection was the reception of the following letter which appeared in Orders on July 1, the day on which the Regiment left Chatham at 9 P.M. for Monmouth :—

Chatham : June 30, 1885.

. . . .

'The Commandant wishes to place on record his appreciation of the high state of efficiency shown by the Royal Monmouth Engineer Militia at his recent inspection. What they were called on to do was well done; their tracing and extending is deserving of special commendation, and elicited the approbation of those who witnessed it. He is glad to be able to add that their stay at Chatham has been marked by an absence of serious crime.'

A further letter, which was printed in Orders on July 2, after the Regiment had reached Monmouth, was received by the Officer Commanding the Regiment from Colonel Gordon :—

Commandant's House, Brompton, Chatham : July 1.

'I cannot allow the Royal Monmouth Engineer Militia to leave Chatham without conveying to you my appreciation of the zealous and efficient manner in which the Regiment has performed both its military and Engineering duties during the annual training which closes this week.

All ranks have shown that they possess the quality which is essential to good soldiers, viz. discipline. The absence of crime during the month of camp life reflects the greatest credit not only on the officers and non-commissioned officers but also on the men themselves, and I trust that they will always strive to preserve to the Regiment its present high standard of efficiency.

'Believe me, &c. &c.,
'(Signed)   E. C. GORDON, Colonel R.E.'

On the day after the Regiment's arrival at Monmouth the men were dismissed. On August 31, a new Regimental Library having been received, members of the Permanent Staff wishing to become subscribers were on payment of one penny a month entitled to take out one volume at a time. The full value of any book lost had to be paid by the subscriber in whose charge the volume was. The amount was assessed by the Adjutant, who charged the same monthly, together with the subscriptions and any sums due for losses.

The District Orders for November 5 contain :—

' The Major-General Commanding has much pleasure in notifying to the Troops that, in reply to his request made on the 16th inst., he has received the permission of His Royal Highness the Field-Marshal Commanding-in-Chief to relax, as an experiment, in this District the restriction as to soldiers smoking in the streets so far as to allow them when off duty to do so after Retreat.

' The privilege is in the first instance permitted only in the first six months, at the expiration of which period the Major-General is to furnish a report on the matter to His Royal Highness.

'Commanding officers of Corps and Stations in the District will therefore on the 1st May next send a report to the A.A. General as to the success or otherwise of this experiment, and the General Officer Commanding trusts that such reports will prove that the soldiers have shown their appreciation of the boon by not allowing it to diminish in any way their smartness and soldierly bearing in the streets, and that it has tended to obviate the necessity of men who wish to smoke resorting to public-houses for that purpose.

' By Order,
'(Signed)   G. DIGBY BARKER, Col., A.A. General.'

During the autumn of 1884 and the whole of the year 1885 many Militia regiments had been embodied, and a large number of Militia officers had been attached to the Regular Army for duty. The names of those of the Royal Monmouthshire Militia who were serving at Chatham have already been given. After the training Captain W. E. C. Curre and Lieutenant Honble. G. W. R. Somerset were again attached to the Royal Engineers, as was also Captain W. H. H. W. Wilson. Captain Curre remained at Chatham, but the other two officers were at Portsmouth and Plymouth respectively. These attachments resulted in the following complimentary letter being addressed by Sir John Stokes, K.C.B., to Colonel McDonnell on January 20, 1886 :

War Office, Horse Guards, S.W. : January 20, 1886.

' Sir,—I am directed by the Field-Marshal Commanding-in-Chief to acquaint you that a report has been received in this office from the Commandant, School of Military Engineering, relative to the officers named in the margin (Captain W. E. C. Curre, and Lieutenant the Honble. G. W. R. Somerset), who have recently quitted Chatham after having been employed for about a year with the Royal Engineers.

' The Commandant brings to notice the able manner in which they have done their work, and the great assistance they have rendered in carrying on the duties of the School, and promoting harmony and good feeling between the seniors and the juniors of the establishment.

' I am therefore to request that you will be good enough to communicate to these officers the expression of His Royal Highness's satisfaction at receiving so favourable a report of their services.

' I have the honour, &c. &c.,

' (Signed)   J. STOKES, D.A.G., R.E.'

Early in 1886 Quartermaster T. H. Perkins was placed on a retired allowance, and was succeeded in the office by Superintending Clerk, George Tucker, R.E., who was promoted Quartermaster. Lieutenant Honble. R. F. Somerset, on August 17, was appointed Lieutenant in the Grenadier Guards vice Lord Raglan, promoted Captain. Later in the year Captain T. M. Reid retired, and Lieutenant E. A. Herbert was appointed Lieutenant in the Inniskilling Dragoons. The new officers were W. J. J. White and A. St. Q. Ricardo, and on October 1 Lieutenant H. E. Morgan Lindsay, R.E., was appointed Adjutant in succession to Captain Noel, and was granted the rank of Captain.

In March it was ordered that all recruits enlisted at Brecon and Builth were to be enlisted for the County of Brecknock and posted to No. 7 Company, and all recruits enlisted at Cardiff, Neath, and Swansea

GODFREY CHARLES, 1ST VISCOUNT TREDEGAR.
Honorary Colonel of the Regiment since 1885.

were to be enlisted for the County of Glamorgan and posted to No. 8 Company. It was explained in Orders of May 10 that the privilege of men being able to smoke in uniform in the streets after 8 P.M. was only a temporary one, which was not to be abused by diminishing the soldier's smartness. It had been instituted with the object of keeping from public-houses the men who had formerly been compelled to retire to them in order to smoke.

The Regiment assembled for forty-one days' training on May 17, and just at this time it was found necessary to appoint a board consisting of Captain R. C. Hanbury-Williams, President, and Lieutenants E. J. B. Buckley and T. R. Symons, to assemble at Pwll-Holm to inquire into and report on 'the loss of Government Stores in possession of the Regiment occasioned by the heavy rains and floods in the vicinity.' On May 27 the attention of officers was called to Section XVI., paragraph 15, of the Queen's Regulations and Orders for the Army, which directed that no armed party consisting of more than twenty men was to be allowed to proceed on any duty unaccompanied by an officer.

Major-General J. C. Lyons, C.B., commanding the Western District, inspected the Regiment in complete marching order this year, and the Commanding Royal Engineer, South Wales, also made the usual official inspection extending over two days.

The year 1887 saw only four changes in the officers of the Regiment. On April 23 Captain Lord Raglan, late Grenadier Guards, was appointed a Captain in the Regiment, and on September 24 F. H. G. Wilkinson was gazetted to a commission as Second Lieutenant. On June 11 Lieutenant L. C. V. Henry and on October 8 Lieutenant F. H. V. Henry resigned their commissions.

The recruits assembled for Preliminary Drill on April 11, when the officers doing duty were Captains W. E. C. Curre and R. C. Hanbury-Williams, and Lieutenants A. St. Q. Ricardo, Honble. G. W. R. Somerset, W. White, and C. M. Crompton-Roberts.

A Corps Memorandum dated May 2, as to the wearing of greatcoats, was issued in these words :—

' Commanding Royal Engineers and Officers Commanding Troops and Companies are informed that when the Great Coat is worn by dismounted non-commissioned Officers and men of the Corps—other than Staff Sergeants—the waist belt should always be worn over the Great Coat.

' In wet weather Capes may be worn with Great Coats to protect the waist belt and side arms.'

The Regiment came out for forty-one days' training on May 23. Officers were reminded that they were expected to acquire certificates in Military Engineering at the School of Military Engineering, Chatham, and that those who did not obtain them could not expect to be promoted.

A detail, consisting of forty-two non-commissioned officers and men under command of Captain W. H. H. W. Wilson, proceeded to Chatham on Tuesday, May 31, to prepare the camp there for the Regiment. They left May-Hill Station by the 9.30 A.M. train. On June 3 the Regiment paraded at 7.30 P.M. in Marching Order and entrained for Chatham at Troy Station at 9 P.M. On June 11 it was inspected in Review Order by the Commandant of the School of Military Engineering, and again on June 28, prior to the departure for Monmouth on the following day, when the tents were struck at 9 A.M. and all camp equipment was returned into store, under the direction of the Quartermaster. The Battalion paraded at 7.30 P.M. in Marching Order to return by special train to Monmouth, and in Orders for July 4 there appeared :—

'The Commanding Officer wishes to convey to the Officers, Non-Commissioned Officers and Sappers of the Royal Monmouthshire Engineer Militia his high appreciation of the steady and soldierlike manner in which the Regiment marched out of Chatham, which he considers reflected the greatest possible credit on all ranks.'

On Tuesday, October 18, the Permanent Staff paraded in Review Order to meet the Old Colours of the 43rd Monmouthshire Light Infantry, which were deposited in St. Mary's Church, as already described in Chapter I.

In 1888 Captain W. C. St. I. Partridge resigned his commission, and Lieutenant W. B. M. Jackson was promoted to command the vacant company. Two new officers joined the Regiment—on January 21 E. W. J. P. H. Smythe[1] and on May 31 R. H. Williams. This was the first year in which the Militia non-commissioned officers kept the registers on the range, an introduction which created much surprise and astonishment on the part of the Permanent Staff, who did not credit the Militiamen with such capabilities. Lord Raglan was instructor of musketry at the time. An Army Order, dated February 1, was circulated to the effect that in the firing exercise the words ' At   yards, ready, present ' were to be superseded by the words ' Ready, at   yards, present.'

---

[1] Edward Walter Joseph Patrick Herbert Smythe, son of Sir Walter Smythe, eighth baronet.

The motions were to be performed in exactly the same way as formerly, the change was merely in the commands. On March 17 it was notified for general information that from April 1, 1888, it had been decided to discontinue until further orders the issue of 'bringing money' for all recruits whether for the Regular Army or for the Militia. Attention was also called at the same time to a change in the designation of the Engineer Militia, Engineer Volunteers, and Submarine Miners as under :—

Existing Designation	New Designation
Engineer Militia	Engineer Militia, Fortress Forces, Royal Engineers. Engineer Militia, Submarine Miners, Royal Engineers.
Engineer Volunteers	Engineer Volunteers, Fortress and Railway Forces, Royal Engineers.
Volunteer Submarine Miners	Engineer Volunteers, Submarine Miners, Royal Engineers.

The new designation was to be used in all official communications referring to the Engineer Auxiliary Forces in the Western District.

The recruits assembled this year on April 23 for Preliminary Drill, when the officers doing duty were Captain E. L. Lister, Lieutenants H. H. Clay, Honble. G. W. R. Somerset, and C. M. Crompton-Roberts, and Second Lieutenants F. H. Green Wilkinson and E. W. J. P. H. Smythe. On May 23 it was notified that 'it had been decided by the Secretary of State for War that grey flannel shirts instead of white cotton ones should be worn by the Royal Monmouthshire Engineer Militia in future.'

A District Order of May 5 runs :—

'Saturday the 2nd June being the day on which Her Majesty's Birthday will be celebrated, the Troops in each Garrison in this District will parade together in Review Order on that day, and will fire at 12 noon a Royal Salute from Batteries of Field Artillery, and where possible a *feu-de-joie* by Garrison Batteries, Battalions, and Depôts.

'A Field state of the Garrison Parade will in each case be sent to this office on Army Form B. 232 by the 31st instant.

'By order,

'(Signed)   H. T. JONES VAUGHAN, Col., A.A. General.

On June 1, Surgeon F. D. Moir, Medical Staff, joined for duty and assumed medical charge of the Regiment. He was assisted during the training by Civil Surgeon C. T. Prosser. On June 4 the Regiment assembled for forty-one days' training, when the daily parades were fixed thus:—

1st Parade, 7 o'clock A.M. . . . Officers not required.
Breakfast, 8 o'clock A.M.
Instructional Parade, 9 o'clock A.M. { All officers, junior to adjutant, all Militia N.C. officers, recruits of this year.
Orderly Room, 10.30 A.M.
2nd Parade, 11 o'clock A.M. . . All officers.
Dinners, 1 o'clock P.M.
3rd Parade, 2.30 P.M. . . . All officers.

A special Army Order as under was received during the training:—

War Office: June 16, 1888.

'His Royal Highness the Commander-in-Chief has received the Queen's Commands to direct on the present melancholy occasion of the death of His Majesty the German Emperor, King of Prussia, son-in-law of Her Majesty the Queen, that the officers of the Army be required to wear, when in uniform, a band of black crape round the left arm as prescribed by the regulations. The mourning will commence from the 16th June and be continued until the 7th July next.

'By command,
'(Signed) WOLSELEY, A.-G.

The Secretary of State for War approved this year of the establishment of non-commissioned officers of the Regiment being increased by the addition of sixteen sergeants and sixteen corporals who received pay as such from the date of their appointments, and of forty-eight lance-corporals who received pay as sappers only. This increase in the number of non-commissioned officers was met by a corresponding reduction in the establishment of sappers.

The Commanding Royal Engineer, Western District, inspected the Regiment on July 13, and these observations were made on the 'Confidential Inspection Report' made by him:—

'His Royal Highness is much satisfied with the Confidential Report on the Royal Monmouthshire Engineer Militia. The Commanding Royal

Engineer of the District, whilst speaking in high terms of the state of this Regiment, remarks that the Engineer work was carried out very well under the direction and personal instruction of the company officers.

'ARTHUR LYON FREMANTLE,
Major-General.'

On August 20 instructions were issued as to the wearing of the haversack, as follows :—

'The haversack will in future be worn over the left instead of the right shoulder.

'The haversack when worn is to be slung across the left shoulder by all dismounted men.

'The haversack sling (both front and hind portion) will be worn under the waist belt. When empty, the haversack is to be neatly rolled up, the top edge close to and parallel with the bottom of the waist belt, resting on the right hip. When full it should be let down so that the top of it comes below and clear of the water-bottle.'

In the year 1889 Lieutenant E. L. J. Murphy resigned on July 20, Lieutenant W. W. J. White on August 3, and Honorary Lieutenant-Colonel W. H. Wheeley on October 26. Lieutenant A. St. Q. Ricardo had also left before the commencement of the year on appointment to the Royal Inniskilling Fusiliers. On February 8 Captain W. H. H. W. Wilson was given the honorary rank of Major. Captain W. E. C. Curre was promoted Major in succession to Lieutenant-Colonel Wheeley on November 15, and Lieutenant Honble. G. W. R. Somerset on the same date was given the vacant company. Second Lieutenant F. H. Green Wilkinson was promoted Lieutenant and B. J. W. Wickham joined on April 3.

The training this year was principally at Chatham again, the Regiment returning to Monmouth two days before the conclusion, when the men were quartered in billets, which resulted in much drunkenness and difficulty in paying off. It was the first year the men were paid in the trains, and this time it was not a great success as most of them were drunk, and after getting into the train got out on the reverse side or else detrained at the next station and returned to Monmouth. Many people in the town hooted as the men were marched to the trains.

The recruits assembled at Monmouth, previous to the training, on April 29 for forty-two days' Preliminary Drill. In conjunction with the 'old hands' they were formed into four companies for pay purposes, commanded respectively by Captain W. H. W. Wilson, Lieutenants H. H. Clay, and C. M. Crompton-Roberts, and Second Lieutenant R. H. Williams. The Regiment came out on June 10, and on the 14th entrained in the evening at Troy Station for Chatham. The daily parades at Chatham, Saturdays and Sundays excepted, were as follows :—

Clean Fatigue dress, 7 A.M. Orderly officer.
1st Working Parade, 9 A.M. One officer per company.
2nd Working Parade, 2 P.M. ,, ,,
Working parties returned to camp by 5 P.M.
Breakfasts were at 8 A.M., and dinners at 1 P.M.
Companies working at Upnor took their rations with them.
The weather was very warm, and a District Order was issued :—

'During the present summer weather parades should be restricted to the morning and evening hours, at the discretion of the Commanding Officers.' The annual inspection took place on July 15, and on the 17th the Regiment proceeded by special train for Monmouth at 9 P.M.

In September of this year it was notified for information that frocks with pockets would shortly be issued to the troops, but that the men must be absolutely forbidden to unstitch the pockets except on service; and a District Order of September 25 stated that the letter 'M' could be removed from the shoulder straps of non-commissioned officers and men of the Militia of all arms.

The Orders for October 17 contain :—

'The attention of the N.C. Officers and Buglers of the Permanent Staff is drawn to the fact that a Military Exhibition will be held in London about the 1st of May next, the particulars of which will be read out on the next parade. It is most desirable that some exhibits should

KNIFE BAYONET, 1889

be sent from this Regiment, and in order to ascertain whether anything suitable can be produced, it is proposed to invite the Non-commissioned Officers and Buglers of the Permanent Staff and also of the Militia in the neighbourhood of Monmouth who may be willing to prepare something for exhibition to give in their names and join a local competition in the first instance from which the exhibits at the London Exhibition will be selected.

'At the local exhibition the following prizes will be offered, viz.:

	£	s.	d.		£	s.	d.
1st Prize	1	5	0	4th Prize	0	10	0
2nd ,,	1	0	0	5th ,,	0	10	0
3rd ,,	0	15	0				

and any reasonable amount expended by anyone on materials *who does not win a prize* will be paid.

'The Exhibits in preparation will have to be sent into the Orderly Room by November 15 in order to ascertain how many of them are likely to be fit for the London Exhibition, so that application can be made for space, but they need not then be complete. The actual date on which they must be sent in will be communicated later.'

A MILITIA GRENADIER CAP, 1759-1765

CHAPTER XII

THE REGIMENT BETWEEN 1890 AND THE SOUTH AFRICAN WAR

IN September 1890 Colonel F. McDonnell, who had been in command of the Regiment since 1879, retired, and he was succeeded in the command by Major and Honorary Lieutenant-Colonel F. B. Vaughan,[1] who was promoted to the rank of Lieutenant-Colonel on November 15. The vacant majority was filled by the promotion of Captain E. L. Lister on December 13, on which date Lieutenant H. H. Clay was also promoted Captain. Second Lieutenant B. J. W. Wickham resigned his commission on June 14. The officers who joined during the year 1890 were Lieutenant C. J. Helbert Helbert, who had been a lieutenant in the Royal Welsh Fusiliers, and Second Lieutenants F. J. D. McDonnell,[2] C. Bathurst,[3] and W. H. Partridge.[4] Lieutenant C. C. E. Morgan was appointed Instructor of Musketry on February 8.

The recruits of the Regiment in this year assembled on April 21 for forty-two days' Preliminary Drill, the officers doing duty being Lieutenants C. M. Crompton-Roberts and F. H. Green Wilkinson, and Second Lieutenant F. J. D. McDonnell. On May 21 the detachment paraded at 11.30 A.M. in review order to do honour to Her Majesty's birthday.

The Regiment came up for forty-one days' training on June 2 at 12 NOON.

The attention of Officers Commanding companies was called to the fact that a great number of articles of clothing returned to regimental stores, although not time-expired, were found unfit for reissue or to wear the unexpired period. It was notified that this damage

---

[1] Francis Baynham Vaughan, son of Colonel John Francis Vaughan, who commanded the Regiment for many years.

[2] Francis J. D. McDonnell, son of Colonel Francis McDonnell, of Usk, who retired from the command of the Regiment in September 1890, and who was nominated a Companion of the Bath in 1902.

[3] Charles Bathurst, son of Charles Bathurst, of Lydney Park, Gloucestershire, a verderer of the Forest of Dean.

[4] William Hamp Partridge, son of William Bailey Partridge, of Llanfoist, Monmouthshire.

should invariably be charged to the men concerned, who should be warned of their liability to pay, and that in future, should any articles be found to be unduly worn or damaged, the amount of such damage would be charged against the company. It was found that clothing in this condition was usually handed in by men who were not going to be present another training.

It was, moreover, notified that 'breaking into camp' did not constitute an offence under the Army Act, and soldiers were consequently not to be so charged. Thirty-two men were invited during this training to volunteer for the Militia Reserve, and one waiting man per company was allowed in addition to this number. After July 1 passes were only granted up to 11 P.M., and only in very exceptional cases could they be obtained for a longer period. The Commanding Officer drew the attention of officers to the fact that passes were only intended for men of very good character, as a reward for previous good conduct.

The Commanding Royal Engineer inspected the Regiment on July 10 and 11. The men paraded in field-day order at 10 A.M., and at 2.30 P.M. the recruits and Militia Reserve were inspected in fatigue dress in the Castle Square. On July 12 the camp was struck before breakfast.

On October 9 was published an extract from Corps Memorandum No. 584, on the subject of the dress of company sergeant-majors:—

'The following detail as to the order of dress for company sergeant-majors is to be strictly adhered to in time of peace:

'*Rifles.*—To be carried on all occasions when carried by the men.

'*Pouches.*—Two to be worn when the rifle is carried.

'*Valises.*—Not to be carried on marching order parades.

'*Great Coats.*—To be carried on marching order parades, rolled as directed in the "Instructions for Fitting Valise Equipment."

'When a company sergeant-major is doing duty as acting regimental sergeant-major of two or more companies the rifle is not to be carried in time of peace, nor the great coat unless actually required.'

It was notified on November 20 that on and after December 1 the Great Western Railway Company would grant non-commissioned officers and men proceeding on furlough third-class return tickets for single fare upon the booking clerk being shown the pass or furlough testifying that the man was on leave.

The year 1891 did not see very many changes in the officers' ranks. Second Lieutenants E. W. J. P. H. Smythe and R. H. Williams were promoted lieutenants on May 13, as also was Second Lieutenant

F. J. D. McDonnell on June 3. Captain Lord Raglan was granted the honorary rank of Major on August 29. G. M. L. Lamotte joined as Second Lieutenant on March 25. Captain H. E. Morgan Lindsay, late Royal Engineers, who had been Adjutant till November, was appointed a Captain in the Regiment on December 2 ; and Lieutenant T. R. Symons resigned his commission on March 11.

The recruits assembled on April 20 for fifty-six days' Preliminary Drill. The officers doing duty were Lieutenant C. C. E. Morgan and Second Lieutenant F. McDonnell. It was notified for information on April 25 that in the absence of the Commanding Officer the senior officer doing duty was in command of the detachment, and no movements could be ordered, leave granted, or old hands taken on except by him. No officer could be considered as doing duty until he had appeared in orders as being taken on the strength. The recruits' course of musketry commenced on May 19, and was carried out under the direction of Lieutenant C. C. E. Morgan, Instructor of Musketry, who was struck off regimental duty for the purpose. A *feu-de-joie* was fired by the detachment on May 30 to celebrate the Queen's birthday.

The orders for June 10 contain :—

' The second pair of boots will be issued to the recruits and old hands who have been up during the preliminary drill, on Saturday, the 13th inst. N.C.O.s and men to be warned that they are only to be worn on occasions when orders are given by captains of companies—which should only be done when necessary through wet weather. The second pair of boots will be kept in good condition, and during the last week of the training they will be taken into company stores for reissue the following year. Great care is to be observed in booking the number, and company sergeant-majors when taking them into store must so mark them as to be able to identify the second pair from the others.'

The Battalion assembled on June 15 for forty-one days' training under Lieut.-Colonel F. B. Vaughan. The recruits and recruit officers proceeded to Pwll-Holm for work, and the remainder were left at the disposal of company officers for the purpose of drawing arms and company drill.

On July 6 it was ordered that, out of respect to the memory of Captain and Honorary Major W. H. H. W. Wilson, who had died at Ilfracombe, officers wear crêpe in accordance with the Queen's Regulations on all occasions when in uniform during the remainder of the training. On July 21 the death occurred of Captain R. C. Hanbury-Williams, and a firing-party under command of Captain W. B. M. Jackson proceeded to Abergavenny on July 24 to take part in the funeral ceremony.

Captain Morgan Lindsay, before relinquishing the Adjutancy, placed on record an appreciation of the services of the Permanent Staff in these words :—

'*November* 13, 1891.—Before giving up his appointment as Adjutant of the Royal Monmouthshire Engineer Militia, Captain H. E. M. Lindsay, R.E., wishes to return his best thanks to Sergeant-Major Wood and the N.C.O.s and Bugles of the Permanent Staff, whose cordial co-operation has made his term of service with them, to him, such a very pleasant one.'

Captain Morgan Lindsay was succeeded as Adjutant by Captain C. D. Learoyd, R.E., who took up his duties on November 14.

In 1892 Lieutenant C. M. Crompton-Roberts was promoted captain on May 14, and Second Lieutenants C. Bathurst, W. H. Partridge, and G. M. L. Lamotte were promoted lieutenants in June. Lieutenant E. J. B. Buckley resigned in April, and the new officers consisted of C. J. Vaughan,[1] Viscount Southwell, and Hon. H. A. Rolls.[2]

Attention was directed in May to the Militia Regulations, 1891, as amended by 'General Amendments,' 1892. Under those Amendments the annual bounty was not paid to Militiamen who on the assembly of their regiment were found to be suffering from disease, certified to have been brought about by their own action, and who had been discharged as temporarily or permanently unfit for duty.

A Militiaman who during any portion of the recruit or preliminary drill or training was in hospital on account of disability which was certified to have been brought about by his own action, was subject to a stoppage from the bounty payable to him for that training at the rate of 8*d*. a day for each day that he was in hospital.

The usual parade of the detachment was held on May 25, at 10.30, for the purpose of celebrating the Queen's birthday. The Regiment did not come out for training until June 20.

A District Order of June 30 states :—

'On the days of nomination and election of Members of Parliament at places in this district, no N.C. officer or soldier is to be allowed to go out of barracks or quarters, unless for the purpose of mounting and relieving guard or giving his vote at the election; and every N.C. officer and

---

[1] Charles Jerome Vaughan, son of Colonel Francis Baynham Vaughan.
[2] Honble. Henry Allan Rolls, son of Lord Llangattock.

man so allowed to go out must return to his quarters with all convenient speed as soon as his vote has been tendered.'

July 7 being election day, no soldier was allowed to leave camp. All men whose names were on the register of voters for the borough of Monmouth were required to give in their names to their company sergeant-majors the previous evening, and at 8.30 A.M. on the morning of the election they were marched to the poll to record their votes.

The inspection this year was made by Colonel R. W. Stewart, R.E., Commanding Royal Engineer, Western District, on July 27 and 28.

In 1893 Lieutenant C. J. Helbert Helbert was promoted captain in September, and Second Lieutenants F. J. Lawrence, C. J. Vaughan, and Viscount Southwell were promoted lieutenants. R. J. S. Price joined the Regiment as a Second Lieutenant on April 14.

The recruits assembled for fifty-six days' Preliminary Drill on April 10, and the officers present were Captain F. H. Green Wilkinson, Lieutenants C. Bathurst, F. J. D. McDonnell, and C. J. Helbert Helbert, and Second Lieutenants Viscount Southwell, Hon. H. A. Rolls, and R. J. S. Price.

Prizes for good shooting were this year awarded to recruits as follows:—

Individual Prizes—

	s.	d.
To the best shot of recruits	8	0
To the best shot in each company	4	0
To the second best shot in each company	2	0

Section Prizes—

	s.	d.
To the section with the highest percentage at volley firing	12	0
To the section with the highest percentage at independent firing	12	0

Any balance of the musketry grant remaining after the above distribution was paid to the best shot in the individual attack practice.

The training of the Regiment took place this year at Chatham. An advance party under the command of Captain C. M. Crompton-Roberts proceeded from Troy Station on June 3 at 8.30 A.M.

On the day before their departure they paraded for inspection at 9 A.M. in marching order, with kit bags. It was notified that every Militiaman must hand in his plain clothes to his company sergeant-major, as no man would be allowed out of barracks, on the morning that the Regiment was dismissed, for the purpose of bringing his clothing from any place in the town. A list of men who had not handed in their clothing was made out, and clothing was purchased for them out of the bounty they would have been entitled to on the termination of the training. This order was read out on three successive parades.

The Regiment paraded in marching order in the Castle Square at 6.45 A.M. on June 8, and left Troy Station at 8 A.M. by special train for Chatham. Before marching to the station, captains told off their companies by sections of *four files*, numbering from the right of sections, a N.C.O., as far as possible, being included in each section, who was in charge of the section in the train. All corporals fell in in the ranks. An officer was detailed to mark the carriages for each company. He marked the first compartment for a guard, the next five for the band and buglers. The last three compartments of the train were left vacant for guard, prisoners, and sick. This officer was accompanied by a marker from each company, and he placed the markers facing the train opposite the rearmost compartment that would be occupied by their companies.

Officers commanding companies were required to furnish to the orderly room by 6 P.M. the previous night the number of men in their companies who would be going. The men were marched on to the platform in sections of fours, halted opposite their own carriages, and ordered to get in, take off their valises, place them under the seats, and lay their rifles, with sight-protectors on, in the racks. They were warned to have their packs on ready to detrain at Chatham, and that a meal would be provided for them at Swindon at about 10.30 A.M. On arrival at Swindon, officers detrained and went to the carriages occupied by their companies, and the 'Halt' was sounded, when the men left the train. When it was time to proceed, the 'Close' was sounded, on which the men re-entered their carriages, the officers reporting all present to the Commanding Officer.

The routine at Chatham consisted of—

Réveille	6 A.M.
Drill Parade (clean fatigue dress, with rifles without slings)	7 A.M.
Rations	7.30 A.M.
Breakfasts	8 A.M.
Working Parade	9 A.M.
Guard Mounting	9.15 A.M.

Orderly Room	9.30 A.M.
Dinners	1 P.M.
Second Working Parade	2 P.M. until 4.30 P.M.
Pay	4.30 P.M.
Retreat as per Garrison Orders.	
First Post	9.30 P.M.
Tattoo	10 P.M.

Saturday afternoon was assigned for the bathing parade of the Royal Monmouthshire Militia. The General Officer Commanding directed that during these parades instruction in swimming should be given, and a list of swimmers was required to be furnished by officers commanding companies on June 26.

The Battalion was inspected in marching order on June 23 by the Inspector-General of Fortifications, and on July 12 by the Major-General commanding the district. A terrific storm was raging at the time, and much of the clothing did not get properly dry before the end of the training, and was thus spoilt. On July 14 the Battalion paraded at 8.30 P.M. in marching order, and left Chatham Station at 10 P.M. for Monmouth. On arrival at Monmouth a breakfast consisting of bread and meat with beer was drawn by officers commanding companies for issue to the men. All clothing and equipment was immediately afterwards handed in, and the men's accounts finally settled; those men whose homes were at or beyond Pontypool Road were marched to the station in time to entrain in a special train leaving Monmouth (Troy Station) at 10 A.M. This train did not stop until it arrived at Pontypool Road. The remainder of the men living away from Monmouth were sent off by the ordinary trains as soon afterwards as possible.

In 1894 there were four new officers: C. T. Kemeys-Tynte,[1] H. M. Vaughan,[2] R. H. Edwards, and E. D. M. H. Cook, and in September Major W. E. C. Curre was granted the honorary rank of Lieutenant-Colonel.

Instructions were issued from the Horse Guards on January 31 to the effect that no Militia recruit was to be enlisted who gave for his address a common lodging-house, except in the case of a man who wished to enlist with a view to qualifying for the Line.

---

[1] Charles Theodore Halswell Kemeys-Tynte, son of Halswell Milborne Kemeys-Tynte, of Cefn Mabli, Glamorganshire.

[2] Herbert Millingchamp Vaughan, son of John Vaughan, of Plás Llangoedmore, Cardigan.

The Preliminary Drill of fifty-six days commenced on April 23, and Lieutenant G. M. L. Lamotte acted as Musketry Instructor. Prizes for shooting were allotted to the recruits as follows:—

	s.	d.
To the best shot of the recruits	6	0
To the best shot in each company	3	0
To the second best shot in each company	1	6
To the section with the highest percentage at volley and independent firing	16	0

The Regiment assembled for forty-two days' training on June 18. During this training the band was detailed to play at the following places:—

Day of the Week	Place	Time
Monday	Camp	4.30 to 5.30 P.M.
Tuesday	Officers' Mess	Dinner
Wednesday	Camp	4.30 to 5.30 P.M.
Thursday	Agincourt Square	6 to 7 P.M.
Friday	Officers' Mess	Dinner
Saturday	Cricket Match	3.30 to 5 P.M.

Major W. E. C. Curre being absent on leave from the training, Captain W. F. Batt acted as Major and Lieutenant C. Bathurst commanded No. 5 Company. Lieutenant-General Sir R. Harrison, K.C.B., commanding the Western District, arrived at Monmouth on July 5 and inspected the Regiment the next day.

The following Horse Guards letter, dated July 14, 1894, was published for information during the training:—

'It having been brought to the notice of the Commander-in-Chief that very lenient sentences have in many instances been passed by courts-martial on absentees from the Militia, although it might naturally have been inferred from Horse Guards letter of February 13 last, in which directions were given for these men to be tried by Court-Martial instead of by Civil Power, that a too lenient view of this crime, which is at present so prevalent, had been taken by the magistrates in dealing with it.

'I have the honour by desire of His Royal Highness to point out that if such sentences as one or two days' imprisonment with hard labour are given, which have been done on several occasions lately, the hoped for result of diminishing this offence cannot possibly be realised.'

On July 26 the Battalion paraded in review order for inspection by

Colonel R. W. Stewart, R.E., the Commanding Royal Engineer, Western District.

Colonel F. B. Vaughan relinquished the command of the Regiment on January 2, 1895, and he was succeeded by Major and Honorary Lieutenant-Colonel W. E. C. Curre, who was promoted Lieutenant-Colonel on February 6 and granted the honorary rank of Colonel on May 29. The vacant majority was filled by the promotion of Captain and Honorary Major Lord Raglan on May 29, who, on October 23, was granted the honorary rank of Lieutenant-Colonel. Other changes among the officers in 1895 consisted of the promotion to Captain of Lieutenant E. W. J. P. H. Smythe, the resignations of Lieutenants W. H. Partridge and F. J. Lawrence, the death of Captain W. F. Batt in October, and the promotion of Second-Lieutenants Honble. H. A. Rolls, R. J. S. Price, and C. T. H. Kemeys-Tynte. The only gentleman who joined this year was R. L. Matthews.

The recruits of the Regiment who had enlisted since July 28, 1894, commenced their fifty-six days' Preliminary Drill on April 22. The officers present were Lieutenants Viscount Southwell and E. W. J. P. H. Smythe and Second-Lieutenants E. D. M. H. Cooke, R. J. S. Price, C. T. H. Kemeys-Tynte, R. H. Edwards, and R. L. Matthews. His Royal Highness the Commander-in-Chief having directed that all officers should make themselves acquainted with the manner of judging the quality of the bread and meat rations for issue to the troops, officers were instructed to provide themselves with a copy of 'Guide to Meat Inspection.'

It was published in orders on April 29 that the Militia Rifle Association had awarded the second prize for the best eight recruits in 1894 to the Royal Monmouthshire Militia.

A lecture was given at the Rolls Hall, Monmouth, on the evening of May 23 by Lieutenant-Colonel Hon. C. Dutton on 'A Soldier's Life.' All non-commissioned officers and men of the Regiment were invited to attend.

The Regiment having assembled for forty-one days' training on June 17, on July 3 General Sir Richard Harrison, Commanding the Western District, arrived at Monmouth and inspected the Field Works and buildings, and visited the Musketry Camp the same afternoon. On the following day the whole Battalion paraded at 9.15 A.M., and was formed up in line at open order on the saluting base at 10 A.M. The official inspection was made on July 24 and 25 by Colonel Bell, V.C., R.E., Commanding Royal Engineer, Western District. He inspected the books

COLONEL WILLIAM EDWARD CARNE CURRIE.
Commanded the Regiment 1895–1901

at 12.30 P.M. on the 24th, and the Field Works on the afternoon of the same day. On the 25th the Regiment paraded at 10.15 A.M. in review order. Afterwards the camp was visited and an inspection was made of the men of the Militia Reserve.

In 1896 Lieutenant Hon. H. A. Rolls resigned. Quartermaster and Honorary Lieutenant G. Tucker was promoted Honorary Captain on April 4, on which date Captain Hon. G. W. R. Somerset was granted the honorary rank of Major. The gentlemen who joined were R. S. Forestier-Walker [1] and P. O. C. Saunders.

A District Order of May 14 states : ' In consequence of the prevalence of smallpox in the district, the annual training of the Royal Monmouth Engineer Militia has been cancelled for the present year.' The non-commissioned officers and buglers serving on the permanent staff were directed to proceed to the dispensary of Surgeon T. G. Prosser for re-vaccination. The wives and families on the married establishment were also asked to be vaccinated by the medical officer, without cost, at their own option.

It was notified on August 11 that the designation of the Regiment had been changed and that in future it would be known as the Royal Monmouthshire Royal Engineers (Militia). It was given out in the same month that the Royal Engineers should follow the exercises laid down for Rifle Regiments in the 'Manual of Rifle and Carbine Exercises, 1896.' On relinquishing the adjutancy in December, Captain Learoyd placed in Orders :—

'On relinquishing the adjutancy of the Royal Monmouthshire Royal Engineers Militia, it gives Captain Learoyd great pleasure to place on record the exemplary conduct of the whole of the Permanent Staff during the term of his appointment. He cannot leave the Regiment without expressing his gratitude to the Regimental Sergeant-Major, the Quartermaster-Sergeant, the Bandmaster, the N.C.O.s and buglers, Company-Sergeant-Major Burnett, and the Orderly Room Staff, for the help they have always so willingly given him, and in bidding them " Good-bye " he feels sure that they will extend the same assistance to his successor.'

Captain Learoyd was succeeded in the adjutancy by Captain G. H. Bland, R.E., who was appointed on December 8.

Special efforts were made to procure recruits at the close of the year 1896.

[1] Roland Stuart Forestier-Walker, son of Sir George Forestier-Walker, second baronet.

The company sergeant-majors and sergeants of the Permanent Staff were instructed to make special efforts in this direction in Monmouth and the neighbouring towns and villages. For this purpose parties were detailed to visit outlying villages weekly, commencing Monday, December 14. All men of 5 foot 5 inches and upwards were to be enlisted for the Regiment. Those from 5 foot 3 inches to 5 foot 5 inches in height were to be enlisted for the South Wales Borderers. The non-commissioned officers on recruiting duty took with them posters and leaflets for distribution in all the villages through which they passed.

Promotions were made as follows during 1897:—

January 20, Lieutenant F. J. D. McDonnell to Captain.

January 20, Second Lieutenant H. M. Vaughan to Lieutenant.

January 20, Second Lieutenant E. W. M. H. Cooke to Lieutenant.

June 21, Captain and Honorary Major Hon. G. W. R. Somerset to Major.

June 21, Lieutenant C. Bathurst to Captain.

June 21, Second Lieutenant R. L. Matthews to Lieutenant.

Second Lieutenants R. H. Edwards and G. D. W. Rooke resigned their commissions early in the year, while the new officers were G. B. Ollivant, W. A. D. Galloway, Hon. W. McClintock-Bunbury, and C. F. J. Galloway.

The Preliminary Drill extended from April 26 to June 20, and the Regiment came out from June 21 to July 31. Lord Raglan was in command during the early portion of the training, Colonel Curre being away on leave. The lack of training during the previous year had had a bad effect on the men, and many were sentenced to cells for insubordination.

Early in the year regulations were framed as to the duties of the Permanent Staff in case of fire at or near the Castle. They were:—

'In case of a fire at the Castle or within 200 yards to windward of the same of a serious nature, likely to involve the safety of the arms, clothing, mess premises, &c., the senior resident member of the Permanent Staff will at once:

'(a) Send to the quarters of the nearest bugler with orders to sound the alarm in the neighbourhood of the non-resident N.C.O.s of the Permanent Staff.

'(b) Ring the Fire Bell at St. Mary's Church.

'(c) Warn the Adjutant, Orderly Sergeant, and any of the Permanent Staff within a quarter of a mile of the Castle.

'(*d*) Return to the Castle for further orders.

'The Senior N.C.O. at the Castle will :—

'(*a*) Turn off the gas from the meter at the first alarm.

'(*b*) Warn, and if necessary remove all the inmates from the Castle.

'(*c*) Take the Keys from the Keyboard in the entrance, open the stores, and see to the removal to a place of safety by the Permanent Staff of all arms and Government property that are in danger of damage by fire or water, and will mount a sentry on same.

'(*d*) Mount a N.C.O. on guard at the entrance of the Castle Square with orders to prevent the entry of unauthorised persons.

'(*e*) Uncover the hydrant in front of the Castle and get the key ready.

'(*f*) Unlock the chains on the ladders and prepare the latter for use if required.

'(*g*) Remove the ammunition from the magazine if in danger.

'As the members of the Permanent Staff arrive at the Castle after being warned, they will report to the senior present and be told off under his orders to assist where required.

'Should the fire be of a really serious nature, a bugler is to be sent to warn the Quartermaster and another to collect any absent members of the Permanent Staff.

'The public are not to be admitted to the Castle Square, except a limited number of known persons who volunteer their services for help with fire buckets, hose, or fire engine.

'The following tools are to be kept on the premises in charge of the Quartermaster for use in case of fire :—

Two Felling Axes	Four Pair Hedging Gloves.
Six Hand Axes.	Two Ropes 2 in. or $2\frac{1}{2}$ in. (about
Four Pick Axes.	15 fathoms).'

In March three hundred recruits were required for the Regiment, and every effort was made to procure them, almost every town and village in the area being visited.

Some amendments were made to the Drill Book this year, such as: 'A battery will open fire with shell and percussion fuze to find the range, and then change to time fuze. Should a pause occur when changing fuzes, it will give an excellent opportunity for infantry to push in.'

Instructions were issued as to the procedure for revolver practice :—

'All officers, non-commissioned officers, and men armed with revolvers in time of war are to be instructed in the drill and practice, firing twenty-four rounds (cavalry will fire forty-eight rounds). Blank firing will be previously carried out as follows :

'Cavalry, ten rounds single practice, mounted;

'Cavalry, ten rounds continuous practice, mounted.

Royal Artillery . . . ⎫
Royal Engineers . . ⎬ Five rounds single practice, mounted.
Army Service Corps and ⎥ Five rounds continuous practice, mounted.
Regimental Transport . ⎭

'*Dismounted*.—Each man will be individually called to the front by the superintending officer : he will load and fire six shots single practice with the right hand, and six shots single practice with the left hand, He will then return to his original position before the next man is called to the front. Continuous practice will afterwards take place in a similar manner.

'*Mounted—Cavalry only*.—The procedure will be as above, excepting that twelve rounds single and twelve rounds continuous practice will be fired with the right hand only. At all practices every possible precaution is to be taken against accidents, the strictest order and discipline being maintained at the firing point.'

Any officers who wished to do duty with the 3rd Welsh Regiment during its annual training at Aldershot from August 9 to September 11 were invited on July 12 to forward their names to the Orderly Room without delay. Confidential Orders as to the action to be taken on receipt of orders to ' Mobilise ' were issued the same day to all concerned. Officers were thoroughly to acquaint themselves with these orders, and to see that they were understood by all ranks of their commands. Officers commanding companies were required to retain in their possession the orders for N.C.O.s and men of their companies, after having explained the same to them.

The company next for duty was required to furnish daily a sergeant to be detailed for regimental duty as sergeant on duty in one of the half-battalion dining sheds during all meals.

The Regimental Orderly Sergeant was to perform a similar duty in the other half-battalion shed, to always take charge of the shed to which his half-battalion belonged, and the other sergeant detailed was to take charge of the other dining shed.

The duties of these N.C.O.s were :—

First to be present during meal time, and

Second, to see that order and discipline were maintained among the men during meal time, and that the sheds were kept tidy and clean during their tour of duty. During the absence of the Orderly Sergeant on this duty the Regimental Orderly Corporal acted for him.

The General Officer Commanding the Western District inspected the Regiment early in July, and on the 29th and 30th of the same month Colonel M. S. Bell, V.C., C.B., A.D.C., Commanding Royal Engineer of the district, made the official annual inspection.

On the 29th he inspected the books in the billiard room at 12.45. Each officer was required to bring with him the latest edition of the following books :—

1. 'Queen's Regulations';
2. 'Infantry Drill';
3. 'Manual of Elementary Field Engineering';

and officers in command of companies produced their company books, including Pay and Mess Books and Pay Lists.

The Battalion paraded for field works at 2 P.M., all officers attending.

The Inspecting Officer visited the rifle range and made his inspection of the field works at Pwll-Holm during the afternoon.

On Friday, the 30th inst., guard mounting was at 6 A.M., and there was no 7 A.M. parade that day.

The Battalion paraded for inspection by Colonel M. S. Bell, formed up in the Drill Field at 10.30 A.M.

Three captains resigned their commissions during the year 1898: F. H. Green Wilkinson on March 23, C. Bathurst on April 20, and E. W. J. P. H. Smythe on August 10. Two captains were brought into the Regiment: J. G. O'Brien from the 4th Battalion Shropshire Light Infantry on March 28, and A. Leetham, late of the 13th Hussars, on September 3, the latter of whom was granted the honorary rank of Major on October 12. The promotions were Lieutenants C. J. Vaughan and G. M. L. Lamotte to be Captains, and Second-Lieutenants R. S. Walker, G. B. Ollivant, and W. A. D. Galloway to be Lieutenants. The gentlemen who joined during the year were K. E. Digby, G. M. Lindsay, W. A. Kennard, and H. Lewis. Lieutenant R. J. S. Price was appointed Instructor of Musketry in succession to Lieutenant G. M. L. Lamotte.

Recruiting was carried on vigorously again this year, and Recruiters were sent out in all directions.

Non-Commissioned Officers on recruiting duty were instructed to be careful to explain to any Volunteers who desired to enlist into the Regiment that they enlisted for the Militia subject to the conditions stated on the Notice Paper given to Militia Recruits. Before such men were enlisted they had to resign from the Volunteers and hand into Store their Volunteer clothing and equipment, and also obtain a statement from the Volunteer Instructor that these conditions had been complied with.

This statement had to be shown to the Recruiter, and was retained by him for reference if required.

In places where or within two miles of which there was no Military Medical Officer the recruit was examined by the Recruiting Officer, or the Recruiter, and if found to be without apparent deformity, of good eyesight when tested by the dot card, and up to the standard of height (5 feet 5 inches) and chest measurement (33 inches), the attestation was proceeded with.

In May was published in Orders :—

'The attention of all concerned is invited to the proclamation of neutrality dated *London Gazette*, April 26, 1898, to be observed during the war between Spain and the United States of America; the directions therein laid down will be strictly complied with.'

The Regiment encamped this year at Chatham.

Advance parties proceeded as follows :—

Fifty rank-and-file under the command of Captain G. M. L. Lamotte and Second Lieutenant Hon. W. McClintock Bunbury on May 16.

Two hundred and fifty rank-and-file commanded by Lieutenant-Colonel Lord Raglan on May 23.

The following officers proceeded with this detachment :—

Lieutenant C. J. Vaughan.

Lieutenant Viscount Southwell.

Second Lieutenant K. E. Digby.

Second Lieutenant G. M. Lindsay.

The Headquarters of the Regiment proceeded to Chatham on the 26th.

A prize was awarded to the best turned out man on the 8.30 A.M. parade for the first Advance Party for Chatham. The distribution of officers at Chatham was :

No. 1 Company.—Captain C. C. E. Morgan, Viscount Southwell, and Second Lieutenant W. A. D. Galloway.

No. 2 Company.—Captain E. W. Smythe, Lieutenant R. S. Forestier-Walker, and Second Lieutenant C. F. J. Galloway.

No. 3 Company.—Captain C. M. Crompton-Roberts and Lieutenant R. L. Matthews.

No. 4 Company.—Captain C. J. Helbert Helbert and Lieutenant C. T. H. Kemeys-Tynte.

No. 5 Company.—Captain C. J. Vaughan and Second Lieutenant Hon. W. McClintock Bunbury.

No. 6 Company.—Captain J. G. O'Brien and Lieutenant R. J. S. Price.

No. 7 Company.—Captain G. M. L. Lamotte, Lieutenant E. D. M. Cooke, and Second Lieutenant G. M. Lindsay.

No. 8 Company.—Captain (Hon. Major) H. E. M. Lindsay, Lieutenant G. B. Ollivant, and Second Lieutenant K. E. Digby.

On June 13 the officers attended the levée held by her Majesty in London.

Major L. C. Jackson, R.E., gave a course of lectures to the officers of the Regiment, commencing on June 10. They were given in the Lecture Theatre of the R.E. Institute. For several days an officers' class for sword exercise was held in the gymnasium between 7 and 8 A.M.

Miss Daniell's Soldiers' Institute at Chatham was placed at the disposal of the men of the Regiment, who were able to find there reading, recreation, bath, and billiard rooms.

A confidential lecture was given in the Lecture Theatre, R.E. Institute, on June 23, on the 5-inch howitzers against earthworks. The Commander-in-Chief was present, and officers in the district were invited to attend in drill order. Afterwards the Commander-in-Chief inspected at Chatham, and saw the Thames defences on June 23 and 24.

The annual inspection took place on Wednesday, June 29, the inspecting officer being Major-General T. Fraser, C.B., C.M.G., commanding the Thames District. Books were shown in the anteroom of the officers' mess at 9.30 A.M.

Officers and staff-sergeants paraded for sword exercise after book inspection.

The Battalion was inspected in drill order on the Great Lines at 11.30 A.M. Tents and kits were inspected next, and the inspecting officer saw the Battalion at field works in the afternoon.

The Regiment proceeded from Chatham for Monmouth by two special trains on July 1. The right half-battalion left Chatham at 9.20 P.M. and arrived at Monmouth at 4.45 A.M. on July 2. The left half-battalion left thirty-five minutes later.

In 1899 there were not many changes in the officers' ranks, perhaps on account of the war in South Africa, which commenced in October of that year. Lieutenant H. M. Vaughan resigned on May 10, Second Lieutenant

Hon. W. McClintock-Bunbury joined the 2nd Dragoons, and Lieutenants E. D. M. H. Cooke and G. B. Ollivant joined the Royal Garrison Artillery and 12th Lancers respectively. Captain C. J. Helbert Helbert was granted the honorary rank of Major on July 19, and the gentlemen who joined during the year were N. W. F. Baynes, B. H. Williams, J. L. Mansel, and N. J. Lyon; the last named, having previously served in the Grenadier Guards, joined on June 12, but the entry in the *Gazette* was cancelled on the 27th of the same month at the officer's own request.

At the commencement of the Preliminary Drill the companies were commanded by the following officers :—

'A' Company (Nos. 1 and 2) by Major A. Leetham.
'B' Company (Nos. 3 and 4) by Lieutenant Viscount Southwell.
'C' Company (Nos. 5 and 6) by Lieutenant R. J. S. Price.
'D' Company (Nos. 7 and 8) by Captain G. M. L. Lamotte.

The weekly detail of Preliminary Drill was :—

Two weeks April 17 to April 29. Squad and company drills, rifle exercise, and physical training.

One week, May 1 to May 8. Squad and company drill and field works as per programme, mornings to 1.30; battalion drill in afternoons, 3.30 ditto.

One week, May 8 to May 13. Ditto.

One week, May 15 to May 20. Three days' field work and drill as above.

One week, May 22 to 27. Six days' musketry preliminary drill.

One week, May 29 to June 3. Six days' musketry target practice.

One week, June 5 to June 10. Two days' musketry, one day field works, three days returning stores and pitching camp.

On June 2 a tactical scheme was carried out by the detachment at the Hendre, the general idea being : 'A force advancing from Abergavenny is reported to have occupied the Hendre and to be preparing a defensive position there, covered by outposts. Orders are received to reconnoitre the position, ascertain its strength, and if not in superior force attack the enemy in position.'

The Regiment assembled for forty-one days' training on Monday, June 12, when the following was the distribution of officers :—

No. 1 Company.—Captain C. C. E. Morgan, Lieutenant Viscount Southwell, Second Lieutenant W. A. Kennard.

No. 2 Company.—Captain and Hon. Major A. Leetham, Lieutenant R. S. Forestier-Walker, Second Lieutenant B. H. Williams.

No. 3 Company.—Captain C. M. Crompton-Roberts, Lieutenant R. L. Matthews, Second Lieutenant C. F. J. Galloway.

No. 4 Company.—Captain C. J. Helbert Helbert, Lieutenant G. B. Ollivant, Second Lieutenant H. Lewis.

No. 5 Company.—Captain C. J. Vaughan, Second Lieutenant N. W. F. Baynes.

No. 6 Company.—Captain J. G. O'Brien, Lieutenant R. J. S. Price, Second Lieutenant J. L. Mansel.

No. 7 Company.—Captain G. M. L. Lamotte, Lieutenant W. A. D. Galloway.

No. 8 Company.—Captain and Hon. Major H. E. M. Lindsay, Second Lieutenant K. E. Digby.

On Monday, July 17, a further field day was arranged, when the following were the general and special ideas:—

General Idea.—(1) ' A "Red Force" advancing on Ross and Abergavenny *via* Monmouth and the Hendre, is opposed by a "Blue Force" occupying a defensive position at the Hendre covered by outposts.'

(2) 'Operations to be confined to the area within the Hendre Deer Park.'

Special Idea (Blue Force).—' The R.M.R.E. (M) strength about 500 of all ranks, representing the advanced guard of a brigade moving from Abergavenny to Monmouth, on arrival at the Hendre receives information that a division of the enemy is advancing from Ross on Abergavenny *via* the Hendre. The advanced guard of the enemy, represented by the 6th Battalion Royal Warwickshire Regiment, strength about 650 of all ranks, is reported to have reached Monmouth. Orders are received to take up a defensive position on the ridge between the Yew Tree Cottage and Bowling Green Wood. Three hours are supposed to be available for work on the position, which is to be held to the last and every effort made to prevent the advance of the enemy.

'An outpost line to be thrown out, extending from Caxton Tower on the right to Survey Mark (433) on the left, so as to watch the approaches from Rockfield and Monmouth, and give timely notice to the main body at the Hendre of the approach and distribution of the enemy.'

The annual inspection was made by Colonel W. R. Purchas, R.E., Commanding Royal Engineer, Western District, on July 19 and 20.

The inspecting officer arrived at Monmouth on Tuesday evening.

On Wednesday, July 19, at 10 A.M., was held the inspection of the books in the billiard room at the Castle, and at 12 NOON the Battalion was formed up ready for inspection in the Drill Field. The inspecting officer heard any complaints, and saw the men of the Militia Reserve on the return of the Regiment to camp. The men of the Militia Reserve were for this purpose formed up on the reverse flank of their companies. At 3.30 P.M. the Battalion was formed up in the Drill Field in drill order, for inspection in company drill, ceremonial and manœuvre, under captains and subalterns, and the inspecting officer visited the camp after this parade.

On Thursday, July 20, the Battalion paraded in working dress at 9 A.M. for field work. The inspecting officer saw the companies at field works at Pwll-Holm, commencing at 10 A.M.

On July 21 was circulated :—

'The inspecting officer wishes to express to Colonel Curre, commanding the Regiment, and to the officers, non-commissioned officers, and men of the R.M.R.E. (M), his entire satisfaction with the efficiency and steadiness of the Regiment in drill and field works. This order to be placed on record in the Regimental Order Book for the information of all ranks.'

MILITIA MEDAL—STRUCK DECEMBER 1904.

PRELIMINARY DRILLS DURING FIRST WEEK'S TRAINING.

Day	Time	Subject	Sections
Monday	4 P.M.	Assembly [1]	..
Tuesday	9.15 to 9.30	General Parade [2]	..
,,	9.30 to 10	Squad Drill	1 to 7
,,	10 to 10.30	Ditto	1 to 7
,,	11.30 to 12	Extension Motions [3]	8
,,	12 to 12.30	Squad Drill	1 to 13
,,	2.30 to 3	Extension Motions [4]	8
,,	3 to 3.30	Squad Drill	1 to 13
,,	4 to 5	Ditto [5]	1 to 13
Wednesday	9.15 to 9.30	General Parade	..
,,	9.30 to 10	Extension Motions [6]	8
,,	10 to 10.30	Squad Drill	1 to 13
,,	11.30 to 12.30	Ditto	1 to 22
,,	2.30 to 3	Physical Exercises	45 (14)
,,	3 to 3.30	Squad Drill	9 to 22
,,	4 to 5	Ditto	9 to 22
Thursday	9.15 to 9.30	General Parade	..
,,	9.30 to 10	Physical Training [7]	46 (14)
,,	10 to 10.30	Squad Drill	1 to 22
,,	11.30 to 12.30	Ditto	22 to 33
,,	2.30 to 3	Extension Motions	46 (15)
,,	3 to 3.30	Squad Drill	22 to 33
,,	4 to 5	Ditto	1 to 33
Friday	9.15 to 9.30	General Parade	..
,,	9.30 to 10	Physical Training	46 (14)
,,	10 to 10.30	Squad Drill	1 to 22
,,	11.30 to 12.30	Ditto	22 to 45
,,	2.30 to 3	Extension Motions	46 (15)
,,	3 to 3.30	Squad Drill	45
,,	4 to 5	Ditto	1 to 45
Saturday	9.15 to 9.30	General Parade	..
,,	9.30 to 10	Physical Training	46 (14)
,,	10 to 10.30	Squad Drill [8]	23 to 33
,,	11.30 to 12.30	Ditto	35 to 45
,,	2.30 to 3.30	Marching [9] and saluting in 'walking out' dress.[10]	

Remarks.

1. Read Orders and General Instructions. Pay.
2. General Parade daily at 9.15. Companies fall in at 9.10. Dinners daily, 12.30 to 2.30. Pay daily after last Parade.
3. All instruction to be as varied as possible, so as to include each subject.
4. Men not to be kept too long at attention or any one exercise.
5. By repeating former exercises it will be easy to vary them.
6. In the event of wet weather preventing instruction on the square, companies will be marched to dining sheds and markets and receive general instruction and lectures in accordance with Appendix 13, Infantry Drill, for first and second weeks.
7. Physical training. Stationary exercises only during this week. Section 46 (14 and 15). Sticks will be provided for use as dummy rifles.
8. Recruit officers will fall in and be instructed with their own companies.
9. Drum and Plummet to attend all marching drill. Bandmaster to arrange accordingly and for Band to attend. 2.30 Parade on Saturday.
10. General instruction on Saturday to include dress and behaviour in church. Duty of soldiers to assist Picquet and Police if required. Cleanliness of person, accoutrements, and clothing.

CHAPTER XIII

THE REGIMENT IN SOUTH AFRICA AND DURING EMBODIMENT AT HOME

THE month of October 1899 had seen the commencement of the war in South Africa—a long and perhaps inglorious struggle which was not concluded until May 1902.

The total British Force engaged amounted to 448,435; that of the Boers approximately to 75,000. Of the British Force 5,744 were killed in action, 22,829 were wounded, and 16,168 died of wounds or disease in South Africa. The total cost of the campaign was about 223,000,000*l*.

Owing to the large number of troops required at the seat of war, it was found necessary to embody the Militia early in the campaign, and many regiments proceeded to South Africa, while others did garrison duty in the Mediterranean, relieving Regular regiments required for service at the front. The Yeomanry and Volunteers also proceeded in large numbers to the war. There was much useful fighting material furnished by the Auxiliary Forces, until methods of recruiting were adopted by which raw and unsuitable men were sent in numbers to satisfy public clamour.

Some remarks on the services of the Royal Monmouthshire Royal Engineers during those critical months, will at this juncture be of interest. The *London Gazette* of February 13, 1900, contains: 'Her Majesty has been graciously pleased to accept the voluntary offer made by the undermentioned section of the Royal Engineers Militia and by embodied battalions to serve at stations out of the United Kingdom, viz. a section of the Royal Monmouthshire Royal Engineers Militia.'

The services of the section were accepted for duty with the Bridging Battalion, Royal Engineers, on active service in South Africa. It assembled at Monmouth on February 26, and consisted of the following officer, non-commissioned officers, and men:—

Lieutenant R. S. Forestier-Walker, 1 Company
No. 9377 Sergeant A. Freeman, 1 Company
,, 1757 Corporal W. Gaston, 5 Company

THE REGIMENT IN SOUTH AFRICA AND AT HOME

No. 2213 Second Corporal T. Llewellyn, 2 Company
" 1781 Sapper W. Cleary, 6 Company
" 1187 " W. Chard, 7 Company
" 9698 " W. Panting, 6 Company
" 1851 " E. Brickley, 1 Company
" 1665 " A. Jenkins, 1 Company
" 1863 " W. Dixon, 8 Company
" 728 " J. Tobin, 7 Company
" 781 " J. Collins, 5 Company
" 771 " W. Padmore, 3 Company
" 1678 " C. Cronin, 3 Company
" 1820 " W. Brown, 5 Company
" 2668 " S. Jeremy, 3 Company
" 1736 " D. Davies, 5 Company
" 1026 " G. Edy, 2 Company
" 1819 " J. Jenkins, 7 Company
" 2003 " W. Baldwin, 5 Company
" 2120 " W. H. Milson, 1 Company
" 1785 " W. Rowan, 4 Company
" 1514 " M. Connor, 4 Company
" 103 " J. Thomas, 8 Company

The following men were rejected as unfit for active service, not being up to the standard of physique for the Bridging Battalion R.E. :—

No. 1441 Sapper E. Hogan, 2 Company
" 1062 " J. Smith, 4 Company
" 1944 " J. Reardon, 8 Company
" 1336 " T. Webb, 7 Company
" 9917 " R. Gould, 8 Company

The section being subsequently increased by the inclusion of Sappers S. Davies and T. Morgan, embarked under the command of Lieutenant R. S. Forestier-Walker on the transport *Nile* at Southampton on March 14.

Meanwhile a District Order of March 10 had intimated that all Militia regiments stationed in the district, if not already embodied, would be called out on or before May 1. On April 9 the recruits enlisted since July 1899 assembled for Preliminary Drill, and on April 21 Company Sergeant-Majors were directed to prepare notice papers calling up the non-commissioned officers and men of their companies for embodiment at Monmouth on May 1. During the embodiment the distribution of officers was :—

No. 1 Company—Captain and Hon. Major C. C. E. Morgan.
　　　　　　　　Second Lieutenant C. H. R. Crawshay.
No. 2 Company—Captain Viscount Southwell.
　　　　　　　　Second Lieutenant F. St. J. Atkinson.
No. 3 Company—Captain and Hon. Major C. M. Crompton-Roberts.
　　　　　　　　Lieutenant C. F. J. Galloway.
No. 4 Company—Captain and Hon. Major C. J. Helbert Helbert.
　　　　　　　　Second Lieutenant H. Lewis.
No. 5 Company—Captain R. J. S. Price.
　　　　　　　　Lieutenant R. L. Matthews.
No. 6 Company—Captain J. G. O'Brien.
　　　　　　　　Second Lieutenant C. T. L. Jenkins.
No. 7 Company—Captain G. M. L. Lamotte.
　　　　　　　　Lieutenant W. A. D. Galloway.
　　　　　　　　Second Lieutenant J. E. C. Partridge.
No. 8 Company—Captain and Hon. Major H. E. M. Lindsay.

Captain and Honorary Major A. Leetham had been on February 14 seconded for service with the 13th Hussars, his former regiment; and Captain and Honorary Major C. C. E. Morgan was seconded while holding the appointment of Aide-de-Camp to the General Officer commanding the Thames District.

Lieutenant R. S. Forestier-Walker, the officer with the Special Service Section, was on May 4 granted the temporary rank of lieutenant in the Army while serving in South Africa.

On May 10 it was notified for general information that the War Office had proposed to accept the services of at least one company of the Regiment for service in South Africa at any early date, conditional on her Majesty's consent being obtained, and that the Commanding Officer had recommended for acceptance the voluntary offer of the Regiment to serve as a whole in South Africa.

The official news of the Relief of Mafeking having been received on May 21, the occasion was celebrated by a torchlight procession in the town of Monmouth.

It was announced on May 22 that orders had been received for the preparation of a company of about 100 rank-and-file to be in readiness to proceed to South Africa and to embark about June 1; and the following officers, non-commissioned officers, and men were selected by the Commanding Officer for duty with the company:—

>Captain and Honorary Major H. E. M. Lindsay in Command.
>Lieutenant R. L. Matthews.
>Second Lieutenant C. H. R. Crawshay.
>Company Sergeant-Major J. Brown.
>Sergeant F. Alder.
>Bugler H. Gilmore and such men of No. 8 Company as were medically fit; the numbers being completed by such men as were selected from those who volunteered from other companies.

On June 6, 1900, the company left Troy Station *en route* for Southampton, and embarked in the s.s. *Aurania*. It landed at Cape Town on June 29, and, after a short stay at Green Point, proceeded by rail to the Orange River Colony for duty under the C.R.E.

On July 12 one section under Lieutenant R. C. Matthews detrained at Springfontein, and the rest proceeded to Bloemfontein.

On the 18th the Headquarters with three sections started by route march for Sannah's Post with orders to put the waterworks, which supplied Bloemfontein, in a good state of defence, which done, the company on August 2 returned to Bloemfontein.

After having been employed for a few days in road making and other duties, the company was, on August 20, placed at the disposal of the Director of Railways in exchange for the 20th Company R.E., which was retransferred to the Engineer-in-Chief.

The Headquarters were then moved to Kroonstad, and Lieutenant Matthews' section was transferred to Bloemfontein.

From that time onwards the company was kept exclusively for work on the Imperial Military Railways in the Orange River Colony, on which portion of the line—some 420 miles in length—the men were practically the only Sappers employed.

At times, when the enemy was specially active and the company was manning four or even five construction trains, every available man was taken up, but in the intervals of comparative peace, as soon as a section could be spared, it was always sent to assist in the reconstruction of the permanent bridges, where the men's work was invariably much appreciated by the Engineers in charge, and on every day on which the construction trains were not out, the men were employed on such works as cutting up and riveting together pieces of old girders from blown-up bridges, constructing sidings, building platforms for detraining horses and waggons, and sometimes, when railway work was slack at any particular station and men were available, doing work for the C.R.E.

After April 1901 the 'breaks to the road by the enemy' were comparatively rare, although in three cases—the derailment of the hospital train at Boschrand, the explosion under the armoured train at America, when Major Heath was killed, and the derailment of the engine of the up-mail at Tredefort Road, when the fireman, Private Dale, 9th Lancers, lost his life—the results were most serious.

It was consequently possible to employ most of the company on permanent bridges (the 100-foot span at Doorn River was launched and riveted and the bridge over the Rhenoster River re-riveted almost entirely by the company) and in refencing the line and fitting up the apparatus for ringing electric bells in the blockhouses.

At the time that the company was transferred to the Imperial Military Railways Major H. E. M. Lindsay was appointed Deputy Superintendent of Works (really Chief Engineer for the Orange River Colony) and O.C. Railway Troops, Orange River Colony, but was provided with no staff for these duties other than the help he could obtain in his own company.

In the latter capacity he had to maintain two offices—at Bloemfontein and Kroonstad—and to look after the pay, clothing, and discipline of the soldiers of all corps employed on the Imperial Military Railways in the Colony. These averaged (in addition to his own company) some 200 men who were continually changing, as in thirteen months at least 400 men passed through his hands. He had to arrange for the testing of these men on their applying for work on the Imperial Military Railways, their transfer from and to their regiments and the Military Imperial Railways, and the transfers to the reserve or the discharges of those who took permanent employment, as well as answering the applications of the hundreds for whom employment could not be found.

This meant the finding, by the company, of an Acting-Sergeant-Major and Quartermaster-Sergeant for the railway troops, two clerks and an orderly, as well as taking up much of the time of two officers of the company.

As Deputy Superintendent of Works, Major Lindsay had his office at Kroonstad, from which the 'outward' letters alone averaged 350 per month, besides telegrams sent out and received at the rate of about twenty a day. Here the services of at least one clerk and an orderly were indispensable, and a great part of Major Lindsay's time was taken up visiting and inspecting the line and the various works under his charge—for this purpose a private coach was placed at his disposal; the company also sent one man to the railway telegraphs, two to the South African Constabulary, and one was employed, for almost the whole time, as fireman on No. 2 armoured train.

That a company of Engineer Militia of this strength should have successfully coped with the works already described is no doubt creditable, but it cannot be doubted that the strength was far too small for the work an Engineer company would probably be called upon to perform, especially when the inevitable waste of active service is considered—indeed in this particular instance it is known that the work could never have been carried through had not the assistance, at a most critical moment, of Lieutenant R. S. Forestier-Walker and the remains of his Special Service Section been obtained.

The company embarked for South Africa on June 6, 1900, with a total strength of three officers and 103 N.C.O.s and men, and when it entrained at Kroonstad for re-embarkation on September 14, 1901 (the Special Service Section had already gone home), the numbers were reduced to two officers and sixty-eight N.C.O.s and men, the wastage being accounted for as follows:—

	Officers	Rank and File
Died [1]	..	2
Sent home, invalided	1	9
,, time expired	..	19
,, under sentence of Court-Martial	..	1
Discharged in South Africa	..	3
Left at Kroonstad under sentence of Court-Martial	..	1
Total	1	35

One man, Sapper Greenfield, was taken prisoner by the enemy when the train was wrecked at Klip River, between Vereeniging and Elaandsfontein (he was afterwards released), but in no other case was anyone either killed, wounded, or made prisoner. It was by no means uncommon for working parties, when repairing the railway line, to be

[1] In St. Mary's Church, Monmouth, is a window dedicated to the memory of those of the county who died in South Africa during the war. The mural tablet beside it bears the names of the dead and includes those of the following members of the Royal Monmouthshire Royal Engineers: Corporals W. Garton and W. A. Roberts; Lance-Corporal C. Westley; Sappers W. Baldwin, E. Brickley, and T. Samuels.

fired upon at long ranges by the enemy, but these attacks were never pushed home. For the ordinary maintenance work of the railway Major Lindsay had under him—in his position as Deputy Superintendent of Works—two civilian District Engineers, but during the first three months of 1901 these gentlemen were both either in hospital or on sick leave, and their places had to be filled by officers of the company —Lieutenant Forestier-Walker took the Bloemfontein District, while Major Lindsay, assisted by Lieutenant R. L. Matthews, took the northern or Kroonstad part of the line, in addition to the other work.

On Major Lindsay taking leave of the Superintendent of Works, Imperial Military Railways, the latter expressed his very high opinion of the work done by the company, an opinion which nothing but the unremitting zeal displayed by all ranks could have enabled them to deserve. The company on arrival in England was disembodied on October 14, 1901.

Meanwhile the Regiment at home, since its embodiment on May 1, 1900, had experienced many vicissitudes. On June 15, 1900, it proceeded from Monmouth to Aldershot. Authority to recruit only having been received three weeks before embodiment, the men who had just joined were only half drilled and the Regiment's drill did not recover for several years.

The advance party, under command of Captain G. M. L. Lamotte, left Troy Station at 12.30 P.M. on June 12. Nos. 5 and 6 Companies, under Lieut.-Colonel Lord Raglan, on the Regiment's arrival, were sent to Bulford, where but very scanty preparations had been made for their comfort. The band of the 4th Gloucestershire Regiment met the detachment and played it to its destination. Colonel W. A. Hill, too, who commanded the 4th Gloucestershire Regiment, went out to meet the two companies. Great difficulty was experienced in ascertaining where to camp and whence to draw rations and stores, and there was a good deal of trouble with the men. The two companies were each brought up to 100 strong from other companies, and it was left to Captains as to what men should be sent, and naturally all the bad characters were cordially transferred, an opportunity which should never be given to Captains, since it is very hard on an officer in charge of a detachment to have all the bad characters of the Regiment handed over to him. In addition to this state of affairs no tools were available, and therefore no work was done for a week or ten days, but drill was proceeded with vigorously, and the other units in camp admired the physique and steadiness of the men, and also their general turn out. The officers were made honorary members of the mess of the 4th Gloucestershire Regiment.

Soon after the arrival of the tools the camp was moved to a better position on a hill overlooking the whole camp. There was a very severe thunderstorm early in August, which killed a man of the Brecon Volunteers and also struck a tent of the 4th Gloucestershire Regiment, knocking down all the men and damaging several rifles. A difference between the 4th Gloucestershire Regiment and some other regiments in the camp resulted in an attack by the latter on the former's camp, during which Second Lieutenant J. E. C. Partridge of the Royal Monmouthshire Royal Engineers had his head cut open by a stone, whereupon the men of his regiment were greatly excited and keen to participate in the affray, but eventually they were persuaded by the officer commanding to go to bed.

The 4th Gloucestershire Regiment moved to another camp and the officers of the Royal Monmouthshire Royal Engineers were made honorary members of the mess of the 4th Battalion Royal Irish Rifles. Soon afterwards (September 1) Nos. 5 and 6 Companies of the Royal Monmouths returned to Aldershot, being relieved by Nos. 1 and 2 Companies of the Regiment. About the middle of October the 4th Royal Irish Rifles left the camp, when the officers gave a farewell dinner at Amesbury. On the termination of the embodiment silver ash-trays were presented to the 4th Gloucestershire Regiment and a silver cup of Irish design to the 4th Royal Irish Rifles by the officers of the Royal Monmouths as some slight recognition of the kindness and hospitality which had been extended to them. On the departure of the 4th Royal Irish Rifles the Royal Monmouths moved into huts, it being very cold, and a scratch mess was improvised of the officers in the camp, Lord Raglan being the officer commanding the troops at Bulford Camp. The other officers of the Royal Monmouths serving under Lieut.-Colonel Lord Raglan were Captains R. J. S. Price and J. G. O'Brien, Lieutenant C. F. J. Galloway, and Second Lieutenants E. T. L. Jenkins and J. E. C. Partridge.

Soon after the arrival of the Regiment at Aldershot it was inspected by Colonel M. H. G. Goldie, R.E., the Commanding Royal Engineer at that station. On June 21 there was formed a riding class for subalterns, and any other officers who wished to join it. Officers attended in plain clothes at 7 A.M. daily except Saturdays and Sundays; the course lasted for six weeks and certificates were given to such as qualified.

The Regiment paraded daily for field works at 9 A.M. and 2 P.M. except when otherwise ordered. The captain of the week attended all working parades, and if he was the senior officer present he received company reports from the companies on parade. When a senior officer was present, the captain of the week collected the reports and reported to him.

The senior officer doing duty with the Regiment as captain was placed in charge of the regimental field works. He was responsible to the commanding officer for the general distribution and employment to the best advantage of the men and material available. He detailed the companies for work, and issued the necessary daily working orders. In the event of his absence, on duty or leave, he handed over charge to the next senior officer present with the Regiment before leaving, and informed him as to any special instructions or directions to be observed in connection with the work.

Such companies as were detailed in orders, or on parade, to draw stores or tools, marched to work independently from the General Parade, the remaining companies being marched to work by the senior officer present, accompanied by the fifes and drums. All companies returned from work to company lines independently.

Officers commanding companies were required to attend company and regimental working parades as under :—

Morning parades : twice weekly.

Afternoon parades : twice weekly.

Officers commanding companies were responsible that their companies were visited, while at work, by an officer of the company at least twice daily.

Captains of companies were responsible to the officer in charge of field works that their companies were employed to the best advantage, in accordance with his directions.

On July 6 the Regiment was inspected by the Inspector-General of Auxiliary Forces on Laffan's Plain. The District Orders of July 5 contained ' the Militia battalions stationed at Aldershot will be inspected by the Inspector-General of Auxiliary Forces on Laffan's Plain on Friday next, the 6th July, at 10.40 A.M. The battalions, as strong as possible, will be drawn up in line of quarter columns, facing south, the centre opposite the flagstaff with twenty paces interval between battalions and in the following order : Royal Monmouthshire Engineer Militia ; Militia battalions of the First Aldershot Division ; Militia battalions of the

Second Aldershot Division; Militia battalions of the Third Aldershot Division according to regimental seniority. Companies to be made up to thirty files approximately. Captain Whateley (Brigade Major First Division) will act as Staff Officer to the Inspector-General and meet him on Laffan's Plain.'

At a parade held a few days afterwards Sappers C. Ryan and R. Evans were awarded bronze medals and certificates for having saved life at Monmouth; and it was also announced that the Regiment had been awarded the '4th Young Soldiers' Team Prize' for 1889 by the Militia Rifle Association.

In accordance with instructions received, No. 4 Company under the command of Captain and Honorary Major C. J. Helbert Helbert proceeded by train on August 21 to Liphook and thence by route march to Longmoor, Woolmer, where it was employed in digging for stone on Weaver Down for the purpose of new roads to the huts which the War Department was erecting there for the reception of troops from South Africa. No. 3 Company, under the command of Captain and Honorary Major C. M. Crompton-Roberts, was also warned on September 6 to be in readiness to proceed to the same place at short notice. It arrived there some ten days after No. 4 Company, the camp equipment being taken from Aldershot in an armoured road train. Both companies were employed in digging for stone, and worked in conjunction with gangs of local civilians, who, from their local knowledge, were the more fortunate in their discoveries. Later, No. 3 Company was occupied for some six weeks in laying drains in connection with the hut encampment, which originally was intended to provide accommodation for four Line battalions and a military hospital of from 300 to 400 beds. Major Helbert having been granted sick leave, Major Crompton-Roberts commanded the detachment until its return to Monmouth to be disembodied together with the rest of the Regiment.

On October 31 the Aldershot companies proceeded by special train at 4.15 A.M. from Aldershot Town to Monmouth (Mayhill) to be disembodied, the Longmoor companies joining the same train *en route*.

On arrival at the Castle, Monmouth, arms were piled on company parades, accoutrements, helmets, and leggings were taken off, and slings removed from rifles and attached to valise straps. Officers commanding companies then furnished the Quartermaster with the actual marching strength of their respective companies (N.C.O.s and men left at Aldershot or at Mayhill station not included), and detailed two N.C.O.s and eight men per company to draw bread and cheese and hot coffee from the hospital kitchen. The coffee was issued in buckets and distributed to the men on company parades, the men using their mess-tins.

When the men of a company had disposed of their refreshments, all accoutrements and public clothing, with the exception of the suit in wear, were handed in to the company store; any deficiencies or damages being noted by an officer of the company.

As soon as each company completed handing in accoutrements and clothing, rifle oil was drawn from the armoury by each section commander. Rifles and bayonets were examined, thoroughly cleaned, and oiled inside and out under the personal supervision of company officers before return to the armoury. This completed, each company formed up near its company store, and the plain clothes marked with the men's names were distributed, and the suit of uniform in wear taken in. During the embodiment Engineer pay was issued temporarily, it not being permanently allowed until 1901.

It can well be imagined that during the embodiment several gentlemen joined the Regiment as Second Lieutenants. No fewer than seven came forward between January and September 1900—E. T. L. Jenkins, C. H. R. Crawshay, J. E. C. Partridge, A. P. Evans, A. Green, T. S. Gist, and E. Browne. Three officers were seconded for other duty—Honorary Major A. Leetham, on February 14, to serve with the 13th Hussars, he being taken back on the establishment on July 25; Lieutenant R. S. Forestier-Walker, while serving with the Royal Engineers in South Africa; and Honorary Major C. C. E. Morgan, while acting as A.D.C. to the General Officer Commanding the Thames District. Four officers resigned—Lieutenant J. L. Mansel joined the 7th Dragoon Guards, Second Lieutenant G. M. Lindsay the Rifle Brigade, and Second Lieutenant N. W. F. Baynes the Gloucestershire Regiment, while Quartermaster and Honorary Captain G. Tucker went on retired pay, his duties being taken up provisionally by Captain G. M. L. Lamotte. Major the Honble. G. W. R. Somerset was granted the honorary rank of Lieutenant-Colonel on July 4; Lieutenants Viscount Southwell and R. J. S. Price were promoted Captains; and Second Lieutenants C. F. J. Galloway, K. E. Digby, and H. Lewis were promoted Lieutenants.

CHAPTER XIV

FROM 1901 TO 1909

THE year 1901 is notable for the fact that it was the first year in which the recruits were camped. Lord Raglan, who had succeeded to the command of the Regiment and who had recently been appointed Under-Secretary of State for War, was detained at his official duties until the conclusion of the Parliamentary Session and consequently the training was fixed for later than usual, the Preliminary Drill commencing on June 3; thus the recruits were able to be camped, and it was found to be a very great improvement on the billeting system, for the men being together were kept under better discipline, and it was altogether a most successful recruiting year.

Lord Raglan had for his Assistant Private Secretary at the War Office Major A. Leetham of the Royal Monmouthshire Royal Engineers, who had since July 26, 1900, been in command of the Field Depôt, Royal Engineers, at Aldershot, where he had under his charge 500 Sappers and Drivers and some eighty horses, and where were raised and organised during his command three field companies of Royal Engineers. On Lord Raglan accepting the appointment of Governor of the Isle of Man, Major Leetham ceased to remain seconded.

The training in 1901 was voluntary, that is to say, only those officers and men came out who wished to do so. The Regiment was worked as four companies, and in spite of many difficulties the immense advantage of the double-company system became at once apparent. A letter had been circulated early in the year from the War Office intimating the likelihood of the compulsory training being dispensed with. It was in these words :—

'War Office, London, S.W. : December 27, 1900.

' Sir,—In view of the prolonged period of embodiment of the various Regiments of Militia, and the uncertainty which prevails as to the Trainings of 1901, I am directed by the Secretary of State for War to request that you will be so good as to cause the following communication to be made to the Militia under your command :—

'1. It is hoped that the usual Annual Training of the Militia will not be required in 1901, but should unlooked-for circumstances make such a training a national necessity, the longest possible notice will be given.

'2. In any case special facilities for leave will be granted in 1901.

'3. The Messing Allowance will be continued to all men entitled to it under the Army Scale.

'4. Non-commissioned Officers will receive the pay of their Army rank.

'5. Extra Duty Pay will be continued under the Army Scale.

'6. In future years an opportunity of earning additional remuneration will be afforded to Militiamen.

'7. The further training of Recruits after they have completed their drill on enlistment will be carried out as usual, but they will be attached to a Regular Unit for the purpose should it be found desirable. In units where preliminary drill takes place, that drill will be carried out as usual.

'8. Facilities will be afforded to all Militiamen who desire to do their annual training to be attached to a regular unit for the purpose.

'I have the honour to be, &c.,
'(Signed)   J. H. LAYE, D.A.G.

'The G.O.C. Western District.'

On January 23 the whole country was plunged into the deepest gloom owing to the death of Queen Victoria. The melancholy news was published in the Daily Orders on January 25 in the undermentioned words :—

MOURNING. DEATH OF HER MAJESTY THE QUEEN.

(SPECIAL WESTERN DISTRICT ORDER, JANUARY 23, 1901.)

With profound sorrow the General Officer Commanding publishes the following telegram received from the War Office to-day :—

'The Commander-in-Chief regrets to inform you of the death of Her Majesty Victoria, Queen of the United Kingdom of Great Britain and Ireland and of the Colonies and Dependencies thereof, Empress of India, who departed this life at 6.30 P.M. yesterday at Osborne House, Isle of Wight.'

Eighty-one guns will be fired from the Citadel Battery and other saluting stations at noon to-day.

All flags will be at half-mast.

GEORGE FITZROY HENRY, 3RD LORD RAGLAN, C.B.
Commanded the Regiment 1900-1903.
(*From an oil painting in the Officers' Mess.*)

Officers will wear mourning.

No bands will play until further orders.

On May 31 it was notified that the officers of the Militia Regiments and Battalions which had been embodied in consequence of the war in South Africa would be granted the local rank in the Army of their Militia regimental rank from the date of the embodiment of their battalions, or, if promoted, or appointed while embodied, from the date of promotion or appointment up to the date of disembodiment.

On disembodiment this local Army rank was to be converted into honorary Army rank.

This local or honorary rank was to lapse in the case of Militia Officers appointed to the Regular Forces, whose only rank would be that which they held in the Regulars.

The Special Service Section arrived at Troy Station on its return from South Africa at 7.12 P.M. on July 9, and was entertained in Camp on its arrival, the men being sent to their homes the next day.

The following promotions for good service in the field were approved by the Commanding Officer on the recommendation of the Officer Commanding the Service Section of the Regiment, *dated July 1, 1901* :—

No. 147, Corporal G. Pyner to be Sergeant, *vice* Lewis discharged.
No. 2008, Lance-Corporal S. Jeremy to be Corporal.
No. 1819, Lance-Corporal J. Jenkins to be Corporal.
No. 1678, Sapper C. Cronin to be Second Corporal.
No. 771, Sapper W. Padmore to be Second Corporal.

The members of the Section who returned on July 9 were :—

No. 1710 Sergeant V. Davis, 2 Company.
,, 1819 Corporal J. Jenkins, 7 Company.
,, 2008 Corporal S. Jeremy, 3 Company.
,, 1678 Second Corporal C. Cronin, 3 Company.
,, 1187 Sapper W. Chard, 7 Company.
,, 781 Sapper J. Collins, 5 Company.
,, 1514 Sapper M. Connors, 4 Company.
,, 2120 Sapper W. Milsom, 1 Company.
,, 1610 Sapper T. Morgan, 7 Company.
,, 147 Sergeant G. Pyner, 6 Company.
,, 1785 Sapper W. Rowan, 4 Company.
,, 103 Sapper J. Thomas, 7 Company.

It was announced on July 25 that the King had graciously intimated his intention of presenting the South African War Medal to a small detachment of the Service Section of the Royal Monmouthshire Royal Engineers (Militia) on July 29 at Marlborough House.

Such officers, non-commissioned officers, and men as had been ordered to attend and receive the medal proceeded from Monmouth to London by the 9.35 A.M. train from May Hill Station, and assembled in Friary Court, St. James's Palace, opposite the garden entrance to Marlborough House at 3 P.M. The dress was Review Order; Dismounted Officers wore the usual mourning band on the arm, and those receiving medals saluted with the hand.

Non-commissioned officers and men receiving medals did not carry carbines or rifles.

The names of those who proceeded to Marlborough House on this occasion were :—

Lieutenants C. H. R. Crawshay and V. T. J. Eyre.
Sergeants A. Freeman and G. Pyner.
Corporals J. Jenkins and S. Jeremy.
Second Corporals T. Llewellyn and C. Cronin.
Sappers W. Chard, J. Collins, M. Connors, W. Milsom, T. Morgan, W. Rowan, J. Thomas.

The voluntary training of the Regiment commenced on July 29. The four double companies were commanded as follows during the training :—

'A' No. 1, *Double Company*—
Major A. Leetham.
Lieutenant W. A. D. Galloway.
Lieutenant V. T. J. Eyre.
Second Lieutenant E. B. K. Norman.

'B' No. 2, *Double Company*—
Major C. M. Crompton-Roberts.
Lieutenant K. E. Digby.
Second Lieutenant H. M. Seton-Karr.

'C' No. 3, *Double Company*—
Captain R. J. S. Price.
Lieutenant C. F. J. Galloway.
Second Lieutenant M. N. Kennard.
Second Lieutenant C. G. Evans.

'D' No. 4, *Double Company*—
    Captain C. H. Paynter.
    Lieutenant J. R. L. Thomas.
    Second Lieutenant J. E. Gunning.

Company Commanders were particularly directed to arrange for proper instruction, by means of lectures, to be given to their non-commissioned officers and men in the Field Work subjects allotted to their respective companies. These lectures were given as a rule on the day previous to the actual execution of the particular subject on the Field Work Ground.

A District Order circulated on July 25 had for its object the supersession of the sword by the carbine for dismounted officers :—

'As dismounted Infantry Officers will in future carry carbines in place of swords on active service and field manœuvres, instructions in "Infantry Sword Exericse" will be discontinued, except as regards the method of drawing and returning the sword and saluting. Swords will not be worn at Musketry Practice or during Field Training by dismounted Infantry Officers.'

A Special Mourning Order was transmitted throughout the District on August 9 on the occasion of the death of Her Imperial Majesty the Dowager-Empress Frederick of Germany. The wording of the Order was :—

'The Commander-in-Chief has received the King's command to direct, on the present melancholy occasion of the death of Her Imperial Majesty the Dowager-Empress Frederick of Germany and Queen of Prussia, Princess Royal of Great Britain and Ireland, Sister of His Majesty the King, that the Officers of the Army be required to wear, when in uniform, a band of crape round the left arm as prescribed by the Regulations. The mourning will commence on August 8 and be continued until September 19 next.'

The funeral was on August 13 and all flags were kept half-mast high until sunset on that day.

A Special Army Order dated August 20, 1901, contained :—

'His Majesty having received from the Royal Monmouthshire Engineers (Militia) an offer to serve in South Africa has been pleased to accept the services of a company from that corps. The company will be formed under the conditions laid down in Army Order No. 130 of 1900, and will be held in readiness to proceed to South Africa on receipt of orders.'

The company paraded under the command of Captain C. H. Paynter on September 7 at 8 A.M. on the Castle Square, and proceeded by the 9 A.M. train from Troy Station to Southampton for conveyance to South Africa in the mail steamer *Dunottar Castle*.

Meanwhile the Regiment was being put through a strenuous training, during which it was inspected on September 5 by Colonel M. H. Goldie, R.E., District Engineer, Western District.

Throughout the year 1901 there had been a perpetual flow of new officers to the Regiment. Those who took commissions were M. N. Kennard, V. T. J. Eyre (late Imperial Yeomanry), E. B. K. Norman, H. M. Seton-Karr, C. G. Evans, O. H. L. Fletcher, and R. E. Greenwell; while Captain E. B. Hawker (late Royal Sussex Regiment) joined as a Captain, as also did Major C. H. Paynter (late Inniskilling Dragoons). Lieutenant and Quartermaster W. F. Field, R.E., joined as Quartermaster of the Regiment.

Honorary Major C. C. E. Morgan on January 6 was absorbed into the establishment on his vacating the appointment of Aide-de-Camp to the General Officer Commanding the Thames District, and on January 9 he was seconded for service with the Remount Department, as were also Captain G. M. L. Lamotte (on January 1) and Second Lieutenant A. P. Evans (on March 15). Captain E. B. Hawker was seconded for service with the Royal Sussex Regiment, Second Lieutenant A. Green for service with the Royal Engineers, and the following for service in South Africa: Captain R. S. Forestier-Walker, Second Lieutenant F. St. J. Atkinson, and Second Lieutenant E. Browne.

Colonel W. E. C. Curre resigned on March 20, and was succeeded by Lord Raglan, who was granted the honorary rank of Colonel on April 27.

Honorary Lieutenant-Colonel the Honble. G. W. R. Somerset resigned on May 21, and Second Lieutenant G. B. K. Norman on December 14, while Lieutenant H. Lewis joined the 16th Lancers and Second Lieutenant A. P. Evans the King's Royal Rifles. Honorary Major H. E. M. Lindsay was promoted Major on March 20 and granted the honorary rank of Lieutenant-Colonel on April 27. Honorary Major C. C. E. Morgan received his majority on June 12, Lieutenant R. L. Matthews was promoted Captain, and the following Second Lieutenants were made Lieutenants: E. T. L. Jenkins, C. H. R. Crawshay, F. St. J. Atkinson, J. E. C. Partridge, C. L. Corry, and J. R. L. Thomas.

Local rank in the Army while serving in South Africa was granted to Captain R. L. Matthews, and Lieutenants E. T. L. Jenkins, C. H. R.

Crawshay, J. E. C. Partridge, C. L. Corry, C. F. J. Galloway, and K. E. Digby.

In 1902 the recruits were again camped and the Castle was purchased by the War Office from the Duke of Beaufort, who sold most of his Monmouthshire property. The training was a very wet one and the camp very muddy. Sir Evelyn Wood, who inspected the Regiment, ordered additional camping ground to be hired so that the men could be removed from the mud; a piece of land was consequently taken—the site of the present officers' lines. The Regiment was this year definitely organised into five service companies and one depôt: the Companies consisted of one Field, two Railway, and two Bridging; and the Depôt comprised the band, drums, and all non-commissioned officers and men on regimental employment. The new organisation was found to possess many advantages and but few, if any, disadvantages. Perhaps the companies were a little large in time of peace, but in war it would be a fault on the right side.

Six gentlemen joined as Second Lieutenants in 1902—F. E. Gill, C. H. Saunders, C. F. T. Bullock, A. G. Thackeray, T. B. Jenkinson, and Honourable FitzR. R. Somerset.[1] Supernumerary Second Lieutenant E. Browne was appointed Second Lieutenant on the establishment and resigned soon afterwards. The Adjutant, Captain E. H. Bland, was promoted Major early in the year, and was succeeded in the Adjutancy on April 2 by Captain N. J. Hopkins, R.E. Supernumerary Major C. C. E. Morgan was appointed a Major on the establishment on January 30; Honorary Major C. M. Crompton-Roberts was promoted Major on July 21; Captain C. H. Paynter was granted the honorary rank of Major on September 13; and Honorary Major C. J. Helbert Helbert was promoted Major on July 21.

The resignations consisted of those of Captains Viscount Southwell and J. G. O'Brien, Lieutenant V. T. J. Eyre, who joined the 1st Life Guards, and Second Lieutenants C. G. Evans, O. H. L. Fletcher, M. N. Kennard, C. H. Saunders, H. M. Seton-Karr, and R. E. Greenwell, the last five of whom all took commissions in Cavalry Regiments. Captain R. L. Matthews was seconded while acting as Aide-de-Camp to Lord Ampthill, the Governor of Madras. Later in the year Lieutenant C. L. Corry joined the Royal Garrison Regiment, and Lieutenant J. R. L. Thomas became Aide-de-Camp to Sir F. M. Hodgson, K.C.M.G., the Governor and Commander-in-Chief of Barbados and its Dependencies.

---

[1] Honble. FitzRoy Richard Somerset, eldest son of the third Lord Raglan.

The Preliminary Drill lasted from May 19 to July 20 and the Annual Training from July 21 to August 30.

It was announced on April 26 that a naval and military exhibition would be held in the Connaught Hall, Portsmouth, from June 16 to August 30 in aid of the Sailors and Soldiers' Families Relief Association, and the Local Hospital. Any non-commissioned officers and men having interesting naval or military relics or works of art appertaining to the services were invited to lend them.

The reorganisation of the Regiment dated from July 1 and during the training the five companies were commanded as under :—

No. 1 Company (Field)—
   Major C. C. E. Morgan, Commanding.
   Captain R. S. Forestier-Walker.
   Second Lieutenant J. E. Gunning.
   Second Lieutenant O. H. L. Fletcher.

No. 2 Company (Bridging)—
   Major A. Leetham, Commanding.
   Lieutenant W. A. D. Galloway.
   Second Lieutenant Hon. FitzRoy R. Somerset.

No. 3 Company (Railway)—
   Major C. M. Crompton-Roberts, Commanding.
   Lieutenant C. F. J. Galloway.
   Second Lieutenant J. B. Jenkinson.
   Second Lieutenant R. Williams, Royal Anglesey, R.E.(M.) attached.

No. 4 Company (Bridging)—
   Major C. J. Helbert Helbert, Commanding.
   Captain R. J. S. Price.
   Second Lieutenant C. F. T. Bullock.
   Second Lieutenant G. A. Jones, Royal Anglesey, R.E.(M.) attached.

No. 5 Company (Railway)—
   Lieutenant-Colonel H. E. M. Lindsay, Commanding.
   Captain C. H. Paynter.
   Lieutenant K. E. Digby.
   Second Lieutenant A. G. Thackeray.

On August 21 officers commanding companies were instructed to select 22 men of their respective companies to be in readiness to proceed to London, on receipt of orders, to take part in the Coronation Ceremonies of King Edward VII. Sergeant J. O'Flynn of the Permanent Staff with one corporal and nine sappers proceeded from May Hill Station to Paddington as an advance party by the 9.35 A.M. train on August 6, and the detachment followed on August 8.

The annual Inspection was made by Lieutenant-General Sir William Butler, K.C.B., Commanding the Western District, on August 28, and after it was finished he directed the Commanding Officer to publish in Regimental Orders, for the general information of all ranks, that he was extremely pleased with all that he had seen during his inspection.

In 1903 the entire camping ground was taken on lease by the War Office. A large amount of railway plant arrived very late in the training and was with great difficulty taken to Pwll-Holm, the plant including an engine,[1] four trucks, and many hundreds of rails and sleepers. The engine was hauled through the town by means of rails laid down and taken up again, and then it was towed to the foot of the lane leading to Pwll-Holm by a traction engine borrowed from Lord Llangattock; here a rail was laid down to Pwll-Holm gate and the engine was hauled up by the men of the railway companies and then let down the slope. During this procedure it broke loose, and with Major Crompton-Roberts, who was on board, ran away. Fortunately Major Crompton-Roberts found some sand in the sand box, and by applying the brakes and sanding vigorously, the engine, assisted by a curve in the line, was finally pulled up.

This same year the field company was furnished with horses and equipment for the first time, but no provision was made for sick horses, only sixteen being allowed. In the same way there were no materials for repairing the four waggons.

With a view to preventing the enlistment into the Regular Army and Militia of undesirable characters who would not bring credit to the Service, the following instructions were ordered to be observed :—

No man was to be accepted for any branch of the Regular Army or Militia who could not produce a satisfactory reference as to his character and antecedents. If this were not forthcoming steps were to be taken

---

[1] The engine, trucks, and rails had originally been used at Suakim in 1885 in the projected Suakim-Berber Railway; the plant was subsequently returned to England and used near Devonport.

to obtain the man's character, and the recruiting Officer was to satisfy himself that the candidate was in every respect a suitable man for enlistment.

In the case of recruits joining the Regular Army from the Militia, the usual steps had to be taken to obtain their character while in the Militia.

In order that desirable men might not be lost to the Army while inquiry was being made as to their character, recruits were allowed to be attested, but were not finally approved until a satisfactory character was forthcoming.

On May 7 it was notified for information that a new scale of clothing for gradual adoption by Militia units had been approved and was as follows:—

1. Militiamen were to have a full dress suit, a Service dress suit, and a canvas suit.

2. The full dress, consisting of frock and trousers, was to last eight trainings; the other two suits four trainings.

3. The wear at Preliminary Drill counted as a training.

Consequent on the foregoing particulars, the following instructions were promulgated:—

(*a*) From May 7 all new frocks and trousers issued to non-commissioned officers and men would be considered full dress, and would be required to last eight trainings.

(*b*) All part-worn frocks and trousers were to be used up by being issued in lieu of the Service dress during the periods for which they were originally issued.

(*c*) As the clothing referred to at (*b*) was used up, Service dress uniforms were issued.

(*d*) Wear at a Preliminary Drill subsequent to May 7 would count as a training for all clothing.

(*e*) As a temporary measure one part-worn suit only was to be issued to N.C.O.s and men coming up for the Preliminary Drill, and in the case of men who had two suits of part-worn clothing allotted to them in the company stores, the best suit would be issued.

The recruits came up for sixty-three days' Preliminary Drill on May 18 and were again camped, and were divided into five companies. A detachment proceeded to Bulford for training in mounted duties, leaving Troy Station by train at 9 A.M. on May 25, and proceeding *via* the Severn Tunnel, Salisbury, and Greatly to Amesbury, where the detachment detrained. It returned to Monmouth on July 13.

An order was circulated on June 16 to the effect that salutes by soldiers would in future be returned by all officers present and not by the senior only.

The distribution of officers during the training of 1903, which commenced on July 20, was as under :—

No. 1 Company—
Major C. C. E. Morgan.
Captain R. S. Forestier-Walker.
Lieutenant T. S. Gist.
Second Lieutenant A. G. Thackeray.

No. 2 Company—
Lieutenant-Colonel A. Leetham.
Captain W. A. D. Galloway.
Lieutenant C. G. Evans.
Second Lieutenant Hon. FitzRoy R. Somerset.

No. 3 Company—
Major C. M. Crompton-Roberts.
Captain R. J. S. Price.
Lieutenant C. F. J. Galloway.

No. 4 Company—
Major G. M. L. Lamotte.
Captain C. J. Vaughan.
Second Lieutenant C. F. T. Bullock.

No. 5 Company—
Lieutenant-Colonel H. E. M. Lindsay.
Major C. H. Paynter.
Lieutenant E. T. L. Jenkins.
Lieutenant J. E. Gunning.
Second Lieutenant F. E. Gill.

Depôt Company—
Lieutenant K. E. Digby.

On August 24 the Regiment was again inspected by Lieutenant-General Sir William Butler, K.C.B., Colonel M. H. G. Goldie, R.E., making his official inspection on the same day.

Regulations for the wearing of the haversack were issued on September 29 as follows :—

'The following will be substituted for the first three lines of paragraph 1963: "King's Regulations," as amended by the instructions issued with Army Order No. 126 of 1902. The haversack will be worn over the right shoulder, except by men of the Royal Horse and Royal Field Artillery, and mounted men of the Royal Engineers and Army Service Corps who will wear it over the left shoulder. The sling will be worn under the waistbelt, the haversack hanging outside the side arm with the top below the lower edge of the belt (in line with the top of the bayonet scabbard, if side arms are worn). If carried in Review Order the haversack sling will, when the belt is worn under the tunic or jacket, be shortened so that the top of the haversack is four inches above the elbow. The haversack will be worn by all ranks in marching order, on other occasions it will only be carried when specially ordered for use, and is not to be worn rolled up.'

The changes in the officers' ranks in 1903 were not many. Honorary Major A. Leetham was promoted Major on March 21 and granted the honorary rank of Lieutenant-Colonel, while Captain G. M. L. Lamotte received his majority on June 6; Lieutenant W. A. D. Galloway was promoted Captain and Lieutenant K. E. Digby was appointed Instructor of Musketry. Captain C. J. Vaughan was re-appointed Captain on May 6. Lieutenants C. G. Evans and T. S. Gist rejoined the Regiment after service with the 3rd Battalion Leicestershire Regiment and 3rd Battalion Scottish Rifles respectively. C. E. H. Perkins, who had served with the Imperial Yeomanry in South Africa and who had been granted the Honorary Rank of Lieutenant in the Army, joined on June 22, the other new officers being M. David, C. A. Vyvyan-Robinson, A. G. H. Barrett-Lennard, J. H. Bradney,[1] and F. G. Phillips. Major C. J. Helbert Helbert died on January 28 and Lieutenant J. E. C. Partridge was appointed to the Welsh Regiment on the same date. Lieutenant T. S. Gist and Second Lieutenant O. H. L. Fletcher both resigned their commissions.

In 1904 Major G. M. L. Lamotte resigned on May 28, Supernumerary Captain E. B. Hawker on December 24, Lieutenant J. E. Gunning on February 27, and Second Lieutenant Hon. FitzR. R. Somerset on August 6. Major C. C. E. Morgan was granted the honorary rank of Lieutenant-Colonel, as also were Major C. H. Paynter (who had received his majority on May 28) and Major C. M. Crompton-Roberts. Lieutenant

---

[1] John Harford Bradney, son of Colonel Joseph Alfred Bradney of Tal-y-Coed, commanding 2nd Battalion Monmouthshire Regiment.

C. F. J. Galloway was promoted Captain, Lieutenant C. G. Evans was appointed Instructor of Musketry, and Second Lieutenants F. E. Gill and C. F. T. Bullock were made Lieutenants. The new officers were E. L. Skinner, R. G. C. Napier, R. G. Wavell, H. FitzR. E. Somerset,[1] Hon. W. FitzR. Somerset,[2] and H. Mackworth,[3] the last-named having been in the Queen's Regiment.

In the Orders for March 19 it was announced:—

'The Army Council has received the King's command to direct on the present melancholy occasion of the death of Field-Marshal His Royal Highness the Duke of Cambridge, K.G., &c., that the Officers of the Army be required to wear when in uniform a band of black crape round the left arm, as prescribed by the Regulations. The mourning will commence from March 18 and be continued until March 24 next.'

The Regiment assembled on July 11 for forty-eight days' training with the exception of the field company which assembled on July 4 for a period of fifty-five days. The officers of the various companies were:—

No. 1 Company—
Lieutenant-Colonel C. C. E. Morgan, Commanding.
Captain C. J. Vaughan.
Lieutenant A. G. Thackeray.
Second Lieutenant A. G. H. Barrett-Lennard.
Second Lieutenant F. G. Phillips (attached).

No. 2 Company—
Lieutenant-Colonel A. Leetham, Commanding.
Captain W. A. D. Galloway.
Lieutenant F. E. Gill.
Second Lieutenant Hon. FitzRoy R. Somerset.
Second Lieutenant Hon. W. FitzR. Somerset (attached).
Second Lieutenant E. L. Skinner (attached).

No. 3 Company—
Major C. M. Crompton-Roberts, Commanding.
Captain C. F. J. Galloway.
Second Lieutenant C. A. Vyvyan-Robinson.
Second Lieutenant F. G. Harris (attached).
Second Lieutenant R. G. Wavell (attached).

---

[1] Henry FitzRoy Edward Somerset, son of Lord Edward Somerset and grandson of the eighth Duke of Beaufort.
[2] Honble. Wellesley FitzRoy Somerset, second son of the third Lord Raglan.
[3] Humphrey Mackworth, son of Colonel Sir Arthur Mackworth, Bt.

No. 4 Company—
  Major C. H. Paynter, Commanding.
  Captain R. S. Forestier-Walker.
  Second Lieutenant M. David.
  Second Lieutenant P. C. R. Moreton (attached).
  Second Lieutenant H. FitzR. E. Somerset (attached).

No. 5 Company—
  Lieutenant-Colonel H. E. M. Lindsay, Commanding.
  Captain K. E. Digby.
  Lieutenant E. T. L. Jenkins.
  Second Lieutenant J. H. Bradney (attached).
  Second Lieutenant R. G. C. Napier (attached).

Depôt Company—
  Captain R. J. S. Price, Commanding.
  Lieutenant C. G. Evans (Instructor of Musketry).

Three officers of the Royal Anglesey Royal Engineers were attached during the training, and at the end of July the Bridging Battalion, Royal Engineers, arrived at Monmouth as follows:—

Advance party on the 27th by rail—one officer and thirty men.

Advance party on the 30th by road—three officers and thirty-six men.

Main body on July 30 by rail—three officers and 147 men.

Horses, nine officers, and sixty-three troop arrived on the 30th.

On December 8 was laid down the manner of proposal of his Majesty's health in R.E. messes:—

'In accordance with instructions contained in the minute of the A.A. General, R.E., dated War Office, November 24, 1904, the health of his Majesty when proposed in R.E. messes should be proposed in the following manner: "The King, our Colonel."'

In December 1904, the King having been graciously pleased to approve of a medal for long service and good conduct being granted to non-commissioned officers and men of the Militia and Imperial Yeomanry, the following instructions were issued for the guidance of all concerned: 'The Militia Long-Service Medal will bear the effigy of His Majesty on the obverse, and on the reverse the inscription, "Militia, for Long Service and Good Conduct," and will be granted to non-commissioned officers and men of good character who are serving on or after November 9, 1904, and have completed eighteen years' service, which need not be continuous, and attended at least fifteen trainings. The colour of the ribbon to be worn with this medal will be blue.'

In 1905 Second Lieutenant R. G. C. Napier went to the Grenadier Guards on probation, and Second Lieutenant R. G. Wavell Paxton to the Coldstream Guards. K. P. Wallis, A. G. Pardoe, H. J. W. Fletcher, and E. J. P. Clarke all joined the Regiment.

The Orders for March 21 contained:—

'It is proposed to hold a Rifle Meeting at Penally at the end of June, open to the Royal Navy, Regular Troops, Militia, and Volunteers stationed in the Welsh and Midland Command. Should any of the non-commissioned officers or men at this station be desirous of entering, subject to the conditions of the various competitions being agreeable to them, they are requested to give in their names at the Orderly Room without delay, in order that it may be ascertained what number of entries are likely to be forthcoming.'

It was intimated to recruiters in April that they would be held responsible that every man brought before the Medical Officer fulfilled the primary conditions as to physical fitness—height, chest measurement, and weight. They were also required to satisfy themselves that the would-be recruits could see the usual dots at the regulation distance with each eye, and that each man was not deficient of more than eight teeth. Recruits seventeen years of age were to be at least 110 lb. in weight if 5 ft. 2 in. in height; 114 lb. if 5 ft. 5 in.; 118 lb. if 5 ft. 8 in.; and 122 lb. if 6 ft. in height, with corresponding chest measurement of $32\frac{1}{2}$ in., 33 in., $33\frac{1}{2}$ in., and $34\frac{1}{2}$ in. when fully expanded. The range of expansion was to be 2 in. except in the case of recruits 6 ft. and over in height when the expansion required was $2\frac{1}{2}$ in.

Recruits above the age of eighteen had to correspond with the tests A, C, and E for the Regular forces of the same arm of the service, except that the chest measurement 'when fully expanded' might be $\frac{1}{2}$ inch lower than in those tests.

The Preliminary Drill in 1905 commenced on May 8 and continued until July 9. The Field Company trained from July 3 until August 26; other companies from July 10 until August 26.

The distribution of officers at the training was:—

No. 1 Company—
    Lieutenant-Colonel C. C. E. Morgan, Commanding.
    Captain C. J. Vaughan.
    Lieutenant A. G. Thackeray.
    Second Lieutenant A. G. H. Barrett-Lennard.
    Second Lieutenant F. G. Phillips.

No. 2 Company—
    Captain R. S. Forestier-Walker, Commanding.
    Captain W. A. D. Galloway.
    Lieutenant F. E. Gill.
    Second Lieutenant Hon. W. FitzR. Somerset.
    Second Lieutenant E. L. Skinner.
    Lieutenant A. Rigby, 7th Liverpool Regiment (attached).

No. 3 Company—
    Lieutenant-Colonel C. M. Crompton-Roberts, Commanding.
    Captain C. F. J. Galloway.
    Second Lieutenant C. A. Vyvyan-Robinson.
    Second Lieutenant F. C. Harris.
    Second Lieutenant F. B. Jarvis.

No. 4 Company—
    Lieutenant-Colonel C. H. Paynter, Commanding.
    Lieutenant H. Mackworth.
    Second Lieutenant H. FitzR. Somerset.
    Second Lieutenant P. C. R. Moreton.
    Second Lieutenant K. P. Wallis.

No. 5 Company—
    Lieutenant-Colonel H. E. M. Lindsay, Commanding.
    Captain K. E. Digby.
    Second Lieutenant M. David.
    Second Lieutenant J. H. Bradney.
    Second Lieutenant C. E. H. Perkins.
    Second Lieutenant A. G. Pardoe.

Depôt Company—
    Lieutenant E. T. H. Jenkins, Commanding.
    Lieutenant C. G. Evans, Instructor of Musketry.

On July 20 a memorial service was held at the parish church, Monmouth, on the occasion of the unveiling of a window in memory of Queen Victoria. The Regiment detailed a firing party for the ceremony, and a general parade, under command of Lieutenant-Colonel C. C. E. Morgan, took place at 4.30 P.M. in Review Order for all who wished to be present at the service.

The Inspection took place on August 11, when Colonel R. Thompson, R.E., Chief Engineer Welsh and Midland Command, was the inspecting

FIELD-MARSHAL HIS ROYAL HIGHNESS THE DUKE OF CONNAUGHT, K.G., AND THE OFFICERS OF THE ROYAL MONMOUTHSHIRE MILITIA, 1906.

First Row

2nd Lieut. T. F. R. Symons. 2nd Lieut. F. B. Jarvis. Lieut. E. C. Harris. 2nd Lieut. P. C. F. Morton. Lieut. J. H. Bradley. Lieut. C. A. Vyvyan-Robinson. 2nd Lieut. E. J. P. Clarke. 2nd Lieut. E. L. Skinner. 2nd Lieut. the Hon. W. F. Somerset. 2nd Lieut. E. H. B. Curties. Lieut. H. Mackworth. 2nd Lieut. R. P. Wallis. Lieut. F. E. Gill.

Middle Row

Lieut. M. David. Lieut. the Hon. C. M. B. Ponsonby, M.V.O., G.Gds. Colonel R. Thompson, *Chief Engineer*. Colonel Lord Raglan. Capt. K. E. Digby. Capt. R. L. Matthews. 2nd Lieut. A. G. Pardoe. 2nd Lieut. H. F. E. Somerset. 2nd Lieut. F. G. Phillips. Captain N. J. Hopkins, R.E. Lieut. & Adjt. J. C. G. Evans. Capt. R. S. Forester-Walker. Lieut. and Q.M. T. L. Whitehead, R.E. Major G. E. F. Talbot, R.G.A. (M.), Lieut. A. G. Thackeray.

Bottom Row

Lieut.-Col. C. M. Crompton-Roberts. Brig.-General Sir J. G. Maxwell, K.C.B. H.R.H. the DUKE OF CONNAUGHT, K.G. Lieut.-Col. H. E. M. Lindsay. Capt. W. A. D. Galloway. Colonel G. Barker, C.B. *Inspector of R.E.* Lieut.-Col. A. Leetham. Colonel Viscount Tredegar. Captain C. J. Vaughan.

officer. Colonel G. Barker, R.E., Inspector of Royal Engineers, also saw the Regiment on August 17. The result of the official inspection was the publication of the following observation by the General Officer Commanding-in-Chief Welsh and Midland Command: 'I am glad to receive such a very satisfactory report, which reflects great credit on the commanding officer and all ranks.'

In 1906 Honorary Lieutenant-Colonel C. H. Paynter, Captain R. J. S. Price, and Second Lieutenant H. J. W. Fletcher resigned their commissions, and Second Lieutenant C. E. H. Perkins went to the 5th Manchester Regiment. Five Second Lieutenants were promoted Lieutenants —M. David, C. A. Vyvyan-Robinson, A. G. H. Barrett-Lennard, J. H. Bradney, and F. C. Harris; while T. E. R. Symons and E. H. B. Curties joined as new officers.

On February 2 was circulated :—

'The Army Council has received the King's commands to direct on the present melancholy occasion of the death of His Majesty Christian IX. King of Denmark, K.G., G.C.B., a General of the British Army, and father of Her Majesty Queen Alexandra, that the officers of the Army be required to wear, when in uniform, a band of black crape round the left arm as prescribed by the Regulations. The mourning will commence from the 1st February and will be continued until the 7th February inclusive.'

The recruits of the Regiment who had enlisted since March 27 assembled on May 7 for sixty-three days' Preliminary Drill, and on June 25 they proceeded to Porthcawl under command of Captain N. J. Hopkins, R.E., the Adjutant, for musketry. Three companies of the Regiment, Nos. 1, 3, and 5, came up for annual training on July 2, and the remainder on July 9.

His Royal Highness the Duke of Connaught visited the Regiment this year, and after his visit there was published ' The Officer Commanding is commanded by His Royal Highness the Inspector-General of the Forces to inform the Regiment that His Royal Highness was much pleased with the appearance and turn-out of the Regiment, with its steadiness on parade, and with the excellence and usefulness of the work done at Pwll-Holm.' In August Lieutenant-Colonel A. Leetham was appointed Field Officer in charge of Field Works at Pwll-Holm.

As it had been decided that the two Railway companies (Nos. 3 and 5) were to spend the last fortnight of their 1906 annual training at Whitehill, Hants, for work on the Woolmer Instructional Railway, under the direction of Major F. Fuller, R.E., Officer Commanding Railway Companies, R.E., the officers commanding those two companies, Lieutenant-Colonel C. M. Crompton-Roberts and Lieutenant-Colonel H. E. M. Lindsay, determined to devote rather more time than usual, while at Monmouth, to the construction of heavy trestle bridging.

Accordingly stock was taken of all the available timber and other materials at Pwll-Holm, and Lieutenants J. H. Bradney (No. 5 Co.) and F. B. Jarvis (No. 3 Co.) were directed to take sections of the river Monnow at 'Bridgehead,' and to send in a report as to the feasibility of constructing a heavy trestle railway-bridge at that spot.

They made three sections and reported the distance from bank to bank at the most favourable site to be 100 feet, the banks to be shelving steeply and muddy, showing a certain amount of probable sinkage; but that the main portion of the river-bed was fairly level, with a hard gravel bottom, and that the greatest depth of water was 11 ft. 4 in.

It was then decided to construct a heavy trestle railway-bridge of ten bays of 10 ft. each, with eleven trestles including the two shore transoms, for which baulks 12 in. by 12 in. were used. Detail drawings of the bridge and of each trestle were prepared, from the information furnished in the report, while the Railway companies were at Ross for their annual musketry course.

The trestles next the shore on either side of the river were placed on footings of courses of sandbags. It was decided to rest the seven centre trestles with their ground-sills on the river bottom, as, owing to the depth of water, it was not considered necessary and scarcely feasible to construct crib piers in these positions.

To enable the heavy trestles to be placed in position more easily, a locomotive tender (on charge as 'wood and water waggon, one') was converted into a species of travelling crane (under the supervision of Major Talbot, R.G.A. (M.), who was attached to No. 3 Company during the training) by having two 30-ft. bull-headed rails fixed on either side of the tender, so as to project some distance in front of it, and duly stayed with wire, &c. The tank of the tender was then filled with about five tons of water to keep it steady, and to prevent its kicking up behind when the weight of the heavy trestles was taken on the projecting crane tackle.

The last heavy trestle was placed in position and the superstructure of the bridge completed on August 8.

It is scarcely necessary to add that on service the construction of a

LAYING TRESTLES WITH AN IMPROVISED CRANE.

THE BRIDGE COMPLETED.

HEAVY TRESTLE BRIDGING ON THE RIVER MONNOW AT PWLL HOLM, 1906.

heavy trestle railway-bridge would scarcely be attempted in such a depth of water; but a deviation of some considerable length of railway line would preferably be laid to some shallower portion of the river. Such a trestle bridge was constructed at this particular spot at Pwll-Holm, because it is only at this spot that any land is owned by the War Department on the further side of the river.

The height of water in the river Monnow varied from day to day during the construction of the bridge, as much as 2 ft. variation being recorded, and this was mainly due to the intermittent working of the turbines of the Monmouth Corporation electric-light station, situated about half a mile below Pwll-Holm.

The tallest trestle was 16 ft. in height; 12 in. by 12 in. baulks were used for the legs, topsills, and groundsills of all the trestles, 12 in. by 6 in. for the side stays, and 12 in. by 3 in. for the back stays from trestle to trestle. The back stays of each trestle were fixed with coach-screws to the inside of the bottom of the legs, at the required angle, while the trestle was suspended from the crane and before it was lowered into position on the river bottom; the tops of the back stays were fixed to the previous trestle after being placed into position. The tops of the trestles were further stayed by 30-ft. rails laid flat and spiked down to the topsill of each trestle.

It was originally intended to lay as road-bearers two baulks of 12 in. by 12 in., one on the top of the other, on each side of bridge; but it was found that there was not sufficient timber available for this, and so one baulk only was used. This was found to be quite strong enough for the load the bridge would have to carry, the trestles being only 10 ft. apart. Sleepers and rails were laid on the road-bearers. The gauge was the standard gauge, 4 ft. $8\frac{1}{2}$ in.

The locomotive weighed fourteen tons, on a 4 ft. 6 in. wheel base. The tender weighed seven tons, and, when converted into a crane, carried five tons water and (say) one ton superstructure of crane, making thirteen tons in all on a 7 ft. 6 in. wheel base.

The locomotive, tender, rails, and sleepers originally formed part of the railway in use at Suakim in 1885.

A barrel-pier raft, which had been constructed by the Bridging companies, was utilised to assist in placing the trestles in position.

During the trainings of 1906 and 1907, while at Longmoor, the Railway companies were employed in the laying and ballasting of the military line from Bordon to Whitehill, in pile-driving, and in other miscellaneous work.

In 1907 Captain W. A. D. Galloway resigned his commission, as did also Lieutenants E. T. L. Jenkins and A. G. H. Barrett-Lennard together with Second Lieutenants F. G. Phillips, E. L. Skinner, and H. F. E. Somerset, while Second Lieutenants the Honourable W. FitzR. Somerset and K. P. Wallis both joined the Welsh Regiment. Captain R. L. Matthews was promoted Major, and Lieutenant C. G. Evans received a Captaincy. The new officers were Captain H. Fulton and Lieutenants C. F. Huth, R. C. Hebden, T. G. H. Studdert, and F. J. Cary, all of whom were transferred from the Submarine Miners, Royal Engineers Militia, on the disbandment of that branch of the Force.

The preliminary drill was from May 6 to July 7, and the annual training of the Regiment commenced on July 1 for the Field Company and on July 8 for other companies, and lasted until August 24. The Railway companies proceeded to Longmoor for the last fourteen days of the training.

The distribution of officers this year was:—

No. 1 Company—
    Lieut.-Col. C. C. E. Morgan, Commanding.
    Captain C. J. Vaughan.
    Lieutenant R. C. Hebden.
    Lieutenant F. J. Cary.
    Second Lieutenant T. E. R. Symons.
    Second Lieutenant R. J. Watts.

No. 2 Company—
    Lieut.-Col. A. Leetham, Commanding.
    Captain C. F. J. Galloway.
    Lieutenant F. E. Gill.
    Lieutenant T. G. H. Studdert.
    Lieutenant A. Rigby.
    Second Lieutenant E. B. Wauton.

No. 3 Company—
    Lieut.-Col. C. M. Crompton-Roberts, Commanding.
    Captain H. Fulton.
    Lieutenant C. A. Vyvyan-Robinson.
    Lieutenant J. H. Bradney.
    Second Lieutenant F. B. Jarvis.

PWLL HOLM, MONMOUTH, SHOWING RAILWAY IN COURSE OF CONSTRUCTION.
1907 Training.

HIGH COMMAND REDOUBT IN COURSE OF CONSTRUCTION.
1907 Training.

No. 4 Company—
  Major R. L. Matthews, Commanding.
  Captain C. G. Evans, Instructor of Musketry.
  Lieutenant H. Mackworth.
  Lieutenant F. C. Harris.
  Second Lieutenant P. C. R. Moreton.
  Second Lieutenant E. H. B. Curties.

No. 5 Company—
  Lieut.-Col. H. E. M. Lindsay, Commanding.
  Captain K. E. Digby.
  Lieutenant M. David.
  Lieutenant C. F. Huth.
  Second Lieutenant A. G. Pardoe.
  Second Lieutenant E. J. P. Clarke.

The Brigadier-General Commanding the Wales Coast Defences inspected the Regiment on August 8, and there appeared in Orders on August 15 :—

'The Brigadier-General Commanding the Wales Coast Defences has expressed his entire satisfaction with the result of his inspection of this Regiment on the 8th instant. He was highly pleased with the general appearance and bearing of all ranks on parade, as well as with the skill with which the Field Works are being carried out. He considers that the high degree of efficiency attained by the Regiment reflects the greatest credit upon all concerned.'

An extract from a War Office letter of August 2, 1907, was published on August 9 for general information :—

'Fragments of rail demolished in the open have been known to fly 1000 yards, and therefore in practising the demolition of rails and girders of small section with high explosives by the ordinary service method, it is essential either that the demolition should take place in a pit blinded with timber and earth, or that the rail should be well covered with filled sand-bags.'

It was announced on August 20 that at a recent examination of officers in foreign languages held in London, Captain K. E. Digby had qualified as an interpreter in Russian.

On October 2 was circulated in Regimental Orders :—

'The Commanding Officer cannot permit Captain N. J. Hopkins, R.E., to go on leave pending the completion of his period as Adjutant of the

Royal Monmouthshire Royal Engineers (Militia) without placing on record his high appreciation of the good work he has done while holding that appointment. During the last six years the establishment of the Regiment has been largely increased, the Field Company has been raised, the remaining companies have been reorganised, and the whole scheme of training altered. The improvement which has taken place in the numbers, physique, and training of the men, and the conduct and bearing of the N.C. Officers is due largely to the exertions of Captain Hopkins and to his ability to secure the best efforts of the Permanent Staff.'

The year 1908 was the last year in which the Regiment trained as a Militia unit previous to its transfer to the Special Reserve, a force created simultaneously with the Territorial Force, but before this event took place there were other important incidents in connection with the Regiment. On March 19 Lord Raglan relinquished the command of the Battalion.

'In relinquishing the command of the Royal Monmouthshire Royal Engineers (Militia), Colonel Lord Raglan wishes to give his best thanks to the officers, non-commissioned officers, and men for the whole-hearted support they have given him for the seven years he has been at the head of the Regiment. During this period the Regiment has been entirely reorganised, as well as largely increased in establishment, and that it is in a high state of efficiency is shown by the fact that His Majesty the King in token of his satisfaction with the Royal Monmouthshire Royal Engineers (Militia) was graciously pleased to confer on the Commanding Officer the Companionship of the Order of the Bath.

'Colonel Lord Raglan has served for nearly twenty-one years in the Regiment, and the happiest days of his life were those on which he wore the uniform of the Royal Monmouthshire.

'He cannot sever his long connection with the Regiment without the deepest regret, his only consolation being the knowledge that he hands over the command to a successor whose love for it is as great as his own.

'Colonel Lord Raglan wishes to assure the officers, non-commissioned officers, and men of his warm interest in their welfare individually and collectively, whether in military or in civil life.

'Whatever may be the effect of present changes, he feels sure that all ranks will unite in keeping up the high character of the Royal Monmouthshire Royal Engineers (Militia)—a character earned in peace

HOWITZER GUN BATTERY
1908 Training.

DEMOLITION OF RAILWAY.
1908 Training.

IMPROVISED GIRDERS FOR RAILWAY BRIDGE.
1908 Training.

and in war by 250 years of loyal and devoted service to Sovereign and Country.'

Lord Raglan was succeeded in the command by Honorary Lieut.-Colonel H. E. M. Lindsay, who was promoted to Lieut.-Colonel on March 19. Consequent on this promotion, Captain R. S. Forestier-Walker was given the vacant majority, and Lieutenants F. E. Gill and H. Mackworth were promoted Captains. During the year Second Lieutenants F. B. Jarvis, A. G. Pardoe, and E. J. P. Clarke all became Lieutenants. The resignations were those of Honorary Lieut.-Colonel C. C. E. Morgan on August 30, Captain C. F. J. Galloway, Lieutenants R. C. Hebden, and A. G. Thackeray; and Second Lieutenant T. E. R. Symons joined the Grenadier Guards. The new officers consisted of T. G. B. Forster, A. G. Cowie, and H. C. Cowie.

A Royal Message from King Edward VII. was conveyed to the Militia throughout the country in February in these words :—

'At this time, when the Militia is to be asked to undertake new duties and fresh liabilities, I take the opportunity of expressing to the Force my keen appreciation of its services in the past. In peace and in war the Militia has never been asked in vain to make sacrifices for the good of the country.

'The devotion to duty which has ever distinguished the Militia will, I am convinced, continue to be shown by the officers and men of the Force, whatever calls may be made on them.

'I express my special thanks for past services to those battalions and other portions of the Militia to which, to my great regret, no place can be assigned in the new organisation.

'I desire that this message may be promulgated for the information of the whole Army.'

The Preliminary Drill for the new special reservists commenced on March 2 and lasted until August 29. From March 2 to April 30 the men were accommodated in billets; after the latter date they went under canvas. The training of the Regiment commenced on July 20 and terminated on August 29. The officers doing duty were :—

No. 1 (Field) Company—
    Captain C. J. Vaughan, Commanding.
    Lieutenant F. J. Stanley-Cary.
    Lieutenant A. G. Pardoe.
    Second Lieutenant R. J. Watts.
    Second Lieutenant A. G. Cowie (attached).

No. 2 (Bridging) Company—
  Lieut.-Colonel A. Leetham, Commanding.
  Captain F. E. Gill.
  Lieutenant T. G. H. Studdert.
  Lieutenant E. J. P. Clarke.
  Second Lieutenant E. B. Wauton.

No. 3 (Railway) Company—
  Lieut.-Colonel C. M. Crompton-Roberts, Commanding.
  Captain H. Fulton.
  Lieutenant J. H. Bradney.
  Lieutenant F. B. Jarvis.
  Second Lieutenant H. C. Cowie (attached).

No. 4 (Bridging) Company—
  Major R. L. Matthews, Commanding.
  Lieutenant F. C. Harris.
  Lieutenant H. C. G. Allen (attached).
  Second Lieutenant E. H. B. Curties.

No. 5 (Railway) Company—
  Major R. S. Forestier-Walker, Commanding.
  Captain K. E. Digby.
  Lieutenant M. David.
  Lieutenant C. F. Huth.
  Second Lieutenant T. G. B. Forster (attached).

Depôt Company.
  Captain C. G. Evans, Commanding.

The Inspector of Royal Engineers visited the Regiment and wrote subsequently :—

'The Inspector of Royal Engineers desires to express his entire satisfaction with what he saw on the occasion of his inspection.

'The instruction at Pwll-Holm was of a very useful nature, all ranks taking an intelligent interest in their work. On parade he particularly noticed the steadiness of the men and the smartness with which the movements were carried out.

'In camp the arrangements were worthy of all praise. It is with the greatest regret that he bids the Regiment farewell as one of Militia, but feels confident that those who continue their connection with it as a Special Reserve to the Corps of Royal Engineers will carry on the good traditions and high standard of excellence of the past.'

FROM 1901 TO 1909

The *London Gazette* dated September 25, 1908, contained :—

'In accordance with the terms of the Order in Council dated 9th April, 1908, the following Militia unit having completed the prescribed period of annual training, is transferred as a unit of the Army Reserve, and the Officers named, having assented to be transferred, are appointed Officers of the Special Reserve of Officers from the date stated, retaining the rank and seniority which they held while in the Militia.

'Royal Monmouthshire Royal Engineers (Militia) to be the Royal Monmouthshire Royal Engineers. Dated 30th August, 1908.

Lieut.-Colonel	H. E. M. Lindsay.
Major and Hon. Lieut.-Col.	C. M. Crompton-Roberts.
,, ,, ,,	A. Leetham.
Major	R. L. Matthews.
,,	R. S. Forestier-Walker.
Captain and Hon. Major	C. J. Vaughan.
Captain	K. E. Digby.
,,	H. Fulton.
,,	C. G. Evans.
,,	H. Mackworth
,,	F. E. Gill.
Lieutenant	M. David.
,,	C. A. Vyvyan-Robinson.
,,	J. H. Bradney.
,,	F. C. Harris.
,,	C. F. Huth.
,,	T. G. H. Studdert.
,,	F. J. Stanley-Cary.
,,	P. C. R. Moreton.
,,	F. B. Jarvis.
,,	A. G. Pardoe.
,,	E. J. P. Clarke.
Second Lieutenant	E. H. B. Curties.
,,	R. J. Watts.
,,	E. B. Wauton.
,,	T. G. B. Forster.
,,	H. C. Cowie.
,,	A. G. Cowie.'

Viscount Tredegar, the Honorary Colonel, was gazetted Honorary Colonel of the Regiment as Special Reserve on August 30, 1908.

The reorganisation of the Regiment consequent on the revised establishment promulgated by Appendix III. of a Special Army Order of December 23, 1907, was carried out as follows :—

No. 1 (Field) Company became No. 1 (Siege) Company.
No. 3 (Railway) Company became No. 2 (Railway) Company.
No. 5 (Railway) Company became No. 3 (Railway) Company.
The old Depôt Company remained the new Depôt Company.

Nos. 2 and 4 (Bridging) Companies were disbanded, and the N.C. officers and men thereof were absorbed by the other companies as detailed.

A form of notice was given to each individual Militiaman belonging to a Militia unit undergoing training, whether the Militiaman was present at the training or absent with leave, or through sickness. It contained the following clauses :—

1. It having been decided to convert the Militia unit to which you belong into a Reserve unit on the completion of the annual training in 1908, you may choose any of the three following courses :—

(i) To join the Special Reserve.

(ii) To remain as you are in the Militia until your term of service expires. In the latter case you will not be called out for annual training after 1908, nor be permitted to re-engage, but you will remain liable to embodiment in time of emergency. Provided your service has not expired, you will be entitled to your non-training bounty on the following dates : 1st October, 1908, 1st December, 1908, and 1st February, 1909.

(iii) To take a free discharge.

2. If you decide to join the Special Reserve :—

(*a*) You will receive the sum of 2*l*. for accepting the liability for service abroad as a Special Reservist.

(*b*) Your non-training bounties whilst in the Special Reserve will also be paid on the usual dates.

(*c*) You will become a member of the Army Reserve, and as a Special Reservist you will be liable for service abroad in time of emergency. That is, you may then be sent to join a Regular unit. No Infantry Militiaman serving on his present engagement who joins the Special Reserve Infantry will be sent to join any battalion other than one of his Territorial Regiment, except with his own consent, and when drafted, the draft will be accompanied by an officer of his Regiment.

(d) You will not be required to undergo any extra drill except as stated below.

(e) Your annual training in the Special Reserve will be—
  (i) Royal Field Artillery and Royal Garrison Artillery, 15 days. Men of the Royal Garrison Artillery Militia who elect to join the Royal Field Reserve Artillery, and men of the Infantry Militia and Royal Engineer Militia who are allowed to join the Royal Field Reserve Artillery, will be called up for 28 days' instruction immediately before the annual training of 1909.
  (ii) Royal Engineers, 15 days. Men of the Royal Engineer Militia who elect to join the Special Reserve Royal Engineers will be called up for one month's training in 1909, instead of 15 days' training.
  (iii) Infantry 15 days and 6 days musketry.

(f) Your pay and allowances in the Special Reserve will be at Army rates, as set out in the accompanying leaflet. You will be eligible for Proficiency Pay, if you join either the Special Reserve of the Artillery or Infantry, but not for Good Conduct Pay.

(g) You may enlist in the Special Reserve to complete the unexpired portion of your Militia engagement, provided you have still one clear year to serve. If you have less than one year to serve, you may enlist for four years, and will be considered as a re-engaged man.

(h) For the unexpired portion of your current engagement or re-engagement under (g), you will continue, though a Special Reservist, to receive your training and non-training bounties at the same rate as you have received in the Militia.

(k) If you wish to purchase your discharge, during the term of your current engagement or re-engagement under (g), you will be allowed to do so at whichever rate is the more advantageous to you, viz. the old Militia rate, or the rate laid down for the Special Reserve.

3. You are requested to fill up the enclosed form, and to sign it according to which decision you make. If you elect to become a Special Reservist, your attestation and final approval for the Special Reserve will be carried out, and will date from the termination of the training of your unit in 1908.

If you join the Special Reserve during the annual training you will not be required to undergo a fresh medical examination.

In case you are absent with leave, or through sickness, from the 1908 training, and elect to join the Special Reserve, you will be required to attend at the nearest recruiting centre, where, if you are found medically fit, your attestation and final approval for the Special Reserve will be carried out. The authorised travelling expenses to and from your home will be allowed, and you will receive a day's pay, ration allowance, and, if eighteen years of age, messing allowance.

If belonging to the Royal Garrison Artillery Militia, you may join the Royal Field Reserve Artillery or Infantry.

If belonging to the Royal Engineer Militia, you may join the Royal Engineer Special Reserve or Special Reserve Infantry, and if medically fit and of the prescribed standard, you may have your name registered for the Royal Field Reserve Artillery should a vacancy exist for you, but in this case you must first join the Royal Engineer Special Reserve, and no guarantee can be given that you will be allowed to join the Royal Field Reserve Artillery.

If belonging to the Cork or Antrim Royal Garrison Artillery Militia, you may join the Royal Garrison Reserve Artillery for Cork or Antrim, or the Royal Field Reserve Artillery or Infantry.

If belonging to the Infantry Militia, you may join the Special Reserve Infantry, and, if medically fit and of the prescribed standard, you may have your name registered for Royal Field Reserve Artillery should a vacancy exist for you, but you must join the Special Reserve of the Infantry in the first case, and no guarantee can be given that you will be allowed to join the Royal Field Reserve Artillery.

The Special Reserve does not come within the scope of this work; therefore, wishing every success to the Regiment in the future, the author here concludes his task.

SWORD-BAYONET ISSUED TO THE ARMY IN 1909

A LIST OF OFFICERS

WHO HAVE SERVED, OR WHO ARE SERVING

IN THE

ROYAL MONMOUTHSHIRE MILITIA

ROYAL MONMOUTHSHIRE MILITIA

† Served in South African War as a Militia Officer. ‡ Has held the office of High Sheriff of Monmouthshire.

Name	Colonel	Lieut.-Col.	Major	Captain	Lieutenant	2nd Lieutenant or * Ensign	Remarks
ABERGAVENNY, HENRY, EARL OF, K.T.	—	Apr. 5, 1793	Apr. 1772	—	—	—	2nd Earl, born 1755, resigned June 30, 1805, died 1843.
ADAMS, GEORGE	—	—	—	—	—	*1799	
ALLAWAY, WILLIAM AUGUSTUS HAMILTON KINNAIRD	—	—	—	May 17, 1869	Apr. 5, 1861	*Sept. 24, 1858	Resigned Aug. 1873.
ARNEY, E. T.	—	—	—	—	—	*Aug. 1, 1857	
ARNOLD, JOHN	—	—	1697	—	—	—	
ARNOLD, NICHOLAS	—	—	1697	—	—	—	
ATKINS, THOMAS	—	—	—	—	Apr. 29, 1809	*Feb. 5, 1808	Resigned Aug. 24, 1809.
ATKINSON, FREDERIC ST. J.†	—	—	—	—	Mar. 14, 1901	Apr. 17, 1900	Joined 2nd Dragoon Guards, Sept. 3, 1902.
BALDWYN, EDWARD JAMES	—	—	—	Sept. 1, 1852	—	*Jan. 1, 1836	Late Lieut. 4th Foot, died June 13, 1857.
BANNERMAN, JAMES MURRAY‡	—	—	—	Mar. 21, 1877	July 22, 1869	—	Joined 4th Regt.
BARRETT-LENNARD, AYLMER GUY H.	—	—	—	—	Apr. 7, 1906	June 22, 1903	Resigned May 31, 1907.
BATHURST, CHARLES	—	—	—	June 21, 1897	June 4, 1892	Aug. 16, 1890	Resigned April 20, 1898.
BATHURST, THE HON. WILLIAM LENNOX	—	—	—	—	—	*May 8, 1821	

LIST OF OFFICERS

Name									Remarks
Batt, Augustine William	—	—	—	—	—	—	May 24, 1798	*June 2, 1794	
Batt, William Ferdinand	—	—	—	—	—	Apr. 16, 1884	July 1, 1881	Jan. 11, 1881	Died Oct. 14, 1895.
Baynes, Nigel William Francis	—	—	—	—	—	—	Feb. 10, 1899		Joined Gloucestershire Regt. March 6, 1900.
Beadnell, A. G. S.	—	—	—	—	—	Apr. 17, 1871	—		
Beale, William	—	—	—	—	—	—	*Aug. 12, 1807		Joined 90th Regt. Sept. 24, 1807.
Beaufort, Henry, 5th Duke of, K.G.	—	Dec. 23, 1771	—	—	—	—	—		Granted Rank of Colonel in Army March 14, 1794. Lord Lieutenant of the Counties of Monmouth, Brecon, and Leicester. Died Oct. 11, 1803.
Beaufort, Henry Charles, 6th Duke of, K.G.	—	Oct. 26, 1803	—	—	—	—	—		See Worcester, Marquis of. Lord Lieutenant of the Counties of Monmouth, Brecon, and Gloucester. Died Nov. 23, 1835.
Beer, Hercules	—	—	—	—	—	—	*Apr. 7, 1808		Resigned 1809.
Beever, William Frederick Holt	—	—	—	—	—	—	Sub. June 1, 1874		Resigned Oct. 15, 1875.
Bellamy, Thomas	—	—	—	—	Capt. Lieut. May 15, 1788 / July 25, 1793	—	—		
Benson, Arthur Edward	—	—	—	—	—	Nov. 18, 1859	—		Late Lieut. 10th Hussars, died 1866.

ROYAL MONMOUTHSHIRE MILITIA

Name	Colonel	Lieut.-Col.	Major	Captain	Lieutenant	2nd Lieutenant or *Ensign	Remarks
BLAKENEY, HENRY ROSS	—	—	—	—	July 1, 1881	Mar. 13, 1880	Resigned Nov. 22, 1881.
BOSANQUET, SAMUEL RICHARD	—	—	—	June 16, 1824	—	—	
BOYS, THOMAS	—	—	—	—	—	*Feb. 5, 1808	Joined 4th Regt. April 10, 1809.
BRADNEY, JOHN HARFORD	—	—	—	—	Apr. 7, 1906	Oct. 31, 1903	Joined Duke of Cornwall's Light Infantry May 22, 1909.
BRADNEY, JOSEPH ALFRED ‡	—	—	—	Jan. 11, 1882	Apr. 19, 1881	—	From Shropshire Militia. Resigned 1892. Subsequently Colonel 2nd Batt. Monmouthshire Regt.
BRAGGE, JOSEPH	—	—	—	—	Mar. 25, 1799	*June 16, 1798	
BREDIN, WILLIAM	—	—	—	—	Mar. 4, 1859	*1858	
BRIDGEWATER, THOMAS	—	—	—	Aug. 29, 1806	May 24, 1798	*Jan. 24, 1798	Joined 36th Regt. Nov. 1799, rejoined Militia in 1803, and afterwards Captain Royal Brecon Militia.
BRIGGES, CLEMENT	—	—	—	—	Feb. 1, 1793	—	
BROOK, THOMAS	—	—	—	May 14, 1855	May 6, 1853	—	Resigned May 17, 1869.
BROWN, WILLIAM	—	—	—	—	May 3, 1798	—	Also Quarter-Master.

LIST OF OFFICERS

Name						Remarks
BROWNE, EVELYN †	—	—	—	—	Sept. 22, 1900	Hon. Lieut. in Army, resigned Dec. 6, 1902.
BROWNE, JAMES	—	—	—	—	June 25, 1856 / *June 13, 1855	Resigned Sept. 3, 1862.
BUCHANAN, THOMAS J.	—	—	—	Apr. 8, 1870	—	From 52nd Foot, resigned 1871.
BUCKLEY, EGERTON JOHN BULKELEY	—	—	—	Apr. 27, 1885	—	Resigned April 19, 1892.
BULLOCK, CLIFFORD FREDERICK TOULMIN	—	—	—	May 28, 1904	May 7, 1902	Resigned Jan. 14, 1905.
BUNBURY (see McClintock-Bunbury)						
BYGRAVE, CHARLES	—	—	—	Apr. 25, 1803	—	Joined 45th Regt. Aug. 1805.
CAPPER, RICHARD HARCOURT	—	—	—	May 1, 1865	—	Resigned Sept. 1869.
CAPPER, RICHARD HARCOURT ORD	—	—	—	July 1, 1881	Apr. 4, 1881	Joined North Staffs Regt. May 23, 1885.
CARLES, J. E.	—	—	—	—	*Aug. 2, 1798	
CARTER, EDWIN	—	—	1831	—	—	Resigned 1843.
CARY (see Stanley-Cary)						
CECIL, WILLIAM	—	—	—	—	*Apr. 5, 1796	
CHAMBRE, CHRISTOPHER.	—	—	Mar. 25, 1813	Jan. 1, 1813	—	

ROYAL MONMOUTHSHIRE MILITIA

Name	Colonel	Lieut.-Col.	Major	Captain	Lieutenant	2nd Lieutenant or *Ensign	Remarks
CHAMBRE, FRANCIS	—	—	Aug. 25, 1812	July 13, 1803	Apr. 26, 1798	—	Joined 36th Regt. Nov. 1799. Afterwards Lieut.-Col. Commandant Royal Brecon Militia.
CHAMBRE, JOHN	—	1761	—	—	—	—	
CLARKE, ERNEST JAMES PROCTOR †	—	—	—	—	May 15, 1908	Dec. 2, 1905	
CLAY, HENRY HASTING ‡	—	—	—	Dec. 13, 1890	Dec. 15, 1883	—	Resigned March 8, 1893.
CLIFFORD, HENRY MORGAN	Mar. 5, 1858	Lieut.-Col. Commndt. July 22, 1847	—	Apr. 18, 1836	—	—	Nine years in 14th Foot, died Feb. 12, 1884.
CLIFFORD, HENRY SOMERS MORGAN	—	—	—	—	Jan. 6, 1855	—	Resigned Jan. 1856.
COOKE, EDWARD DOUGLAS MONTAGUE HUNTER	—	—	—	—	Jan. 20, 1897	July 6, 1894	Joined R.G.A. June 14, 1899.
COOKE, JOSEPH JOHN	—	—	—	—	Sept. 25, 1812	*Feb. 14, 1811	Resigned July 6, 1813.
CORRY, CLAUDE LINDSAY †	—	—	—	—	Mar. 14, 1901	May 1, 1900	Joined Royal Garrison Regt. Nov. 5, 1902.
COSENS, GEORGE	—	—	—	—	Jan. 25, 1808	Aug. 8, 1807	Resigned Jan. 12, 1809.
COWARD, ISAAC TOOGOOD	—	—	—	—	—	*Jan. 16, 1814	Joined Royal Wagon Train Feb. 25, 1814.
COWARD, THOMAS TOOGOOD	—	—	—	—	—	*July 17, 1810	Joined Royal Wagon Train 1810.

LIST OF OFFICERS

Name					Remarks
COWIE, ALEXANDER GORDON	—	—	—	—	Dec. 19, 1907	
COWIE, HUGH CAMERON	—	—	—	—	Dec. 18, 1907	
COXE, C. W.	—	—	May 14, 1779	—	—	
CRAWSHAY, CODRINGTON H. REES †	—	—	—	Mar. 14, 1901	Apr. 9, 1900	Joined Royal Welsh Fusiliers July 27, 1901.
CROKER, EDWARD WILLIAM	—	—	—	July 1, 1881	Apr. 4, 1881	Resigned May 1, 1883.
CROMPTON-ROBERTS, CHARLES MONTAGU ‡	—	—	July 21, 1902	May 14, 1892	Mar. 21, 1885	—	Hon. Lieut.-Colonel Dec. 3, 1904. Hon. Captain in Army Nov. 1, 1900.
CURRE, WILLIAM EDWARD CARNE ‡	—	—	Feb. 6, 1895	Nov. 16, 1889	Aug. 16, 1879	May 6, 1874	—	Hon. Colonel May 20, 1895, Hon. Lieut.-Colonel in Army Oct. 31, 1900. Resigned March 19, 1901.
CURTIES, EUSTACE H. BESSEMER	—	—	—	—	June 14, 1906	
CURZON, ERNEST CHARLES PENN	—	—	—	Oct. 16, 1875	—	Joined 18th Hussars.
DASHWOOD, DE COURCY PITCAIRN	—	—	—	May 15, 1867	—	Resigned April 1870.
DAUNT, GEORGE BOWERBANK	—	—	—	June 25, 1856	*June 13, 1855	Resigned March 1, 1861.
DAVID, MARKHAM	—	—	—	Apr. 7, 1906	Apr. 22, 1903	
DAVIES, FRASER	—	—	—	Mar. 26, 1780	*Apr. 1778	Also Surgeon.

ROYAL MONMOUTHSHIRE MILITIA

Name	Colonel	Lieut.-Col.	Major	Captain	Lieutenant	2nd Lieutenant or Ensign	Remarks
DAVIES, JAMES	—	—	Mar. 21, 1877	May 21, 1853	Oct. 17, 1852	—	Hon. Lieut.-Colonel, May 8, 1877, resigned Dec. 2, 1881.
DAVIS, THOMAS WATKINS	—	—	Nov. 25, 1803	May 25, 1796	—	—	Resigned Aug. 24, 1812.
DE LAPASTURE, HY.	—	—	—	—	Feb. 13, 1869	—	Resigned May 25, 1869.
DELISLE, GEO.	—	—	—	—	July 7, 1803	—	Resigned May 27, 1804.
DENNY, THOMAS STOUGHTON	—	—	—	—	May 25, 1808	*Jan. 14, 1808	Resigned Jan. 25, 1810.
DIGBY, KENELM E. †	—	—	—	May 28, 1904	Feb. 14, 1900	Jan. 1, 1898	Qualified Interpreter in French, German, and Russian.
DIXON, CHARLES CECIL	—	—	—	—	—	*July 5, 1798	Also Surgeon.
DONNELLAN, N. N.	—	—	—	Oct. 25, 1803	Mar. 25, 1799	—	Died Aug. 28, 1806.
DOWLING, REGINALD B.	—	—	—	—	Mar. 1, 1859	*Feb. 8, 1858	Joined 25th Regt.
DURBIN, JOSEPH G.	—	—	—	Oct. 24, 1798	Mar. 26, 1796	—	Joined 36th Regt. Nov. 1799.
EDIE, JOHN	—	—	—	—	June 25, 1798	—	
EDWARDS, RICHARD H.	—	—	—	—	—	May 17, 1894	Resigned Jan. 20, 1897.
EDWARDS, ROGER	—	—	—	—	1761	—	

LIST OF OFFICERS

Name								Remarks
Edwards, Thomas Ferrers	—	—	—	—	Sept. 18, 1821	—	—	—
Ellis, Thomas	—	—	—	1831	—	—	—	—
Elton, Arthur Bayard	—	—	—	—	July 19, 1879	—	Oct. 27, 1877	Joined 19th Regt. Aug. 12, 1879.
Evans, Arthur Percival	—	—	—	—	—	—	Aug. 20, 1900	Joined King's Royal Rifles Dec. 3, 1901.
Evans, Charles Gilbert†	—	—	—	—	June 1, 1907	June 23, 1902	June 8, 1901	Hon. Lieut. in Army Oct. 1902.
Eyre, Vincent Thomas Joseph	—	—	—	—	Jan. 7, 1901	—	—	Joined 1st Life Guards Jan. 29, 1902.
Feetham, Edward	—	—	—	—	July 1, 1881	—	—	Joined Royal Berkshire Regt. May 12, 1883.
Fletcher, Horatio John Walpole	—	—	—	—	—	—	Nov. 11, 1905	Resigned March 28, 1906.
Fletcher, Owen Heaton Lynch	—	—	—	—	—	—	Sept. 21, 1901	Resigned March 21, 1903.
Fludyer, Sir Samuel, Bt.	—	July 1, 1805	—	Mar. 25, 1799	—	—	*June 25, 1781	2nd Baronet. Resigned Aug. 24, 1812.
Fludyer, Sir Samuel, Bt.	—	—	1835	Feb. 9, 1821	—	—	—	3rd Baronet. Resigned 1843.
Foord, William	—	—	—	—	Aug. 2, 1810	—	*May 2, 1810	Paymaster. Died April 8, 1826.
Foote, Charles S.	—	—	—	—	Mar. 21, 1877	—	—	Joined 40th Regt. Oct. 18, 1878.

266 ROYAL MONMOUTHSHIRE MILITIA

Name	Colonel	Lieut.-Col.	Major	Captain	Lieutenant	2nd Lieutenant or *Ensign	Remarks
Forestier-Walker, Roland Stuart †	—	—	Mar. 19, 1908	Mar. 20, 1901	Apr. 20, 1898	Apr. 4, 1896	Hon. Captain in Army Oct. 15, 1901.
Forrest, Houghton	—	—	—	—	Mar. 26, 1855	*July 3, 1854	Resigned 1856.
Forster, Thomas Guy Burton	—	—	—	—	—	Dec. 1, 1907	
Freeston, William Lockyer	—	—	—	—	—	*Feb. 25, 1811	Joined 3rd Regt. Aug. 1811.
Fry, William Jones	—	—	—	—	—	*Dec. 11, 1793	
Fryer, George	—	—	—	—	—	*1761	
Fulton, Henry †	—	—	—	May 1, 1907 Mar. 3, 1904	—	—	Hon. Lieut. in Army. Joined from Portsmouth Div. Submarine Miners R.E. Militia.
Gabb, George	—	—	—	—	—	*Nov. 9, 1811	Joined 4th Regt. Nov. 24, 1812.
Gabb, James Ashe	—	—	—	—	Oct. 27, 1803	July 29, 1803	Resigned April 14, 1807.
Galloway, Christian F. J. †	—	—	—	Mar. 19, 1904	Feb. 14, 1900	Dec. 1, 1897	Hon. Lieut. in Army Nov. 1, 1900, resigned Jan. 15, 1908.
Galloway, William A. D.	—	—	—	June 6, 1903	Dec. 7, 1898	Mar. 10, 1897	Hon. Lieut. in Army, resigned April 30, 1907.
Gill, Francis Edwin †	—	—	—	Mar. 9, 1908	May 28, 1904	Dec. 21, 1901	Hon. Second Lieut. in Army Oct. 5, 1902.

LIST OF OFFICERS

Name					Remarks
Gilliat, Sydney William E.	—	—	—	Jan. 11, 1882	Resigned Jan. 30, 1883.
Gist, Thomas Sillick	—	—	Mar. 28, 1903	Aug. 23, 1900	Resigned Dec. 5, 1903.
Goodlake, Henry Selwyn	—	—	—	Apr. 24, 1878	From South Gloucester Militia. Subsequently joined 40th Regt. Oct. 11, 1879.
Gray, John Michael Zamoiski-	—	—	May 23, 1866	Aug. 9, 1858*June 23, 1856	Hon. Major June 13, 1876, resigned May 9, 1879.
Green, Andrew	—	—	—	Aug. 22, 1900	Resigned April 30, 1904.
Greenwell, Ronald Eyre	—	—	—	Oct. 26, 1901	Joined 13th Hussars March 26, 1909.
Green Wilkinson, F. H.	—	—	Mar. 4, 1893	Sept. 4, 1889 Sept. 24, 1887	Resigned March 23, 1898.
Gunning, John E.	—	—	—	Jan. 7, 1903	Jan. 2, 1901	Resigned Feb. 27, 1904.
Gwyn, Matthew	—	—	Feb. 25, 1793	—	Captain Glamorgan Militia Oct. 22, 1780.
Gwynne, Roderick	—	—	Mar. 14, 1803	—	Resigned 1804.
Gwynne, Sackville	—	—	Sept. 1, 1798	—	Resigned Oct. 25, 1803.
Haldane, Edward H. V.	—	—	—	Feb. 26, 1876	—	Resigned Feb. 1, 1877.
Hanbury-Williams, Richard Capel	—	—	Apr. 26, 1882	July 1, 1881	Sept. 26, 1879	Died in camp with the Regiment July 21, 1891.

ROYAL MONMOUTHSHIRE MILITIA

Name	Colonel	Lieut.-Col.	Major	Captain	Lieutenant	2nd Lieutenant or * Ensign	Remarks
HARRIS, FREDERIC C.	—	—	—	—	Apr. 1, 1906	May 9, 1904	
HASWELL, JOHN	—	—	—	—	Mar. 7, 1792	*June 10, 1779	Adjutant Aug. 1778.
HAWKER, EDMUND BULTEEL	—	—	—	June 3, 1901	—	—	From Royal Sussex Regt., resigned Dec. 24, 1904.
HEBDEN, ROBERT C.	—	—	—	—	Apr. 1, 1907; July 29, 1900	—	From Humber Division Submarine Miners Militia, resigned April 15, 1908.
HEDGES, KILLINGWORTH WILLIAM	—	—	—	—	—	Mar. 25, 1878	Resigned June 17, 1879.
HELBERT HELBERT, CHARLES J.	—	—	July 21, 1902	Sept. 2, 1893	Mar. 22, 1890	—	From Royal Welsh Fusiliers. Hon. Captain in Army Nov. 1, 1900. Died Jan. 28, 1903.
HENRY, F. H. VAUGHAN.	—	—	—	—	Jan. 31, 1883	—	Resigned Oct. 8, 1887.
HENRY, LORENZO C. V.	—	—	—	—	Apr. 26, 1883	—	Resigned June 11, 1887.
HERBERT, EDMUND ARTHUR, M.V.O.	—	—	—	—	Mar. 7, 1885	—	Joined Inniskilling Dragoons and commanded the Regiment.
HERBERT, EDMUND PHILIP	—	—	Jan. 6, 1855	Dec. 11, 1848	—	—	Chief Constable of Monmouthshire, resigned 1857.
HEYLIN, CHARLES	—	—	—	—	—	*1761	Also Adjutant and Quarter Master.

LIST OF OFFICERS

Name							Remarks
Hicken, Henry	—	—	—	—	—	Aug. 25, 1806	Mar. 1806	Resigned 1808.
Hodges, John	—	—	—	—	—	—	*June 16, 1793	
Hogsflesh, Benjamin	—	—	—	—	—	—	*Jan. 6, 1820	
Hollingdale, William	—	—	—	—	—	—	*June 5, 1812	Also Assistant Surgeon, resigned May 10, 1813.
Hollister, Luke	—	—	—	—	June 25, 1781	—	*Feb. 25, 1779	
Homfray, Augustus Devereux	—	—	—	—	—	Apr. 24, 1880	Dec. 11, 1878	Joined 35th Regt. Oct. 22, 1880.
Homfray, Charles	—	—	—	—	—	June 13, 1855	*July 15, 1854	Resigned Dec. 31, 1855.
Homfray, Samuel George	—	—	—	—	Mar. 26, 1855	May 6, 1853	—	Resigned 1857.
Hopkins, Herbert Frederick Northey	—	—	—	—	—	July 19, 1879	Feb. 6, 1878	Joined Essex Regt. July 29, 1882.
Huth, Charles F.	—	—	—	—	—	Apr. 1, 1907 July 29, 1900	—	From Harwich Div. Submarine Miners Militia. Hon. Lieut. in Army July 14, 1901.
Hyde-Clarke, Rochfort	—	—	—	—	—	Nov. 13, 1875	—	
Isaacson, Anthony Allett	—	—	—	—	—	Mar. 25, 1813	June 25, 1812	Resigned 1816, and took Holy Orders. Died 1843.

ROYAL MONMOUTHSHIRE MILITIA

Name	Colonel	Lieut.-Col.	Major	Captain	Lieutenant	2nd Lieutenant or *Ensign	Remarks
ISAACSON, ANTHONY HARVEST	—	—	—	—	Apr. 5, 1793	—	Also Quarter-Master. Ensign 34th Regt. March 1783. Also served in the 2nd (Queen's) Regt. and the 41st Regt. Appointed Adjutant Monmouth and Brecon Militia Feb. 19, 1792. Brevet Captain, 1798. Adjutant West Monmouth Local Militia Sept. 1808.
ISAACSON, EGERTON CHARLES HARVEST	—	—	—	—	—	*Sept. 25, 1812	Later Ensign 51st Regt. Adjutant Brecon Militia 1823-46.
JACKSON, WILLIAM BIRKENHEAD MATHER	—	—	—	May 26, 1888	Apr. 25, 1883	—	Resigned March 4, 1893.
JARVIS, FRANK B.	—	—	—	—	Mar. 19, 1908	May 8, 1905	
JENKINS, EDWARD TUBERVILLE LLEWELLIN†	—	—	—	—	Mar. 14, 1901	Jan. 24, 1900	Hon. Second Lieut. in Army Nov. 1, 1900, resigned April 30, 1907.
†JENKINS, GEORGE T.	—	—	—	—	Feb. 25, 1809	—	Resigned April 24, 1814.
JENKINS, RICHARD	—	—	—	Apr. 25, 1798	Dec. 3, 1795	*Apr. 2, 1794	Resigned 1811.
JENKINSON, THOMAS BANKS	—	—	—	—	—	May 13, 1902	Resigned Nov. 5, 1902.
JOHNSTONE, THOMAS JAMES	—	—	—	—	Aug. 12, 1807	*Apr. 25, 1807	Resigned Aug. 24, 1809.

LIST OF OFFICERS

Name							Remarks
JOHNSTONE, THOMAS JAMES	—	—	—	—	July 5, 1810	Aug. 25, 1806	Died Dec. 15, 1812.
JONES, GEORGE	—	—	—	—	Aug. 25, 1794	—	
JONES, JOHN	—	—	Oct. 1, 1798	—	—	—	
JONES, RICHARD	—	—	—	—	—	—	Paymaster 1854, resigned April 28, 1863. Joined the Hanoverian Hussars and became A.D.C. to King George V. of Hanover.
JONES, THOMAS	—	—	—	Sept. 20, 1798	Mar. 25, 1794 Capt.-Lieut. April 5, 1793	—	Resigned June 24, 1803.
KANE, CHARLES GEORGE	—	—	—	—	—	*Feb. 8, 1858	Joined 9th Regt. 1858.
KEMEYS, SIR CHARLES, BT.	—	—	—	—	1684	—	
KEMEYS-TYNTE, CHARLES THEODORE HASWELL	—	—	—	—	Sept. 4, 1895	Jan. 6, 1894	Resigned Sept. 28, 1898.
KENNARD, MAURICE N.	—	—	—	—	—	Apr. 3, 1901	Joined 6th Dragoon Guards March 26, 1902.
KENNARD, WILLOUGHBY A.	—	—	—	—	—	Oct. 26, 1898	Joined 13th Hussars March 21, 1900.
KENNEDY, ERNEST ARTHUR	—	—	—	—	July 1, 1881	Nov. 14, 1879	Resigned Jan. 24, 1882.
KETTLEBY, JAMES	—	—	Sept. 18, 1812	Aug. 10, 1812	—	—	Captain 51st Regt. Jan. 8, 1814.

ROYAL MONMOUTHSHIRE MILITIA

Name	Colonel	Lieut.-Col.	Major	Captain	Lieutenant	2nd Lieutenant or *Ensign	Remarks
KING, JAMES PEARCE	—	—	—	—	Nov. 15, 1852	—	Resigned Sept. 25, 1854.
KING, WILLIAM	—	—	—	—	July 10, 1778	—	
LAMOTTE, GEORGE M. L.†	—	—	June 6, 1903	Mar. 27, 1898	June 4, 1892	Mar. 25, 1891	Hon. Captain in Army Nov. 1, 1900, resigned May 28, 1904.
LANGSLOW, ROBERT	—	—	—	—	Dec. 25, 1810	*Sept. 10, 1810	Captain Wiltshire Militia, Aug. 10, 1812.
LAVICOURT, JOHN	—	—	—	—	—	*May 9, 1813	Resigned Feb. 24, 1814.
LAWRENCE, ARTHUR SEELY	—	—	—	—	—	*June 14, 1813	Also Assistant Surgeon.
LAWRENCE, FREDERIC J.	—	—	—	—	Apr. 15, 1893	Apr. 4, 1891	Resigned April 15, 1893.
LAWRENCE, JOHN	—	—	—	—	—	*Apr. 18, 1854	Joined 23rd Regt. Nov. 28, 1854.
LAWRENCE, RICHARD A.	—	—	—	—	Dec. 11, 1848	—	Died April 1, 1856.
LEETHAM, ARTHUR	—	—	Mar. 21, 1903	Sept. 3, 1898	—	—	Late Capt. 13th Hussars. Served in Egypt 1885–6. Maj. Res. of Officers. Hon. Lieut.-Col. May 9, 1903. Assistant Private Secretary to Under Secretary of State for War Feb. 13, 1901. Secretary, Royal United Service Institution, Jan. 1904.

LIST OF OFFICERS

Name							Remarks
LEIGH, WM.	—	—	—	—	Mar. 1, 1859	Jan. 11, 1856	*Aug. 25, 1854	Resigned April 2, 1861.
LESLIE, LEWIS	—	—	—	—	—	—	*Dec. 25, 1812	Joined 16th Regt. Feb. 25, 1814.
LEWIS, AYTHAN	—	—	—	—	Feb. 25, 1798	Capt.-Lt. and Capt. Mar. 25, 1796 Lieut. Apr. 5, 1793	—	Adjutant Brecon Local Militia, April 25, 1809.
LEWIS, CHARLES EDWARD	—	—	—	—	May 21, 1853	Oct. 17, 1852	—	Resigned May 5, 1855.
LEWIS, FRANCIS	—	—	—	—	—	—	*1697	
LEWIS, GEORGE	—	—	—	—	1697	—	—	
LEWIS, HENRY	—	—	—	—	1704	June 6, 1900	Oct. 26, 1898	Hon. Lieut. in Army, Nov. 1, 1900. Joined 16th Lancers Jan. 5, 1901.
LEWIS, THOMAS	—	Nov. 23, 1835	Aug. 25, 1812	July 7, 1803	—	—	—	
LEWIS, THOMAS	—	—	—	—	—	—	—	Died April 24, 1847.
LEWIS, THOMAS FREKE	—	—	—	—	—	Dec. 20, 1853	—	Joined 23rd Regt, Jan. 5, 1855.
LIDCARD, CHARLES	—	—	—	—	—	—	*1831	
LINDSAY, GEORGE MACKINTOSH	—	—	—	—	—	—	Feb. 2, 1898	Joined Rifle Brigade Jan. 23, 1900.

ROYAL MONMOUTHSHIRE MILITIA

Name	Colonel	Lieut.-Col.	Major	Captain	Lieutenant	2nd Lieutenant or *Ensign	Remarks
LINDSAY, HENRY EDZELL MORGAN†	—	Mar. 19, 1908	Mar. 20, 1901	Dec. 2, 1891	—	—	Captain late R.E., Major Reserve of Officers. Served in Eastern Sudan 1885. Adjutant 1887–1891.
LISTER, EDWARD LONGWORTH	—	—	Dec. 13, 1890	May 12, 1881	Oct. 29, 1879	31 Aug. 1878	Died July 29, 1896.
LLOYD, A.	—	—	—	—	May 24, 1798	*July 18, 1779	
LLOYD, GEORGE ARTHUR	—	—	—	Apr. 5, 1861	Apr. 2, 1856	*May 28, 1855	Resigned May 22, 1866.
LORYMER, JAMES	—	—	—	Dec. 25, 1810	Nov. 16, 1805	—	Disembodied Jan. 6, 1816. Died Feb. 16, 1820.
LOWLEY, MILES	—	—	—	—	—	*Sept. 23, 1793	
LUCAS, RICHARD	—	—	—	Apr. 29, 1772	—	—	
LYON, NATHANIEL JOHN	—	—	—	—	June 12, 1899	—	Resigned Oct. 3, 1899. Late Grenadier Guards.
McCLINTOCK-BUNBURY, HON. W.†	—	—	—	—	—	Sept. 28, 1897	Joined 2nd Dragoons Jan. 4, 1899. Killed at the Relief of Kimberley.
McDONNELL, FRANCIS, C.B.	—	Apr. 30, 1879	Mar. 1, 1859	May 6, 1853	—	—	From 71st Foot. Hon. Colonel July 25, 1879. Resigned Sept. 27, 1890.
McDONNELL, FRANCIS J. D.	—	—	—	Jan. 20, 1897	June 3, 1891	Apr. 7, 1890	Resigned April 2, 1898.

LIST OF OFFICERS

Name						Remarks
McGregor, John Stewart	—	—	—	—	—	
Mackworth, Humphrey†	—	—	Jan. 16, 1908	Dec. 10, 1904	—	Formerly Lieutenant 3rd Queen's Royal West Surrey Regt. Hon. Lieut. in Army, Feb. 7, 1903.
Mansel, Jestyn Llewelyn	—	—	—	—	Feb. 11, 1899	Joined 7th Dragoon Guards Jan. 10, 1900. Resigned June 24, 1909.
Matthews, Robert L.†	—	Nov. 11, 1906	Mar. 14, 1901	June 21, 1897	Mar. 27, 1895	Hon. Captain in Army, Oct. 14, 1901, Extra A.D.C. to Lord Ampthill, Governor of Madras, April 12, 1902.
Mayberry, Walter	—	—	—	Dec. 25, 1804	—	Lieut. 35th Regt., May 1805.
Meredith, Evan J.	—	—	—	June 25, 1798	—	Lieut. 35th Regt., May 1805.
Meredith, John C.	—	—	May 25, 1809	—	—	Adjutant Brecon Local Militia, Mar. 24, 1813.
Metcalfe, John A.	—	—	Feb. 1, 1873	Apr. 2, 1864	—	Transferred to Durham Militia June 1, 1874.
Milman, Henry Salisbury	—	—	Oct. 30, 1852	—	—	Resigned 1856.
Moffatt, Harold Charles	—	—	—	Feb. 4, 1882	—	Resigned Jan. 26, 1883.

ROYAL MONMOUTHSHIRE MILITIA

Name	Colonel	Lieut.-Col.	Major	Captain	Lieutenant	2nd Lieutenant or *Ensign	Remarks
MOGRIDGE, JOHN ANTILL	—	—	—	—	July 19, 1879	Oct. 6, 1877	Joined 40th Foot Aug. 12, 1879.
MORETON, PERCY C. R.	—	—	—	—	Jan. 16, 1908	Mar. 19, 1904	
MORGAN, CHARLES COURTENAY EVAN†	—	—	June 12, 1901	Dec. 30, 1891	Oct. 18, 1884	—	A.D.C. to General Officer Commanding Thames District, May 16, 1900. Hon. Lieut.-Colonel June 23, 1904. Resigned Aug. 29, 1908.
MORGAN, HENRY	—	—	—	1697	—	—	
MORGAN, PAUL	—	—	—	1761	—	—	
MORGAN, R.	1759	—	—	—	—	—	
MORGAN, THOMAS	—	—	—	Mar. 26, 1778	—	—	
MORGAN, THOMAS	—	—	—	Oct. 25, 1811	Aug. 15, 1796	—	Brigadier-General of Militia for Brecknock and Monmouth, 1760
MORGAN, THOMAS	—	—	—	1761	—	—	Died Dec. 20, 1821.
MORGAN, WILLIAM F. H.	—	—	—	—	—	Aug. 16, 1879	Resigned March 11, 1881.
MORRIS, GEORGE L.	—	—	—	—	Oct. 18, 1879	Apr. 4, 1878	Resigned Apr. 5, 1881.
MORSE, GEORGE	—	—	—	—	Sept. 25, 1803	—	Also Assistant Surgeon. Resigned Sept. 26, 1807.

LIST OF OFFICERS

Name						
Murphy, Eugene L. J.	—	—	—	—	Nov. 28, 1883	—	Resigned July 20, 1889.
Napier, Rupert George C.	—	—	—	—	—	June 4, 1904	Joined Grenadier Guards May 10, 1905.
Nash, William Llewellyn	—	—	—	—	Sept. 28, 1807	*Mar. 25, 1800	Also Assistant Surgeon and, later, Surgeon. Resigned May 3, 1812.
Neville, Hon. S. H. (see Abergavenny)	—	April 5, 1793	Apr. 1772	—	—	—	Resigned June 30, 1805.
Newland, Charles	—	—	—	—	—	*Sept. 28, 1807	Also Assistant Surgeon. Resigned Aug. 14, 1809.
Nicholson, William	—	—	—	—	Nov. 19, 1807	May 3, 1796	
Norman, Edward Brise Kensit	—	—	—	—	—	June 26, 1901	Resigned Dec. 14, 1901.
Nunn, Joshua Arthur, C.B., C.I.E., D.S.O.	—	—	—	—	Mar. 24, 1871	—	Joined Army Vet. Dept., Apr. 24, 1877. Became Colonel, and died in 1908.
Oakes, Edward	—	—	—	—	—	Mar. 13, 1880	
Oakley, Thomas Robert	—	—	—	—	Apr. 30, 1873	—	Resigned Jan. 13, 1874.
O'Brien, J. G.	—	—	—	Mar. 27, 1898	—	—	Resigned June 18, 1902. Late Captain 4th Batt. King's Shropshire Light Infantry.
Ollivant, George B.	—	—	—	—	May 18, 1898	Mar. 3, 1897	Joined 12th Lancers, Nov. 15, 1899.

ROYAL MONMOUTHSHIRE MILITIA

Name	Colonel	Lieut.-Col.	Major	Captain	Lieutenant	2nd Lieutenant or *Ensign	Remarks
OWEN, WM.	—	—	—	—	Jan. 11, 1856	*Nov. 28, 1854	Joined 52nd Regt. June 24, 1856.
OXNARD, EDWARD	—	—	—	—	—	*Feb. 24, 1779	
PARDOE, ARTHUR GEORGE	—	—	—	—	Apr. 15, 1908	June 1, 1905	Resigned Feb. 23, 1883.
PARDOE, ARTHUR JOHN	—	—	—	Feb. 28, 1881	July 19, 1879	Feb. 6, 1878	Resigned Feb. 23, 1883.
PARRY, FLETCHER	—	—	—	—	—	*May 4, 1813	Resigned July 17, 1813.
PARSONS, JOHN DUNGATE	—	—	—	Nov. 13, 1803	—	—	Ensign 9th Foot, May 12, 1796. Adjutant Monmouth and Brecon Militia, Aug. 24, 1802. Died Aug. 26, 1821.
PARTRIDGE, EDWARD OTTO	—	—	—	Oct. 30, 1852	—	—	Resigned March 26, 1855.
PARTRIDGE, JOHN CROKER	—	—	—	—	Mar. 27, 1871	—	Resigned Nov. 30, 1877.
PARTRIDGE, JOSEPH E. C.†	—	—	—	—	Mar. 14, 1901	Apr. 25, 1900	Joined the Welsh Regiment Jan. 28, 1903.
PARTRIDGE, WALTER CROKER ST. IVES	—	—	—	Rejoined Jan. 12, 1884	Oct. 25, 1873	Oct. 25, 1873	Joined 61st Regt. Nov. 21, 1875.
PARTRIDGE, WILLIAM HAMP	—	—	—	—	June 4, 1892	Oct. 11, 1890	Resigned March 20, 1895.
PAXTON (see Wavell-Paxton)							

LIST OF OFFICERS

Name						Remarks
PAYNE, JOHN SELWYN	—	Feb. 24, 1877	Aug. 9, 1858	May 6, 1853	—	From 14th Regt. Hon. Colonel, April 1, 1877. Resigned April 29, 1879.
PAYNE, RICHARD LLOYD, C.B., D.S.O.	—	—	—	—	Feb. 21, 1874	Transferred to Tower Hamlets Militia. Joined Army. Now Major-General.
PAYNTER, CAMBORNE HAWEIS †	—	—	May 28, 1904	Feb. 3, 1900 July 10, 1901	—	Hon. Lieut.-Col. Nov. 26, 1904. Maj. late Inniskilling Dragoons. Major Comdg. Cornwall R.E. (T.F.) 1909.
PEARCE, JOHN	—	—	—	—	July 25, 1813 *Nov. 13, 1795	
PEARCE, JOHN	—	—	—	—	July 17, 1813 *Aug. 25, 1794	Also Paymaster and Quartermaster. Died, July 29, 1820.
PENNY, HENRY	—	—	—	—	June 11, 1809 Feb. 25, 1809	
PERKINS, CHARLES EDWARD HARRISON †	—	—	—	—	June 22, 1903	Hon. Lieut. in Army, Sept. 5, 1902. Joined 5th Batt. Manchester Regt., March 14, 1906.
PERKINS, EDWARD	—	—	—	1697	—	
PHILLIPS, CHARLES	—	—	—	—	July 25, 1778	Joined 89th Regt.
PHILLIPS, FREDERICK GORDON	—	—	—	—	Nov. 28, 1903	Resigned Feb. 28, 1907.
PHILLIPS, THOMAS JONES	—	—	—	—	June 25, 1781 *Apr. 27, 1780	

ROYAL MONMOUTHSHIRE MILITIA

Name	Colonel	Lieut.-Col.	Major	Captain	Lieutenant	2nd Lieutenant or *Ensign	Remarks
PHILLPOTS, JOHN MORGAN	—	—	—	—	May 25, 1798	*Nov. 15, 1796	Ensign 35th Regt., 1805.
PIDDING, JAMES	—	—	—	—	—	*Feb. 2, 1793	Also Surgeon.
PITT, WILLIAM GREY	—	—	—	—	—	*Aug. 2, 1854	From 11th Dragoons. Resigned Nov. 15, 1854.
POLLOCK-GORE, WILLIAM A. M.	—	—	—	—	Apr. 5, 1882	—	Joined Royal Scots, Feb. 28, 1885.
POWELL, CHARLES HARRISON	—	—	—	June 16, 1807	Oct. 27, 1803	*July 28, 1803	Paymaster, June 25, 1826.
POWELL, L. P.	—	—	—	—	—	*May 12, 1798	
POWELL, WILLIAM	—	—	—	—	—	*Mar. 1, 1814	Joined 43rd Regt. 1814.
POWELL, WILLIAM RHYS BRYCHAN	—	—	—	—	Mar. 1, 1859	*Sept. 17, 1858	Resigned Jan. 2, 1863.
PRICE, CHARLES	—	—	—	1697	—	—	
PRICE, DAVID	—	—	—	—	—	*Mar. 4, 1793	
PRICE, JOHN D.	—	—	—	Oct. 27, 1803	1803	—	Resigned March 24, 1857.
PRICE, REGINALD J. S.	—	—	—	Mar. 28, 1900	May 15, 1895	Apr. 14, 1893	Hon. Captain in Army, Nov. 1, 1900. Resigned June 23, 1908.
PRICE, THOMAS PHILLIPS	—	—	—	Dec. 10, 1879	July 19, 1879	Aug. 8, 1877	Resigned April 3, 1883.

LIST OF OFFICERS

PRICE, WILLIAM	—	—	—	—	May 24, 1798	*Apr. 5, 1793	Also Surgeon.
PRITCHARD, JOSEPH JAMES	—	—	—	—	—	*Apr. 25, 1803	Resigned May 31, 1805.
PROBERT, HENRY	—	1697	—	—	—	—	
PROCTOR, THOMAS	—	—	—	—	Aug. 20, 1814	*Feb. 25, 1814	Lieut. 43rd Regt., Oct. 1815.
PROCTOR, THOMAS	—	—	—	—	—	*Mar. 3, 1794	
RAGLAN, GEORGE FITZ ROY HENRY, LORD, C.B.	—	—	—	Mar. 20, 1901	May 29, 1895	Apr. 23, 1887	Late Captain Grenadier Guards. Served in Afghan War 1879–80. Hon. Colonel, April 27, 1901. Hon. Major in Army, Nov. 1, 1900. Afterwards Under-Secretary of State for War and Governor of the Isle of Man. Resigned Mar. 19, 1908.
RAWLINGS, PHILIP	—	—	—	—	—	*July 17, 1794	
REES-CRAWSHAY (see Crawshay)							
REID, FRASER J. D.	—	—	—	—	Jan. 21, 1874	—	From 6th Dragoons. Resigned March 31, 1874.
REID, THOMAS MAITLAND	—	—	—	—	Mar. 24, 1871	Apr. 24, 1871	From 6th Lancashire Militia. Resigned Sept. 24, 1886.
RICARDO, AMBROSE ST. Q.	—	—	—	—	Dec. 11, 1886	—	Joined Royal Inniskilling Fusiliers.

Name	Colonel	Lieut.-Col.	Major	Captain	Lieutenant	2nd Lieutenant or *Ensign	Remarks
RICHARDS, JAMES	—	—	—	—	—	Oct. 25, 1811	Joined 50th Regt. 1813.
RICHARDS, T. W.	—	—	—	Dec. 12, 1803	—	—	Resigned Feb. 28, 1805.
RICHARDS, WILLIAM	—	—	—	Nov. 26, 1803	—	—	
ROBERTS, JOHN CHAPMAN	—	—	—	Sept. 18, 1821	Jan. 6, 1810	—	From 37th Regt.
ROBERTS, THOMAS	—	—	—	—	July 25, 1778	—	
ROLLS, ALEXANDER	—	—	Apr. 26, 1853	1848	—	—	From 4th Dragoon Grds. Resigned Jan. 5, 1855.
ROLLS, HON. HENRY ALLAN	—	—	—	—	May 15, 1895	Aug. 27, 1892	Resigned April 4, 1896.
ROMART, EDWARD FRANCIS	—	—	—	—	Mar. 25, 1799	*May 29, 1798	
ROOKE, GEORGE DOUGLAS WILLOUGHBY†	—	—	—	—	—	Aug. 28, 1895	Resigned Feb. 17, 1897.
ROSSER, SAMUEL	—	—	—	—	1761	—	
ROUSSEAU, JOHN JAMES	—	—	—	—	—	*Feb. 10, 1804	Resigned May 27, 1804.
ROWARD, J.	—	—	—	—	—	*Oct. 24, 1780	
RUDDOCK, F. G.	—	—	—	—	—	*June 25, 1781	
RUDHALL, JACOB	—	—	—	Feb. 1, 1793	Apr. 1778	—	Also Quartermaster. Capt.-Lieut., July 7, 1779.

LIST OF OFFICERS

Name								Remarks
Rumsey, John	—	—	—	—	—	—	—	—
Russell, John Richard	—	—	—	Jan. 1, 1856	Dec. 20, 1853	May 6, 1853	—	Resigned May 31, 1869.
Salvin, Bryan John Francis	—	—	—	—	Mar. 24, 1871	—	—	Resigned Feb. 20, 1874.
Sargeaunt, John	—	—	—	—	Oct. 27, 1803	*Apr. 2, 1803	—	Joined 61st Regt. July 31, 1806.
Saunders, Cecil H.	—	—	—	—	—	Dec. 25, 1901	—	Joined 6th Dragoon Guards March 26, 1902.
Saunders, Percy O. C.	—	—	—	—	—	Dec. 9, 1896	—	Died March 6, 1898.
Savery, Almericus Blakeney	—	—	—	Aug. 1, 1857	May 6, 1853	—	—	Resigned May 7, 1865.
Segrave, Francis	—	—	—	—	Apr. 26, 1862	—	—	Resigned May 31, 1869.
Segrave, John	—	—	—	—	Jan. 29, 1855	*Mar. 29, 1854	—	Joined 4th Regt. March 25, 1855.
Selwyn, George	—	—	—	—	—	*Sept. 2, 1798	—	—
Seton-Karr, Henry Malcolm	—	—	—	—	—	July 2, 1901	—	Joined 2nd Dragoons March 26, 1902.
Sheehy, Bryan	—	—	Aug. 16, 1879	Nov. 2, 1858	July 23, 1855	*Aug. 25, 1854	—	Hon. Lieut.-Col. Sept. 19, 1879. Resigned Nov. 21, 1882.

Capt.-Lt. and Capt. May 8, 1799

Name	Colonel	Lieut.-Col.	Major	Captain	Lieutenant	2nd Lieutenant or *Ensign	Remarks
SIMMONS, SAMUEL	—	—	—	—	—	*1800	
SKINNER, EDGAR LOUIS	—	—	—	—	—	Feb. 20, 1904	Resigned March 21, 1907.
SMITH, HORATIO SHAW	—	—	—	—	Apr. 26, 1875	—	From Tower Hamlets Militia. Resigned April 23, 1878.
SMITH, RICHARD	—	—	—	—	Dec. 25, 1810	*Oct. 30, 1810	Disembodied, Jan. 6, 1816.
SMYTHE, EDWARD WALTER JOSEPH PATRICK HERBERT	—	—	—	June 6, 1895	May 13, 1891	Jan. 21, 1888	Resigned Aug. 10, 1898.
SOMERSET, HENRY FITZROY EDWARD	—	—	—	—	—	June 1, 1904	Resigned July 8, 1907.
SOMERSET, HON. FITZROY RICHARD	—	—	—	—	—	June 10, 1902	Resigned Aug. 6, 1904. Afterwards joined Grenadier Guards.
SOMERSET, HON. GRANVILLE WM. RICHARD	—	—	June 21, 1897	Nov. 16, 1889	Feb. 7, 1885	—	Previously in Royal Navy. Served in Egypt 1883, and in East Indies 1882. Hon. Lieut.-Colonel July 4, 1900. Resigned May 22, 1901.
SOMERSET, HON. RICHARD FITZROY	—	—	—	—	Jan. 31, 1883	—	Joined Grenadier Guards Aug. 17, 1886.
SOMERSET, HON. WELLESLEY FITZROY	—	—	—	—	—	July 16, 1904	Joined Welsh Regiment March 2, 1907.

LIST OF OFFICERS

Name						Notes
SOMERSET, LORD ARTHUR	—	—	Aug. 25, 1803	June 24, 1803	—	Resigned March 1805.
SOMERSET, LORD HENRY EDWARD BRUDENELL	—	—	—	Mar. 24, 1871	—	4th son of the 8th Duke of Beaufort. Resigned Feb. 20, 1874.
SOMERSET, VERE FRANCIS JOHN	—	—	—	Mar. 20, 1872	—	Resigned Feb. 2, 1875.
SOUTHWELL, ARTHUR R. P. VISCOUNT	—	—	Feb. 4, 1900	Sept. 2, 1893	Apr. 20, 1892	Resigned Feb. 5, 1902.
SPRY, JOHN	—	—	—	—	*Aug. 15, 1809	Also Assistant Surgeon. Resigned Aug. 10, 1811.
STANLEY-CARY, F. J.	—	—	—	May 2, 1905	—	From Humber Div. R.E. Submarine Miners Militia. Hon. Lieut. in Army, Sept. 16, 1902. Private Secretary to the Secretary of the War Office, April 1, 1907.
STEPNEY, T.	—	—	—	Apr. 1778	—	
STEWARD, WILLIAM JAMES	—	—	Sept. 24, 1873	Nov. 19, 1864	—	
STOUGHTON, T. A.	—	—	—	Apr. 29, 1809	*July 12, 1808	Resigned June 10, 1809.
STRACHAN, HORACE WARD	—	—	—	July 1, 1881	Jan. 14, 1880	Resigned Jan. 26, 1883.
STUDDERT, THOMAS G. H.	—	—	—	Apr. 1, 1907 Feb. 20, 1904	—	From Milford Haven Div. R.E. Submarine Miners Militia.
SYMONS, THOMAS EDWARD RAYMOND	—	—	—	—	Apr. 23, 1906	Joined Grenadier Guards Aug. 5, 1908.

ROYAL MONMOUTHSHIRE MILITIA

Name	Colonel	Lieut.-Col.	Major	Captain	Lieutenant	2nd Lieutenant or *Ensign	Remarks
SYMONS, THOMAS RAYMOND	—	—	—	—	Dec. 9, 1885	—	Resigned Mar. 11, 1891. Served as Lieutenant in Imperial Yeomanry in South African War.
THACKERAY, ALEX. GUY	—	—	—	—	May 28, 1904	May 15, 1902	Resigned May 15, 1908. Died 1909.
THATCHER, CHARLES	—	—	—	—	Dec. 19, 1804	*May 26, 1804	Resigned Sept. 24, 1809.
THIRKILL, JOHN	—	—	—	—	Mar. 24, 1871	—	
THOMAS, JOHN R. L.	—	—	—	—	Mar. 14, 1901	May 1, 1900	A.D.C. to Governor of Barbadoes June 11, 1902. Resigned Dec. 3, 1902.
THOMAS, OLIVER	—	—	—	—	—	*Aug. 9, 1811	Also Assistant Surgeon. Surgeon, May 4, 1812. Resigned May 5, 1855.
THYNNE, FREDERICK CHARLES	—	—	—	—	—	*July 13, 1855	
TOZER, ARTHUR G. M.	—	—	—	—	Oct. 22, 1881	—	Joined Northumberland Fusiliers May 14, 1884.
TREDEGAR, GODFREY CHARLES, VISCT.	Dec. 9, 1885	—	—	—	—	—	Late Capt. 17th Lancers. Rode in the Balaclava Charge. Son of the 1st Baron; created a Viscount 1902. Is Lord Lieutenant of the County of Monmouth.

LIST OF OFFICERS

Name							Remarks
TYLER, EDWARD JAMES	—	—	—	—	Jan. 25, 1856	*Jan. 29, 1855	Joined 5th Fusiliers, June 24, 1856.
TYLER, GEORGE GRIFFIN	—	—	—	Jan. 6, 1855	Nov. 3, 1852	—	Took out a draft of Militiamen to the Crimea.
VAN, CHARLES	—	—	—	1761	—	—	
VAUGHAN, CHARLES JEROME †	—	—	—	May 18, 1898 / May 6, 1903	Apr. 15, 1893	Feb. 5, 1892	Hon. Major, Aug. 6, 1908. To 7th Dragoon Guards, 1900–1902.
VAUGHAN, BAYNHAM FRANCIS	—	—	Nov. 15, 1890	Jan. 6, 1883	June 1, 1874	May 24, 1866	Hon. Colonel, Aug. 1, 1892. Resigned Jan. 2, 1895.
VAUGHAN, HERBERT MILLINGCHAMP	—	—	—	—	Jan. 20, 1897	Jan. 20, 1894	Resigned May 10, 1899.
VAUGHAN, JOHN FRANCIS	—	—	July 16, 1853	July 22, 1847	Aug. 27, 1836	—	Hon. Colonel, Mar. 19, 1858. Served in the Crimea. Resigned Jan. 9, 1877.
VYVYAN-ROBINSON, CECIL ALBERT	—	—	—	—	Apr. 7, 1906	May 6, 1903	
WAKEMAN, WILLIAM PLOWDEN	—	—	—	—	Mar. 2, 1861	—	
WALBEOFFE, THOMAS	—	—	—	—	—	*Sept. 8, 1820	Afterwards joined 79th Highlanders.
WALKER, GEORGE FERDINAND	—	—	—	—	Apr. 1, 1874	—	Resigned Mar. 12, 1875. Afterwards Sir G. F. Forestier-Walker, Bart., 3rd Baronet.

Name	Colonel	Lieut.-Col.	Major	Captain	Lieutenant	2nd Lieutenant or *Ensign	Remarks
WALKER, ROLAND STUART (see Forestier-Walker)							
WALLIS, KENNETH PERCIVAL	—	—	—	—	—	Mar. 29, 1905	Joined Welsh Regt. Mar. 2, 1907.
WALTON ROBERT BARON	—	—	—	—	—	*Dec. 25, 1812	Joined 51st Regt. Feb. 25, 1814.
WARD, JOHN	—	—	—	—	Jan. 25, 1808	*Sept. 21, 1807	
WATTS, ROGER J.	—	—	—	—	—	Nov. 1, 1906	Joined 5th Batt. Worcestershire Regt., July 29, 1909.
WAUTON, EDRIC BRENTON†	—	—	—	—	—	May 1, 1907	Assist. Commr., S. Nigeria, May 17, 1909.
WAVELL-PAXTON, RAYMOND GEORGE	—	—	—	—	—	June 11, 1904	Joined Coldstream Guards May 10, 1905. Took additional surname of Paxton, Mar. 28, 1905.
WHEELEY, JOHN GRIFFITHS	—	—	—	Aug. 9, 1858	Sept. 18, 1854	Dec. 20, 1853	Hon. Major, May 1873. Resigned Mar. 22, 1878.
WHEELEY, WILLIAM HENRY	—	—	Apr. 26, 1879	June 1, 1869	Apr. 5, 1861	*Aug. 8, 1859	Hon. Lieut.-Colonel, Aug. 8, 1884. Resigned Oct. 26, 1889.
WHITE, WILLIAM JASPER JOSEPH	—	—	—	—	Dec. 11, 1886	—	Resigned Aug. 3, 1889.

LIST OF OFFICERS

Name						
WICKHAM, BERTRAM J. W.	—	—	—	—	Apr. 3, 1889	Resigned June 13, 1890.
WILLIAMS, BASIL HENRY	—	—	—	—	Feb. 10, 1899	Joined Royal Warwickshire Regt. April 21, 1900.
WILLIAMS, DAVID	—	—	—	—	*Feb. 26, 1793	
WILLIAMS, EDWARD	—	—	—	—	*Feb. 25, 1811	Joined 3rd Regt. May 24, 1811.
WILLIAMS, SIR HOPTON, BT.	1704	—	—	1694	—	
WILLIAMS, SIR JOHN, BT.	1697	—	—	—	—	
WILLIAMS, JOHN	—	—	—	—	*Nov. 25, 1813	Joined Royal Wagon Train Feb. 25, 1814.
WILLIAMS, ROBERT H.	—	—	—	May 13, 1891	May 31, 1888	Resigned Mar. 11, 1893.
WILLIAMS, WILLIAM	—	—	Oct. 26, 1803	Mar. 14, 1803	—	Disembodied Jan. 6, 1816.
WILLIAMSON, ROBERT REDDALL	—	Dec. 3, 1881	May 3, 1865	Aug. 1, 1857	*Sept. 7, 1855	Hon. Lieut.-Colonel, Jan. 17, 1882. Resigned Mar. 14, 1882.
WILSON, GEORGE	—	—	—	—	*May 6, 1853	Surgeon Oct. 10, 1854. Surgeon-Major Mar. 11, 1873. Resigned Dec. 20, 1882.

ROYAL MONMOUTHSHIRE MILITIA

Name	Colonel	Lieut.-Col.	Major	Captain	Lieutenant	2nd Lieutenant or *Ensign	Remarks
Wilson, William Henry Herbert Walbeoffe	—	—	—	Jan. 30, 1883	—	—	Hon. Major, Feb. 8, 1889. Late Capt. 3rd Batt. Welsh Regt. Died July 2, 1891.
Wiseman-Clarke, William E.	—	—	—	—	—	Feb. 24, 1875	Resigned Dec. 9, 1879.
Witherington, Thomas	—	—	—	—	—	*Jan. 25, 1808	Joined 57th Regt. Oct. 25, 1808.
Wood, Simon	—	—	—	—	Jan. 14, 1804	—	
Worcester, Charles, 4th Marquis of	1684	—	—	—	—	—	Died July 13, 1698.
Worcester, Henry Charles, Marquis of	—	—	Feb. 1, 1793	—	—	—	See 6th Duke of Beaufort.
Worsley, Henry Arthur Mant	—	—	—	—	July 1, 1881	Dec. 23, 1879	Resigned Mar. 13, 1883.
Wright, Robert	—	—	—	—	July 25, 1793	*Feb. 1, 1793	
Zamoiski-Gray (see Gray)							

† Served in South African War as a Militia Officer. ‡ Has held the office of High Sheriff of Monmouthshire.

ADJUTANTS.

WITH RANK ON APPOINTMENT.

HASWELL, J. Lieutenant	August, 1778
ISAACSON, A. H. Lieutenant	March 12, 1803
PARSONS, L. Lieutenant	June 7, 1820
KANE, J. J. Captain	August 27, 1821
CARTER, J. M. Captain	January 19, 1846
HICKMAN, R. J. Captain	March 9, 1867
MACKWORTH, SIR A. W., BART. Captain	April 1, 1877
NOEL, W. F. N. Captain	October 1, 1881
LINDSAY, H. E. M. Captain	October 1, 1886
LEAROYD, C. D. Captain	November 14, 1891
BLAND, E. H. Captain	December 8, 1896
HOPKINS, N. J. Captain	April 2, 1902
GILES, F. L. N. Captain	October 2, 1907

SURGEONS.

WITH RANK ON APPOINTMENT.

PIDDING, J. Ensign	February 7, 1793
PRICE, W. Lieutenant	May 5, 1793
NASH, W. L. Lieutenant	April 25, 1803
THOMAS, O. G. Ensign	May 5, 1812
WILSON, GEORGE (Assistant Surgeon) Ensign	May 6, 1853
WILSON, J. G. Lieutenant	October 10, 1854
COWARD, J. E. Ensign	January 25, 1856
WILLS, J. M. Lieutenant	March 13, 1861
WILLIS, G. (Assistant Surgeon) Lieutenant	April 17, 1862
NORMAN, G. A. Lieutenant	May 28, 1873
WILSON, GEORGE (Surgeon) Captain	March 1, 1873

QUARTERMASTERS.

WITH RANK ON APPOINTMENT

JONES, T. Major	January 11, 1793
ISAACSON, A. H. Lieutenant	January 12, 1794
PEARCE, J. Lieutenant	August 25, 1794
BURLEY, G. Lieutenant	October 25, 1805
FINNERTY, J. Lieutenant	October 10, 1859
PERKINS, T. H. Captain	April 1, 1877
TUCKER, G. Captain	April 1, 1886
FIELD, W. F. Lieutenant	May 13, 1901
WHITEHEAD, T. L. Lieutenant	March 31, 1904

PAYMASTERS.

WITH RANK ON APPOINTMENT.

FOORD, WILLIAM Lieutenant	1820
POWELL, C. H. Lieutenant	1827
JONES, R. Lieutenant	June 26, 1854

APPENDIX I.

ROLL OF PAST AND PRESENT WARRANT AND NON-COMMISSIONED OFFICERS OF THE PERMANENT STAFF.

(*Compiled December* 1909.)

Name	Date From	Date To	Former Regiment	Rank on Leaving or at Present	Cause of Leaving
ABBOTSON, T.	April 5, 1880	Mar. 8, 1896	25th Foot	Sergt.	Discharged
ADAMS, R.	Dec. 1, 1882	Dec. 31, 1896	R.E.	C.S.M.	Discharged
ALDER, F.	Feb. 21, 1898	May 2, 1904	R.E.	C.S.M.	Discharged
ALLAN, F. J.	Aug. 21, 1902	Feb. 17, 1907	R.E.	Sergt.	Discharged
ALLINSON, W.	Feb. 14, 1855	Nov. 18, 1861	48th Foot	Sergt.	Died
ARCH, J.	Sept. 13, 1879	Feb. 28, 1891	23rd Foot	C.S.M.	Discharged
AUGER, I.	June 6, 1862	May 7, 1863	Royal Mon.	Sergt.	To join Police Force
AUSTIN, J.	Jan. 22, 1894	Dec. 17, 1903	R.E.	C.S.M.	Discharged
BANNISTER, T. H.	Nov. 8, 1903	Nov. 30, 1908	R.E.	C.S.M.	Discharged
BARROW, D.	Feb. 19, 1907	To date	R.E.	Q.M.S.	
BARTIE, J.	Mar. 28, 1878	Mar. 27, 1888	87th Foot	C.S.M.	Discharged
BAYNHAM, A.	Apr. 7, 1853	Sept. 16, 1855	Scots Grds.	Sergt.	Discharged
BAYTON, T.	July 31, 1856	Mar. 6, 1873	Royal Mon.	Sergt.	Discharged
BEARMAN, J.	Mar. 14, 1893	Mar. 18, 1895	R.E.	Sergt.	Discharged
BEAVER, R. G.	May 11, 1903	Sept. 23, 1908	R.E.	C.S.M.	Discharged
BELL, W.	Apr. 2, 1896	Apr. 2, 1901	R.E.	Sergt.	Discharged
BELLINGER, R.	Apr. 21, 1891	Mar. 15, 1898	R.E.	Sergt.	Discharged
BLACK, W.	Oct. 15, 1853	Feb. 29, 1856	21st Foot	Sergt.	Transferred to Inverness Militia
BLACKMORE, W.	Dec. 1, 1853	Sept. 27, 1854	Royal Mon.	Private	Reverted to Regiment as Militiaman
BOND, J.	Nov. 20, 1877	Oct. 27, 1885	99th Foot	Sergt.	Discharged
BOURNE, F.	Nov. 9, 1885	Jan. 31, 1894	R.E.	C.S.M.	Discharged

ROYAL MONMOUTHSHIRE MILITIA

Name	Date From	Date To	Former Regiment	Rank on Leaving or at Present	Cause of Leaving
BOWERS, F. W.	Feb. 18, 1907	To date	R.E.	Sergt.	
BOWRON, T.	Mar. 19, 1895	July 31, 1902	R.E.	C.S.M.	Discharged
BOWKETT, W.	June 16, 1873	Aug. 16, 1873	37th Foot	Paid pensioner recruiter	Discharged
BRAIN, T.	Feb. 18, 1907	Jan. 21, 1909	R.E.	Sergt.	Transferred to Ch'hre Field Coy. R.E. (Territorial Force)
BRICKNELL, S.	Oct. 27, 1902	Feb. 17, 1907	R.E.	Sergt.	Discharged
BROWN, J.	Apr. 6, 1887	Mar. 19, 1905	R.E.	C.S.M.	Discharged
BRUDERELL, G.	Apr. 3, 1854	Apr. 2, 1859	31st Foot	Colour-Sergt.	Discharged
BUNGAY, J. J.	Feb. 18, 1907	To date	R.E.	Sergt.	
BURNETT, J. J.	Apr. 1, 1891	Oct. 14, 1906	R.E.	Q.M.S. Engnr. Clerk	Discharged
BYRNE, P.	Dec. 1, 1877	July 29, 1878	11th Foot	Private	Returned to 11th Foot on reduction
BYRNES, M.	Apr. 14, 1868	Dec. 13, 1871	85th Foot	Colour-Sergt.	Discharged
CAFFREY, P.	Jan. 21, 1879	Jan. 21, 1894	8th Foot	C.S.M.	Discharged
CARR, S. G.	June 24, 1902	June 15, 1905	R.E.	C.S.M.	Discharged
CHARLES, T.	Sept. 30, 1852	Sept. 30, 1862	46th Foot	Colour-Sergt.	Discharged
CHARLESWORTH, C. G.	Nov. 16, 1898	Sept. 1, 1906	R.E.	Sergt.	Died
CHOTE, H. J.	Oct. 1, 1909	To date	R.E.	Civilian clerk	
COATES, J.	Mar. 31, 1892	Oct. 1, 1899	R.E.	C.S.M.	Trans. to Per. Staff R.A., R.E. (Militia)
COCHRANE, J.	Feb. 13, 1863	Feb. 13, 1868	47th Foot	Sergt.	Discharged
COLE, J.	Dec. 5, 1888	Oct. 15, 1897	R.E.	Q.M.S.	Discharged
CORDELL, T.	Apr. 17, 1893	Feb. 19, 1898	R.E.	Sergt.	Discharged
CORDER, A. G.	Oct. 15, 1908	To date	R.E.	R.S.M.	
CROSS, E.	May 11, 1859	June 22, 1861	77th Foot	O.R. Sergt.	Discharged
DAY, P.	Feb. 2, 1878	Sept. 7, 1890	58th Foot	Sergt.	Discharged
DEANE, J.	Feb. 16, 1863	1864	95th Foot	Sergt.	Discharged
DALANEY, J.	Sept. 18, 1874	Apr. 15, 1882	54th Foot	Paymstr.-Sergt.	Discharged
DUKES, H. B.	Mar. 6, 1900	Feb. 17, 1907	R.E.	C.Q.M.-Sergt.	Discharged

APPENDICES

Name	Date From	Date To	Former Regiment	Rank on Leaving or at Present	Cause of Leaving
EDWARDS, F.	Oct. 26, 1906	Sept. 30, 1909	R.E.	Corpl. T.E. Clrk.	Transferred to the Balloon School
EDWARDS, J.	Feb. 14, 1853	Dec. 18, 1857	73rd Foot	Colour Sergt.	Discharged.
EVERSON, R.	Dec. 21, 1906	Jan. 1, 1909	R.E.	Sergt.	Transferred to the 42nd Coy. R.E.
FAIRMAN, S.	Aug. 16, 1898	To date	R.E.	Q.M.S. Engr. Clerk	
FASSON, G.	Feb. 1, 1894	Feb. 17, 1907	R.E.	C.M.S.	Discharged
FERGUSON, P.	Apr. 17, 1866	July 18, 1874	58th Foot	Sergt.	Discharged
FINNERBY, J.	Sept. 30, 1852	Oct. 10, 1859	47th Foot	R.S.M.	Promoted Qrtrmastr.
FITZGERALD, J.	Mar. 15, 1861	Nov. 20, 1865	73rd Foot	R.S.M.	Died
FORBES, A.	Oct. 7, 1907	Sept. 15, 1908	R.E.	C.Q.M.-Sergt.	Transferred to the 33rd Coy. R.E.
FORD, J.	Oct. 20, 1853	Jan. 3, 1858	47th Foot	Q.M.S.	Transferred to Barrack Dept.
FROST, F.	July 11, 1901	Oct. 30, 1906	R.E.	C.Q.M.-Sergt.	Discharged
FURZE, W.	June 16, 1890	Oct. 7, 1898	R.E.	Sergt.	Discharged
GARLAND, M.	Feb. 19, 1866	Apr. 14, 1885	85th Foot	R.S.M.	Died
GILES, N. E.	Aug. 4, 1905	To date	R.E.	C.Q.M.-Sergt.	
GORDON, J.	June 9, 1868	July 17, 1869	92nd Foot	Paymstr.-Sergt	Discharged
GOSS, H.	Oct. 5, 1858	Oct. 17, 1870	48th Foot	Q.M.S.	Discharged
GRAY, G.	Sept. 1, 1904	To date	R.E.	Sergt.-Bugler	
GREENE, J.	July 31, 1856	Aug. 10, 1876	Royal Mon.	Colour-Sergt.	Discharged
GREGORY, J.	Sept. 3, 1871	Aug. 17, 1877	77th Foot	Sergt.	Transferred to West Essex Militia
GUY, J.	July 9, 1907	To date	R.E.	Sergt.	
GUYATT, J.	May 22, 1854	Aug. 3, 1855	83rd Foot	Sergt.	Died
HAMILTON, J.	Apr. 17, 1909	To date	R.E.	C.S.M.	
HARRIS, G.	Dec. 11, 1873	July 26, 1877	24th Foot	Sergt.	Transferred to South Wales Bord. Militia
HAYES, R.	Nov. 26, 1897	Feb. 17, 1907	R.E.	Q.M.S.	Discharged

ROYAL MONMOUTHSHIRE MILITIA

Name	Date From	Date To	Former Regiment	Rank on Leaving or at Present	Cause of Leaving
HEAL, A.	1872	June 25, 1874	23rd Foot	Sergt.	Dismissed by order of S. of S. for War
HEARD, H.	Oct. 11, 1901	Apr. 16, 1909	R.E.	C.S.M.	Discharged
HAFFERMAN, A.	Oct. 10, 1863	Jan. 13, 1870	30th Foot	Sergt.	Died
HEWITT, H.	Oct. 27, 1876	Feb. 16, 1889	28th Foot	Sergt.-Bugler	Discharged
HILL, C. C.	Nov. 19, 1900	July 5, 1904	R.E.	Sergt.-Bugler	Discharged
HISCOCKS, P.	1873	July 20, 1874	Royal Mon.	Sergt.	Discharged
HOCKADAY, F.	Jan. 15, 1909	To date	R.E.	C.Q.M.-Sergt.	
HOLMES, W.	Mar. 23, 1871	Mar. 22, 1876	Royal Mon.	O.R. Sergt.	Discharged
HOSIE, J.	Feb. 12, 1904	Mar. 17, 1907	R.E.	Sergt.	Discharged
HUGHES, E.	Mar. 21, 1898	Oct. 14, 1908	R.E.	R.S.M.	Discharged
ISHERWOOD, J.	May 5, 1862	Oct. 22, 1870	Royal Mon.	O.R. Sergt.	Discharged
JAMES, T.	May 17, 1860	Feb. 26, 1880	Royal Mon.	Sergt.	Died
JARRATT, W.	May 25, 1889	May 9, 1901	R.E.	C.S.M.	Discharged
JOHNS, W.	July 31, 1856	Not known	Royal Mon.	Not known	Not known
JONES, J.	June 24, 1829	July 31, 1854	Royal Mon.	Sergt.	Discharged
JONES, R.	July 31, 1856	1859	Royal Mon.	Drum-Major	Discharged
JONES, T.	Sept. 9, 1858	Jan. 16, 1865	57th Foot	Colour-Sergt.	Died
KEARVELL, H. F.	Feb. 18, 1907	To date	R.E.	Sergt.	
KERNICK, F.	May 21, 1907	To date	R.E.	Sergt.	
KNOFF, H.	Mar. 21, 1864	Sept. 26, 1866	30th Foot	Sergt.	Discharged
LARRY, F.	Feb. 14, 1909	To date	R.E.	Sergt.	
LINCOLN, S.	Aug. 16, 1853	Dec. 26, 1859	21st Foot	Colour-Sergt.	Discharged
LITTLE, M.	Mar. 16, 1898	Feb. 17, 1907	R.E.	C.S.M.	Discharged
MACKINTOSH, J.	June 1, 1904	Nov. 11, 1908	R.E.	Sergt.	Discharged
MARSHALL, G.	1885	Dec. 21, 1886	R.E.	Sergt.	Discharged
MARTIN, W.	Apr. 6, 1891	Feb. 17, 1907	R.E.	C.S.M.	Discharged
MCCARTHY, D.	Oct. 24, 1863	Aug. 23, 1865	37th Foot	Drum-Major	Discharged
MCDOUGALL, D.	Apr. 15, 1854	Apr. 15, 1869	59th Foot	Colour-Sergt.	Discharged

APPENDICES

Name	Date From	Date To	Former Regiment	Rank on Leaving or at Present	Cause of Leaving
McDougall, H.	April 1, 1869	May 31, 1906	Royal Mon.	C.S.M.	Discharged
McDowell, A.	1854	1855	Royal Mon.	Paymstr.-Sergt.	Not known
McManus, T.	Sept. 17, 1897	Aug. 2, 1899	R.E.	Sergt.	Discharged
McQuarrie, A.	Apr. 25, 1862	Apr. 1, 1877	73rd Foot	Colour-Sergt.	Transferred to Royal Antrim Militia
Meaken, E. A.	Dec. 15, 1906	Dec. 4, 1908	R.E.	C.Q.M.-Sergt.	Transferred to "M" Coy. R.E.
Meighen, J. P.	Dec. 25, 1906	Aug. 11, 1908	R.E.	Sergt.	Discharged
Miles, W.	Apr. 19, 1854	Feb. 2, 1861	20th Foot	Colour-Sergt.	Died
Morgan, J.	Apr. 23, 1863	Apr. 26, 1868	Royal Mon.	O.R. Sergt.	Died
Murray, H. W.	June 8, 1892	Aug. 15, 1898	R.E.	Corpl. T.E. clrk.	Transferred to "G" Coy. R.E.
Nash, W. J.	Apr. 15, 1862	Apr. 1, 1867	Surrey Mil.	Sergt.	Transferred to Hereford Militia
Newbery, J.	June 30, 1902	Feb. 9, 1905	R.E.	Sergt.	Transferred to Perm. Staff R.A., R.E. (M.)
Nixon, W.	Aug. 25, 1877	Sept. 2, 1894	41st Foot	Sergt.	Discharged
O'Flynn, J.	Sept. 5, 1899	Feb. 17, 1907	R.E.	C.S.M.	Discharged
Pascoe, J.	Nov. 4, 1859	Oct. 21, 1881	Royal Mon.	Hosp. Sergt.	Died
Parker, J.	Nov. 28, 1894	Feb. 1, 1899	R.E.	Sergt.	Transferred to Perm. Staff R.A., R.E.(M.)
Perkins, T. H.	June 19, 1860	Apr. 1, 1877	4th Foot	Q.M.S.	Promoted Qr.-Mstr.
Perry, W.	July 31, 1856	June 19, 1869	Royal Mon.	Sergt.	Discharged
Phillpott, C. W.	May 9, 1903	To date	R.E.	C.S.M.	
Powell, T.	Feb. 16, 1880	Mar. 10, 1893	R.M.A.	Sergt.	Discharged
Power, D.	Apr. 18, 1899	Feb. 15, 1900	R.E.	Sergt.	Discharged
Power, P.	1872	Nov. 11, 1875	85th Foot	Sergt.	Discharged
Powles, W.	1855	1857	Royal Mon.	Armr.-Sergt.	Discharged
Preece, T.	July 31, 1856	Nov. 5, 1871	Royal Mon.	Sergt.	Discharged
Prendergast, J.	Mar. 18, 1854	July 17, 1862	30th Foot	Paymstr.-Sergt.	Died
Prendergast, T.	May 15, 1865	Aug. 21, 1877	2nd Foot	Sergt., I. of M.	Transferred to 2nd Lon. Rifle Vols.

Name	Date From	Date To	Former Regiment	Rank on Leaving or at Present	Cause of Leaving
Pugh, E.	July 25, 1853	Apr. 21, 1862	Royal Mon.	Colour-Sergt.	Discharged
Purcell, J.	Nov. 14, 1869	Sept. 7, 1872	47th Foot	Paymstr.-Sergt.	Died
Quaine, M.	Nov. 13, 1877	Apr. 27, 1889	11th Foot	O.R.-Sergt.	Discharged
Quarman, T.	Mar. 11, 1875	Aug. 17, 1877	24th Foot	Sergt.	Transferred to West Essex Militia
Redgrave, E.	Oct. 22, 1907	To date	R.E.	Sergt.	
Redman, T.	Feb. 1, 1870	Oct. 2, 1870	R.M.L.I.	Sergt.	Discharged
Redpath, R.	June 21, 1906	To date	R.E.	C.S.M., I. of M.	
Rees, C.	April 1, 1867	Feb. 25, 1892	Royal Mon.	C.S.M.	Discharged
Reilly, H.	May 3, 1869	Nov. 30, 1876	58th Foot	Sergt.	Discharged
Reneeles, G.	Mar. 1, 1889	Nov. 30, 1900	R.E.	Sergt.-Bugler	Discharged
Renwick, J.	1871	Dec. 1, 1873	Coldst. Gds.	Drum-Major	Transferred to 5th Lancs. Militia
Robbins, R.	Apr. 1, 1854	Nov. 12, 1855	R.M.A.	Sergt.	Discharged
Robinson, J. E.	June 30, 1902	Dec. 14, 1906	R.E.	C.Q.M. Sergt.	Transferred to the Jersey Militia
Rogers, J. G.	Jan. 5, 1878	Mar. 31, 1891	29th Foot	C.S.M.	Discharged
Ruane, P.	Feb. 15, 1897	Oct. 6, 1907	R.E.	C.S.M.	Discharged
Sartin, W.	Nov. 30, 1899	To date	R.E.	C.S.M.	
Scott, T.	July 31, 1856	July 30, 1871	Royal Mon.	Colour-Sergt.	Discharged
Scott, W.	July 31, 1856	June 18, 1870	Royal Mon.	Sergt.	Discharged
Shaw, J. W.	Mar. 1, 1879	Aug. 27, 1884	30th Foot	C.S.M.	Transferred to 1st East Lancs. Regt.
Sheppard, G.	Oct. 25, 1906	To date	R.E.	C.Q.M. Sergt.	
Shergold, A. E.	May 20, 1903	Sept. 25, 1908	R.E.	C.Q.M. Sergt.	Transferred to 2nd North Mid. Field Coy. R.E. (Territorial Force)
Simpson, S.	May 17, 1860	Oct. 12, 1861	94th Foot	Sergt.	Discharged
Smith, J.	June 24, 1889	Feb. 15, 1902	R.E.	C.S.M.	Discharged
Smith, T.	Mar. 1, 1883	Aug. 18, 1897	R.E.	C.S.M.	Discharged
Stewart, J.	Nov. 22, 1877	Mar. 31, 1891	47th Foot	Sergt.	Discharged

APPENDICES

Name	Date From	Date To	Former Regiment	Rank on Leaving or at Present	Cause of Leaving
STUART, A.	Sept. 25, 1866	Oct. 12, 1886	1st Royals	Q.M.S.	Discharged
STUART, R.	Jan. 20, 1876	Oct. 9, 1883	16th Foot	C.S.M.	Discharged
SUTTON, R.	Apr. 5, 1861	June 10, 1862	Royal Mon.	Colour-Sergt.	Discharged
SYKES, J. W.	June 30, 1902	Nov. 8, 1903	R.E.	Sergt.	Transferred to "G" Coy. R.E.
TATAM, A. A. E.	May 1, 1905	To date	R.E.	C.Q.M. Sergt.	
THOMAS, C.	Oct. 1, 1852	Sept. 30, 1862	Royal Mon.	Colour-Sergt.	Discharged
THOMPSON, W.	Jan. 15, 1866	Sept. 15, 1868	64th Foot	Bugle-Major	Discharged
THORPE, W.	May 15, 1862	May 14, 1876	Royal Mon.	Sergt.	Discharged
THORPE, W.	May 15, 1867	Jan. 30, 1883	58th Foot	C.S.M.	Discharged
VINNICOMBE, W.	Dec. 14, 1906	Sept. 3, 1907	R.E.	Sergt.	Discharged
WADE, H.	Mar. 1, 1907	To date	R.E.	Sergt.	
WALSH, M.	May 7, 1862	June 6, 1863	Royal Mon.	Sergt.	Disqualified
WARREN, J. A.	Oct. 29, 1902	To date	R.E.	C.S.M.	
WATKINS, D.	Jan. 24, 1829	July 31, 1854	Royal Mon.	Sergt.	Discharged
WATKINS, T.	Dec. 9, 1852	July 8, 1876	Royal Mon.	Bugle-Major	Discharged
WATKINS, T.	Dec. 13, 1906	Feb. 2, 1909	R.E.	Sergt.	Discharged
WHALLEY, G.	Apr. 1, 1884	May 31, 1892	R.E.	Q.M.S.Engr.Clk	Discharged
WHELAN, W.	June 12, 1863	June 13, 1874	12th Foot	Sergt.	Dismissed by order of H.R.H. the C. in C.
WILKINSON, H. E.	Feb. 14, 1905	July 8, 1907	R.E.	Sergt.	Discharged
WILLIAMS, C.	July 31, 1856	July 30, 1861	Royal Mon.	Sergt.	Discharged
WILLIAMS, T.	Nov. 15, 1877	Jan. 29, 1893	2nd Foot	C.S.M.	Discharged
WILLIAMS, W.	July 31, 1856	Mar. 7, 1863	Royal Mon.	Colour-Sergt.	Discharged
WILLIAMS, W.	Mar. 8, 1858	Aug. 10, 1871	Royal Mon.	Sergt.	Discharged
WILLIAMS, W.	May 30, 1903	Feb. 17, 1907	R.E.	C.Q.M. Sergt.	Discharged
WOOD, R.	May 30, 1885	Mar. 20, 1898	R.E.	R.S.M.	Discharged

APPENDIX II.
Roll of Regimental Sergeant-Majors.

Regtl. No.	Name	Corps	Date From	Date To	Remarks
—	Finnerty, J.	R.M.R.E. (M.)	Sept. 30, 1852	Oct. 9, 1859	No permanent regimental numbers
—	Fitzgerald, J.	Do.	Mar. 15, 1861	Nov. 20, 1865	
—	Garland, M.	Do.	Feb. 19, 1866	Apr. 14, 1885	
9471	Wood, R. L.	Royal Engrs.	May 30, 1885	Mar. 20, 1898	Warrant officer
16748	Hughes, E.	Do.	Mar. 21, 1898	Oct. 14, 1908	Warrant officer from Apr. 1, 1900
22745	Corder, A. G.	Do.	Oct. 15, 1908	To date	Warrant officer

APPENDIX III.
N.-C. Officers and Men who have been Awarded the Militia Good Conduct Medal.

Regtl. No.	Rank.	Name.	Remarks.
8718	C.-S.-Major	McDougall, H.	Serving on Permanent Staff at the time of award
9217	Sergeant	Bevan, W.	Discharged
9777	,,	Cumbley, J.	Still serving
9377	,,	Freeman, A.	Do.
1600	Sapper	Evans, A. E.	Do.
5101	,,	Fletcher, J.	Do.
3320	,,	Hawkins, G.	Discharged
9902	,,	Kelly, J.	Do.
104	,,	Robinson, W.	Do.

APPENDIX IV.

Inspection Returns, 1854—1909.

Date	Officers	Warrant and N.C.O.s	Privates	Permanent Staff N.C.O.	Permanent Staff Drummers	Total
1854	30	49	546	—	—	625
1855	27	53	562	—	—	642
1859	20	40	792	—	—	852
1860	23	43	400	—	—	466
1861	25	45	651	—	—	721
1862	25	43	761	—	—	829
1863	23	41	734	—	—	798
1864	24	34	732	—	—	790
1865	25	48	628	—	—	701
1875	23	47	783	20	8	881
1876	24	47	732	18	8	829
1877	25	46	678	15	8	772
1878	25	47	722	20	8	822
1879	24	48	635	20	8	735
1880	26	46	677	21	8	778
1881	25	46	739	21	8	839
1882	24	48	649	20	8	749
1883	19	47	676	21	8	771
1884	21	48	525	21	8	623
1886	25	48	530	21	8	632
1887	24	47	683	21	8	783
1888	25	73	697	21	8	824
1889	25	91	702	21	8	847
1890	23	92	615	19	8	757
1891	23	103	602	19	8	755
1892	24	105	595	19	8	751
1893	23	111	711	19	8	872
1894	27	113	715	19	8	882
1895	25	112	698	19	8	862
1896*	—	—	—	—	—	—
1897	25	123	648	19	8	823
1898	26	128	731	19	8	912
1899	28	133	689	19	8	877
1900	24	107	673	19	8	831
1901	23	125	746	18	8	920
1902	23	104	848	21	8	1004
1903	27	118	928	28	10	1111
1904	32	83	889	27	10	1041
1905	33	79	952	27	8	1099
1906	35	85	1005	28	10	1163
1907	30	99	1024	28	10	1191
1908	31	100	800	27	10	968
1909	28	92	612	20	6	758

* Training cancelled.

www.ingramcontent.com/pod-product-compliance
Lightning Source LLC
Chambersburg PA
CBHW080611230426
43664CB00019B/2861